Handbook of Schooling
in Urban America

HANDBOOK OF SCHOOLING IN URBAN AMERICA

EDITED BY

Stanley William Rothstein

GREENWOOD PRESS

Westport, Connecticut • London

Library of Congress Cataloging-in-Publication Data

Handbook of schooling in urban America / edited by Stanley William
    Rothstein.
        p.   cm.
    Includes bibliographical references and index.
    ISBN 0–313–28412–1 (alk. paper)
        1. Education, Urban—United States—Handbooks, manuals, etc.
    2. School management and organization—United States—Handbooks,
    manuals, etc.   I. Rothstein, Stanley William.
    LC5131.H35   1993
    370.19'348'0973—dc20   93–9323

British Library Cataloguing in Publication Data is available.

Library of Congress Catalog Card Number: 93–9323
ISBN: 0–313–28412–1

First published in 1993

Greenwood Press, 88 Post Road West, Westport, CT   06881
An imprint of Greenwood Publishing Group, Inc.

Printed in the United States of America

The paper used in this book complies with the
Permanent Paper Standard issued by the National
Information Standards Organization (Z39.48–1984).

10 9 8 7 6 5 4 3 2 1

Contents

III. Minority Perspectives

IV. Teacher-Pupil Relations

V. The Urban Battleground

VI. Pedagogical Problems

VII. What Can Be Done?

Preface

There is a growing commentary on urban problems, especially urban educational problems, all of which point to a deepening crisis and concern: huge numbers of Americans now live and learn in ever-expanding cities and megalopolises. This reference work is a guide to the most critical issues at the heart of schooling in these urban areas. Each chapter in this reference is written by an authority on a particular aspect of urban schooling. Together, the chapters in this reference provide a comprehensive overview of historical and contemporary facets of urban education and point to new directions for future research.

The first section of this *Handbook of Schooling in Urban America* takes a historical view of the development of urban education and its problems. The section begins with a short history of urban education, followed by chapters on particular case histories of the urban educational experience.

The second section of this reference examines political and organizational perspectives and their effects on urban schooling. A brief introductory chapter overviews criticism of urban schools and provides a context for the more specific chapters that follow. The first of these chapters carefully examines the role of policymakers and politics in urban education. The next chapter looks more particularly at politics and the curriculum. A chapter then discusses bureaucratic organizational structures in urban school systems, and a final chapter addresses administrative and supervisory perceptions of teacher competency.

The third section provides an insightful look at minority perspectives on urban education. The first chapter gives special attention to multiculturalism and the Puerto Rican experience in urban schools. The second explores the difficulties of African-American, Hispanic, and Vietnamese students. A final chapter considers the special needs of girls in urban schools and whether those needs are adequately met.

Teacher-pupil relations have a strong impact on the urban educational experience, and the fourth section of this reference considers the topic in detail. An introductory chapter explores the fundamental importance of communication between teachers and students. A chapter then looks at the particular case of Latino students and analyzes how the culture of the teacher shapes the experiences of these students in the classroom. The next chapter closely examines the place of special needs children in urban schools.

Urban schools exist within the larger environment of the city and do not offer a safe refuge from urban problems. The fifth section of this reference looks at some of the social problems that plague urban schools because of their place within the culture of the city. An introductory chapter briefly overviews the problems typical of urban environments and how those problems impact urban school systems. The next chapter looks at the particular case of Latino churches and schools as urban battlegrounds. The third chapter considers one of the most troublesome problems of urban education, the impact of urban drug culture on schoolchildren.

Pedagogical issues are at the heart of all schooling, and the sixth section of this reference gives close attention to pedagogical problems of special significance to urban schools. An introductory chapter analyzes the nature of pedagogy and provides a theoretical frame for the remaining chapters. The next chapter discusses problems related to mathematics and science education and offers some suggestions for improving student mastery of these subjects. A chapter then considers the social and educational problem of school dropouts.

The seventh section of this reference discusses solutions to the problems of urban schooling. An introductory chapter appropriately discusses what needs to be done. A chapter then considers what urban schools can do about crime, violence, gangs, and drug abuse. The next chapter discusses the importance of reading in the urban environment. The following chapter offers suggestions for involving minorities in urban education, and a final chapter examines the all-important role of the principal in urban schools.

As a reference work, this volume provides a broad vision of the historical, political, social, and pedagogical factors that shape and define urban schooling in America. The reference lists at the end of each chapter direct the reader to more specific sources of current information, and the bibliography at the end of the volume includes the most important sources of additional information.

Introduction

Stanley William Rothstein

A survey of the vast literature on schooling in urban America reveals recurring themes connecting the cramped, congested environments of urban centers with the technological innovations, world trade, and commerce of industrial society. In this view, the deleterious effects of urban life are a natural consequence of advanced society and should be viewed as an unfortunate imbalance. Further, urban educational systems have been developing for several centuries; they are related to spatial conditions in inner-city schools and the populations concentrating there. Urban education, then, is the socialization process wherein children find their places and know precisely how they must behave in an impersonal and mechanistic world. It presents messages that reinforce those of the churches, schools, and media. In this ideological viewpoint, the problems associated with inner-city schools are thought to be related to spatial conditions: space and its characteristics are given the power to cause the social contradictions and relationships observed in ghetto schools (and urban workplaces). Scholars cannot easily counter this ideology of the environment because it seems to make sense: overcrowded, underfunded, dysfunctional schools are most often seen in urban concentrations. Their size and diverse populations appear to be dictated by crowds of immigrants and the urban poor. State governments are unable to deal with these populations and the deteriorating conditions of the inner cities: shrinking tax bases have forced them to lessen severely their financial support for mass transport, health care, welfare, housing, and education.

The unexamined premise that urban education can be apprehended in a commonsense way makes it more difficult for us to understand the ideological nature these words have in our culture. The terms are very difficult to define, although most people believe they "know" when they are in an urban school. Unfortunately, all of the characteristics of urban schools can be found, more and more, in schools that are located in suburban areas as well.

The premise that urban education can be understood by focusing attention on the way space affects the behavior of individuals gives to the environment a causal effect: the social relations that develop in urban schools are seen as an outgrowth of spatial considerations. Such thinking ignores the economic and historical determinants that caused these particular social formations to take hold. Inculcation, the primary task of state schools, is neglected, and we are asked to look at the arbitrary curricula and disciplinary practices as though they were beyond rational criticism or analysis. Once the ideological nature of the term *urban education* has been assimilated, a theoretical framework of urban schooling can be constructed. Such a framework requires a historical development of schooling tied to the economic and social needs that first propelled compulsory education into national law.

By tracing the development of urbanism and urban schools in American society, we are able to understand how old the urban question really is. Such an approach helps us to see how and why urban, charity schools were first established after the revolutionary war: the ethical and economic reasons for their creation are uncovered, and education comes to be viewed as a "socialization" or an inculcation that has deep social status biases. Ideological understandings of these first charity schools caused Americans to accept them at face value. They were presented as a natural response to social and economic problems, as an evolution from previous, less civilized ways of doing things.

From this we can say that the evolving dominance of urban educational forms has been a constant and persistent social phenomenon existing across historical periods. In fact, the size and density of urban areas and educational systems have been increasing throughout recent history, especially in the past century. Our incapacity to control or deal with their worst excesses has been a continuing concern, especially now that inner cities have become uninhabitable wastelands where the poorest of our citizens live. The increasing levels of lawlessness, normlessness, and social isolation in the midst of ever-increasing populations and the movement of millions of citizens to the suburbs are just some of the more obvious consequences of our use of space in the twentieth century. But most studies of these problems have only provided a quantitative basis for describing and analyzing urban education and the urbanism phenomenon itself; the real problems of qualitative changes and deteriorating life-styles have been ignored or left to the media.

Apart from its obvious population density and bureaucratic structures, urban education has its own forms and practices. The grimness of urban schools and classrooms and their rigid pedagogical style have evolved naturally from their internal structures and historical traditions. These include the use of partitioned classrooms to divide students into smaller, more manageable groups; the grade system with its graduated curricula and tracking mechanisms; the interdependency with the state and economy; and the need to prepare urban youth for a future in the increasingly competitive labor market.

Within urban schools themselves one finds two activities that never vary: an overly corrective pedagogy of inculcation and a bureaucratic impersonality that often deadens the curiosities of inquiring minds. Urban schools are involved in the production of replacement workers; their educational efforts are directed at reproducing the social relations of educational and economic production. They are responsible for sorting out and evaluating the merit of students and assigning them to various tracks in the educational system and, later, in the work force. These activities can be seen more clearly in inner-city schools, where children attend state institutions that have a history and a culture of failure. But they are also found in the outer rings of the urban setting and in the suburbs, where urbanism has made significant inroads. In all of these state schools there are a similar organizational ethos and structure: bureaucratic and hierarchical lines of communication facilitate the reproductive functions of schooling in mass society. Urban schools bring together licensed teachers and educational buildings that belong to the state. Some of these schools are more successful than others, based on the class position of children who attend them. The more successful schools cater to middle-class students and organize themselves around college-bound curricula and standards of discipline. But urban schools are characterized by educational practices that are much less successful than their suburban counterparts: their locations in inner cities cause them to reflect some of the worst aspects of urban blight as it is developing in the United States at the end of the twentieth century.

Educational progress has been measured mostly by standardized test scores and the numbers of children falling under the compulsory education laws that were first passed in the 1840s and 1850s. The role played by education in the transformation of urban areas has been well documented. This has been played out by graduates and dropouts alike, both of whom accepted without question the ideological assumptions and legitimacy of the public schooling establishment. The new methods of technology and production influenced urban educational systems; but the class nature of American society meant that schooling had to prepare children for differential fates in a changing and unequal labor market.

The technological revolutions have permitted urban centers to grow ever larger and less manageable. With this has come a need to concentrate labor power near the industrial and administrative centers of modern capitalism. New forms of transport allowed for greater mobility and an integration of productive methods. The automobile made possible the suburban areas that now circle our largest cities. Life has become more regimented and work more rationalized and boring.

THE URBAN CRISIS

From this we can conclude that the inner cities of the United States have been in a steep decline for many years. Because of an expanding world trade and the exportation of production jobs overseas, high unemployment and despair have become widespread in our depressed urban areas. Just as serious has been the development of suburban areas and the deterioration of urban housing, public transport, and health and educational services.

An unfortunate legacy of this urban crisis has been a more intense socioeconomic and racial segregation and the collapse of the public school system in inner-city districts. Governmental policies have contributed to these difficult problems. Yet they are not alone in bearing responsibility. We must take note of the new global economy and the marginalization of unskilled and skilled American workers in the new order, developments that occurred with the encouragement and consent of the American government. Allowing multinational corporations to relocate to low-wage, low-tax countries in the less-developed parts of the world was wholly incompatible with any hope of maintaining high-wage jobs and an effective, assertive union movement. The failure to limit these practices accelerated the exportation of jobs and capital and further depressed the conditions of workers, especially in our inner cities.

Our ability to correct these problems is reduced because business now transcends national boundaries while, as yet, no international political government exists for regulating and controlling these modern-day robber barons. In short, the urban crisis has developed because of unwise and unrestrained economic policies, the flight of the middle classes to the suburbs, and the resulting inability of local governments to provide adequate services for their residents.

The urban crisis is worsening because so many unemployed people are migrating to our large cities and towns. With unemployment and under-employment running at increasingly high levels, it seems obvious that the tax base of urban governments will not increase. Adding to these problems are the further growth in crime, homelessness, and poverty and their savage consequences for racial minorities, women, and children. The more the urban crisis goes unchecked, the more family life is destroyed by single-parent homes and the pernicious welfare system. Further, unattended children are usually a factor in developing gang cultures and criminal activities.

I

HISTORICAL PERSPECTIVES

1

A Short History of Urban Education

Stanley William Rothstein

Those who have studied such matters are in agreement that urban education—
the long and arduous training of youth in cultural and political decorum—is an
outgrowth of the state's need to condition the minds of its citizens. Urban
education has a history and reason for being. It is common in many societies
but especially noticeable in modern industrialist systems, where it must prepare
students for an impersonal and uncertain future in the labor market. Scholars
are not certain whether urban schooling is a unique cultural phenomenon or
whether its characteristics can also be found in suburban and rural schools. But
they do ask questions that reveal the essential nature of schooling's social functions. Would any government support expensive educational systems if it did
not believe in the need to inculcate and train youth to accept the cultural and
economic demands of civil society? Did urban schooling perform a significant
function for an emerging industrial America in the nineteenth century, or were
its failures an embarrassment?

Some things can be said with reasonable certainty. Urban education can be
traced to the desire of religious and political leaders to propagate ideas and
beliefs that would benefit the prevailing social order.[1] On the other hand, there
is a gulf separating religious education from the urban schooling that teaches
secular communities the rudiments of reading, writing, and arithmetic. Second,
historical evidence for urban schooling before the Protestant revolution is largely
confined to the clergy and nobility in most European nations. As an approved
state program, urban schooling began with certain German duchies and Frederick
the Great in Central Europe and was made popular by its success in binding
youth to the nationalistic and religious aims of monarchical governments. In
these preindustrial instances the state dictated that such schooling should occur
as regularly as possible, but less often during the planting and harvesting seasons,
and that it should be paid for by townspeople.

By the seventeenth and eighteenth centuries, there is evidence that urban schooling is more widely accepted in Europe and less so in the English colonies.[2] We now have the charity and Lancastrian schools strung out in the cities and towns of America and some ''public'' schools in New England. Older students were used in the Lancastrian schools, along with unpaid volunteers, and urban classroom space was arranged with military precision to increase schooling's efficiency. Hierarchy was strictly observed: the teacher sat high above the students on a platform. Teachers could see at a glance what was happening in the classroom even as monitors and assistants scurried back and forth along long lines of pauper boys, giving them instructions and maintaining order and control. Students were punished when they talked, when they were inattentive, when they were out of their seats, and so on. If they were saucy to monitors or snatched slates or books from one another, their names were reported to the teacher for further disciplinary action. Of course, there were many other infractions during the long school day.

Lancastrian students attended school as a punishment of birth, seeking to learn correct conduct and moral training from their betters. They accomplished their schooling by acts of deference and obedience in enormous classrooms of 365 to 1,000 pupils per teacher. They were taught in regimental fashion by young monitors or corporals while standing on assigned spots at slate boards on either side of long rows of seats or benches. The pauper boys were first taught reading and catechism and later, subjects of greater difficulty and complexity. Schooling the poor was seen as the Christian duty of the faithful: the pauper boys were predominantly Anglo-Saxons who, with proper training, could be rehabilitated and cured of their social and educational defects.[3]

Of course, these charity schools were born in poverty, and poverty was their excuse for being; they began to lose much of their popularity after 1830, when their defects were more clearly understood and talk of common, free schools was heard in the northern part of the United States. Prior to that time, the military discipline of the Lancastrian schools had been accepted without much thought. Poor students had taken the role of the dependent, subservient, unworthy individuals with effects that were to be felt in the infant schools and free state-supported schools that followed them.

The common schools were an extension of the old charity schools, but with this important difference: they sought to provide common training for all. Business favored the development of these common schools, whose founder, Horace Mann, assured them they would extend the wealth and security of their property and lives. Thus, the business-oriented ideologies that dominated the economy and cultural life of the nation triumphed also in its schools; there was a consolidation of some of the military structures and practices that had characterized the pauper schools and their Lancastrian variants.[4]

From the 1830s onward, free schools were founded throughout the cities and urban communities of the United States. Already, Horace Mann had accepted the post of secretary of the State Board of Education in 1834. When he assumed the position, education still was not valued, and the post had low status and pay.[5] But Mann had an unshakable faith in the improvability of the race; he believed that the schools needed to be reformed and democratized, educating all classes of American society. He came to his post with a great deal of enthusiasm, vision, and courage; and he was a politician with practical legislative experience. He realized that the schools needed to expand the range of instruction they offered: schools and their practices were not in harmony with the new social conditions created by industrialism and urbanization. He began to present his views throughout Massachusetts and other nearby states. Soon he had awakened interest and enthusiasm in establishing free schools that would be more purposeful in their secular orientations. In these years, the struggle to secure state-supported schools began in earnest; the church had always had possession of the education of the young, and the states continued to recognize their dominion in this area by donating land and money to their schools. These endowments ceased about 1800, but grants of state aid for parochial schools continued for the next half century and more.[6] Finally, with the rise of state-supported common schools, these church and private schools were taken over, and funding was provided on the same basis as the new state schools. The urban schools of this period were obviously moral and religious institutions and part of the churches' training program. The first Industrial Revolution began to make Americans aware of new secular needs created by more urban environments and greater pockets of poverty and crime.

Whether the notion of common schools was approved of by most Americans is another question. We only know that by the 1840s and 1850s most of the states had some form of compulsory education laws. Did they fully support them? Or, when left to their own devices, did they ignore these compulsory education laws and continue to underfund common schools?

What seems certain is that every state, every county, every city eventually accepted schooling as a bastion against the pressing problems of crime, poverty, and rising immigration that were now so widespread in urban centers.[7] In the past, schooling was thought to be the responsibility of the family and local communities, which could be relied on to teach socially and economically accepted doctrines to children. People believed that the communal bonds would automatically create harmony and order between the members of the state and city, maintaining the stability of the family and community. These assumptions seemed reasonable, since tradition-based schooling had worked in the past and teachers were inevitably chosen from among like-minded persons in the community.

A DULL UNIFORMITY

Despite the struggle for free common schools, the criticism of such schools throughout the nineteenth century had an unchanging theme. In 1880, Charles Francis Adams called educators "drill sargents," saying their schools resembled cotton mills and prisons more than institutions of learning.[8] When Dr. Joseph

Rice described the schools two year later, no one seem surprised by his charges of extreme regimentation; no one questioned the accuracy of his observations. Charles W. Eliot of Harvard echoed these sentiments, deploring the public school's "military and mechanical methods" and their dull uniformity. Among his criticisms were descriptions of military discipline and uninteresting lessons. Schoolmasters, he believed, accepted a system and discipline that clearly predated the institutional forms of both the charity schools and the newer common schools. Eliot saw in the rigid social status system a training for authoritarian workplaces: the strict control of the student's bodily movements, the youngster's dependency upon the goodwill of schoolmasters who had absolute authority over them, the consequences of social rankings and class and the estrangement of urban youth from their own families and cultures as they learned an arbitrary curriculum in a military fashion.[9] These urban schools were regimented, poorly lit, poorly staffed, and poorly heated buildings where the children of the poor and immigrant families learned the language and customs of America in the most stressful of circumstances.

But if the free schools were characterized by so much social and educational rejection, why did they persist and flourish? Why does the figure of the pompous, self-righteous schoolmaster remain with us a century later? Why, from the practices of the charity and common schools, did these militaristic forms of discipline prevail?

Perhaps one answer was in the traditions of European schooling that so influenced our own efforts. In 1890, William Torrey Harris, twice commissioner of education, made his influence felt on the administration of schools. He developed the practices of graded schools, schedules, supervision, and selection based on examinations that characterize urban schools to this day. The practice of keeping attendance records and providing salary schedules for employees was introduced, and by a series of directives, the authoritarian atmosphere of the urban school was assured. Harris established a school system in which order and purposeful activity were venerated: the goal of the urban school was to limit the freedom and aimless behavior of youth, to urge students to greater effort and interest. The schools were prescriptive institutions rather than places where youngsters or teachers could choose their activities and curricula. They were agencies where routine and regularity were prized and demanded, where silence and industry were needed to preserve and maintain order and instruction.[10]

The idea of common experiences and curriculum, so central to the thought of the original common school reformers, was quickly discarded. Since the poor were to do the lesser work, their education would have to prepare them to accept their lower positions in society. They were identified at an early age and trained to accept their future in the labor market.

Ungraded schools disappeared, or almost so; the concern for individual preferences and needs vanished. A corrective-dominated, punishment-oriented ethos with its roots firmly embedded in the free school movement of the past remained. Whipping posts were abandoned; schoolmasters no longer carried bundles of switches. But the excess of drill and military command remained, along with corporal punishments and various forms of paddling; blows with rods, rulers, and the hand were frequently used to impose order and maintain control. Students were bombarded with commands by voice, bells, whistles, and gestures during the school day.[11]

These corrective and punitive practices were used without thought or reflection. Where did they come from, and what were their original purposes in urban schools? Methods for distributing individuals, locating them in confined spatial areas, sorting them, forcing them to engage in purposeful activity, training their minds and bodies to fit a preconceived mold, evaluating their performances and recording those judgments, forcing them to interact in open areas where they could be easily observed—all were features of penal, religious, and military communities in the pre-capitalist period. The methods of forcing individuals to respond to commands predate modern organizational forms; the desire of those in authority to create obedient, responsive soldiers, disciples, inmates, or students by constraining their bodily movements had its beginnings in the prehistory of the human condition.

What was this fascination with discipline that so dominated the urban schools of the late nineteenth and early twentieth centuries? Two aspects of these organizational practices deserve attention. First, discipline in urban schools was always exercised in the service of educational goals. The rules and regulations were almost always invoked to justify pedagogical practices, forcing students to accept their role as students in arbitrary fashion. This was the regimentation that so many observers reported. The mechanisms of organizational control sought to eliminate confusion, aimless movements, and emotionalism in the interests of coordination and directed, purposeful activity. Uniform behavior and work patterns were desired. Students were seen as objects of a larger social organization: they had to be controlled and manipulated for their own good and for the common safety of the school.[12]

Second, these rules and regulations occurred within a power structure based on legal-rational authority: every member of the staff was licensed by the state to perform his or her duties in the classroom. This system met with a great deal of success because of its inherent simplicity: schoolteachers had certain rights and responsibilities in the urban schooling situation. Inside the building, they were in control; they were the ones who decided, who judged, who observed and evaluated all student deportment and achievement.

Finally, urban schools had for their historical model the military organization. That organization also confronted the problem of controlling, training, and moving large numbers of people in confined spatial areas. Prisons and asylums were confronted with similar organizational dilemmas. Such institutions felt a strong affinity for geometric and uniform formations and constructions. Buildings and tents were assigned specific locations, entrances, and exits. A malfunctioning soldier or inmate could be discovered by simply observing whether his actions deviated from the prescribed geometric norms. This was the essence of surveillance in human affairs, and it was adopted eagerly by schoolteachers in crowded urban classrooms.

These schools were structured, even then, to provide schooling for children of the immigrant and urban poor.[13] They were to provide a better example of proper deportment, thereby assuring society more disciplined citizens and workers. In the twentieth century, high schools were developed and used as retention centers, especially during hard times and the Great Depression.

The essential features of the discipline system in urban schools included these characteristics: (1) Discipline was concerned with the way students were moved about in time and space. In the urban elementary and secondary urban schools, this demanded enclosures in a distinct, walled community. The coercive nature of the discipline could thus be carried out without interference from outsiders. Here the students—that collection of idlers from diverse backgrounds and cultures—had to be put in their place; fighting and disorderly conduct were not tolerated; the order and safety of the surrounding community had to be preserved, and the fears of merchants and others calmed. Truancy had to be punished, and the costs of education restricted. The urban school had to be bounded, thereby helping teachers to maintain order, control, and authority in the building. (2) Disciplinary needs, however, acted upon the enclosed spatial area of the urban school in a particular manner, through separation and partitioning. Each student had his or her own classroom, seat, and clothing hook. Uniformity had to be as complete as possible, with students forced to toe a crack when they were unruly or worse. Youngsters could not be allowed to wander aimlessly in the halls; they could not be permitted to absent themselves from scheduled classes. Everything had to be done to force students to concentrate, to attend to the arbitrary curriculum, to obey the authority of the classroom teacher. In this way students were classified as either present or absent, and schoolmasters could locate them inside the building at any time of the school day. Also, lessons could be planned and meetings held; supervision could occur in a systematic fashion. To assess, to judge, to record, and to correct: these were the characteristics of urban disciplinary systems. (3) Certain areas of the urban school were left to the discretion of the educational authorities: spaces where supervision could take place, where disciplinary interviews could occur, where the sick could be isolated and cared for—yet even these areas employed surveillance methods to control the children who congregated there. Teaching and deportment were part of the larger control problems in urban schools: the control over the body of the youngsters had to be complete. Thus it was necessary to separate the urban schooling community and to partition off areas where students were assigned a permanent location. (4) Discipline, in the urban schools especially, was defined by an individual's right to be present in a place and circumstance. A person's rank was of the utmost importance in determining what role he or she might play in normal interaction inside the building. Discipline was merely one way that rank was affirmed and strengthened inside the school itself. It designated the status and authority of persons as they conducted their business together. In earlier periods, rank among students was shown by a youngster's seat in a particular row and file, by a class position or placard placed in the corridors or assembly rooms.[14]

By assigning places to students, the routinization and regimentation of schoolwork became possible; supervision became a simple matter of noticing whether students were deviating from the prescribed norms of teachers. Urban children were seen as raw materials that had to be molded into dependable, efficient workers and Americans. They had to be trained to perform routine, uninteresting work in the factories and offices of the commercial world. This explains, in part, the constant demand for standardization, predigested lessons and learning materials, and the physical arrangements of the urban classroom. They facilitated surveillance and evaluation by teachers and administrators. Purposeful movements were encouraged, as they were in the industrial workplace and the world of trade and commerce.[15]

The most difficult problem regarding urban education concerned its relationship to the poor, the immigrant, and the minorities. Since these groups were without sufficient property and power, their schooling was of less concern to politicians and educators alike. By the middle of the nineteenth century, records show that poor youth of Massachusetts were already being incarcerated in reform schools in order to force them to attend school regularly. It was expected that Irish Catholic students and families would willingly send their children to schools that preached Protestant values and doctrines, but this did not happen. In many an urban town or city, parochial schools were built so that Irish youth would not become estranged from the values and beliefs of their families and kinfolk.

THE REFORM SCHOOL AT WESTBOROUGH

When the Westborough state reform school was opened in Massachusetts in 1848, it was intended as a place for neglected, wayward children. It was not to be thought of as a children's prison. It was to look as little as possible like a penitentiary while ensuring that students could not escape their incarceration. The commissioners made a distinction between character formation and reform, and punishment: "The fact must never be lost sight of that the prime object of the school is the reformation of the boy, and not his punishment. . . . It is to prevent him from becoming a criminal, and to make him a man."[16]

The same principles of public education were affirmed: "respect for authority, self-control, self-discipline, self-reliance, and self-respect." The goal was, according to Westborough's first superintendent, the acquisition by the boy of a fixed character and a complete transformation of his inner self and personality.

There were attempts to simulate family life in order to make the experience at Westborough more palatable. Each cottage in the family system was supervised by a married couple with authority to manage and control the boys in their households. Sixty boys were given the opportunity to live in these domestic, homelike settings. Such efforts touched only the most compliant and cooperative of youngsters. Efforts were made to place some of the boys on farms where they could learn to perform productive labor. An attempt was also made to counteract the vicious effects of urban life, providing youth with the moral teachings they would need in their adult lives. Still, most students lived in more impersonal, institutional settings where tight scheduling, punitive discipline, and work took up most of their time. During the 1860s, the students made shoes and chairs, but in the beginning most worked on sewing and knitting chores while others performed domestic labor. The chair making was done for a private contractor who paid "the school one and one quarter cents per hour for the labor of each boy."[17]

The reform school used confinement as a means of character reformation: it sought to teach boys to subordinate themselves to their responsibilities in the institutional community; it controlled the environment in which students worked and studied; and it acted as a substitute parent. Education and ignorance were thought to be in invidious opposition to one another. One possessed a moral authority while the other was almost akin to sinfulness itself. Education's effectiveness was affirmed by the growing industries and bureaucracies of the nation. Since earliest times, education has been thought of as the mark of a cultured and gentlemanly person. It was not only these ideological and legal requirements that directed the schools to teach urban youth, but also the pressing needs of machine society.

The obligation to reform the delinquent youth of urban Massachusetts was used as the rationale for establishing Westborough and the common schools. The Board of State Charities believed that social reform had to come through an enlightenment of conscience of the prosperous, as well as the indigent, of the commonwealth. Here is their admonition, concluding their 1865 report: citizens had to understand the root causes of poverty and crime so they could "take interest and direct action in social improvement, by levelling from below upward." Where "the degree of poverty that excludes education exists," it "abases and finally destroys self-respect, breeding diseases, indolence and vice. The property of all becomes unsafe and the morals of the community weakened."[18] School reformers believed that authority, kindliness, enlightenment of conscience, and constant labor were the four primary elements of social redemption. This commitment to purposeful activity, to which religion and industrial society were deeply bound, had as its counterpoint the hatred of aimlessness and indolence. Those who waited for charity, luck, or God to come to their aid in this life were sinful, since they disobeyed the commandment of the Scriptures: "Thou shalt not tempt the Lord thy God." As Calvin had taught centuries earlier, the reluctance of the poor to work meant that they were "trying beyond measure the power of God." They were seeking a miracle, but the miracle of labor and labor's rewards was granted to people every day of their life. If it is true that idleness is the pathway to evil and sin, then purposeful work is the way to the realization of God's will on earth. This was why idleness was considered akin to rebellion by the people of Boston: it burdened them with a sinful and ever-increasing welfare population. Indolence was the sin of humankind in the Garden of Eden, but the sin was more keenly present in newly industrialized America. In the factory, where the workers had to be disciplined like their machines, idleness and insubordination were grievous faults.

So it was not surprising that urban delinquents were incarcerated in reform schools: these institutions emphasized discipline, work, obedience to the rules, and attention to authority structures. From the beginning, students were forced to follow strict schedules and work assignments or be punished by more severe forms of confinement and physical abuse. One investigating team, discovered a group of boys manacled, in dismal "unsanitary cells," and in 1860, one newspaper described the "method of treatment . . . the vulgar and harsh method of convict discipline, enforced by the carrying of bludgeons and loaded weapons by some of the officers" that existed in the reform school.[19] Like prisoners in the penitentiary, students were forced to accept the conditions of forced labor.

In the workshops where they toiled long hours each day, boys were graded for reliability and productivity. Those who could be trusted were sometimes rewarded by placement in the farm school. The other 90 percent were confined in cells and provided a special regime designed for urban delinquents. By the mid 1850s education was firmly linked to social purposefulness in the minds of many Americans. Schools of all types condemned youth who were disruptive and unresponsive to teacher commands, suspending and transferring the worst offenders.

The relationship between the practice of compulsory attendance and routines in public schools was dictated by the large numbers of youth teachers had to serve in urban settings. The nation needed trained workers who could function well in the mechanistic world of work of the nineteenth century. A moral imperative supported and sustained pedagogical activities in these urban schools. When school authorities published their annual reports on the poor, it was made quite clear that the condition of their poverty was a result of their weak self-discipline and moral laxness. Both the common schools and the first reform school at Westborough were a way of rendering urban youth more tractable and useful in industrial society.

In this context, then, early reformers saw the growing urban and immigrant populations as a moral dilemma more than an economic one—hence the compulsory education laws that kept urban youth off the streets and out of the labor market. The student who could accept the authority and routines of the reform school could be released after a year or two, not so much because he would be less impoverished in the outside world, but because he had accepted the ethical standards and authority of the adult community. Schools specified that work must occupy the greater part of each day and must be interspersed with readings from pious books. This moral basis gave schoolmen and reform school officers their legitimacy and the right constantly to observe, judge, and punish perceived infractions in the name of society and the child's welfare. Only when students accepted the unquestioned pedagogic authority of the adult staff could they be taught the things they needed to know as adults. Finally, every fault was to be punished by a reduction of rations, by an increase in laboring time, by more severe forms of incarceration, and by other punishments that fit perceived transgressions.

THE URBAN HIGH SCHOOL

In the late 1800s, opinion about urban schooling began to shift more toward a training that prepared the student for his occupational future and taught him the language and culture of native Americans. The ideal urban school blended together the moral and ethical demands of the past with the secular requirements of an emerging industrialism; that ideal, however, took place in ways that were unsatisfactory to many educators and citizens. But it was not until the reform period and the establishment of people's colleges or high schools, that urban schooling as we now know it came into being. It was not until then that it became normal for teenagers to be kept in huge, impersonal urban schools and out of the labor market; it was not until then that people accepted the idea that workers in factories and bureaucracies needed to be certified by urban educational systems. Once this idea was accepted, the nature of urban schooling came to be regarded as a training experience for future citizens and workers, and more attention was paid to the labor power needs of business and industry.

What were the myths surrounding this expansion of secondary education? Foremost among them was the idea there would be people's colleges, opening up the system for the poorer and emerging lower middle classes. Authorities assured parents that all the resources of the state would be used to provide youngsters with equality of opportunity. All were promised an education that would be all things to all people. To immigrants and workers, the high school offered industrial and craft training; to merchants and businessmen, bookkeeping skills; to the college-bound, logic, language, and science; to the wealthy, the inner joys of a liberal arts education. To those who were concerned with the welfare of democracy, the high school promised to provide youth with the understandings and insights needed to participate effectively in self-government. To those who were concerned with discipline in the workplace, it promised to discipline students into accepting the authority of those who were in positions of power. Those were the ideologies of the system. But the real world of the high school was quite different. While it was being advertised as a gesture toward greater equality and democracy, its own structures were increasingly autocratic, and its methods of instruction were passive and dominated by rote recitations and a military discipline. Its goals were compromised and obscured by the demands for order and control in mass school buildings. Essentially, secondary education was encouraged as a way of counterbalancing the lack of industrial skills and poor attitudes of the urban immigrant and poor. It was seen as a way of safeguarding the American system during the period immediately following World War I, when changes in technology, bureaucracy, and urban life caused great confusion and discontent in all classes of society. The idea was to place urban youth in environments where they would be in constant contact with the more advanced concepts associated with modern life—skills in science, technology, and discipline.

Correction and coercion appeared as integral parts of the organizational structure of the urban high school; youngsters were to be confined there during their teens and discouraged from entering the already crowded labor market in any meaningful way. But this only reinforced the ideas of the old common schools of the late nineteenth century. Sites were chosen away from the surrounding urban community, and high schools of great size and density were built. Yet the pedagogy practiced in these new urban secondary schools was of a much greater intensity than anything seen in the lower grades. The power to transform students (that wretched refuse spoken about in the Statue of Liberty's inscription), to direct them, to correct their every movement and thought, and to command their obedience in all things allowed urban high schools to function as legitimate institutions of social selection and constraint. Here youth soon found that they could not disrupt or degrade the educational process without facing stern punishment—they were under adult domination and control during their most disorganized developmental period. The task of civilizing the urban young and teaching them to accept their place in an already constituted social and economic firmament became the urban high school's primary responsibility.

In summary, the urban high schools were institutions of symbolic and social control because they continued to track youth as the lower grades had done. They devised school districts that segregated students along racial and socio-economic lines, using curriculum and language that discriminated against the urban poor and minority students. They also provided urban youth with pedagogical experiences that were predicated upon the presumed future occupational role of youngsters, thus strengthening the status quo. They assaulted the self of students by forcing them to play the ignorant, incompetent person in the school setting. Finally, they created a mythology of fair competition that forced urban youth to experience their failures as personal ones.

The urban high school was, first and foremost, a state apparatus. It was a place of inculcation, of ethical transformation and regimentation of an immigrant and poor population into compliant Americans. Everything that was foreign was sacrificed to the demands of the native culture and bureaucratic efficiency. The evidences of personal identities were erased and replaced by institutional roles. In the first three decades of the twentieth century, the urban high schools were asked to bridge the gap between youth in America; they were commanded to open their doors to urban poor and immigrant youth who had been excluded in the past. The values of work and obedient enterprise, so important in modern industry and commerce, now governed the pedagogical actions in secondary schools. They were more effective than they had been in the primary grades. First, urban high schools controlled the bodily movements during the crucial years of teenage development. Second, the disorder and confusion of the adolescent, who seemed interested in little else than idleness and frivolity, required an iron discipline. The routines of work, as imitated in schoolwork, were to be emphasized.

These new urban high schools sought to reduce the differences between students; they sought to eliminate all that was spontaneous, irregular, unannounced, and alien. There were unintended effects to these pedagogies of social rejection: indifference and drop-out rates remained high into our present period. The urban high school was, in its urban manifestations, an agency of moral control and social transformation. Its problem was to impose an arbitrary language and culture upon urban youth, forcing them to denounce their own values and the cultural heritage of their families. The urban high school was to be a constant reminder to urban youth of their impoverished condition; it acted, by constant use of a corrective pedagogy, to fix in the students' mind an awareness of their class, ethnic and racial backgrounds, and status in American society. The tracking on the secondary level was easily established, from the first: to effect a social class stratification, urban high schools were given districts that were already segregated along racial and socioeconomic lines. The "better" high schools served the middle- and upper middle-class families while the "poorer" ones were to be found in the communities of the poorer, immigrant folk. To refine the system of tracking further, students were placed in classes according to their linguistic achievements. These pedagogical decisions assured an ethical basis for the ranking of urban youth, much as in the nineteenth-century common schools.[20]

Today, the role of urban schooling is less obscure than one might suppose: the bureaucratization of the entire urban culture and the belief that science and industry require educated managers and workers have led to mass urban schools in which millions of youngsters are processed in order to provide some with the credentials needed to succeed in the better occupations. In few past societies has schooling been given so important a role in the culture and economy of a nation, nor has it been elevated to such preeminence as it has in the personnel offices of the business world.

Here it should be pointed out that present-day urban schools are not endangered because of very high student failure rates. It must be remembered that these rates of failure have been with us for more than a century, and urban schooling has continued to expand. From the first, urban educational systems were reporting failure rates that were astounding by any measure. In Chicago in 1898, the schools reported 60 percent of their students at "normal age" grade level while 40 percent were failing! Urban schooling elsewhere reported these same soaring failure rates: 40 percent of those attending schools were listed as below "normal age" grade levels in Boston, Detroit, Philadelphia, Pittsburgh, New York, and Minneapolis. In Pittsburgh, 51 percent of the students were below "normal age"; in Minneapolis the number failing rose to 65 percent! Of course, these failure rates dealt only with schooling's survivors: those who had dropped out were no longer counted as failures![21]

From this, we can say that urban schooling has acted as a screen or sorting mechanism for American youth: it is a means of terminating ambition and desire in the poorer classes while validating the worth and privileges of the richer ones. The consequences for all were a sort of acceptance of the status quo that strengthened the social order and made most people feel that those in positions of power and control had gotten there fairly and on merits. The point should also be made that urban schooling in the nineteenth century acted as an ideological social glue, helping the poorer families to accept their condition as a reasonably fair one.[22]

THE SITUATION TODAY

Preparing youth to accept the economic system of a society happens in every society we know of, but social acceptability in the past was supported by oral imperatives and rigid class systems that were mutually supporting. We are in a similar situation today in that our nation is still suffused with moralistic and egalitarian ideologies that cause many to believe in the supposedly "fair and open competition" between youth in urban schools. Successful urban schooling is generally accepted as the validation of an individual's right to go on to higher forms of learning and earning; and discrimination is rejected by the poorer classes and minorities whenever it is identified. Behind all this lie a basic contradiction, a restless rejection of failure as it is being experienced by urban children in today's schools.

Most of the dissatisfaction with urban schooling and competition is unique to our period. It seems to indicate that people in the past did not see their failures as a systemwide problem as many of us do today. These people from the past— even our own grandparents—were more willing to accept their failures in schools and the workplace as personal ones. In this, they thought about things in ways that are increasingly different from the thinking of many of us and our children.

NOTES

1. Elwood P. Cubberley, *The History of Education* (Cambridge, MA: Houghton-Mifflin, 1920), 4–7.

2. Ibid., 8–10.

3. Nathan Edwards and H. G. Richey, *The School in the American Social Order* (Boston: Houghton-Mifflin, 1963), 237–38.

4. David Nasaw, *Schooled to Order* (New York: Oxford University Press, 1979), 20; see also John Karabel and Arthur H. Halsey eds., *Power and Ideology in Education* (New York: Oxford University Press, 1977).

5. Ibid., 80–81.

6. Elwood P. Cubberley, *Public Education in the United States* (Cambridge, MA: Houghton-Mifflin, 1934), 163–68.

7. Ibid., 189–94.

8. Stanley K. Schultz, *The Culture Factory* (New York: Oxford University Press, 1973), 298–300; see also the work of Basil Bernstein, *Pedagogic Discourse Vol. 4 Class, Codes and Control* (London: Routledge, 1991).

9. Michael B. Katz, "The New Departure in Quincy, 1873–1881," in Michael B. Katz, ed., *Education in American History* (New York: Praeger, 1973), 68–71.

10. Ibid., 84.

11. Robert C. Hummell and John M. Nagle, *Urban Education in America* (New York: Oxford University Press, 1973), 31–35.

12. Cubberley, *Public Education*, 322, 328.

13. David Tyack, "Bureaucracy and the Common School: The Example of Portland Oregon 1851–1913" in Michael Katz, ed., *Education in American History* (New York: Praeger, 1973), 166–67.

14. Ibid., 168–69. See also Michel Foucault, *Discipline and Punishment: The Birth of the Prison*, trans. Alan Sheridan (New York: Pantheon Books, 1961), 125–55.

15. Cubberley, *Public Education*, 321–22. See also David Tyack, *Turning Points in American Educational History*, (Waltham, MA: Blaisdell, 1967), 355–57.

16. W. David Lewis, *From Newgate to Dannemora: The Rise of the Penitentiary in New York 1796–1848* (Ithaca, NY: Cornell University Press, 1965), 201–2; see also Lawrence Cremin, *Transformation of the School* (New York: Knopf, 1961).

17. Michael S. Katz, *The Irony of School Reform* (Cambridge, MA: Harvard University Press, 1968), 185–94.

18. Joseph A. Allen, *Westborough State Reform School Reminiscences* (Boston: Century, 1877).

19. Katz, *The Irony*, 195–96.

20. Richard Rothstein, "How Tracking Works," in *Demystifying School*, (New York: Praeger, 1974), 61–73.

21. David Tyack, "Bureaucracy and the Common School: The Example of Portland Oregon 1851–1913," in Katz, *Education*, 164–65.

22. Colin Greer, *The Great School Legend* (New York: Basic Books, 1972), 13–22.

SELECTED BIBLIOGRAPHY

Allen, W. David. *From Newgate to Dannemora: The Rise of the Penitentiary in New York 1796–1848*. Ithaca, NY: Cornell University Press, 1965.

Bernstein, Basil. *Pedagogic Discourse Vol. 4 Class, Codes and Control*, London: Routledge, 1991.

Cremin, Lawrence. *Transformation of the School*. New York: Knopf, 1961.

Cubberley, Elwood P. *The History of Education*. Cambridge, MA: Houghton-Mifflin Company, 1920.

———. *Public Education in the United States*. Cambridge, MA: Houghton-Mifflin, 1934.

Edwards, Nathan, and Richey, H. G. *The School in the American Social Order*. Boston: Houghton-Mifflin, 1963.

Foucault, Michel. *Discipline and Punishment: The Birth of the Prison*, trans. Alan Sheridan. New York: Pantheon Books, Doubleday, 1961.

Greer, Colin. *The Great School Legend*. New York: Basic Books, 1972.

Hummel, Robert C., and Nagle, John N. *Urban Education in America*. New York: Oxford University Press, 1973.

Karabel, John, and Halsey, Arthur H., eds., *Power and Ideology in Education*. New York: Oxford University Press, 1977.

Katz, Michael S. *The Irony of School Reform*. Cambridge, MA: Harvard University Press, 1968.

———. "The New Departure in Quincy, 1873–1881." In Michael B. Katz, ed., *Education in American History*. New York: Praeger, 1973.

Lewis, W. David. *From Newgate to Dannemora: The Rise of the Penitentiary in New York 1796–1848*. Ithaca, NY: Cornell University Press, 1965.

Nasaw, David. *Schooled to Order*. New York: Oxford University Press, 1979.

Schultz, Stanley K. *The Culture Factory*. New York: Oxford University Press, 1973.

Tyack, David. *Turning Points in American Educational History*. Waltham, MA: Blaisdell, 1967.

———. "Bureaucracy and the Common School: The Example of Portland Oregon 1851–1913." In Michael Katz, ed., *Education in American History*. New York: Praeger, 1973.

2

Families, Children, Schools, and the Workplace

Richard J. Altenbaugh

Without education you can't get a job.

—Anonymous student

Many poor and working-class urban students no longer view schooling as either an intellectual experience or a socialization mechanism; rather it simply represents an institution designed to prepare them for work and possibly serving as a mode of social mobility. While the perception of social mobility claims historical precedent, the work preparation view does not. Children, for better or worse, have always had access to the workplace; but in recent decades this has changed. The avenue to work now runs through schooling.

This represents the most consistent finding of in-depth interviews of fifty-eight Pittsburgh "stopouts," that is, dropouts who have resumed schooling. Rough national data indicate that 10 to 35 percent of all dropouts return to school and that 90 percent of these continue their education onto postsecondary levels.[1] One hundred percent of the Pittsburgh narrators, when asked why they decided to return, responded that they "needed" to complete their general equivalency diploma (GED) and obtain some job training. "You need your education to get a job," they typically stated, or "I just wanted to have my GED and a trade."[2] The irony here was that these school leavers, who once found schooling so distasteful that they chose to abandon it, now conveyed an almost desperate tone, seeing their economic survival dependent on schooling. They needed jobs and saw no other alternative. Many observers would not express surprise by this response; some may even applaud it. However, as the students perceived it, schooling represented the only institutional bridge to the workplace. How can we explain this phenomenon?

These dropouts' comments need to be placed within a historical context. This chapter argues that transformations in American political economy, characterized by alterations in both social relations and workplace structure, during the past 150 years, have profoundly changed the institutional relationships among families, children, schools, and work. On the surface, this pretends to be an ambitious, synthetic chapter, but it represents more of a pencil sketch, proposing a different way to view "education" in urban society.[3] Further, this study, which revels in generalizations, skips from city to city in order to illustrate the universality of this experience. As David Nasaw, a social historian, comments about early twentieth-century part-time child laborers:

Working-class Irish kids in Toledo and Philadelphia, Jews in Youngstown and Syracuse, Poles in Chicago and Pittsburgh, Italians in Los Angeles and Cleveland, and "natives" in cities across the country earned their money after school by scavenging for the same kind of junk, selling afternoon papers, blacking boots, and peddling spearmint gum and chocolate bars to commuters, tourists, and people out for a good time on a Saturday night. Wherever they came from, they were expected to turn in their money to their parents.[4]

Social class bound these urban children together, regardless of their locale, religion, race, or ethnicity.

This chapter is divided into two parts: conceptual and chronological. The first section reviews the prevailing functionalist and radical explanations of these shifts. It builds on them by analyzing these social institutions within a historical context, tapping British social history as a model. The second part of this study analyzes the cumulative changes in relationships among families, children, and schools against the backdrop of American political economy. Because it stresses a political-economic approach, it defies traditional periodization. It begins with industrial capitalism during the early nineteenth century, then moves to monopoly capitalism in the late nineteenth century, and finally, briefly focuses on deindustrialization, which is presently unfolding.

CONCEPTUAL

Social Theories

Sociologist James Coleman addresses the relationships between social institutions in his insightful contributions on "social capital." As his thesis in "Families and Schools" warns, "America is at a watershed for families as socializing institutions and, more generally, as welfare institutions, for their dependent young." Social capital, that is, "the norms, the social networks, and the relationships between adults and children that are of value for the child's growing up," has undergone "extensive erosion" since the early 1960s. This decrease in social capital has occurred at the same time, overall, that parents' human capital ("increased levels of educational attainments") has risen. Although universal, this experience has significant implications for poor and working-class children, "for the loss of social capital in the community hurts most the children with least human and social capital in their families."[5]

Coleman explains this recent institutional shift by briefly tracing the historical "change of the locus of dominant activities in society." This all began with the household: "The whole structure of social and economic organization had as its basic building block the family." He relies on a technocratic, modernization model, pointing to the Industrial Revolution as the cause of removing "economically productive activities" from the home. More importantly, "when men left the household in great numbers for daily work outside of it, in the late nineteenth and early twentieth centuries, an extensive public investment was made in a new form of social capital, mass public schooling." Children began to acquire their occupational skills and learn their social values outside the family. Coleman then points to one of the current institutional changes, that more women are entering the work force, as one of "even greater magnitude in the lives of children." Although he treats this latter trend as a culmination of the earlier institutional shifts, he points to individualism and narcissism as additional causes. Coleman concludes, "As corporate actors have swallowed up an increasingly large portion of first men's and then women's activities and attention, the family has become a kind of backwater in society, cut off from the mainstream."[6] As a result, formal social capital has replaced informal social capital.

However, these transitions have been neither this smooth nor this simple. Coleman illuminates this subject, yet underplays broader political-economic transformations that have generated profound and complex alterations in the relationships not only between families and schools but also between children and the workplace. Moreover, conflict, not consensus, marked these changes.

The analysis of the connections between the political economy and educational change was pioneered in the work of Samuel Bowles and Herbert Gintis. As political economists, they see the workplace as a key variable in the relationship between schooling and the household. This becomes apparent as they describe a mechanistic "correspondence" between education and work:

The educational system helps integrate youth into the economic system . . . through a structured correspondence between its social relations and those of production. The structure of social relations in education not only inures the student to the discipline of the workplace, but develops the types of personal demeanor, modes of self-presentation, self-image, and social-class identifications, which are crucial ingredients of job adequacy.[7]

While they appear clear about how schooling reproduces the social division of labor, Bowles and Gintis seem ambivalent about the family. On one hand, family structure, too, parallels job structure: "Through family socialization, children tend to acquire orientations toward work, aspirations, and self-concepts, preparing them for similar economic positions themselves." Bowles and Gintis thus see other linkages between "family background and economic success." On the other hand, the family "exhibits social patterns that are quite uncharacteristic of the social relations of production.'' Here Bowles and Gintis emphasize the remoteness of intimate family life, contrasting ''the personal and emotional relationships, from the impersonal bureaucracy of the wage-labor system.''[8] Because of this experience, schooling has assumed the role as the sole integrator for the workplace.

This analysis reflects the culmination of a gradual shift in institutional roles, which grew directly from political economy transformations; Bowles and Gintis contend that this represents a blantant causal explanation. As factory production supplanted the family economy and as wages replaced ''prices'' and ''piece rates,'' workers and their children needed to become acclimated to this new reality, in which they had little control. This expansion of capital undermined not only the family's economic role but its socialization function as well. With growing inequality and poverty, ''economic leaders sought a mechanism to insure political stability and the continued profitability of their enterprises.'' For the capitalist class and school reformers, like Horace Mann of Massachusetts, universal elementary schooling served to instill acceptable industrial values, like subordination, obedience, discipline, punctuality, neatness, and courtesy. ''Upbringing in the family . . . was not adequate training for work in the rising industrial sector.''[9]

Cultural capital, in this theoretical scheme, simply and quietly shifted from the family to a new institution, public schooling. By the 1840s, the Lowell school committee ''saw the schools as a partial substitute for the home.'' Between 1820 and 1850, the percentage of school-aged children attending school experienced a ''significant increase'' as the percentage of the work force involved in nonagricultural pursuits rose. Bowles and Gintis further allude to the fact that many wage workers embraced schooling as a panacea, promising ''the respectability of security which they sought.'' Worker acquiescence had thus been achieved: common school reform, like that pioneered in Massachusetts, ''had the intent . . . of forestalling the development of class consciousness among the working people . . . and preserving the legal and economic foundations of society.''[10]

Bowles and Gintis perceive the same pattern when they analyze the consolidation of corporate capital between 1890 and 1930. They correctly characterize this period as the ''increasing centralization of capital and the associated increase in the size of the firms.'' Employers consequently exercised more control in the workplace through ''a complicated vertical segmentation of the labor force.'' This impersonal bureaucracy required a different type of worker. Employers needed ''more than obedience and punctuality from their workers; they began to look for workers who had internalized the production-related values of the firm's managers.'' ''Elites'' pushed for the expansion of schooling, with labor supporting these efforts: ''With the closing of the western frontier and the declining prospects for workers going into self-employment, small business, or cooperative trades, labor itself often stood behind educational expansion as the only remaining path toward mobility, security, and social respectability.'' The introduction of standardized testing and high school vocational curricula served as the sorting and stratification instruments that reproduced the division of labor.[11] This concept of expanded schooling implied a concomitant further shrinkage of the family's educational role, as well as consensual continuity.

Finally, Bowles and Gintis come full circle, outlining the rudiments of the more recent political-economic transformation and subsequent educational change. "The continued expansion of the corporate and state sectors of the economy" has produced an "emerging white-collar proletariat." Following their correspondence theory, this has prompted a significant change in the structure of higher education. A "multitiered system" of four- and two-year universities and colleges, with cosmopolitan Ivy League universities at one end of the spectrum and parochial community colleges at the other end, "reflects the social status of the families of the students and the hierarchy of work relationships into which each type of student will move after graduation."[12]

These analyses by Coleman and by Bowles and Gintis—one functionalist and the other radical—sound remarkably similar. Like Coleman, Bowles and Gintis see cultural capital solely controlled by schooling, not families. Furthermore, both Coleman and Bowles and Gintis present largely consensus arguments, implying that all poor and working-class families willingly, quietly, and even gladly surrendered their children to school authorities. This simply was not the case; historically, this has been a reluctant transition. Bowles and Gintis correctly reason that transformations in political economy profoundly affected school-family-work interactions, but workers were never so easily anesthetized, and the dynamics between poor and working-class families and schools proved more complex, variegated, and conflict-ridden than this social control model suggests; families struggled economically and socially to retain control of their workplaces and their children. The remainder of this chapter taps scattered secondary sources and some primary documents to recapture these struggles, stressing how poor and working-class parents and children proved to be vital and effective historical actors.

The British Experience

Many poor and working-class parents chose not to send their children to school, but that experience has too often been obfuscated or relegated to minor contextual material. American educational historians, who usually maintain a Whig approach, focusing on the institutional evolution of schools, or a revisionist interpretation, ignoring human agency, habitually overlooks parents' and children's perspectives and actions.[13]

J. S. Hurt, a British historian, has taken a different path, and his treatment of English and Welsh parents could be instructive for American social and educational historians. Prior to the Elementary Education Act of 1870, which mandated compulsory but not free schooling, laboring parents placed minimal, if not marginal, value on temporal knowledge for their children, who would spend their working lives toiling with their hands. These families also saw no need for the school to assume socialization or religious roles; inculcation of values remained the parents' prerogative. For them, schooling simply served the utilitarian function of literacy training, and they appeared willing to pay for this purpose. "Parents faced a double cost. They had not only to find money for school fees but they also had to forgo the child's earnings. The opportunity cost of losing a child's wages was a far greater burden than mere payment of the weekly fee." Parents therefore had alternatives, but "after the decade of the 1870s they lost this freedom of choice." This dramatically altered working-class culture:

No longer could parents take for granted the services of their children in the home and their contributions to the family budget. Traditional working-class patterns of behavior, when continued, did so in defiance of the law. The state had interfered with the pattern of family life by coming between parent and child, reducing family income, and imposing new patterns of behavior on both parent and child.[14]

Hurt elaborates the struggles between families and school officials over children, in an insightful chapter, titled "Schools, Parents, and Children." During the 1870s, school authorities conducted less-than-legal sweeps through urban neighborhoods "to round up the children and haul them off to school. In Manchester these sorties into the urban jungle had led to affrays when parents had tried to rescue captives. People then had to be summoned to rescue the would-be captors." Many families also objected to the schooling process, particularly corporal punishment. They occasionally dragged a schoolmaster before a magistrate because of excessive abuse. However, few working-class parents challenged school content, usually acquiescing over religious instruction in the schools. They chose "not to exercise their legal rights. The 'fear of incurring the displeasure of their superiors in the neighborhood and imperiling their employment' was enough to deter them."[15]

Human agency culminates in Hurt's final chapter, "Unwillingly to School." Employers and families alike cooperated to evade the law, as one factory inspector recalled: "As soon as an inspector pays one of his rare visits to a stocking village, his coming is at once made known, and children are quickly hidden away, under steps or baskets and in cupboards and holes, and when his back is turned, employers and parents congratulated themselves on their good luck and adroitness in escaping detection."[16] This collusion included boys and girls, working full-time and part-time, and encompassed a variety of industries. One brickfield inspector recounted, "Report has it that once I stepped on a girl under some matting without discovering her."[17] Seemingly clever inspectors resorted to a variety of ploys in order to surprise their prey, but often to no avail. Unfenced iron mills, for instance, worked against them: "The boys dropped their tongs and ran like rabbits."[18]

School attendance remained problematic well into the twentieth century. Even as late as 1967, many poor and working-class families placed little economic value on schooling: "In the working-class home the bright child was the one who demonstrated his academic prowess by leaving as early as legally possible."[19] Thus, as Hurt concludes about the English and Welsh experience, many working-class parents did not support school attendance. Contrary to traditional interpretations and popular notions, a similar mixed pattern existed in the United States.

The relationships among families, children, schooling, and work have profoundly changed during the past 150 years, and American historians, like their British counterparts, can capture this experience. What follows is a speculative approach, arguing that the centrality of work serves as the key to understanding these interactions. Since the workplace and working-class culture represent the foci of this chapter, each of the following sections, which treat each political-economic transformation, begins with an analysis of workplace and structural issues.

AMERICAN POLITICAL ECONOMY

Industrial Capitalism

In order to understand American worker response to industrial capitalism, we must first grasp preindustrial structure, "behavior and attitudes." Labor historian David Montgomery reconstructed the preindustrial working classes of Baltimore, Boston, New York, and Philadelphia, leading cities in the early national period, and found three distinct components. First, "journeymen mechanics," or craftsmen, represented a class distinct from poor and common laborers. These printers, shoemakers, tailors, carpenters, stonecutters, and other artisans controlled the work process in their skilled areas as well as set prices, and remained ever proud and protective of their traditions. Second, "male wage laborers," whose occupations ranged from "seamen and longshoremen at one end of the scale to journeymen at the other," contrasted sharply with skilled mechanics; this "seaport poor" sold their labor power rather than skill, relinquishing control of their work. They consequently experienced deteriorating conditions, growth, and greater visibility. By 1830, this segment of the unskilled constituted 40 percent of Philadelphia's working classes and 25 percent of that city's total population. Third, women and children often served as the initial manufacturing labor force, operating spinning jennies in Philadelphia and Boston. In 1814, eighty-seven cotton mills nationwide maintained a "labor force of 500 men and 3,500 women and children."[20]

Some early industrialists, as educational historian Lawrence Cremin points out, even hired whole families for the emerging factory system. In 1800, Samuel Slater recruited parents and their children for his new and enlarged cotton mill in Pawtucket, Rhode Island: "The new arrangement relieved Slater and his partners of the responsibilities of oversight in the factories: the parents themselves supervised the children at work and in the process not only maintained social discipline but provided substantial legitimatization for the employment of young children."[21] This use of the "so-called family system" not only became widespread, used in Rhode Island, Connecticut, and Massachusetts, but persisted through the early twentieth century, as Tamara Hareven argues in her study of the Amoskeag Mills.[22]

Thus, a highly varied, deeply textured, and extremely dynamic working-class structure and culture began to assert themselves before industrial capitalism. Many of those class trends continued through the nineteenth century. More importantly, working-class families responded in a variety of ways to public schooling, which began in Massachusetts during the 1840s.

Even with the transformation of mercantile capitalism to industrial capitalism, as workers began their struggles for control of their work, they continued to maintain autonomy over their children. Like their English and Welsh counterparts, American families and schools clashed over the fundamental notion of authority. In Carl Kaestle's balanced study of nineteenth-century educational history, "School reformers argued for the precedence of state responsibility over traditional parental responsibility for education." Some parents disagreed, however. "They took their children's side in cases of school discipline, disrupting school sessions to argue with teachers, in some cases assaulting the teacher and in others having the teacher arrested and brought before a magistrate." Other parents, protesting school policies, simply kept their children at home; still others subverted school authority and sowed student defiance by openly criticizing teachers in front of their children. As Kaestle aptly summarizes:

Parents and teachers in the antebellum Northeast were not in a state of declared war, but neither was their relation blissful. The indifference of many parents to school exhibitions, the persistent belligerence of some others resisting school discipline, and the anti-parental propaganda of antebellum educators belie the notion of consensus and collaboration.[23]

The "family labor system," as Thomas Dublin, a social historian, labels it, appeared to be a universal phenomenon during the nineteenth century. In the Lowell mills, children earned from 51 to 71 percent of family income, depending on family structure and family cycle. "Children's earnings must have amounted to more than 80 percent of family income in female-headed households." In other families, more children, of course, meant increased family earnings, and older children raised family income as they gradually became adult wage earners. This system appeared to be so integrated that "payroll records for 1850 and 1860 provide repeated instances in which fathers signed for and probably picked up their children's pay envelopes." School enrollment reflected this reality; "only 24 percent of the children attended school." Gender represented an important distinction, however:

The vast majority of boys in the 10–13 year old age group remained in school and did not work, in contrast to girls of the same age. About 74 percent of boys in this age attended school and did not work, compared to only 52 percent among girls. Conversely, almost 42 percent of girls worked, while only 13 percent of boys of this age did so. Between 14 and 17 the gap in employment rates between boys and girls narrowed until by age 18 the work patterns of the two groups were roughly the same.

Parents believed that schooling possessed more value for boys. Because of a paucity of evidence, Dublin presents a speculative explanation, that families attempted to extract greater earnings from their soon-to-wed daughters. Moreover, families saw some vague connection between schooling and the enhanced earnings of their sons, who would serve as breadwinners.[24]

In Milwaukee, between 1840 and 1860, Kathleen Neils Conzen, an urban historian, found that school attendance depended on social class and ethnicity. Germans maintained the lowest attendance level regardless of social position yet retained the highest literacy rate. In 1850, they comprised 38 percent of that town's work force and occupied "high visibility at all levels of the city's economic ladder," with 20 percent nonmanual, 50 percent skilled, 5 percent semiskilled, and 20 percent unskilled. School attendance, public or private, appeared most problematic for the latter two groups. Children of casual laborers found work to provide immediate relief for their families, particularly if the father had suffered illness or injury. In fact, the whole family found work: "The mother did laundry, the young boys sawed wood, and the sisters entered domestic service. Other families even more desperate set their younger children to begging or raiding backyard swill barrels for garbage and grease to feed the hogs." However, some semiskilled and unskilled families managed to apprentice their twelve- to fourteen-year-old sons as machinists, carpenters, or masons. "For families who could do without immediate income from their sons, such apprenticeships were a means of ensuring a more secure future for their children."[25]

A similar strategy guided decisions about Milwaukee's German daughters. Boys, as in Lowell, attended school more often than girls, who usually found employment as live-in servants. "Parents were assured that domestic service involved no loss of status, that it meant training for the household the girl would hope to run after her marriage, and a chance to earn a nest egg in the meantime."[26]

Apprenticeship represented a direct relationship among families, children, and work. Cremin describes its colonial antecedents:

It involved a formal contract between a youngster (most often a boy, occasionally a girl), a master craftsman or tradesman, and the youngster's parent(s) or guardian. The most important elements in the contract were the youngster's promise to serve the master in all lawful commands and capacities over a stipulated period of time and the master's promise in turn to teach the youngster the arts and mysteries associated with a particular craft or trade.[27]

This implied systematic instruction in the workplace. With the expansion of shop production and a persistent labor shortage throughout the nineteenth century, this relationship became less formal, with traditional apprenticeship experiences shrinking from seven to six, or even five, years; nevertheless, ''apprenticeship remained the most common form of craft training.''[28] The Boston school board rationalized low attendance during the early nineteenth century: ''The parents of scholars are able to find places to put them out as apprentices, or in counting houses.''[29] This experience was changing, however. As the deskilling of labor continued, artisans saw apprenticeship erode further. Master printers and shoemakers virtually disappeared by mid-century. Others would soon follow, as we shall see.

Parents reasoned therefore that work and work training, not schooling, not only ensured that they and their children would be financially secure but could facilitate occupational mobility. They had direct access to the workplace for jobs and, better yet, apprenticeship experience.

These strategies of choice may be generalized for the antebellum period. The common school movement certainly appeared to increase school enrollment. According to Kaestle's analysis, a 50 percent attendance rate represented the northern ''norm'' by 1850. ''Indeed, investigation of enrollments for eight towns in Massachusetts in 1860, for Washtenaw County, Michigan, in 1850, and Chicago in 1860 reveal rates of 85 to 95 percent at the prime common-school ages, seven to thirteen, for all ethnic and occupational groups.'' However, ''pockets'' of nonattenders still concerned educators, particularly in ''urban slums and factory tenements.'' In Philadelphia's cotton mills ''the working day for children and adults alike ranged from eleven to fourteen hours. One-fifth of the employees were under age twelve, and no provision was made for their education. Of all the employees under eighteen, only one-third could read or write.'' Kaestle, too, points out that employers appeared to be ambivalent concerning child labor; some complied with the weak child labor laws while others painlessly ignored them. Some parents likewise violated these child labor restrictions: ''Factory workers needed the extra income.''[30]

The emergence of public high schools, seemingly fulfilling the democratic ideal of free schooling for all, again failed to reflect all social classes. For Kaestle, ''precise studies of high schools in Chicago, New York, and Salem in the 1850s'' indicate that

sons of clerks, merchants, proprietors, craftsmen, and professionals attended these high schools. A few factory workers' sons appear on the rolls, but the lower working class is severely underrepresented. The trend in graduates' careers was toward white-collar work, both clerical and professional, regardless of whether the boys' fathers worked in manual or nonmanual jobs. The New York graduates of 1858 included a brass turner's son who became a lawyer, a machinist's son who became a bookkeeper.[31]

Kaestle further speculates that the ongoing deskilling of labor prompted craftsmen, more and more, to send their sons to high school instead of arranging an apprenticeship experience for them: ''Some fathers with such artisan labels may have been substantial craftsmen or even proprietors of their own businesses;

however, because of changes from craft to factory production, some members of this artisan group may have felt anxious about their positions and their sons' futures.''[32]

The need to work and changes in the work process therefore shaped family decisions concerning the importance of schooling. For the children of unskilled parents, the workplace remained open to them, with the growing demand for unskilled labor. Some parents needed their children's income to ensure the survival of the family, while other parents saw work as educational, teaching values and skills necessary for economic survival. Yet, ever so gradually, as witnessed by mid-century attendance patterns among some craftsmen's sons, schooling was beginning to function as a bridge to a job. With the decline of crafts, they saw schooling as the source of new values, skills, and job security.

Nevertheless, resistance characterized the relationship of many poor and working-class parents and their children to schooling with the transformation from mercantile capitalism to industrial capitalism. First, in general, some parents resisted the imposition of school authority over their children, confronting teachers and administrators about school values and procedures. Second, in particular, many poor and working-class parents continued to withhold their children from school throughout the nineteenth century. According to 1880 data from the St. Louis schools, "Eighty percent of the sons of professional fathers and 64 percent of the sons of white-collar workers between the ages of thirteen and sixteen were in school, compared to only 32 percent of the sons of unskilled laborers." While many boys chose not to attend high school, girls did, often in overwhelming numbers: one rough, 1866 estimate indicates that female secondary students outnumbered males by a margin of two to one.[33] Families thus continued to retain control of their children as work grew increasingly unskilled and the struggle for the workplace intensified.

Monopoly Capitalism

David Montgomery analyzes the meaning of, and changes in, worker control during the late nineteenth and early twentieth centuries. Workers exercised power over the "direction of production processes" at the end of the century. "This control became increasingly collective, deliberate and aggressive," only to be confronted by scientific management and the corporate structure and counterattacked by the open shop movement of the early twentieth century. Montgomery points to three evolving strategies—the "autonomous craftsman," "union work rules," and "mutual support"—employed by workers to assert and maintain their power in the workplace. The first level of resistance implied an unwritten agreement among skilled workers over work rules, encompassing both the quantity and the quality of goods produced. "The functional autonomy of craftsmen rested on both their superior knowledge, which made them self-directing at their tasks, and the supervision which they gave to one or more helpers." This often assumed outright defiance, or "manliness," as Montgomery labels it. The next tier of control struggles involved the codification of work rules. Some unions "legislated" a "fixed term of apprenticeship for any prospective journeyman, established a standard wage for the trade, prohibited helpers or handymen from performing journeymen's work, and forbade any member from running more than one machine at a time or accepting any form of piecework payment." After 1886, unions increasingly enforced these work regulations with employers through strikes. The third level of resistance assumed mutual aid through sympathy strikes, clearly characterizing a growing sense of worker solidarity. This strategy peaked between 1890 and 1892: "The number of establishments shut by sympathetic strikes rose from an average of 166 yearly between 1886 and 1889 to 732 in 1890, 639 in 1891, and 738 in 1892." These efforts proved to be deliberate and methodical; they represented "part of the struggle for craftsmen's control—its most aggressive and far-reaching manifestation."[34]

Employers responded by purposefully and systematically accelerating the deskilling process through the introduction of scientific management, ultimately destroying "work practices which had been the taproot of whatever strength organized labor enjoyed in the late nineteenth century." Widespread adoption of the corporate structure, expanding the scale of industry, further alienated workers. This alteration in work patterns and relationships, the key features of the transformation to monopoly capitalism, did not easily deter unskilled workers, however. They now resorted to a new tactic, mass walkouts, in order to counter large-scale industry. Between 1909 and 1910, tens of thousands of workers participated in strikes against the garment industry in New York City, the Pressed Steel Car Company near Pittsburgh, the great armament works of Bethlehem Steel, and the city government of Philadelphia. True, protests now centered on job conditions,, like the eight-hour day, rather than work rules. Nevertheless, this militancy grew directly from the workplace, as Montgomery stresses: "That most large strikes of the epoch ended in total defeat for the workers testifies both to the audacity of the strikers' pretentions and to their willingness to act in defiance of warnings from experienced union leaders that chances of victory were slim." This attitude, part of a long-term and changing pattern of worker efforts to control their workplace, would continue. "The direct, mass-involvement challenge to managerial authority and contempt for accepted AFL [American Federation of Labor] practice workers exhibited in 1909–10 were to remain the outstanding characteristics of American labor struggles, not episodically but continuously for the next dozen years."[35]

The persistent deskilling of work profoundly affected family income and roles. An 1893 statistical analysis of workers in the coal, iron, and steel industries revealed that the "husband's" average earnings only accounted for 85 percent of the total income necessary to support his family. This report included only the wages of skilled workers, such as "foremen, miners, engineers, masons, etc."[36] Skilled workers, of course, received the highest wages, which allowed them to support their families better than their semiskilled and unskilled counterparts. These latter groups faced serious financial deficiencies. Yet, in spite of the disruptions of industrial life, the working-class family, growing increasingly unskilled and often unemployed, remained intact and stable. According to Virginia Yans-McLaughlin, the family functioned as a "working productive unit" in order to resolve the income shortfall of the paternal parent. It employed a variety of strategies, either singularly or in combination, such as taking in boarders, finding employment for mothers, and sending the children to work.[37]

The former two often proved difficult. Lodgers could be accommodated only if the family rented a larger apartment or purchased a house. The money collected from the boarders supplied extra income as well as defrayed higher rent or mortgage costs. If successful, this tactic could add at least 25 percent to the family's income. This arrangement produced a speculative financial situation, however. If the lodgers suddenly moved out, the family immediately had to find a replacement or assume this heavy debt out of their already meager earnings. Moreover, as Margaret Byington found in her 1910 study of Slavic steelworkers in Homestead, boarders often disrupted family life, exacerbated cramped living quarters, and created considerably more work for the mothers and female children. Finally, like their middle-class counterparts, they guarded their privacy.[38]

Working mothers, because of cultural barriers and industrial obstacles, represented another unevenly utilized strategy. In 1905,, "Buffalo's Irish, Polish, Swedish, and German women commonly sought employment as domestics in middle-class homes." However, not all ethnic groups tolerated working mothers employed outside the home; some 86 percent of southern Italian women "did not sacrifice child-rearing responsibilities for work."[39] Further, as Byington noted in 1910, local "industrial conditions . . . determine the family life."[40] Towns dominated by heavy industries, such as iron and steel, offered few employment opportunities for women.

This left child labor as the only viable option to augment the income of the hard-pressed working-class family. Therefore, in order to survive, poor and working-class families chose, among a variety of strategies, to send their children to work. They often saw little connection between schooling and the workplace. They had access to work and exploited it. Few obstacles existed. "In 1898, there were still twenty-four states and the District of Columbia without a minimum age requirement for children employed in manufacturing." With the existence of weak state compulsory attendance laws, like that passed in Massachusetts in 1852 and Connecticut in 1871, which excused poor children from school in order to work, schooling became even more easily expendable.[41] Schooling through the nineteenth and early twentieth centuries appeared to be a matter of choice rather than compulsion. Cultural patterns, as we have seen, reinforced this notion, with working children a common characteristic of rural, preindustrial, and early industrial life. This is precisely what Angus and Mirel, two educational historians, found in their detailed investigation of the entry into the work force by the children of textile workers. Focusing on the 1888 to 1890 period, they conclude: "The decision for a child to enter the work force was exactly that—a decision. . . . At any level of father's income, at any occupational level, at any birth position, some children were at school and some at the same age were at work." Work at a young age was seen as a virtue, not a vice, teaching children diligence, discipline, and responsibility: "Overwork . . . was a preferable alternative to overcoddling."[42]

Children of all ages represented a universal source of labor in industrial America. During a Senate investigation of relations between labor and capital in the 1880s, George Blair, a box manufacturer, testified that children produced between 40 and 50 percent of the manufactured goods in New York State. A New York City tailor confessed that he saw six-year-olds working in the nation's largest cotton mill.[43] In 1880, 29 percent of all males employed in the glass industry were under sixteen years of age.[44] According to the 1910 census, an estimated 2 million children below the age of sixteen worked; 26 percent of cotton textile workers in 1907 claimed to be younger than sixteen.[45] Schooling became so expendable that, in 1914, 60 to 65 percent of all children abandoned it by the fifth or sixth grade. This trend assumed gender and class differences, however. During the first decade of the twentieth century, "17 percent more girls than boys completed elementary school." By the twelfth grade, girls constituted 61 percent and boys 39 percent of the student body. Tyack and Hansot juxtaposed social class and found "fewer working-class boys than working-class girls continued in school, suggesting that males dropped out more often to work." For Angus and Mirel, class more than any other variable shaped work force entry: "Families opting to keep their children in school longer were 'better off' in a number of ways; their fathers had higher incomes and higher status jobs, they lived in less crowded homes which they were more likely to own, and they found it possible to live within their means."[46] Working children's high visibility caused one manufacturer to relate an ironic analogy to Helen Todd, a factory inspector, who published her 1909 survey of Chicago's child labor: "Ever see that box factory in the next block? It's worth seeing. Go into one of those rooms, and you'd think you were in the fourth grade of a Polish school."[47]

Child workers faced brutal conditions. While the majority of cotton textile workers earned between $5.00 and $6.00 per week in 1910, full-time working children younger than sixteen seldom made more than $3.00. Almost half of the children employed in industry worked at least ten hours a day. In the metal trades, 92 percent of the children under sixteen worked more than fifty-four hours a week, and 32 percent of these worked a sixty-hour week.[48] Schooling did little to increase their earning power, as one young factory worker expressed it to Todd: "What ye learn in school ain't no good. Ye git paid as much in the factory if ye never was there. Our boss he never went to school."[49]

These children learned well their lessons on the job. Like their working parents, they occasionally asserted their control over the workplace, as Nasaw describes in his treatment of street workers. In 1899, New York City newsies protested against the distribution procedures implemented by Joseph Pulitzer's *World* and William Randolph Hearst's *Post* by forming a union and organizing a large and successful strike. "They cemented their informal communities of the street into quasi-formal unions, held mass meetings, elected officers, declared strikes, paraded through the streets shouting their demands, 'soaked scabs,' and held together as long as they possibly could.'' Messengers and bootblacks initiated a sympathy strike, joining the newsies in ''what nearly became a children's general strike.'' This militancy spread to other cities, like Rochester, Syracuse, Philadelphia, Pittsburgh, Boston, Cincinnati, and Lexington, Kentucky. Nevertheless, while these strikers acted to protect their workplace, ''the New York City union, like most of the other children's unions, was an ephemeral organization with a limited life span.'' A second wave of strikes broke out between 1916 and 1918 but ended with mixed results.[50]

The cultural milieu aside, early twentieth-century children, like many of their nineteenth-century predecessors, worked primarily because of economic necessity. As Todd wrote in 1912, ''A great part of child labor comes from the premature death or disability of the father through industrial accident or disease, or the unemployment of the father through being engaged in an industry which occupies its people only a portion of the year at low wages.'' According to one factory owner she interviewed, ''As far as I can make out, the women and children support the entire family.'' Children realized the crucial trade-off between school and work, as one related it to Todd: ''Oncet I worked in a night school in the Settlement, an' in the day school too. Gee I humped myself. I got three cards with 'excellent' on 'em. An' they never did me no good. My mother she kept 'em in the Bible, an' they never did her no good, neither. They ain't like a pay envelope.''[51] Schooling offered long-term intangible rewards while work, which remained easily accessible, guaranteed immediate monetary gains and potential future opportunities. A 1916 U.S. Department of Labor study of the conditions of child and women wage earners determined the value of this trade-off. The report encompassed the cotton and silk textile, clothing, and glass industries and found that children, aged fourteen and fifteen, accounted for 18.3 percent of their family's incomes.[52]

Many children also preferred work because they so disliked schooling. Public schools often employed harsh methods. As Todd pointed out in her survey, ''Of some 800 children questioned, 269 gave as their one reason for preferring a factory to a school, that they were hit there.'' One child described his school experiences: ''They hits ye if ye don't learn, and they hits ye if ye whisper, and they hits ye if ye have string in yer pocket, and they hits ye if yer seat squeaks, and they hits ye if ye don't stan' up in time, and they hits ye if yer late, and they hits ye if ye forget the page.'' At times, school discipline proved more oppressive than factory work. ''Nothing that a factory sets them to do,'' Todd concluded, ''is so hard as learning.''[53]

However, the reign of the street traders in particular and child laborers in general was beginning to wane. Child labor declined between 1900 and 1930 from 186,358 to under 30,000 for children aged ten to thirteen. Technological, cultural, and educational changes took their toll. ''By the 1920s,'' according to Nasaw, ''the children of the city had been pushed to the side by the automobile, which cut off their play and work space, by tougher and better-enforced child labor laws, and by adults who moved into the trades they once monopolized."[54] Sociologist Viviana Zelizer takes a slightly different stance than Nasaw, moving beyond "the effect of structural, economic, and technological changes on child labor trends." Certainly the growing labor supply squeezed children out of the workplace, and rising real income allowed families to keep their children in school. These factors for Zelizer initiated a gradual change, profoundly transforming "children's economic roles." Children thus became "emotional and moral assets" rather than raw economic partners. Much improved "compulsory education laws further accelerated the unemployment of children." These factors best explain the ebbing of child labor, since "effective federal regulation of child labor was only obtained after the Depression, first with the National Industrial Recovery Act and in 1938 with the Fair Labor Standards Act, which introduced a section on child labor."[55]

More importantly, the lines between the workplace and schooling began to blur, thus continuing the long process of marginalizing the family. The cooperative education movement signified one of the early formalized expressions of special education for poor and working-class students. With the support of the National Society for the Promotion of Industrial Education (NSPIE), an amalgamation of educators and industrialists, thirteen cooperative schools were developed in eastern industrial centers. In Beverly, Massachusetts, the Union Shoe Company contracted with the local high school in 1909 to train students at its plant for four years. Students worked fifty hours a week for twenty-five weeks at the shoe factory and attended classes at the high school for thirty hours a week during the following twenty-five weeks. While at the high school, however, students continued to participate in industrial training classes for fifteen hours a week.[56]

The Union Shoe Company, as Paul McBride, an educational historian, demonstrates, greatly profited from this arrangement. First, state and local school authorities reimbursed the company for expenses, such as light, heat, electricity, and machine rental, that it incurred in the training process. The company therefore subsidized part of its fixed overhead through its participation in this educational venture. Second, the company paid students only one-quarter of the normal wage scale. In this manner, the company, claiming inexperienced labor, had a ready pool of extremely cheap labor. Third, the company deducted half of the students' meager wages in order to defray its operating costs further. Finally, "the company made at least normal profits from all the shoes which it purchased from the students at established prices."[57]

In Fitchburg, Massachusetts, "educators designed the high school course to produce the 'right attitude' in the co-op students." In English class, students read *Romance of Industry and Invention*, *Romance of Modern Electricity*, *Story of the Railroad*, *Careers of Danger and Daring*, and other histories of "successful men"; the biographies and stories of noted industrialists received considerable attention. The Fitchburg school also established rigid guidelines that students had to obey: "Remember the object of work is production. . . . It is your business to get along smoothly with the workmen and foremen; not theirs to get along with you. . . . Don't be a kicker and don't continually bother your foreman for higher wages." As McBride summarizes, "Educators and industrialists carefully planned the academic education for the participants in the industrial program to instill obedience and docility."[58] Training the working class through vocational education programs became a universal experience. Educational historian Paul Violas notes that in 1909, 25 percent of New York's high school population attended a vocational program. The statistics from other cities prove even more dramatic, with 33 percent in Chicago in 1913, 57 percent in Cincinnati in 1911, and 56 percent in Elyria, Ohio, in 1918.[59] The 1917 Smith-Hughes Act legitimized the juxtaposition of schooling with work.

With the Great Depression, the "youth problem" no longer focused on child labor but concentrated on youth unemployment. Mirel and Angus note a "profound and permanent shift in the basic relationships between youth, schools, and unemployment." In order to attract and retain the remaining 50 percent of dropouts, school officials began to shift curricular emphases. National leaders like Charles M. Prosser, an advocate of secondary vocational preparation and NSPIE executive secretary, supported a "life-education curriculum in which vocational education played a diminished role." The rationale for this approach stemmed from the perceived death of entrepreneurship and the emergence of persistent unemployment, with school dropouts threatening to become a "permanent underclass." Thus, in the Detroit schools, the majority of students now enrolled in courses like Personal Service, studying diet, etiquette, and dating. The results appeared dramatic: "While high school enrollments rose in Detroit by 61 percent from 1929 to 1939, the number of graduates increased by 237 percent." The schools in this case appeared in withdrawing students from the labor market. Mirel and Angus, generalizing from this depression-era Detroit school experience, maintain that educators "shifted the purpose of their institutions away from college and vocational preparation and toward a custodialship of the young based on the conviction that there were not meaningful jobs for them and that their task was to adjust youth to that state of affairs."[60]

Hogan illustrates a similar attendance trend in Chicago. Between 1880 and 1930, school enrollment gradually increased for all ethnic, racial, and social class groups. In 1930, 97 percent of the seven–thirteen age group went to school, 94.6 percent of the fourteen–fifteen age cohort, and 56.6 percent for the sixteen–seventeen year-olds. This represented a changed attitude:

Different ethnic groups developed distinctive patterns of educational behavior, creating varying matrices of child labor, boarding and lodging, home ownership, and school attendance, in their efforts to ensure survival or enhance their position in the wage labor society. But over time, whatever the initial matrix of educationally related behavior, all ethnic and population groups kept their children at school for longer and longer periods in order to enhance the economic welfare of their children. It was this positive, instrumental attitude toward education that underlay the increasing levels of school attendance over and above the age of compulsory attendance.

Ethnic culture certainly played a role in these decisions. However, eventually most groups, like Chicago's Slavic immigrants, with the security of home ownership, recognized the "significance of educational credentials in a wage labor system."[61]

Deindustrialization

The union-organizing drives of the 1930s maintained the continuity of worker control struggles, representing an attempt to regain "leverage over working conditions." The percentage of organizing manufacturing workers likewise leapt from 9 percent in 1930 to 34 percent in 1940. "The number of strikes per year," according to political economists Gordon, Edwards, and Reich, "jumped from an average of 753 a year in 1927–1932 to an annual average of 2,542 a year from 1933 to 1938, reaching a peak of 4,740 strikes." This class conflict turned to class cooperation during the postwar years, however. With "rising real wages, reliable employment security, and improving working conditions" through the 1960s, union and corporate compromise appeared assured. Unions thus slowed their organizing activities, "apparently contributing to a declining union share of the nonagricultural labor force." The increased spread of technology and the decline in unionization have culminated in the present-day "period of decay." From the 1970s to the present, wages, security, and job conditions have deteriorated. This transformation in the political economy has again restructured work. Gordon, Edwards, and Reich summarize these changes as corporate increases "in the intensity of supervision and management" in the workplace; the acceleration of corporate "relocation of fixed capital in manufacturing, disinvesting in the Northeast and expanding rapidly in the Sunbelt and overseas"; "intensified antiunion activity"; and contract stripping.[62] These transformations have seriously challenged workers' access to, let alone control of, their work. The schools now serve as the bridge to the workplace. Poor and working-class parents have no other choices. The gradual and constant restructuring of the workplace has fundamentally altered the relationship among families, children, and schooling.

To illustrate the significance of this recent, and still unfolding, shift, we return to a modernization perspective. Economists Inkeles and Smith, writing during the early 1970s, analyzed the "factory as school" concept. They worked from the premise that "work is one of the most important elements in most men's [*sic*] lives" and demonstrated how factory and school, in a developing capitalist society, contributed equally to economic and social progress; work and school at that time appeared virtually interchangeable:

We anticipated that . . . [workers] would be open to the lessons the factory had to teach, incorporating and adopting as their own standard the norms embedded in a modern factory organization. This learning . . . would come about through the same processes of socialization identified . . . earlier as the basis for learning modern attitudes and values in the school.

An individual "sense of efficacy" developed due to factory work, and this encompassed cultural sophistication as well as technological growth and organizational experience. Inkeles and Smith dismissed variables, such as the rural-urban nexus, educational background, and family influences to arrive at their conclusions: *"The factory is an effective school in modernity."*[63] Thus, in the early 1970s, it was believed by leading theorists that capitalist societies could rely on either the workplace or schooling to generate economic development and ensure individual security.

The more recent findings from the Pittsburgh school leavers study now indicate a different trend, recognizing no alternative with the current political-economic transformation. As one dropback explained, "Without education you can't get a job."

We began this project in 1985, when the Pittsburgh Board of Education approached us. Board authorities possessed ample quantitative data, describing students' ethnic, racial, and gender backgrounds and their family income, neighborhoods, and achievement scores but lacked concrete reasons students abandoned schooling. We began to locate and interview dropouts. Much to our surprise we discovered a unique and seldom studied cohort called stopouts, or dropbacks. They presented us with an irony: returning to school defies most traditional reasons for leaving. As Borus and Carpenter summarize it:

Family background variables, including father's education, poverty status, and absence of mother and/or father in the home at age 14, all which increased the probability of dropping out of school, seemed not to alter the rate for returning. . . . Having had or parenting a child . . . was not a significant factor after marital status was accounted for.[64]

Statistical analyses of this phenomenon are helpful but limited, because researchers examine the results of school leavers' decisions, not the decision-making process or the political-economic context. Partially funded by the Buhl Foundation, we have been interviewing these stopouts, using the Pittsburgh Job Corps Center as our contact institution; these school leavers specifically returned to a job training program.

A November 1991 Associated Press article, reflecting the desperate sentiment expressed by Pittsburgh school leavers, proclaimed: "Recession Hits Young Workers Hardest." It cited and extensively quoted a study sponsored by the Children's Defense Fund. The article, in a disturbing tone, noted that the "biggest job losses occurred among high school dropouts, suggesting that better-educated workers are competing with them for low-skill positions." Hence, schooling did not serve as the key variable, but workplace structure did. It went on to quote the study's findings, which " 'confirm a new era . . . in which disproportionate economic pain falls on the youngest and most vulnerable Americans.' "[65] While this article identified the effects of profound changes in the social structure, it failed to describe the causes for them.

CONCLUSIONS

Current preoccupation with school reform must be placed within the context of political economy. As we have seen, poor and working-class children and their parents seldom recognized connections between schooling and work. In the early nineteenth century, with the emergence of industrial capitalism, the family still assumed responsibility for the vocational training of their children through, for example, apprenticeship. During the late nineteenth and early twentieth centuries, with the transformation to monopoly capitalism, parents, while losing control of skilled work, could still secure unskilled jobs for their children in the burgeoning and massive unskilled labor market; this facilitated the household's, as well as the child's survival. As schools assumed vocational and custodial responsibilities, the family's role became marginal.

The ongoing political-economic transformation has generated yet another shift in these institutional relationships. Poor and working-class parents have essentially lost access to the workplace, thus losing even more control of it and their children's futures. Schools now supplant, not complement, families in this role, but schooling does not replicate the intimate and durable human relationships of family life. This has serious repercussions for schooling and society. Many of these children recognize the bleak reality that schooling simply serves as a means to work, nothing more. Schooling, as they perceive it, is not intellectually or politically liberating. Schooling has gone beyond serving mere utilitarian ends; it represents grim survival.

This chapter does not argue that work, particularly the onerous conditions that children encountered, was preferable to schooling. However, schooling's often harsh methods and purposeful attempt to replace parental authority and assume control over children cannot be always viewed in a positive light. The workplace, not parental values, family structure, or schooling, has determined social and cultural capital. Changes in social relations and work structure have fundamentally altered the interactions between these institutions. As long as the workplace remained accessible, parents possessed choices for themselves and their children's security. As the workplace became less open, schools usurped parental power.

We now criticize poor and working-class parents for not fulfilling their obligations toward their children and cajole them to resume their long-lost role. Yet workplace changes and the concomitant gradual and systematic increased value placed on schooling have depreciated the family's value. The historical irony here is that our children are now totally dependent on the schools for work, and we blame families for this phenomenon!

NOTES

I want to thank Bruce Nelson, Department of History, Central Michigan University, and William Thomas and Kevin Moran, Administrative and Policy Studies, University of Pittsburgh, for their comments and insights on earlier drafts of this chapter. They are in no way responsible for the interpretation expressed in this study or any mistakes that may appear in it.

1. Dale Mann, "Can We Help Dropouts: Thinking About the Doable," *Teachers College Record*, 87 (Spring 1986), p. 315; Michael E. Borus and Susan A. Carpenter, "A Note on the Return of Dropouts to High School," *Youth and Society*, 14 (June 1983), p. 501.

2. This ongoing study of Pittsburgh school leavers began in 1985. This chapter draws heavily from that larger study. I want to thank my colleagues, David Engel and Don Martin, Administrative and Policy Studies, University of Pittsburgh, for their permission to use some of that material for this chapter. A further note: we use the term *school leavers* in the Pittsburgh study because the common label of *dropouts* obfuscates complex and subtle cases of pushouts, fadeouts, and easeouts. This term also overlooks those students who resume schooling, that is, stopouts or dropbacks.

3. In an award-winning essay, David Hogan, "Education and the Making of the Chicago Working Class, 1880–1930," *History of Education Quarterly*, 18 (Fall 1978), p. 259, called for such "a need to shift attention away from the analysis of the stratification system, including inequalities of educational achievement and performance, toward the analysis of the structure, dynamics and processes of social change in society." Also refer to a highly speculative essay by Michael B. Katz and David Hogan, "Schools, Work and Family Life: Social History," in John H. Best, ed., *Historical Inquiry in Education: A Research Agenda* (Washington, DC: American Educational Research Association, 1983), pp. 282–304. Barbara Finkelstein's insightful article, "Dollars and Dreams: Classrooms as Fictitious Message Systems, 1790–1930," *History of Education Quarterly*, 31 (Winter 1991), p. 464, likewise excavates "relationships between school and work as they evolved between 1790, when the United States was a fledgling nation, and 1930, when the educational structures that we live with today were set in place." Her emphasis is pedagogical rather than structural, however.

4. David Nasaw, *Children of the City: At Work and at Play* (New York: Oxford University Press, 1985), p. x.

5. James S. Coleman, "Families and Schools," *Educational Researcher*, 16 (1987), pp. 36, 37. Also see James S. Coleman, *Policy Perspectives: Parental Involvement in Education*, Office of Educational Research and Improvement, Department of Education (Washington, DC: U.S. Government Printing Office, 1991).

6. Coleman, "Families and Schools," pp. 32, 37–38.

7. Samuel Bowles and Herbert Gintis, *Schooling in Capitalist America: Educational Reform and the Contradictions of Economic Life* (New York: Basic Books, 1976), p. 131. For reviews of this work, see "Symposium: 'Schooling in Capitalist America,' " *History of Education Quarterly*, 17 (Summer 1977), pp. 113–68.

8. Ibid., pp. 139, 141, 144.

9. Ibid., pp. 159, 162, 224. See British social historian E. P. Thompson, "Time, Work-Discipline, and Industrial Capitalism," *Past and Present*, 38 (1967), pp. 56–97, where he argues, within a political context, that schools served an important role in

spreading the new industrial values in England. "Once within the school gates," he explains on p. 84, "the child entered the new universe of disciplined time." Just as time regulated the workplace, it also dominated the school routine. Bells began the school day, divided the day into distinct periods of study, and finally ended the school day for the students. Schools not only taught students to be punctual and regular but socialized children to be industrious, frugal, and orderly as well.

10. Bowles and Gintis, pp. 159, 162, 165, 173.

11. Ibid., pp. 184–85, 186, 194.

12. Ibid., pp. 201, 204, 205, 209.

13. See Lawrence A. Cremin, *The Wonderful World of Ellwood Patterson Cubberley: An Essay on the Historiography of American Education* (New York: Teachers College Press, 1965); N. Ray Hiner and Joseph M. Hawes, *Growing Up in America: Children in Historical Perspective* (Urbana: University of Illinois Press, 1985); Richard J. Altenbaugh, " 'Our Children Are Being Trained Like Dogs and Ponies': Schooling, Social Control, and the Working Class," *History of Education Quarterly*, 21 (1981), pp. 213–22.

14. J. S. Hurt, *Elementary Schooling and the Working Classes, 1860–1918* (London: Routledge and Kegan Paul, 1979), pp. 3, 25, 30–31, 34.

15. Ibid., pp. 156, 174.

16. Quoted in Hurt, p. 194.

17. Quoted in Hurt, p. 196.

18. Hurt, p. 196.

19. Ibid., p. 211. E. P. Thompson also notes the impact of industrial capitalism on working-class culture.

20. David Montgomery, "The Working Classes of the Pre-Industrial American City, 1780–1830," *Labor History*, 9 (1968), pp. 12–13, 15, 17–18. Also refer to Gary B. Nash, "The Social Evolution of Preindustrial American Cities, 1700–1820: Reflections and New Directions," *Journal of Urban History*, 13 (February 1987), pp. 115–45.

21. Lawrence A. Cremin, *American Education: The National Experience, 1783–1876* (New York: Harper and Row, 1980), p. 349.

22. Ibid.; Tamara K. Hareven, *Family Time and Industrial Time* (New York: Cambridge University Press, 1982). See Patrick M. Horan and Peggy G. Hargis, "Children's Work and Schooling in the Late Nineteenth-Century Family Economy," *American Sociological Review*, 56 (October 1991), pp. 583–96, for their thorough treatment of "family economy theories." They state, on p. 593, that "higher levels of family resources and lower levels of demand on these resources are associated with higher rates of children's participation in school and lower rates of children's participation in wage labor."

23. Carl F. Kaestle, *Pillars of the Republic: Common Schools and American Society, 1780–1860* (New York: Hill and Wang, 1983), pp. 158, 160.

24. Thomas Dublin, *Women at Work: The Transformation of Work and Community in Lowell, Massachusetts, 1826–1860* (New York: Columbia University Press, 1979), pp. 171, 173, 174, 178, 179.

25. Kathleen Neils Conzen, *Immigrant Milwaukee, 1836–1860: Accommodation and Community in a Frontier City* (Cambridge: Harvard University Press, 1976), pp. 59–60, 69, 73, 90, 91.

26. Ibid., p. 92.

27. Cremin, *American Education*, p. 343. Also refer to W. J. Rorabaugh, *The Craft*

Apprentice: From Franklin to the Machine Age in America (New York: Oxford University Press, 1986).

28. Ibid., p. 344.

29. This remark by the Boston school board is quoted in David Tyack and Elisabeth Hansot, *Learning Together: A History of Coeducation in American Public Schools* (New Haven, Conn.: Yale University Press, 1990), p. 125.

30. Kaestle, pp. 106, 107, 109.

31. Ibid., p. 121. Tyack and Hansot, p. 125, paint a similar picture.

32. Kaestle, p. 121. In addition to being segmented by skill, the working class also appeared to be divided by race, ethnicity, and gender. See Philip S. Foner, *Organized Labor and the Black Worker, 1619–1973* (New York: International, 1974); Herbert G. Gutman, "Work, Culture, and Society in Industrializing America, 1815–1919," in Herbert G. Gutman, ed., *Work, Culture and Society in Industrializing America* (New York: Vintage, 1977); Alice Kessler-Harris, *Out to Work: A History of Wage-Earning Women in the United States* (New York: Oxford University Press, 1982).

33. Tyack and Hansot, pp. 131, 143.

34. David Montgomery, *Workers' Control in America* (New York: Cambridge University Press, 1979), pp. 9, 11, 13, 15, 16, 22, 23.

35. Ibid., pp. 27, 93, 94. Also refer to Harry Braverman, *Labor and Monopoly Capital: The Degradation of Work in the Twentieth Century* (New York: Monthly Review Press, 1974).

36. E.R.L. Gould, *The Social Condition of Labor* (Baltimore: Johns Hopkins University Press, 1893), pp. 17, 25.

37. Virginia Yans-McLaughlin, "Patterns of Work and Family Organization: Buffalo's Italians," *Journal of Interdisciplinary History*, 2 (Autumn 1971), pp. 302, 308. Also refer to her fine book, *Family and Community: Italian Immigrants in Buffalo, 1880–1930* (Ithaca, N.Y.: Cornell University Press, 1977), and Leslie Woodcock Tentler, *Wage Earning Women: Industrial Work and Family Life in the United States, 1900–1930* (New York: Oxford University Press, 1979).

38. Margaret Byington, *Homestead: The Households of a Mill Town* (1910; rpt. Pittsburgh: University Center for International Studies, 1974), pp. 142–44; John Bodnar, *The Transplanted: A History of Immigrants in Urban America* (Bloomington: Indiana University Press, 1985), p. 83.

39. Yans-McLaughlin, p. 306.

40. Byington, p. 107; Yans-McLaughlin, p. 301.

41. Viviana A. Zelizer, *Pricing the Priceless Child: The Changing Social Value of Children* (New York: Basic Books, 1985), p. 75, states: "By nineteenth-century standards, the employment of a nine- or ten-year-old had been legitimate and for the most part legal. In fact, age was not considered a very important criterion of legitimacy until after the 1860s. Before then, only four states limited the age of employment for children." Forest C. Ensign, *Compulsory School Attendance and Child Labor* (1921; rpt. New York: Arno Press, 1969), pp. 68–69, 96–97.

42. David L. Angus and Jeffrey E. Mirel, "From Spellers to Spindles: Work-Force Entry by the Children of Textile Workers, 1888–1890," *Social Science History*, 9 (Spring 1985), p. 139. Nasaw, p. 42, and Zelizer, pp. 59, 100–101, maintain strong cultural arguments. The last quote is by Zelizer, p. 67.

43. United States Senate, *Report Upon the Relations Between Labor and Capital*

(Washington, DC: U.S. Government Printing Office, 1885), vol. 1, p. 851, vol. 2, p. 67; see vol. 2, p. 6, for testimony about eight-year-olds employed in a glass factory.

44. United States Department of Labor, Bureau of Labor Statistics, Bulletin No. 175, *Summary of the Report on Conditions of Women and Child Wage Earners in the United States* (Washington, D.C.: U.S. Government Printing Office, 1916), p. 130.

45. Richard O. Boyer and Herbert M. Morais, *Labor's Untold Story* (New York: United Electrical, Radio & Machine Workers of America, 1976), p. 184; U.S. Dept. of Labor, p. 40; Zelizer, p. 57.

46. S. Alexander Rippa, *Education in a Free Society: An American History* (New York: David McKay, 1976), pp. 157, 159; Tyack and Hansot, p. 171; Angus and Mirel, p. 139.

47. Helen M. Todd, "Why Children Work: The Children's Answer," *McClure's Magazine*, 40 (November–April 1912–1913), pp. 69–70. I first encountered a reference to Todd's colorful survey in David Hogan's article in the *History of Education Quarterly*.

48. U.S. Dept. of Labor, Bureau of Labor Statistics, *Report on the Condition of Women and Child Wage Earners in the United States: Employment of Women in Metal Trades* (Washington, DC: U.S. Government Printing Office, 1911), p. 28.

49. Todd, p. 74.

50. Nasaw, pp. 168, 177, 182–83.

51. U.S. Dept. of Labor (1916), p. 30.

52. Todd, pp. 75–76. Angus and Mirel, p. 139, conclude that their set of "findings gives confirmation to the arguments of nineteenth-century labor leaders that the cause of child labor was the low wages paid to household heads."

53. Ibid.

54. Zelizer, p. 50; Nasaw, p. 187.

55. Zelizer, pp. 62, 63, 112.

56. Paul W. McBride, "The Co-Op Industrial Education Experience, 1900–1917," *History of Education Quarterly*, 14 (Summer 1974), p. 211; Paul C. Violas, *The Training of the Urban Working Class: A History of Twentieth-Century American Education* (Chicago: Rand McNally, 1978), pp. 169–92; Sol Cohen, "The Industrial Education Movement, 1906–1917," *American Quarterly*, 20 (1968), pp. 95–110.

57. McBride, pp. 211–12.

58. Ibid., pp. 213, 215, 218.

59. Violas, p. 15.

60. Jeffrey Mirel and David Angus, "Youth, Work, and Schooling in the Great Depression," *Journal of Early Adolescence*, 5 (1985), pp. 490, 499, 501, 502.

61. Hogan, pp. 227, 231, 255.

62. David M. Gordon, Richard Edwards, and Michael Reich, *Segmented Work, Divided Workers: The Historical Transformation of Labor in the United States* (New York: Cambridge University Press, 1982), pp. 177, 179, 215, 216, 217, 218–19, 221.

63. Alex Inkeles and David H. Smith, *Becoming Modern: Individual Change in Six Developing Countries* (Cambridge: Harvard University Press, 1974), pp. 157, 158, 159, 163, 174. Emphasis is authors'.

64. Borus and Carpenter, p. 505.

65. "Recession Hits Young Workers Hardest," *Pittsburgh Press*, 24 November 1991, p. 1, col. 1.

3

City Schools and School Systems: Sources of Centralization and Bureaucratization

H. Warren Button

INTRODUCTION

City schools have not been good places to learn, as achievement scores and ample other evidence show. They have not been good places to teach, as burn out and teachers' testimony demonstrate. They have been slow to respond, or have not responded at all, to changing circumstances, changing clienteles, changing criticisms. After decades as minor participant and intent observer, I conclude that their shortcomings have been due more than anything else to their intricate bureaucracies, which are primarily due to longtime patterns of centralizing: on their first intellectual antecedents, on bureaucratization, and on the ideology of efficiency.

As to the effects of bureaucratization, I am in agreement with Michael Katz[1] and other revisionist historians. I shall not argue, however, that bureaucratization, centralization, and standardization have necessarily been linked to, or arisen from, social class structure as it is conventionally defined. Neither is it to be argued that central authority and control or bureaucracy or technology has no value. For some ends, centralization is entirely appropriate. For some purposes, bureaucracy is without an alternative. In some instances, technology and the specialized and sometimes guarded knowledge of technocrats have substantial utility. But overcentralization, overbureaucratization, and inappropriate reliance on technology have far too often disabled urban schools. Therefore, I concentrate here on these matters.

The centralization of the administration of schools and the consequent bureaucratization have been an outcome of concurrent modes of thought, the evolution of society, and the efforts and persuasiveness of a few prominent men. Central control and the bureaucratization of school systems were based on ways of thought developed far earlier, during the Enlightenment, in the 1600s and 1700s. Science then provided belief in natural "laws" and in reason and logic.

Michel Foucault provides a plausible explanation for shifts in authority from traditional to rationalized and categorizes the means of the new rational control.[2] The means of control were exemplified by Jeremy Bentham's design for a wheel-like prison. It is not feasible here to do much more than mention the men who have played important parts in the development of centralized school systems.

The monitorial school was the epitome of centralized control within a school. The means of centralizing and standardizing, "systemizing," what would become school systems appeared in rudimentary form about 1800, not long after the establishment of the United States. Improvement of rural schools was the first concern of state superintendents. City systems, intended to regularize and exercise central control of city schools, first appeared in 1837. Their organization was a response to several needs. They provided order for nearly chaotic schools in cities, diminished petty graft and crass political interference, were a means for managing schools as enrollments increased enormously, were evidence of civic virtue, and perhaps perpetuated the power of those most influential. By 1876, the centennial year, the virtues of greater centralized control were voiced.

In the thirty-five years that followed, society was reshaped. The reputation and prestige of businessmen were in ascendancy. Massive factories were built and put into operation. Engineers devoted part of their efforts to developing ways of improving factory management. Beginnings of an empirical, usually quantitative "science of education" made their appearance. In the 1910s "efficiency" became a motto, and the efficiency methods of Frederick W. Taylor and others shaped discussions and justified further centralization and standardization and the rise of large bureaucratic "experts."

But teachers balked at being thought of and treated as machines powered only by money. Monolithic, top-down control could not be maintained on that basis, lost plausibility, and was inappropriate in the intellectual climate of the 1930s and 1940s. "Democracy" in administration, derived from social philosophy, seemed more appropriate then and in the early 1950s. "Human relations" in administration, supported by social scientists' research, served, among other ends, as an improved ideology and more effective means of management. That thinking declined in the 1950s, when there was renewed confidence in businessmen, business methods, and science. Presently, teachers' "reflective thinking" is an advocated mode, but its effect in counteracting centralization of control seems doubtful. An overwhelming hindrance to the reform of school governance is the durability and tenacity of bureaucracies, far more readily assembled than dismantled.

There are several limitations to this mode of analysis. One, always implicit, should be explicit: we have reasonably good records of what was written or, sometimes, said about school administration, but it cannot be guaranteed that what was written or said was what the writer or speaker thought. Our systematic information about what school administrators did is limited to a few relatively recent surveys and other studies. It could be added that in a brief account only prominent or, occasionally, typical individuals can be dealt with. There always have been and still are administrators whose mode of thought is that of previous eras, and other deviant cases.

ORIGINS

Centralization, standardization, bureaucracies, and technocracies as we know them depend in part on modes of thought that appeared during the Enlightenment. All these appeared in what would be their modern forms because of changes in social structure. Descriptions of both thought and configurations of society are necessary for an explanation that approaches adequacy.

Modes of Thought

The earliest origins of the conceptual bases for school centralization (and coincidentally of the "science of education") seem to lie in classical history. However, my interest is in the postmedieval reappearances of these concepts, although their first reappearances are unclear, perhaps unidentifiable. The mode of thought contributing to practices of control and management gained ascendancy with the new science, which we would now describe as empirical. At risk of caricature, this is thought based on observation and experience, eschewing appeals to faith, at least seemingly "objective," emotion-free.

Near the beginning of Enlightenment science, English philosopher and official Francis Bacon, more popularizer than innovator, was influential in the matter. His *Advancement of Learning* appeared in 1603–1605. René Descartes, French philosopher and scientist, was more widely influential in the early 1600s, especially on the Continent. In Descartes's view, there were at least potential explanations of all of nature in mechanical and mathematical terms. Isaac Newton, English mathematician, physicist, and astronomer of the late 1600s was not only important for his discoveries but a widely revered paragon of that mode of thought. Natural science, as explicitly or implicitly defined by Bacon, Descartes, and Newton, developed rapidly in their lifetimes and for much of a century thereafter.

In these views, the world was to be seen as mechanical and governed by natural "laws," discovered or to be discovered (but not at first formulated) by humans. Julien Offray de la Mettrie's *L'Homme Machine* (Man as machine), published in 1748, is representative of the extension of laws like those of physics to explain human actions. This was plausible if behavior was determined mechanistically, as the result of heredity and environment. The latter could be changed by those in authority.

With faith in the new science and its prospects, a new faith in logic and reason appeared. Its most effective proponent, though not its originator, was Voltaire (1694–1778), popularizer of Newton and slashing critic of the established church.[3] The church, as he saw it, rested on, and was encrusted with, objectionable superstition. (Voltaire wrote of *"l'infame,"* which seems untranslatable.[4]) The church had accumulated formidable and objectionable power and wealth. France was governed by the church and by long-since obsolete feudal lords, by innumerable functionaries of the royal court, and by other officials. They were demeaning, repressive, and exploitative, to be attacked by any argument.

Social Structure

The development of a new mode of thought, a part of intellectual history, seems insufficient to explain the appearance of centralization of control and power. That must also be explained on the grounds of social change, although such functional explanations seem also to be in themselves inadequate: outcomes are affected by thought as well as circumstance and by individuals as well as social forces.

Foucault described a global social change in the seventeenth century.[5] Certainly his description could be amplified, but it serves the present purpose. Need for new patterns of control, he argued, rose because of increases in wealth, because of growth of population, and because of an increase in crime. This line of argument appears to be in terms of functional structuralism, which Foucault largely conceded in another context.[6] In this view, systematic centralization and control grew from social necessity.

For Foucault, change in the configurations of society implied the need for systematic control, which was the central subject of *Discipline and Punish: The Birth of the Prison*.[7] Foucault traced the development of modes of control and discipline in workshops, in armies, in prisons, in hospitals, and in schools. By these new means of control, a workshop could be made more productive; the army could transform an impressed rustic into an upstanding soldier; a criminal would become a lawful and "docile" citizen. By the same methods a child could best be educated.

At most, only an approximate summary of Foucault's formulations and their corollaries can be provided here to provide a taxonomy of modes of control under the new rational regime. For Foucault the first necessity was observation. To observe was, to some degree, to control. This necessity would shape the environments of inmates, soldiers, patients, workmen, and pupils. Designs of prisons, encampments, hospitals, workshops and factories, and schools mirrored the imperative of observation.

Beyond observation, control could be exercised by examination, as to the demeanor of the prisoner, the condition of the patient, or the learning of the pupil. Examinations were to be frequent, even daily. The examination, Foucault wrote, "manifests the subjection of those who are perceived as objects and the objectification of those who are subjected."[8] Examinations were visible exercises of power and were an integral part of teaching. "The school becomes a sort of apparatus of uninterrupted examination," he wrote.[9] Examination and observation made it possible to distinguish between individuals and to aid in a "better calibration of their treatment.''[10] From observations and examinations case records could be compiled, which enhanced control. It is to be interjected that, although bureaucrats would have other duties, the compilation of records would make them a necessity. Records would allow individuals to be compared, "normalized." "Enclosure" of institutions was necessary, to shut out and shut in. Within, space was to be "partitioned": "Every individual has his own place, each space is to be individual."[11] A part of environment was time, which was also controlled. It was to be carefully measured and apportioned.[12]

Observation, testing and measurement, case records, "normalization," enclosing of the institution and partitioning within it, and the allocation of time all re-enforced and supported control and power, Foucault wrote. The similarities of military camps, hospitals, asylums, prisons, and schools have a long and, we might add, painful history.

Panopticon

The first essential for control was observation. The epitome of physical design for control was the panopticon (all-seeing). It had its origins in the most unlikely of places, growing out of the plans of Prince Grigory Aleksandrovich Potemkin (1739–1791), adviser of Catherine the Great, Empress of Russia. Englishman Samuel Bentham (1757–1831) was placed in charge of Potemkin's workshop on a tributary of the Dnieper River. All but a few of Bentham's workmen were unskilled countrymen or soldiers. For observation and control of the workers and to use to best advantage his few knowledgeable subordinates, Bentham developed what would be known as the panopticon.[13] All the workshop's rooms were arranged so that they could all be seen from the supervisor's central post.

The fame of the panopticon design came from the efforts of Jeremy Bentham (1748–1832), Samuel's older brother, best known as advocate of legal reforms and as the founder of "utilitarian" philosophy. The aim of the "greatest good for the greatest number" was to be implemented by knowledgeable reformers— utilitarians were often not only reformers but also authoritarian. He was also a staunch advocate of prisons built on panopticon principles:

> The building *circular*—the cells occupying the circumference—. . . The centre—an *intermediate annular well*, all the way up. . . . The cells laid open to it. . . .
>
> By *blinds* and other contrivances, the keeper concealed from the observation of the prisoners . . . hence, on their part, the sentiment of an invisible omnipresence.[14]

The general design reappeared in American penitentiaries into the twentieth century.[15] Bentham spent several years trying to erect a panopticon prison, which would rehabilitate its inmates by control, supervision, and instruction. His effort was not successful: in England the time for prison reform had not yet come.

SCHOOLS

There were scattered precedents in the use in schools of observation, examination, and control, of course; Foucault and John Ralston Saul point out Jesuit
schools as precedents.[16] But the exemplar of centralization of control of schools
was the monitorial school. The monitorial school and its system were developed
by Andrew Bell and Joseph Lancaster, probably by each of them independently.
Bell, a onetime colonial American schoolmaster and Anglican cleric, developed
the monitorial school in India.[17] Lancaster, born in London, was driven to
America by debts (and suspicions of sadism) and was more influential in the
United States. As prescribed by Lancaster and Bell, the monitorial schoolmaster
was to be in complete charge, was to oversee all aspects of the monitorial school.
The school's tasks were divided into tiny increments. Pupils, serving as "monitors," taught other pupils knowledge divided into minute fragments. Other
monitors tested, and still other monitors took attendance. The master oversaw
the school.

The mechanistic view extended to pupils. One writer said, "Every boy seems
to be a cog of a wheel—the whole school a perfect machine." It also extended
the mechanistic view to the school: "A new machine of immense power, parallel
and rival to . . . the greatest of the greatest of acquisitions to mechanical observation."[18] Katz quotes Dewitt Clinton, who would become governor of New
York State, as saying the monitorial system was "in education, what the . . .
machines for abridging labor and expense are in the mechanic arts . . . the least
possible trouble and at the least possible expense."[19] In the school, observation
was omnipresent, centralization of control complete.

Monitorial schools appeared in New York City, St. Louis, Buffalo, and many
other cities and other places.[20] Not surprisingly, Jeremy Bentham was an avid
supporter of monitorial schools. A school in which one schoolmaster observed
and controlled 1,400 pupils was the subject of Bentham's enthusiastic essay. A
mode of complete, centralized control within the individual school had been
realized. But the monitorial school, in spite of its virtues of centralization of
control and economy of means, had such obvious shortcomings that it was
superseded by other patterns of schooling and other, more general modes of
control.

State

Lawrence Cremin, taking as always the benign and affirmative view, dealt
with the beginnings of American school administration as the building of "systems": "a functional organization of individual schools that put them into regular
relationship with one another and with the polity."[21] He began his account with
New York State (always outstanding for centralization). The first step there was
the establishment in 1784 of the Regents of the University of the State of New
York, intended to govern first, Columbia College, and then, all colleges and
academies in the state. In New York State, as in some others, the need for

central administration of common schools arose after the establishment of the state Common School Fund, which allocated state funds in partial support of common schools. New York State did name Gideon Hawley as superintendent of schools in 1812.[22] However, even in New York State, unity of organization would not be complete until the beginning of the twentieth century.

During the common school revival (ca. 1830–1860), "reformers," many of them at one time or another school administrators, had little power but substantial influence. Their highest hope was the improvement of schooling; an important mode of improvement was the establishment of central, systematic control. Horace Mann's selection as secretary of the state Board of Education in Massachusetts in 1837 was a landmark in systemization and centralization. Early nineteenth-century school administration was seen by Katz, especially citing the efforts of Mann, as demonstrating the appearance of incipient bureaucratization of the schools.[23] From Mann's point of view he and the state board had too little power. His opponents said the state Board of Education was a "system of centralization and of monopoly in a few hands, contrary, in every respect, to the true spirit of our democratic institutions" and Prussian-inspired.[24]

The earliest general plan for centralization of a comprehensive system was the Michigan plan for a (almost unpronounceable) "Catholepistemiad." At the apex of the system was to be a university, perhaps modeled after Thomas Jefferson's plans for the University of Virginia. The plan also included colleges, academies, and other schools. John D. Pierce, Michigan's first state supperintendent of education, saw himself as responsible for all the state's public schools.[25] But systemization and centralization were local, episodic, and uneven. The state superintendency of schools in New York, to which Hawley had been named, was abolished in 1821. Its functions as allocator of state funds and administrative judge were transferred to New York's secretary of state.

Usually, common school revivalists were most greatly concerned with improving rural district schools, far the most numerous and attended by most pupils. Mann and Henry Barnard, the two most eminent, visited hundreds of such schools and schoolhouses. Persuasion was the most common tactic for improvement at the beginning. Also, they might be improved by control. In 1856, the secretary of state being overburdened, the office of the state superintendent of schools was reinstituted in New York State. Victor M. Rice, formerly Buffalo superintendent of schools, became the state superintendent. He compiled a 375-page *Code of Public Instruction*, which was published that year. It dealt primarily with one-room rural schools.

Going beyond the allocation of funds, the positions of "district school commissioners" were then established.[26] The *Code*'s description and explanation of the duties of the commissioners were nineteen pages long, in rather small type.[27] The district commissioners were to "visit and examine [observe] all the schools . . . as often in each year as shall be practicable"[28]—

To inquire into all matters relating to the management, the course and mode of instruction, the books, studies and discipline of the schools, the conditions of the school-

houses, out buildings, and appendages. . . . To advise and counsel . . . particularly in
relation to the construction, ventilation and warming of schoolhouses, and the improving
and adorning of the school grounds, and to recommend . . . the proper studies, discipline,
and management of the schools, the course of instruction to be pursued.[29]

The district commissioners were also to examine and certify teachers. They were
to report to the state superintendent of schools, serving as a link in the centralization of control.

Anticipating future development of state education department bureaucracies,
the *Code* listed thirty-five necessary forms recommended or mandated for use
by the commissioners or by local trustees.[30] The *Code* was explicit—as only a
bona fide pen pusher could be—as to proper forms for correspondence to the
state superintendent: "To facilitate the business of the department . . . it is desirable that all letters should be written on foolscap paper, with a clear margin
of one inch on the inside edge of the page."[31]

City

The first city superintendent appeared in 1837. Again, city superintendents'
appearance was sporadic; the long-familiar New York City Board of Education
organization was not completed until the twentieth century. Lack of systemization
was obvious and painful. It was argued that individual city or country schools
under local trustees or boards were likely to succumb to political pressure and
to offer opportunities for graft and dishonesty, and there is evidence to support
some of those suspicions.[32] City governments were being regularized, rationalized. City "boosters" supported the establishment of city school systems.
Sheer size and growth supplied arguments for centralization. Another line of
argument is that city school systems and city school superintendents served to
protect or perpetuate power.

Apparently the first city school system was the one organized in Buffalo in
1837. Oliver Steele, bookbinder and proprietor of a bookstore, was the de facto
first city school superintendent. He later described Buffalo's public schools as
he found them: some common school districts overlapped, and there were gaps
between others. One trustee habitually held the teacher's salary until the end of
the school year; in another the teacher acted as trustee. Teacher pay and qualifications varied widely. Financial support for the schools was spotty. Schools
were in houses, and one shared a building with a church.[33] (The school's quarters
were in the cellar.) Creditable schools would make the city of Buffalo more
attractive, hence more prosperous.

Steele was a sincere proponent of public schools in Buffalo—he would later
support the establishment of a city high school. He was also a "booster," sharing
in the convictions that led others to improve harbors, establish colleges, found
hospitals, and undertake other civic improvements. Beyond Steele's concern for

schools, he aided the establishment of Buffalo's sewage and illuminating gas systems.[34]

The centralization and systemization of control of schools were part of a general plan of centralization and rationalization of civic services. Bayard Still, discussing the development of city government in Milwaukee, pointed out that city fire departments were replacing then-traditional volunteer departments, sometimes better renowned for intramural battles than for the suppression of fires.[35] (Some New York City volunteer firemen became an army regiment, the New York Fire Zouaves, and marched off to fight in the Civil War.[36]) Milwaukee and other cities organized police departments to replace the traditional night watchmen. Systemization and centralization of control of city school systems were not isolated phenomena, but, incidentally, they had begun to take place before the appearance of large business. There were only a very few large manufacturing enterprises then; there would be ample business impact later, with the transplanting of thought from factory to school, but not at the beginnings of centralization of control of schools.

The sheer growth in enrollments in city schools, following the growth of the cities themselves and the increasing public acceptance of the value of elementary schooling, probably added an impetus to the establishment of city school systems. In Chicago, the fastest growing city in mid-nineteenth–century America, the first city superintendent of schools, John Dore, was appointed in 1854. Chicago's school enrollment even by 1860 was only 6,900, and Dore's appointment may have been for civic betterment. But in the following ten years enrollment increased nearly sixfold, to 40,000. Size and increased costs seemed to indicate the need for centralized control.[37] But, again, the New York City school system's centralization, under Superintendent William H. Maxwell, was not complete until 1901.

Another explanation of the impetus for centralization of control of city schools was advanced by Virginia Marie Foley.[38] She noted that there was no obvious geographic pattern in the establishment of city superintendencies—from east to west, for instance. Nor was there a demographic pattern—large city to small city. Following a suggestion by Kenneth Boulding, she argued that centralization of control of city schools, of which the establishment of a city superintendent was an indicator, took place at least in part to assure continued control when established groups saw themselves as risking loss of control to others, for example, Germans in Buffalo, Hispanics in Los Angeles, African-Americans in post–Civil War Charleston. Though the evidence was not, of course, conclusive, her argument was straightforward. It is consonant with what seems to be Foucault's unspoken axiom, that discipline and control were power exercised to enhance power.

The year of the first national centennial, 1876, is a convenient stopping point. By 1876 there were fervent advocates of centralization and central control. At one of the educators' conferences at the Centennial Exhibit, three of the most prominent speakers were David Murray, John G. Hodgins, and James Pyle

Wickersham. Murray was then serving as Japan's "superintendent of educational affairs," de facto under secretary of education. He was a staunch proponent of centralization of control in Japan and would later be secretary of the New York State Board of Regents and advocate of more stringent examinations of students. Hodgins was deputy superintendent of education in the Canadian province of Ontario and spoke with satisfaction of the merits of close control and supervision. In his annual report that year, Wickersham, Pennsylvania state superintendent of schools, wrote in favor of centralization and minimization of local control: "No system of schools can reach a high degree of efficiency without close and constant supervision by competent officers."[39] The impulse for centralization and control had ended its embryonic state.

Sages and Businessmen

The development of school administration at the end of the nineteenth century was affected by changes in society. Rural farm life, which had prevailed, became marginal. Villages that had been centers of trade and local interests were losing their places, and many of them would die. Urban, rather than rural, life was becoming the norm. Most immigrants, who arrived annually by the hundreds of thousands, even millions, settled in the cities, where there were jobs.

Progressivism was at its height at the end of the nineteenth and beginning of the twentieth centuries. One aspect of progressivism was political and governmental; Theodore Roosevelt was its most prominent proponent. Progressive, muckraking journalists—now styled as "investigative reporters"—exposed graft and fraud in city governments. The aims of progressives were reform and efficiency in government, which were to be accomplished by centralizing control, by appointing a competent leader, and by providing him with wide control. This approach, "administrative progressivism," would be what was also recommended for school superintendents and other school administrators.

Another change was the rise of big business, of awesome concentrations of power and wealth, of massive corporations, pools, and trusts. A new group of professional executives and managers appeared. With the growth of business the prestige of the businessman, at first the proprietor and later the business manager, was ascendant. The ways of business were respected, and school administrators began to emulate them.[40]

Railroads had supplemented and then largely displaced inland water transportation, and costs of freight had dropped. Improved transportation opened markets and made feasible more large-scale mass production.[41] Massive cotton mills had been built before the Civil War, but even relatively large mills and factories were the exception then. Before 1900, factories employing hundreds, even thousands, of workers were almost commonplace. In 1900 three steel mills and a locomotive factory each employed more than 8,000 workers; more than 4,000 workers were employed in each of eighteen other factories. Steam engines had displaced water power as the usual source of power. In factories, gas lighting was obsolete by the 1890s, and by 1900 electricity powered factory cranes and railways.[42] Craftsmen were displaced by factory workers. The old-time general foreman became obsolete. Scale of production increased, more complicated industrial processes were developed, and factory management became more complex. Before 1870, engineers had shown "little interest" in factory and shop management, but that became more important because of the improvement of machinery and the growth of scale. In the 1870s, 15 articles on management appeared in engineering journals; in the 1880s there were 143 articles, and in the 1890s, 253.[43]

School administrators acclimatized to their new environment by claiming and exerting their expertise. The earlier evangelists of education of the generations of Mann and Barnard had not made education a career. Their successors were, though, professional "schoolmen," as they called themselves, most often pursuing careers in education. They thought of themselves as experts and were often accepted by the public as such. After roughly 1900, the most influential would extend their areas of purported expertise by adopting the methods of businessmen and engineers.

Schoolmen believed in the "science of education," although their definition of science was far removed from definitions of science a century later, and their definition of education was more narrow—for them, education was schooling. Most often the schoolmen believed in "social science," a widely envisioned unitary discipline including education and what have come to be sociology, history, political science, and history.[44] Social science, reasoned and logical, was to be the basis of practice and policy in all social endeavors, including education. With this was linked Protestant faith, maybe a heritage from the past. School administrators still saw themselves as "guardians of virtue," to use Tyack's felicitous term.

James P. Slade, Andrew S. Draper, and Ellwood P. Cubberley serve as examples of turn-of-the-century schoolmen.

Slade, whose career was probably most typical, was born in New York State in 1837.[45] He attended academies in New York State, but not college. He went to Illinois after teaching a year. In Illinois he taught in a country school and then in the schools of Belleville, Illinois, and was principal of the new Belleville high school. In 1867 he became county superintendent, though continuing at first as teacher and principal. As county superintendent he examined and certified teachers and compiled reports for the state superintendent. There were 140 schools in the country by then. Slade often visited (observed?) them. "It was my custom while Co. Supt. to do . . . much of the traveling before and after the hours of school that I might devote the six hours of school to school inspection. . . . I usually devoted a half day to each school."[46]

In 1878 Slade, running as a Republican, was elected state superintendent of public instruction, the authority of which he worked to strengthen. Speaking before the National Education Association (NEA) in 1882 as to supervision and control, he said: "There would still be much need of school visitation if there were a competent teacher in every ungraded school. 'Even the best masters will not do so well without this aid as with it,' is the opinion of the English Commissioners of Education. 'A school is not a clock, which you can wind up and then leave by itself.' '[47]

Slade was not renominated in 1882 and probably preferred not to run against an old friend and formidable opponent. That year he became the president of Elmira College, after having, with admirable simplicity, bought it. The college, however, suffered financial losses, and in 1890 Slade became superintendent of schools in East St. Louis, Illinois, with enrollment of 1,900 pupils. The city was thriving, and it was expected that enrollments would double. After six years, in 1894, Slade was discharged by a new Board of Education and returned to the classroom and principalship. He died suddenly in 1908, aged seventy-one.

Draper (1848–1913) was born in Westford, New York.[48] After graduating from Albany Academy, he taught, then attended law school and was admitted to the bar. A faithful Republican, he was elected to the state legislature and in 1885 was named by President Arthur as a judge in a claims court. In 1886 the legislature elected him state superintendent of schools; Draper was a politician of great skill and acumen. He left the state superintendency at the end of his second term to become superintendent of schools in Cleveland. He was already a strong advocate of centralization of control of schools. The report of the subcommittee of the Committee of Fifteen, which he chaired, recommended in 1893 that the city superintendent be given wide powers, except over school financial matters.[49] Perhaps that recommendation reflected both the hopes and reality of the Cleveland school system, which had that arrangement. In 1894, he resigned the Cleveland superintendency to become president of the University of Illinois, where he had the reputation of being a bold innovator and autocratic administrator. In 1904 he returned to New York State as state commissioner of schools, a more powerful office than that of state superintendent of schools, which it had replaced.

New York State's Board of Regents had control over colleges and academies. Common schools had been under the state superintendent. (The control of high schools was in dispute.) The new statutes unified the Board of Regents and the office of the state commissioner of schools. Draper maneuvered successfully to control the Board of Regents. He strengthened the power of the New York State district superintendents and greatly elaborated the State Department of Education's bureaucracy. Control of the state normal schools was centralized in the state education department. Draper saw centralization of control by himself and by New York State's mushrooming state education department's bureaucracy as the way to reform schools. Draper also directed the construction of the New York State Education Department's new building, massive and forbidding, it has been said, as his own lasting monument. He died in office.

Cubberley (1868–1941) was the son of a druggist in a small Indiana town and worked in his father's pharmacy. As a college student, he submitted to his father records of his own annual expenses and budgets for the following year; his devotion to his father's business methods and values was lifelong. He majored in physics at Indiana University after a year of teaching at a country school, then taught at a Baptist college, then at Vincennes University in Indiana, 1891–1896, where he became president at the age of twenty-three. In 1896 he was named superintendent of schools in San Diego. Two years later he was appointed assistant professor at Stanford University. On leave from Stanford, he completed his master's degree at Teachers College, Columbia University, in 1902. His doctorate in school administration was completed there in 1905. Cubberley was an early and fervent supporter of centralization of school administration and of business and scientific management of the schools. In 1917 he became dean of the Stanford University School of Education. He continued as dean until his retirement. He died in 1941, leaving to the School of Education $700,000.[50]

Slade and Cubberley devoted whole careers to education. Draper's later commitments to education might have been typical a generation or two earlier but was the exception in his time. Draper and Cubberley were prolific authors, Cubberley of education texts, Draper on a variety of subjects. When school administrators thought of themselves as scholars, many were authors or editors, and Draper and Cubberley were prolific writers and nationally influential. Slade and Draper were administrators in city school systems (though, of course, the Cleveland system was far larger). They were both college presidents (obviously, Elmira College was far smaller.) Administration of higher education and of public schools seemed then to have much in common, and administrators often went from one to the other. Of these three, Slade was the only one dismissed from a superintendency, though that was all too commonplace in the new profession.

These men extended centralization of control of schools in several ways. As state superintendent, Slade attempted to extend the authority of the county superintendents, an effort with which Rice had been familiar, and to which Draper would return. City superintendents introduced the "corporate model" of control, and school boards were reduced in size, heterogeneity, and authority.[51] If school administration was to be like business administration, school board members were, ideally, businessmen, like members of business boards of directors. In the administrative progressive view, powerful superintendents were to depend upon school boards to support them and their decisions.

Some prominent schoolmen who saw themselves as businesslike augmented their power by gaining control of budgets and expenditures. In 1899 the NEA Committee on Uniform Financial Reports wrote:

One of the chief studies of a wise administrator of the schools is to make the cost of education per child as low as is consistent with the best service. Attention to this and to the comparative study of reports for a period of years . . . should give an idea of the average or standard cost of education per child. . . . By careful comparative study, railroad men know the average cost of hauling freight per ton mile, and the cost of transporting a passenger. Those administering schools should be as well informed upon the cost of education.[52]

Frank Spaulding, superintendent of schools in Newton, Massachusetts, grasped business accounting concepts clearly. In an NEA address in 1913 he said:

Why is a pupil recitation in English costing 7.2 cents in the vocational school while it costs only 5 cents in the technical school? Is the "vocational" English 44 per cent superior to the technical English or 44 per cent more difficult to secure? Why are we paying 80% more in vocational than in technical school for the same unit of instruction in mathematics? Why does a pupil-recitation in science cost from 55 per cent to 67 per cent more in the Newton High than in either of the other schools?[53]

Some of the new school administrators had attended Teachers College and Stanford University. George D. Strayer at Teachers College and Cubberley at Stanford gathered faithful retinues of administrators who offered mutual support and pooled practices. Some school administrators and professors of school administration met annually at the winter meeting of the Department of Superintendence (later the American Association of School Administration) and at the summertime meetings of the NEA. Acquaintanceship with each other's practices was an important part of the formation of the "one best system."

Additions to curriculum, for instance, of kindergartens and vocational education, provided further reason for the elaboration of city school bureaucracies. Enrollments still increased; the Chicago school system's enrollment increased from 60,000 on the eve of the Civil War to 300,000 in 1910.[54] In the times of the businessmen and sages, centralization of school control based on business had continued. These convictions and procedures supporting centralization would later be merged with procedures borrowed from factory management.

Factory Management and School Efficiency

Efficiency, as used here, is in the sense of frugality of means. In schooling, its meaning was derived from (but not at all identical to) engineers' usage. There were other meanings: "commendable" and "industrious."[55] In the later two senses, it appeared occasionally prior to the twentieth century, which has occasionally led to misconceptions. The original account of the efficiency movement in education was Raymond E. Callahan's.

The undisputed originator of the efficiency movement in engineering was Frederick W. Taylor (1856–1915), subject of at least three book-length biographies, two of them published after Callahan's.[56] Taylor was a Philadelphian, son of a wealthy family. He attended Philips Exeter Academy, but instead of enrolling at Harvard as originally planned, in 1874 he became an apprentice in the Midvale Steel Company. Even at that late date, an apprenticeship by a son of the well-to-do was not unusual. Taylor's first experiments were on methods of machining steel and would lead eventually to the development of high-speed, chromium-tungsten, alloy-cutting tools, which, Nelson wrote, "precipitated a revolution in machine shop practice."[57]

Improvement of machinery and more complicated production processes made older factory management methods more costly. Taylor formulated systematic, rationalized principles to increase plant efficiency. After preliminary study, a production control system was to be formed, "based on a specific planning department. The general foreman was to be superseded by functional foremen with specific duties: handling materials, keeping tool inventories, shipping, and so on. The functional foremen would share close supervision of the workmen. Stopwatch time-and-motion studies would then follow, when appropriate."[58]

Functional foremen, supervisors, would:

develop a science for each element of a man's work. . . . scientifically select and then train, teach and develop the workman . . . heartily cooperate with the men so as to insure all of the work being done in accordance with the principles of the science which has been developed.

. . . There is an almost equal division of work and the responsibility of work between the management and the workmen. The management take over all work for which they are better fitted than the workman, while in the past almost all of the work and greater part of the responsibility were thrown upon the men.[59]

The most famous and most blatant example of the application of Taylor's methods was to Schmidt, who loaded ninety-pound iron pigs into railroad boxcars under the direction of one of Taylor's associates. This example appeared in Taylor's *Shop Management.*[60] First, there was a step-by-step, time-and-motion analysis, beginning with "(a) picking up the pig from the ground or pile . . . ; (b) walking with it on a level . . . ; (c) walking with it up an incline to the car . . . ; (d) throwing the pig down . . . ; (e) walking back empty to get a load." Each part of the task was timed in hundredths of minutes.[61]

This was logical and fully in the mode of "scientific" thought. Schmidt was observed and examined, if timing is considered examination. A careful case history was compiled. Time was measured, allocated, and controlled. Control of Schmidt was nearly complete.

Taylor was convinced that money was the sole motive for work, in a way a simplifying view, since costs of men and machines could be measured in the same units. Another efficiency expert wrote in 1913: "On a punch press costing $3,000, the yearly cost . . . would be $450. The operator of this machine would probably be paid $3 a day, a total of about $900 a year. The only apparent difference is that the machine is paid for in advance, while the labor is paid for in weekly, bimonthly, or monthly installments."[62] The conclusion is clear: as Taylor and other efficiency experts saw him, the worker was no more than a machine, a machine powered by money.

The widespread enthusiasm for Taylor's efficiency is hard to overstate. Testimony elicited by Louis Brandeis at an Interstate Commerce Hearing in 1910 popularized it. The size and range of Taylor's and his collaborators' clients are indicators: Pullman, Remington Typewriter, Pierce-Arrow, Santa Fe Railroad, manufacturers of textiles and clothing, and printers. In France, Peugot and

Michellin were devoted clients.[63] Taylor described his system in *Atlantic Monthly* articles. His book, *Principles of Scientific Management*, was translated into nine languages.[64] In France Georges Clemenceau would order efficiency studies during World War I.[65] Vladimir Lenin and Joseph Stalin would endorse Taylorism, and it is said that the USSR's first five-year plans were based on Taylor's "scientific management."[66] Saul also argues that Harvard Business School and its case study method were shaped by Taylor's concepts.[67]

Educators promptly applied the concepts of efficiency, because of their "vulnerability" or their desire to emulate high-status businessmen or augment their control.[68] However that may be, efficiency and business management were the occupational ideology of the time. Franklin Bobbitt of the University of Chicago formulated that approach in detail in a yearbook of the National Society for the Study of Education (NSSE), which was the most prestigious of scholarly educators' organizations:

> In any organization, the directive and supervisory members must clearly define the ends toward which the organization strives. They must co-ordinate the labors of all so as to attain those ends. They must find the best methods of work and they must enforce the use of these methods on the part of the workers. . . . Directors and supervisors must keep the workers supplied with detailed instructions as to the work to be done, the standards to be reached, the methods to be employed, and the materials and appliances.[69]

Bobbitt provided four management "principles" for city schools:

> *Definite qualitative and quantitative standards must be determined for the Product.*
> . . .
> *Where the material that is acted upon by the labor processes passes through a number of progressive stages on its way from the raw material to the ultimate product, definite qualitative and quantitative standards must be determined for the product at each of these stages. . . .*
> *Scientific Management finds the methods of procedure which are most efficient under actual conditions, and secures their use on the part of the workers. . . . Standard qualifications must be determined for the workers. . . .*
> *The management must train its workers previous to service.*[70]

Bobbitt held the conviction that schools should be like factories. Appropriate patterns for school administration should be like those of efficient factories, with specialist planners and central control by superintendents, of course. This was a rationale for complete control by administrators. Factories organized in the general pattern for efficiency depended upon technicians for planning, measurement, routing, and so on; school systems could not be efficient without technologists—some call them technocrats. If schools were to be run like factories and the teachers were the workers, then teachers were to be controlled as factory workers were to be controlled. For systematic observations and their recording, teacher "rating" forms were developed; these appeared quickly, perhaps beginning with Edward C. Elliott.[71] The most comprehensive form appeared in 1915 as another NSSE yearbook, *Methods for Measuring Teachers' Efficiency.*[72] If the pupil was to be seen as raw material, work in progress, tests of pupils would measure teacher efficiency by presumably objective data. In a sense, the school was "partitioned," teachers in isolation from one another. Time, of course, was rigidly controlled, by schedules and bells.

Achievement tests, beginning with Cliff Winfield Stone's arithmetic test,[73] were intended to measure output, ostensibly, maybe as the number of iron pigs carried by Schmidt did. A reviewer said Stone "provides the educational world with the means of beginning to standardize its products."[74] (Group IQ tests, which appeared after World War I, accessed qualities of the raw materials, that is, of the pupils.)

Business and factory management practices would continue into the 1930s. A case study by William B. Thomas of a Buffalo superintendent in the 1920s showed that a superintendent's claims of efficiency and scientific management were used to exercise greater control over the system.[75] Most educational research was intended to be of use in scientific management. A wide range of achievement tests became available. Jesse H. Newlon's analysis of courses in school administration showed "clearly the emphasis on the technical and the factual, the external. Most of the topics have to do with the mechanics of administration."[76] It was not coincidental that what would become the American Educational Research Association came into existence at the instance of administrators in charge of budgeting and expenditures.

Democratic Administration, Respite

Although long unavailing, there were critics of centralization and scientific management.[77] Ella Flagg Young, superintendent of schools in Chicago, argued for democracy in the schools, democracy that might be defined, to borrow from Walter Lippmann, as "a way to live in which men proceed by unending enquiry and debate, having agreed to agree as best they can."[78]

The American Federation of Teachers (AFT) also argued that case. Speakers before the NEA Department of Teaching, beginning in 1914, were emphatic, indignant: "I mean . . . very frankly that the status of the teachers is becoming more and more akin to that of the 'hands' in a factory, working under foremen and superintendents who assume real responsibility."[79] In 1916 John Dewey, in *Democracy and Education*, criticized scientific management and its emphasis on efficiency at the cost of social relationships. Three years later Strayer wrote: "We believe that participation by teachers is indispensable to the best development of the public schools. We believe that such participation should be the right and responsibility of every teacher."[80] In 1926 A. S. Barr and W. H. Burton, authors of *The Supervision of Instruction*, advocated "democratic leadership in a group of co-workers to the end that the pupils of the schools may make the largest possible growth in desirable ideals, interests, knowledge, power, and skills."[81] (As an aside, this passage was probably written by Burton.) In the early 1930s John Dewey, William Kilpatrick, and others, most of them at Teachers College, Columbia University, were arguing in *The Educational Frontier* that "social reconstruction's" time had come. Influential then, their arguments could be ignored only with difficulty.

In a 1928 NEA *Research Bulletin* bibliography, entries on democratic administration were twice as frequent as those on scientific management. Thomas Fleming's tabulation shows that in *Education Index* the number of article titles including the word *democracy* increased from two in 1928 to approximately twenty-five in 1951, then declined, at first slowly. After the mid–1950s there was only a scattering of such articles; more than four-fifths of them appeared between 1935 and 1955.[82]

Newlon was the best-known and most effective protagonist of democratic administration. Callahan called him "one of the most able of American school administrators." Formerly teacher, principal, and superintendent of schools, he had said in 1925 that "the greatest danger that besets superintendents at the present time is that they will become merely business managers."[83] In 1927 he became a professor at Teachers College, Columbia University, and was influenced by progressives there. His *Educational Administration as Social Policy*,[84] with articles, addresses, and the courses he taught, were important for their support of democratic administration.

Naturally it was easier to espouse democracy in schools than to practice it, but two surveys confirmed that it was widely practiced, at least to an extent.[85] Though this evidence is slight, it is nevertheless reasonable to conclude that centralization of control was for a time slowed or halted. But the bureaucratic top-hamper, the echelons of specialists and technocrats in city systems' central offices, survived and surely continued to exercise some forms of control. "Democratic administration" later fused with "human relations," as business management and the efficiency movement had.

Human Relations: "Engineered Concurrence"

Democratic administration was based upon social philosophy: "human relations" was said to have rested upon the social sciences. More specifically, in 1923 Elton Mayo, a faculty member at the Harvard Graduate School of Business, influenced by psychology and social psychology, suggested that the limits of workers' production were set by "irrational factors," by affect, emotions, and attitudes. Mayo would later direct the Hawthorne studies. When its results were published in 1939, they seemed to demonstrate that "the limits of human collaboration are determined far more by the informal than by the formal organization of the plant. . . . None of the results give the slightest substantiation to the theory that the worker is primarily motivated by economic interest."[86]

The other most often cited later research upon which the human relations rationale was based was that of Kurt Lewin. Lewin, well known, a refugee from

Nazi Germany, professor at University of Iowa, was interested primarily in personality psychology, but also in industrial research. In 1938 he directed experiments on the effects of leadership style on children's behavior. The study's finding was that "democratic" leadership was more effective than laissez-faire or autocratic leadership.[87] That was a welcome conclusion in a time of totalitarian threats. The study was cited again and again, into the 1980s at least. Lewin later aided the establishment of the National Training Laboratories, the Research Center for Group Dynamics, and Tavistock Institute, centers for research and dissemination of information on group dynamics.[88]

As a matter of interest, the Hawthorne studies have been criticized because data did not support the conclusions. The Lewin, Lippitt, White study has not been able to be replicated in spite of many efforts. Aside from that, in the first seven volumes of *Educational Leadership* only 8 of 568 articles were by social scientists or employed quantitative information. Perhaps the behavioral basis for human relations was selected to support prior convictions.

Bureaucrats, Bureaucracies: Return to Rationalism

It was our hope and expectation in the early 1960s that a science of administration could be formed and that it would be applied to educational administration.[89] Only with great equivocation could it be said that our hopes were even partly fulfilled.

Study of schools as organizations, following the older rational approach of scientific management, abated but did not vanish. Renewed interest in rationality of school organizations drew on Max Weber's work, which, though written decades earlier, was not translated into English until the later 1940s. Weber's description of the ideal bureaucracy is so familiar it need not be repeated here. It was a description of a rationalized organization, systematic and orderly, proof against favoritism and efficiently fulfilling predetermined goals. Weber argued that the scale of contemporary organizations made bureaucratization inevitable, though in some ways detrimental.

But accumulated evidence from human relations studies contradicted in some ways Weber's formulation. In 1923 Mayo had written of "irrational" influences that affected production. The Hawthorne studies had confirmed that, ideal types aside, personal interrelationships greatly affected outcomes. Amitai Etzioni in *Modern Organizations*[90] provided a synthesis; organizations had both formal and informal components. A further complication arose from the presence of professionals, holders of special knowledge, in the organization. It was apparent that school systems were not independent of their social environments. An analogy from biology served as a framework for describing these environmental effects, and writers on school organizations used the term *open system*. These perspectives provided frameworks for research, even if their application to school administration in practice was not obvious. Almost inevitably there were exceptions, for instance, Halpin's *Leadership Behavior of School Administrators*[91] and his

Leadership Behavior Descriptive Questionnaire, which did suggest the effectiveness of some leadership styles, but that was somewhat unusual.

In administrative practice there were new rationales for centralization of control. MBO, management by objectives, incorporated assumptions that predicated top-down control. PERT, by amassing knowledge of production, had similar effects. It would reasonably be supposed that the "reflective teacher," just now in vogue, might feel control less. But that is a matter of doubt, misgivings.[92]

CONCLUSION

Centralization of control, at least to some degree, and bureaucracies, at least to some extent, are nearly essential for large-scale enterprises. It follows that control, to some extent, is also nearly essential. But there are limits to desirable centralization, and these have been greatly exceeded. One route to school reform is centralization of control, which the common school evangelists sought—but reforms from top down are too seldom successful; Kelly and Seller's case study of New York State demonstrates that.[93] If, to put the best face on it, turn-of-the-century schoolmen were wise and knowledgeable and if teachers in the city schools were ill-prepared and inexperienced, then perhaps centralization was justified. But administrators and bureaucrats are no longer the near-exclusive possessors of wisdom and knowledge. Granted that technocrat members of the city school system staff have esoteric and half-secret knowledge, it concerns matters usually peripheral.

Max Weber's view of the ways bureaucratization would develop is not cheering. He wrote that it "is at work to set up the iron cage of that bondage of the future to which some day men like the fellaheen in ancient Egypt will hopelessly be forced to submit"[94] and that "disciplinization as a universal phenomenon will make irresistible headway in every sphere of human life."[95] Therefore, the charismatic leader (as opposed to manager) would appear far less often.[96] More specifically, it seems unlikely that city school superintendents, especially bedeviled as they are by political pressures, will often be leaders, especially leaders in the dismantling of bureaucracy. Weber's predictions have proven uncomfortably true.

There are possible remedies. One alternative now being implemented in Chicago is to turn over control of individual schools to "local school improvement councils," largely freeing them from the system's bureaucrats and regulations.[96] Another is James P. Comer's approach, which stood the usual school reform formula on its head. School performance is, implicitly, the dependent variable. The independent or input variable is the social organization of the school, initially one school. The Comer plan calls for "teamwork," the unpartitioning of teachers, cooperation of counselors and child psychologists and teachers, reestablishment of strong relations among parents, community, and the school.[97] The Chicago way of governance or the Comer schools may be ways for schools to escape "the iron cage" of bureaucracy and central control. But they are only possibilities. The "iron cage" has been centuries in the building, and escape will not be easy.

NOTES

1. Michael B. Katz, *Class, Bureaucracy and the Schools* (New York: Praeger, 1975).

2. Michel Foucault, *Discipline and Punish*, trans. Alan Sheridan (New York: Vintage/ Random House, 1979).

3. John Ralston Saul, in *Voltaire's Bastards* (New York: Free Press, 1992), assigns a more important role to Voltaire, as his title suggests.

4. Redman, Ben Ray, ed., *Portable Voltaire* (New York: Viking, 1969), 24.

5. Foucault argues that the beginnings of formal, hierarchical disciplining organizations had appeared more than a century earlier, as a result of the beginning of the shift in social perspectives.

6. Michel Foucault, *The Archeology of Knowledge*, trans. A. M. Sheridan Smith (New York: Harper and Row, 1972), 200–201.

7. Originally published as *Surveiller et Punior* (Paris: Editions Gallimard, 1975); there seems to be no exact translation for Foucault's title.

8. Foucault, *Discipline and Punish*, 184–85.

9. Ibid.

10. Ibid., 172.

11. Ibid., 143.

12. Ibid., 149, 156.

13. "Samuel Bentham," *Dictionary of National Biography*, 2 (London: Oxford University Press, 1959–1960), 281–84.

14. Jeremy Bentham, "Outline of a Plan of Construction of a Panoptican Penitenary House, as Designed by Jeremy Bentham of Lincoln's Inn, Esq.," in Mary Peter Mack, ed., *A Bentham Reader* (New York: Pegasus, 1969), 194.

15. Blake McKelvey, *American Prisons* (Montclair, NJ: Patterson Smith, 1977), 282.

16. Foucault, *Discipline and Punish*, 146–47; John Ralston Saul, *Voltaire's Bastards* (New York: Free Press, 1992), 31, 45–47, passim.

17. Plausibly, Bell's formulation of his plan for monitorial schools was at least to some extent modeled upon the methods of the British government in India, methods for the control of many by the few. But apparently this possible link has not been investigated.

18. H. Warren Button and Eugene F. Provenzo, Jr., *History of Education in American Culture* (Englewood Cliffs, NJ: Prentice-Hall, 1983), 78.

19. Katz, 10.

20. Button and Provenzo, 77–78.

21. Lawrence A. Cremin, *American Education: The National Experience* (New York: Harper and Row, 1980), 148.

22. Fred Gerald Loveland, "Victor M. Rice and Andrew S. Draper: The Origins of Educational Centralization in Rural New York State" (Ph.D. diss., University at Buffalo, State University of New York, forthcoming).

23. Katz's definition of bureaucracy, p. 59, is somewhat different from the usual Weberian definition; Katz, 33–36.

24. David Tyack and Elisabeth Hansot, *Managers of Virtue* (New York: Basic Books, 1982), 60.

25. Cremin, 160–63.

26. *Code of Public Instruction* (Albany: Superintendent of Public Instruction, 1856).

27. Ibid., 157.

28. Ibid.

29. Ibid., 158.

30. Ibid., 366.

31. Ibid., 32.

32. Cf. D. Wood, "A Case Study in Local Control of Schools," *Urban Education* 10:1 (April 1975): 7–26; Diane Ravitch, *The Great School Wars* (New York: Basic Books, 1974), 85.

33. Oliver G. Steele, "The Buffalo Common Schools," *Publications of the Buffalo Historical Society* 1 (1879): 406–32.

34. George W. Hosmer, "Oliver Gray Steele," *Publications of the Buffalo Historical Society* 2 (1880): 145–56.

35. Bayard Still, *Milwaukee: History of a City* (Madison: State Historical Society of Wisconsin, 1965).

36. Bruce Catton, *Centennial History of the Civil War*, Vol. 1, *The Coming Fury* (Garden City, NY: Doubleday, 1961), 390–91.

37. Mary J. Herrick, *The Chicago Schools: A Social and Political History* (Beverly Hills, CA: Sage, 1971), 116–17.

38. Virginia Marie Foley, "The Establishment of the City Superintendency of Public Schools in Five Nineteenth Century American Cities" (Ph.D. diss., State University of New York at Buffalo, 1972).

39. *Report of the Superintendent of Instruction of the Commonwealth of Pennsylvania for the Year Ending June 1, 1876* (Harrisburg, PA: B. F. Meyers, 1876), xx.

40. Thomas C. Cochran, *The American Business System: A Historical Perspective, 1900–1955* (New York: Harper and Row, 1957).

41. Thomas C. Cochran and William Miller, *The Age of Enterprise* (New York: Harper and Brothers, 1961), 6–8.

42. David Nelson, *Managers and Workers: Origins of the New Factory System in the United States, 1880–1920* (Madison: University of Wisconsin, 1975), 21–22.

43. Ibid., 49.

44. Luther Lee Bernard and Jessie Bernard, *The Social Science Movement in the United States* (New York: Thomas Crowell, 1943).

45. Henry Warren Button, "James Park Slade—Nineteenth Century Schoolman," *Journal of the Illinois State Historical Society* 44:4 (Winter 1961), 374–91.

46. Ibid., 377.

47. James P. Slade, "Country Schools," *NEA Proceedings* (1882): 26.

48. This account is drawn primarily from Loveland and Harlan Hoyt Horner, *Life and Work of Andrew Sloan Draper* (Urbana: University of Illinois, 1934).

49. "Report on the Committee of Fifteen," *NEA Proceedings* (1895): 344–48.

50. Jesse B. Sears and Alvin Henderson, *Cubberley of Stanford* (Stanford, CA: Stanford University Press, 1957); Harold Benjamin, "Ellwood Patterson Cubberley—A Biographical Sketch," in John C. Almack, ed., *Modern School Administration: Its Problems and Progress* (Boston: Houghton Mifflin, 1933), 349–77.

51. Tyack, 126–27.

52. "Report on the Committee on Uniform Financial Reports," *NEA Proceedings* (1899): 345.

53. Raymond E. Callahan, *Education and the Cult of Efficiency* (Chicago, University of Chicago Press, 1962), 54.

54. Herrick, 403, 406.

55. Samuel Haber, *Efficiency and Uplift* (Chicago: University of Chicago Press, 1964).

56. Frank B. Copeley, *Frederick W. Taylor* (New York: Harper and Brothers, 1923); Sudhir Kakar, *Frederick Taylor: A Study of Personality and Innovation* (Cambridge, MA: MIT Press, 1970); Nelson.

57. Nelson, 127.

58. Ibid., 102.

59. Callahan, 27.

60. Frederick W. Taylor, *Shop Management* (Cambridge, MA: M.I.T. Press, 1913).

61. Callahan, 35.

62. Irving A. Berndt, "The Value of a Dollar's Worth of Labor," *Efficiency* (September 1913): 13.

63. Nelson, 7.

64. Callahan, 22.

65. Ibid., 23.

66. Saul, 119.

67. Callahan; Button, "Vulnerability: A Concept Reconsidered," *Educational Administration Quarterly* 27:3 (August 1991): 378–91, is my argument for emulation. B. Berman, in "Business Efficiency, American Schooling and the Public School Superintendency: A Reconsideration of the Callahan Thesis," *History of Education Quarterly* 23 (1983): 297–321, argued that the growth of public schools made business management a necessity. William B. Thomas and Kevin J. Moran, "The Politicization of Efficiency Concepts in the Progressive Period, 1918–1922," *Journal of Urban History* 17 (August 1991): 390–409, demonstrates that one school superintendent employed an efficiency ideology to increase his power.

68. Franklin Bobbitt, *The Supervision of City Schools: Some General Principles of Management Applied to City-School Systems*, 12th Yearbook of the NSSE, Pt. 1 (Chicago: University Chicago Press, 1913), 7–8.

69. Ibid., 11–74.

70. Edward C. Elliott, *Tentative Scheme for the Measurement of Teaching Efficiency* (Madison: University Wisconsin Press, 1910).

71. Arthur Clifton Boyce, *Methods for Measuring Teacher's Efficiency*, 14th Yearbook of the NSSE, Pt. 2 (Chicago: University of Chicago Press, 1915).

72. Cliff Winfield Stone, *Arithmetical Abilities and Some Factors Affecting Them* (New York: Teachers College, Columbia University Press, 1908).

73. Elmer E. Jones, review of Stone, *Arithmetical Abilities, Educational Review* 38 (1909): 195.

74. Thomas.

75. Callahan, 78.

76. Concerning democratic administration I rely heavily on Fleming and Raymond E. Callahan, "The Superintendent of Schools—An Historical Analysis," Report ED 010 410 (Washington, DC: U.S. Office of Education).

77. Thomas Fleming, "Management by Consensus: Democratic Administration and Human Relations" (Ph.D. diss., University of Oregon, 1982).

78. William C. Bagley, "The Status of the Classroom Teacher," *NEA Proceedings* (1915): 1162.

79. Fleming, 76.

80. Ibid., 83.

81. Ibid., 56–57.

82. Callahan, *Cult*, 203.

83. (New York: Scribner, 1934).

84. Roald F. Campbell et al., *A History of Thought and Practice in Educational Administration* (New York: Teachers College Press, 1987), 142.

85. Fleming, 249–50.

86. Kurt Lewin, Ronald Lippitt, and R. K. White, "Patterns of Aggressive Behavior in Experimentally Created Social Climates," *Journal of Experimental Psychology* 10 (1939): 271–99.

87. Fleming, 255.

88. D. E. Griffiths, ed., *Behavioral Science and Educational Administration*, 63rd Yearbook of the NSSE, Part 2 (Chicago: University of Chicago Press, 1964).

89. (Englewood Cliffs, NJ: Prentice-Hall, 1964).

90. (Columbus: Ohio University Research Foundation, 1962).

91. John Smyth, "Teachers' Work and the Politics of Reflection," *American Educational Research Journal* 29:2 (Summer 1992): 267–300.

92. Gail P. Kelly and Maxine S. Seller, "Considerations: Historical Perspectives on Reform in New York State," in Philip G. Altbach, Gail P. Kelly, and Lois Weis, eds., *Excelence in Education* (Buffalo, NY: Prometheus, 1985), 253–74.

93. Wolfgang J. Mommsen, *The Age of Bureaucracy: Perspectives on the Political Sociology of Max Weber* (New York: Harper and Row, 1974), 58–59.

94. Ibid., 112.

95. Ibid.

96. G. Alfred Hess, Jr., *School Restructuring, Chicago Style* (Newbury Park, CA: Corwin, 1991).

97. James T. Comer, *School Power: Implications of an Intervention Project* (New York: Free Press, 1980); Amy R. Anson, et al., "The Comer School Development Program: A Theoretical Analysis," *Urban Education* 26:1 (April 1991): 8–24. Comparing Chicago's restructuring and the Comer plan: Charles Payne, "The Comer Intervention Model and School Reform in Chicago," *Urban Education* 26:1 (April 1991): 8–24.

II

POLITICAL AND ORGANIZATIONAL PERSPECTIVES

4

The Criticism of Urban Schools

Stanley William Rothstein

The criticism of urban schools in more recent times has been noted by both the right and the left in American politics. This general agreement that something is wrong with our educational system has given birth to new political explanations that rediscovered the old problems of a nonacademic teaching staff: overcrowding, watered-down curricula, and legions of student failures. But political tendencies looking for explanations of social inequities among schooling's practices missed the point again. These conditions have existed since the beginning of the common school era and continue to exist because of one overriding reason: they work. Since the 1970s the steadily decreasing test scores of students have been cited as evidence of a deeper malaise; but these scores merely reflected a trend in student failures going back at least to the 1890s, when the schools first began to publish such statistics in a vain attempt to get more money from the states. The themes of schooling have been couched in terms like democracy and citizenship, even as its practices were overly concerned with producing dronelike workers for the factories and bureaucracies of mass society.

If the schools have been able to maintain themselves and expand in their present forms, it is because they have benefited from the direct and indirect support of business and political interests. On one hand, the states have consistently underfunded the public school systems since their inception; and they have been questioned by the most wealthy, conservative elements in government and industry. On the other, the federal government has done little more than pay lip service to educational funding needs while calling for a reform of today's practices.

The understandings of schooling's plight under these circumstances have been plagued with political effects. They are similar in content to struggles that occurred during earlier periods, when reform of the schools was also deemed a dire necessity for national salvation. An idealist, humanist perspective was adopted by Horace Mann in the early 1840s, when he assured business leaders that an educated work force would benefit them while purging youth of their tendencies toward idleness and sloth. Here it would suffice to remember that in the 1890s school superintendents were struggling to bring classroom sizes down to sixty students per teacher! This entire effort to educate and socialize immigrant and urban youth in the virtues of capitalism and American political and social institutions is still with us today, though most of our students are not immigrants and few of them need the practices and curricula of a bygone age. To move back to more recent problems, the following remarks seem germane. The present demands for urban school reform can now be seen as political in nature, with little real muscle behind them. Political ideology may be part of our social reality, yet the effects of such thinking cannot but hinder any rational attempts to understand the schooling phenomenon.

The urbanization of America in the nineteenth century developed before the advent of the Industrial Revolution and the decay of agrarian social structures. The migration of Americans toward urban centers developed as a response to industry's need for labor that was literate and easily available. In our period, this need to concentrate labor power and markets in urban centers was essential if the industrial period was to flourish. Cities and large towns attracted industry and commerce because they provided a ready market for goods and services and because the infrastructure and labor power were near at hand. Of course, there were other reasons for the urbanization phenomenon: when gold was discovered in California, urban centers appeared overnight, and cities grew rapidly when they were easily accessible by land or sea.

Thus industry was the essential element in the further development of urban centers that already existed in the United States. The need for workers who were literate and able to function in increasingly large and complex organizations fueled the demand for urban education during this period. A specialization of labor, peculiar to bureaucratic organization, also fueled the schooling phenomenon, along with a need to assimilate huge numbers of immigrants and urban poor.

The politicalization of urban educational problems in our own period is directly influenced by class biases in the system and the hesitancy to educate urban youth in ways that might prove socially destabilizing. We are witnessing a generation and more of state governments that have underfunded and devalued the concepts of public education while offering private schools and vouchers as panaceas. The need for skilled labor power may be lessening as productive industries leave the United States for countries with cheaper costs and labor. As a result, more and more Americans find themselves trapped in inner cities where the schools are inferior and unable to teach the skills workers will need in the twenty-first century. Against this condition, community movements and some local boards of education have struggled with differential success. Unions, on the other hand, have been significantly weakened and are no longer able to provide their members with higher-paying jobs. Urban schools have steadily deteriorated.

The ever-expanding control of the state apparatus in the area of urban education is based on its ability to fund and license educators. States are, more and more, replacing local school boards as the de facto policy bodies of public schools. This has further politicized the entire urban education problem, even when community control groups have won control of their schools and district offices. The arbitrary curriculum and pedagogical practices have not been eliminated, and minority and poor students have continued to fail much as they did in the past.

The globalization of the urban education problem has further complicated our understanding of this phenomenon. Now urban schools are seen as a weapon in the economic war of survival, and learning is justified as something that is imperative for national defense. This has made it easier for state bureaucracies to impose a military discipline in education, drowning local school boards in reams of new rules and regulations. The school reform movement of the 1980s can be seen as a return to basics, to a mythical time when schooling was more humane and effective.

In the first chapter of this section, Professors Frank Lutz and Laurence Iannaccone provide us with a comparative study of urban school boards, focusing upon administrative practices and their effects on the people they govern. Then Professor Louise Adler discusses the politics of curriculum as it is played out in urban schools, focusing especially on the social control aspects of pedagogical action and its arbitrary nature. Finally, Professor Joseph Weeres analyzes the organizational structures of urban educational systems, tracing its evolution over the past seventy-five years.

5

Policymakers and Politics in Urban Education

Frank W. Lutz and Laurence Iannaccone

The empirical realities of urban school governance stands in stark contrast to the interests and concerns of the parents and children they serve. This should come as no surprise. American governance systems on the federal, state, and local levels demonstrate a fundamental lack of representation for their poor, undereducated, and minority citizens. Urban schools will not likely improve until this condition is corrected. That will require serious modification of the structure of the governance system presently in place. Such a modification must recognize several factors:

1. The reform movement from ward-based machine politics, over the last sixty to seventy years, removed considerable corruption from the schools but also removed the urban schools from the people they are constituted to serve.

2. In the place of ward-based school boards, reform boards were elected at-large or were appointed from among the socioeconomically privileged elite.

3. Such reform boards installed a civil service system of "professionalism" among both administration and teachers that currently exercises an enormous amount of power and operates as a "professional machine," replacing the old machines with a new one that controls resources and jobs while serving the interests of the professionals rather than those of their clients.

4. Such an organization cannot be counted upon to reform itself or to act as a selfless or disinterested party when confronted with conflicting demands of its own constituency as opposed to those of its clients.

5. The very numbers of pupils/families presumed to be represented by urban school boards, whose values often conflict with their constituents, legislate against effective representation.

6. Finally, as the democratic process has eroded in the governance of urban schools, the public has lost faith in their close-to-home, "grass roots" model—and lost hope in using the democratic process as an effective means to change their circumstances.

Without hope in that process, the urban poor are left with the tool of insurrection, expressed sadly in urban riots, as a means to protest and draw to public attention their pathetic conditions.

Urban school governance must be restructured, providing better representation of those who attend urban schools—not only for the sake of urban education but for the sake of the nation and its democratic institutions.

PLURALISTIC OR POLLYANNAS?

Writing in 1985, P. E. Peterson takes an optimistic, if not pollyanna, view of the world of urban education, its "reformers," and its politicians.[1] Peterson rejects R. E. Callahan's[2] position that there has been a generally monolithic and business-oriented control of public education. Peterson says: "Like all social movements, school reform was a complex, pluralistic, multifaceted undertaking . . . alliances were subtle, numerous and subject to change, and its objective varied with time and circumstances. . . . Oh how well reformers would have fared if they had been as unified and powerful . . . as some now would have us remember them."[3]

Further, Peterson says: "The diverse sources of reform came into evidence in the late nineteenth century and began to flourish in the early twentieth . . . [and] it did not end in the 1930's. . . . [It] would achieve its greatest success after World War II. Urban reform especially in education, was at its zenith . . . with the close of World War II and continuing into the 1960's."[4]

Finally, he writes in 1985: "A dark day has not come over American education. But the elan, emerging confidence, and self-esteem that accompany times of educational reform and expansion must constantly be renewed if American schools are to *continue* to enjoy the *multi-class popular* appeal that has historically been theirs."[5] (italics added).

Perhaps Peterson saw some different urban schools than most others saw and still see. Perhaps he saw some different school results than the authors of *A Nation at Risk*, who wrote at approximately the same time.[6] Perhaps urban school decisions are not the result of the action and control of a single, stable, unchanging power elite. But they are hardly the result of a polyarchy broadly representative of the racial, ethnic, and socioeconomic groups that send their children to urban public schools.

A NEW MACHINE IN URBAN EDUCATION?

Under pressure of scientific management and the general reform movement in the cities (see Wilson[7]), urban school boards moved from ward-based and machine-grounded politics. In their place at large elections, appointed boards were positioned. In doing so a "deal was cut" with the professionals. Local boards remained in power to make policy, and superintendents were "enshrined" as expert and professionally trained managers of the organization, largely free from board interference in the administration of the schools.[8] J. M. Cronin reported that this move was largely a success by the mid-1930s.[9]

What happened when urban school boards went from fifty plus to five or seven members? The machine retreated or was put out of business, and local boards could operate in "elite" fashion and left matters of education largely to the professionals. The professionals took over. D. Rogers reports a new machine had been positioned in the New York City public schools by the 1960s. He says: "The independence from party politics should have led to more professionalism, it has not. Under the guise of professionalism, a number of protective practices that are distinctly non-professional have begun . . . and a new form of 'educational politics' has evolved."[10]

This is the "professional" machine. It controls jobs, it controls resources, it controls programs, and it distributes all of them according to its own values. The recipients of rewards are often not the poor and undereducated of the urban inner cities. E. E. Schattschnieder concludes: "Pressure politics is essentially the politics of small groups. . . . The flaw in the pluralist explanations is that the heavenly chorus sings with a strong upper-class accent."[11] A corollary might posit that urban interest groups in education sing with a strong middle-class voice, and the usual song is the welfare of school-related jobs. The "friends" made by the new machine are the "insider-local" professionals who pay their "dues" and give their loyalty to the professional bureaucracy and its top power structure. The Illinois state legislature has tried to challenge Chicago's professional bureaucracy with its reform legislation of 1988. New York still struggles with its professional machine, and Dallas recently exposed its machine when, in 1991–1992 teachers were fired only to be rehired, and many "irregularities" were discovered in the renovation/repair functions that were directly responsible to the professional hierarchy.

DO POLITICS OF PROFESSIONAL BUREAUCRACIES SERVE URBAN CITIES WELL?

Recalling that Peterson[12] finds that urban schools are largely pluralistically governed and that, in general, their reforms have served the people, what can be said to counter the accusation that the reform revolution merely installed a different type of oligarchical machine? P. A. Cusick does an interesting and careful study of today's schools, using heavily his own ethnographic work and that of others.[13] His book is interesting and well done. The descriptive material, which he integrates so well, is alone worth the effort.

Cusick's conclusions provide his answers to the question of how well the professional machine serves American education. He says: "At the base, school is a bureaucracy . . . [that] provides a dynamic with which schools address change (211). . . . The organization co-opts outsiders and critics; it moderates both among competing parts of the overall system and among its internal groups. . . . And even with its somewhat fragmented governance, it behaves as do large, successful corporations."[14] Cusick sees a great deal of individual freedom within the schools. "It is true that schools appear narrow and restrictive, but their appearance is only a facade of a crowded and busy system where individuals, with and without formal status, do to a great degree as each sees fit. The freedom of conscience and choice is a basic characteristic of the system."[15]

Cusick finds the school bureaucracy responsive to diverse values and even change. He notes: "It is true that the bureaucracy does not initiate reforms, but . . . it lends itself naturally to reforms that argue for equality, as most do. Indeed, every one of the initiatives described in this book . . . all argued from the view that education could increase equality, or put another way, decrease inequality." [Cusick argues that] "it makes little sense to criticize a system that so well reflects society . . . coalitions of interested and appreciative citizens, students, teachers, and administrators keep the school stable. They also make the school hard to change [but] . . . not unresponsive."[16] Thus, Cusick makes a strong case supporting Peterson's picture of pluralistically governed urban schools that generally find a way to meet the needs and satisfy the values of the citizens they serve.

ARE THERE MULTIPLE REALITIES?

If Cusick is correct, why are there consistent criticism, cries for school reform, and breast-beating over school results? Cusick would probably say that such is an expression of the tension, the pressure that, through a system of adapting and co-optation, changes schooling and includes the needs and values of the pluralistic society. That is one truth, one picture. But there is another.

IS THERE AN OLIGARCHY?

The phrase "iron law of oligarchy"[17] can be loosely interpreted to mean that regardless of how the governance of any social/political enterprise begins, no matter how many people are originally involved (or participate) in the governance, over time fewer and fewer people will make the decisions for a greater and greater number of people. Lord Acton suggested that "power corrupts and absolute power corrupts absolutely." What does this have to do with the governance and policy in urban schools or, for that matter, public schools in general?

In 1941–1942 there were 115,493 school districts in the United States but only 15,912 in 1981–1982.[18] That number declined only slightly to approximately 15,000 by 1992–1993. In 1940, figuring seven persons to each school board, there were 808,451 local board members governing local education for a population of less than 135 million in the United States (1 per 169). By 1980, again assuming seven members per board, there were 111,384 local board members governing local education for a population of 250 million (1 per 224). That is the iron law of oligarchy operationalized in local school governance. Fewer and fewer people were making the political decisions and allocating values for more and more of the people. More and more power was vested in a smaller and smaller oligarchy. Less power was in the hands of "the people." These data are further exacerbated when one considers that the majority of students in the United States attend urban/city schools while a majority of school boards are located in small town/rural districts.[19]

Consider that urban school districts have more schools and pupils per school board and usually no more board members than do rural districts in the same state. For instance, Dallas Independent School District (ISD), Texas, has 135,320 students and seven board members. Blue Ridge ISD, Texas, has 434 students and seven board members. Blue Ridge ISD is within thirty miles of Dallas ISD.[20] Each Blue Ridge board member represents about 62 school students, and each Dallas board member represents nearly 20,000 students. In New York City, seven board members represent over 2 million students (1 per 285,714). It took seven transfer calls to the New York City Board Office to verify those numbers and they got it wrong at that. In Los Angeles Unified District, seven board members represent approximately 800,000 students (1 per 114,000). That information took only one transfer to confirm, and they got it right. Can one board member represent 285,714 students and their parents as well as one board member can represent the values and needs of 62 students and their parents? Could the answer to that question have some influence on the ability, or lack of it, to govern the school system in New York, Dallas, or Los Angeles?

LESS OPTIMISTIC VIEWS OF PLURALISM IN PUBLIC EDUCATION

Three major models of public school governance take considerably less charitable views of the manner in which public schools are governed than did Peterson.

Competition/Participation Theory

L. H. Zeigler, M. K. Jennings, and G. W. Peak suggested that competition and participation in the political arena are the major measures of democracy.[21] They found that competition for school board membership was vertically non-existent, describing the "pathways to board membership . . . [as] apolitical, circumscribed, and insulated."[22] Further, "the early educational reformers, those who wanted to keep politics and education separate, succeeded too well,"[23] and "the prescribed norms of democratic leadership selection run in the contrary direction [to those seen in school governance]."[24] Those authors found that "the less complex the district, and the higher the mass support, the more likelihood there was of finding a school board responsive to individual preference. . . . To solve the racial and social ills of urban education, it is proposed that control be radically decentralized in the central cities.[25] These authors were less positive than Peterson about the nature of urban schools, and they preempted the idea of "site-based management" by fifteen years.

When speaking particularly of urban school boards, Zeigler, Jennings, and Peak suggested that although urban boards represent a more diffuse electorate, they are even less likely than rural/small school boards to respond to citizen demands, and their election is not the result of heavy competition or large voter participation. The authors say: "Our overall conclusion is that [urban] boards are likely to become spokesmen *for* the superintendent *to* the community; their representational roles are revised, and the superintendent becomes the dominant policy maker. Here is, of course, a serious gap in the chain of governance . . . school board members are inclined to view their role as 'trustee,' e.g., standing aloof from community opinion."[26] (italics added) In the end those authors view the political process of school governance, particularly urban school governance, as undemocratic!

Input/Output System Theory

F. M. Wirt and M. W. Kirst[27] suggest a model of school governance based on D. Easton's[28] definition of politics as the authoritative allocation of values. That definition is important to the Wirt and Kirst model and the arguments offered in this chapter. Essentially, the notion of value allocation assumes a finite pool of resources and a seemingly infinite pool of interests and demands upon those resources. Thus, when a legislative, judicial, or administrative branch makes a decision for the people, that decision favors one set of values as opposed to some other set held by some other group. The values are allocated with the authority vested in the government. At that moment citizens have a simple choice: comply or not, abide by the law or break it.

Like Zeigler, Jennings, and Peak, Wirt and Kirst see the referendum as a critical part of the political process but find it falls short of its democratic promise in school governance. They say:

The promise of referendum control by citizens [in school governance] . . . has not been matched by reality. . . . Yet the promise is not completely hollow . . . these devices *can* be resorted to if their [policymakers'] actions are too offensive . . . the referendum is more significant for education than other areas of public policy. . . . [It] may be viewed as a conversion process that bypasses the school board and authoritatively allocates values, a direct policy-making process. . . . The act of voting for or against—or not at all—links the individual citizen to the school in a direct and intimate way that is unparalleled for other major public policies.[29]

Thus, Wirt and Kirst disagree with Zeigler, Jennings, and Peak about the degree of democracy possible within the school governance system as it actually operates. Wirt and Kirst see the general process of day-to-day political decision making as just as undemocratic, however, although "increasingly and more openly politicized."[30]

In chapters 2 and 3 Wirt and Kirst provide the foundation for their "system theory" of school governance. In chapter 13 they develop a wide array of inputs on local school governance, including resources, values, interests, and demands. They define the political process as one in which school boards (as legislative and judicial decision makers), along with top school administrators, particularly the superintendent, produce outputs, that is, programs and policy. Finally, they see those outputs as operational responses of the political process that, if viewed in terms of the demands, are the ultimate measure of democracy. Such outputs provide "feedback" for further inputs. Thus, failed policy output can effect a defeat for a school bond referendum.

Wirt and Kirst see this process as generally closed, although "episodic inputs . . . challenge this closed system of policy making and make it more pluralistic. . . . The past saw little of this model in local politics, [however]."[31] The authors continue: "We see school administrators as the key decision makers whose leadership role stems from the power of their expertise as professionals. In a context where community voices were few and faint, and where boards had limited policy initiatives, school administrators have filled a vacuum."[32] A vacuum, they might have added, that was largely manufactured by school administrators and their professional associations. This description, to a large extent accurate, can hardly be considered the epitome of democracy. Again, although not as emphatically as the Zeigler, Jennings, and Peak model, the Wirt and Kirst model leaves an impression of local school governance as largely undemocratic!

Dissatisfaction Theory

F. W. Lutz and L. Iannaccone[33] agree with many of the specific points made by the individuals previously reviewed here. In their dissatisfaction theory of American democracy they agree:

1. with Peterson that a type of pluralism does operate, at least periodically, within local school districts in order to form coalitions; the one representing the plurality of the electorate is, according to R. Dahl,[34] a governing polyarchy as opposed to an oligarchy;

2. with Zeigler, Jennings, and Peak that the democratic process is best seen when, periodically, there is competition among candidates for the board seats and when larger numbers of voters participate in the board's election or referenda and

3. with Wirt and Kirst that often the large array of inputs into the political process of local public school decision making is dominated by the superintendent and an elite school board acting in consensus and with their superintendent.

Yet, there is a major difference or exception suggested by the dissatisfaction theory. The authors of the dissatisfaction theory choose to look at the continuing process of political behavior in diachronic time, as opposed to stop-action time frames of synchronic time. Thus, at any particular time, public school governance may be uncompetitive and lack participation; it is dominated by an oligarchy comprised of the superintendent and the board, which tends to be unresponsive to the needs and values held by other racial/ethnic SES groups; and the policy outputs are incongruent with many public demands.

At such a time, especially, public dissatisfaction with the local district policy becomes sufficient so that (1) more citizens vote, (2) more candidates run, (3) incumbents are defeated, and (4) superintendents are more likely to lose their jobs. Then school policy and programs change. The "people" get their way. The democratic process becomes fulfilled. "From the viewpoint of dissatisfaction theory, continuous competition and decision output theories appear to present us with a Hobson's choice. Their respective central concepts . . . doom the local school district to disappearance as a democratic governmental unit, the one by calling for . . . nearly universal participation, the other by subjecting us to the old tyranny, for administrator representation is despotism writ small."[35]

Unlike its counterpart theories, the dissatisfaction theory of American democracy declares the local education political process not only democratic but the grass roots model of American democracy. This is a tremendous difference! American democracy not only guarantees its citizens the right to vote but, unlike some other democracies (e.g., Sweden), provides the right not to vote. In American elections, even national presidential elections, usually less than 60 percent of eligible voters bother to vote. One can only conclude that although voters are not necessarily satisfied with the government, they are not dissatisfied enough to do anything about changing the government and, thus, public policy. When they are dissatisfied enough, they vote—and often, in this manner, they throw the incumbents out. That is American democracy, and that is the way the local school political process actually works. This has important meaning for what is happening in America's urban schools.

URBAN SCHOOLS—IN RETROSPECT

For decades minorities in our urban cities have been either apathetic or alienated citizens, failing to participate effectively in political decisions about their schools, or much else for that matter. This is largely due to poverty and undereducation conditions, which lead to powerlessness in the political system, which in turn continues their poverty and undereducated condition. Until 1954 blacks and Hispanics were legally excluded from white schools in many states. They were also effectively excluded from most school boards, even when their children were admitted, except in nearly totally black communities. These individuals are no longer the minorities in the urban cities. They are increasingly discontent with their representatives on school boards and the operational outputs of the urban schools, as seen in the percent of school dropouts and in the failure and illiteracy of those who remain in school. They are moving toward increased participation and representation. From now on, if mistakes are to be made (and there will surely be mistakes), they will demand to make their own mistakes. They will also, when mistakes are recognized, move to correct those mistakes.

That is what democracy is about, and there are no more important political issues to them than the education, or lack of it, of their children.

Speaking of the dissatisfaction theory, Lutz and C. Merz ask:

How long can people be turned away? How long will they tolerate being given no real evidence that their special interest is of concern to those policymakers who are supposed to represent them? How long can those in power neglect special interest groups without creating a plurality of people "dissatisfied enough" to vote against the incumbents, the taxes they levy, and the bond issues they propose?[36]

The answer in today's American urban schools is, Not much longer!

THE OLD POLITICAL MACHINE

During the late nineteenth century and early twentieth centuries machine politics and corruption dominated urban politics in America. Public schools, although perhaps not the major example of such corruption, did not escape the notice of city machines.[37] In order to understand what happened while the machine had a hold on public education and how the demise of the machine affected it, two conceptual notions must be understood. But first, a given must be emphasized. Neither author of this chapter favors crime, kickbacks, or corruption, under the guise of either machine or reform government. Corruption had occurred within both types of government, although "theoretically" machine government is supposed to be totally corrupt and reform government is supposed to be totally void of corruption.

R. K. Merton[38] introduced the concepts of latent and manifest functions, which G. Ritzer[39] claims were a major contribution to sociology in general and specifically to structural/functionalism. When discussing latent/manifest functions, Merton wrote: "The distinction between manifest and latent functions was devised to preclude the inadvertent confusion . . . between conscious motivations for social behavior and its objective consequences. [It therefore] . . . clarifies the analysis of seemingly irrational patterns."[40] As his prototypic example of a latent function, Merton cites the persistence of machine government in large cities. Merton points out that while it was the intent of reformers to remove all vestiges of the machine from city government, many remain. This, he notes, is unintended and not functional, given a rational and legal reform city government working as it was supposed to work. But sometimes that rational system fails to meet the needs of certain citizens. Therefore, machine government continued to exist where it did, just because it met those otherwise unmet needs of the social/political system.

In their classic work, *City Politics*, E. C. Banfield and J. Q. Wilson point out, "People will exchange their votes for 'friendship' more readily than for cash or other material benefits; and the machine cannot afford to pay cash for many of the votes it needs."[41] The machine did favors for the people, and the people returned those favors at the ballot box, at least once an election.

The general removal of machine government from city and urban schools may have removed much of the corruption. It may also have removed a historically useful avenue for the poor and undereducated, the very people who remain in our urban centers, to influence politics, including the politics of education. Banfield and Wilson go further: "Even though in the abstract one may prefer a government that gets its influence from reasonable discussion about the common goods rather than from giving jobs, favors and friendship . . . even though in the abstract he may prefer the rule of professional administrators to that of politicians, he may nevertheless favor the machine in some particular circumstance."[42]

Lutz and Merz suggest that the people may be ready for a new type of corruption-free, but machinelike, government in local education to replace the "professional machine" that now operates.[43] This new government, although generally uncorrupt, would "deliver the goods" not on a "common good" basis but on a concrete and specific individual level; would respond to the needs of the people who send their children to urban schools; and would teach inner-city kids reading and writing and keep drugs and weapons out of the schools. Corruption should not and need not be part of that system. The people who send their children to urban schools are tired of government by an oligarchy of professional bureaucrats who think they are serving "all the kids" while large groups of those kids are dropping out or failing. Perhaps site-based management provides such an opportunity, if permitted by the "professional machine" to have a chance.

NEW YORK CITY SCHOOLS, MID-1960s

What is today called "site-based management" was called "local control" in New York City (NYC) during the 1960s. Driven by failure of the New York schools to meet the needs of many of its students, the Ford Foundation, the United Federation of Teachers (UFT), parents, and NYC government, under the leadership of reform mayor John Lindsay, all called for major school reform. The UFT, which had first backed inner-city school reform and even struck the schools to save the "More Effective Schools" program, broke with the school reformers and joined the school board and school administrators when it came to an assault on the professional bureaucracy threatening to impose citizens' control on local schools. Even with the massive resources of the Ford Foundation, even after Lindsay's intervention in school board politics by "packing the board" (going from seven to thirteen members) in order to get more reform, the effort to wrest control from the professional bureaucracy failed. The New York State legislature failed to pass local control legislation. The "compromise" resulted in little local control and little actual school reform.[44] During the battle one indigenous black female leader told a district school board (of all white males) "You don't prepare our men for college; you prepare them for the penitentiary." Probably more black males who once attended NYC schools are residents of penal institutions than institutions of higher education. If this is how the bureaucracy accommodates and adopts, there is a real problem. There is reality in Cusick's statements. There is also reality in the words of the black leader speaking in the 1960s. There are still more black males in prison than in universities.

CHICAGO IN THE 1990s

Late in the 1980s then secretary of education William Bennett called the Chicago school system the worst school system in the country.[45] Perhaps stimulated by that charge and perhaps in an effort to reform the Chicago schools before the legislature was itself "reformed," the Illinois state legislature passed a law mandating elected school councils for every public school in Chicago. Not only did the original bill give the community-dominated councils real power in personnel, budgets, and curriculum matters, but it cut the "downtown" professional bureaucracy nearly in half. This plan was challenged by the professional bureaucracy in the state courts, and its ability to survive and provide real local control is still in question.

OTHER AREAS IN THE 1990s

States like California, Florida, Minnesota, New York, Tennessee, and Texas have provided some form of state legislation mandating and/or permitting site- or school-based management. The Texas legislation was immediately emasculated by state school board regulations forbidding any site decision making that would undermine the authority of the local school board or superintendent. That regulation was lobbied by the state administrator and school board associations. Today there is a mounting rhetoric, but a dearth of evidence, indicating much large-scale movement toward community control of public education—except through the periodic political process of school board elections and, in some states, the election of local superintendents. The urban school systems, with their hundreds of thousands of student/family units, all represented by the same few members that comprise small and rural districts, might best be served by community, site-based management. These same urban districts have the strongest professional bureaucracies opposing effective lay participation in education policy-making.

ARE URBAN SCHOOLS MONOLITHIC?

We tend to speak of and seek solutions for urban school problems as if all urban schools were the same. They surely have some similarities. If nothing else, they are all very large, there has been "white flight" (whether stimulated by jobs' moving to suburbs or by racism), and there are the more massive problems of poverty, drugs, and violence.

But there are differences as well. Almost any urban school system can point to one or more high schools demonstrating excellence in academic outcomes, while other schools in the same district experience 100 percent turnover during any school year and high percentages of dropouts and failures. Schools within an urban district differ. On a larger scale, however, there are differences that should affect the politics and fundings.

T. N. Clark,[46] having once proposed the concept of the "Northeast syndrome,"[47] suggests there is only a weak link between the city's fiscal spending, its population decline and so on, and the age and location of that city. He states, "Political processes better explain the fiscal policies of city governments."[48] Yet, there are differences between the cities in the Northeast and Midwest, and the cities of the Sunbelt and West. Most of the Northeast/Midwest urban cities are older and more racially separated than those of the Sunbelt and West. Most have more decay in their infrastructure and greater decline by property values. Cities like Dallas, Houston, Phoenix, even Denver are relatively property-wealthy school districts when compared with the poor rural areas in their separate states. P. A. Jargowsky and M. J. Bone point out that poverty decreased in the South and West (as measured by percent of people living in poverty) while it increased in the Northeast and Midwest.[49] New York, Chicago, Philadelphia, Newark, and Detroit had the greatest increases in percent living in poverty, a variable strongly associated with the general poverty level of those cities. Thus, the fiscal plans to fund urban schools, developed in the Northeast and Midwest, should not be unthinkingly transplanted to every urban district in the nation. The basic problem in funding public schools is that ad valorem tax remains, in most states, the major source of school revenue. It is a regressive tax, penalizing the very poor whose schools it hopes to improve. Additionally, assessed property valuation per pupil in urban school districts, as compared with nonurban school districts in the same state or across regional areas of the country, is not usually similar. Money surely won't fix urban schools if that money must come from the poor themselves. Nor will it likely fix urban schools if it is controlled by the same "professional machines."

CRACK, CONDEMN, AND CRISIS

All problems faced by urban schools are not "urban school problems." Rather, many are urban problems that come to school with the "kids." Since the 1940s great emphasis has been placed in keeping all children in school through high school. That effort, while not totally successful, has greatly increased the number of children who do stay in school. "Youth Indicators" describes a decline of those between the ages twenty-five and twenty-nine with less than four years of high school from 62 percent in 1940 to only 12 percent in 1988.[50] Previously, unable to succeed in school, many had left, taking their problems with them. Now, apparently 88 percent stay in school and bring their problems to school with them. The use of drugs has increased enormously since 1960. Recently the use of crack and other drugs by pregnant women has imposed a generation of "crack kids" on the schools whom J. V. Greer referred to as a "bio-underclass."[51] The schools must educate these children.

Birthrates for unmarried women, ages fifteen–nineteen (high school ages) increased from 12.6 per 1,000 in 1950 to 36.8 per 1,000 in 1988. In 1950 the school bothered little about pregnant students except to be rid of them. Today the school assumes major responsibility for their continued education, nutrition, and health. In 1950 there were 385,000 divorces involving 299,000 children; in 1987 there were 1,183,000 divorces involving 1,038,000 children. In 1950, 4.1 per 1,000 children under seventeen years of age were arrested; in 1988 there were 117 per 1,000. Additionally, there were 128.9 per 1,000 children (under the age of nineteen) who were victims of violent crime in 1988.[52] In 1991, in Dallas, Texas, there were 9,875 juvenile offenses, of which 957 were violent felony offenses. Of those, 31 were homicides, 103 were sexual assaults, 315 were robberies, and 335 were assaults by students still attending school.[53]

The Los Angeles riots of 1992 have an important message for urban schools. First, there is the potential for massive violence in our cities, and the teenage urban gang is one center of that potential violence. Second, pent-up violence can use any excuse to loot, burn, and murder, anywhere. Third, the violence is an expression of generalized frustration and hate directed at racial and ethnic differences among teenage gangs as much as against any social injustice. These gangs exist in urban schools. Often, they exercise some control of those urban schools. To some extent these gangs are substitutes for family and community relationships that have declined in our society in the last several decades, as demonstrated by Youth Indicators.[54] Strengthening the family, the schools, and the community is a unitary job. It cannot be accomplished without concern for the entire social/political network of relationships.

Finally, there is the problem of autoimmune deficiency syndrome (AIDS). Given the data about sexually active high school students, the nature of AIDS, and the unlikelihood that anyone, much less everyone, always practices "safe sex" as a teenager, this disease threatens a whole generation of teenage schoolgoers. These are not problems instigated by the school. They are problems that come to school with children. They come massively to urban schools, affecting school politics and policy.

THE PROBLEM OF POLITICAL REPRESENTATION IN URBAN SCHOOLS

Once we faced a rural urban bias in state and federal legislatures that greatly disadvantaged urban areas.[55] This has largely shifted due to the "one-man, one-vote" principal and legislative reapportionment. Now urban centers generally hold the numerical advantage in state and federal legislatures. But with this advantage they have not been able to solve urban, school, fiscal, or other problems. Like always, politicians in state and federal legislatures must form coalitions, make deals, and get reelected, if they are to accomplish anything.

Peterson says that federal policy aimed at solving the problems of urban cities often has only increased the urban problems.[56] He argues that federal policies intended to affect other than urban problems often have unanticipated urban consequences, such as making it easy for industry and the middle class to flee the city. He suggests the use of such latent policy to affect the cities positively. In one area alone he makes a specific policy suggestion, however. "At a time when the federal government . . . was enabling most American firms and workers to choose from an ever-widening array of locales the site best suited to their tastes and needs, one segment of the population—those dependent on welfare— was refused the same degree of flexibility and choice.[57] He also said:

Finally, the United States needs a much more flexible and adaptable educational system in the core areas of cities, a system that can enhance the country's human capital, strengthen the institutional position of the family, and reduce the alienation between minority youth and the mainstream institutions of society. The current expensive, bureaucratically controlled, hierarchical, rule-bound, stratified, gang-infested system of urban education needs to be drastically changed. We need to redesign our urban school systems to give families more choice and more control, provide harbors for young people seeking to escape the neighborhood peer culture, and create a learning environment that respects the culture of the low-income, minority community."[58]

These authors could not agree more strongly with that statement of Peterson's. The means to accomplish that goal may be a matter of disagreement, however. We argue for changing the political process of governing local education rather than changing fiscal policy, moving toward vouchers and tax credits that could result in further ethnic and racial polarization, in the guise of "choice." The best schools in this nation choose their students, not the reverse. That fact seems to be missed by most reformers.

From 1980 to 1992 the United States tried the "free market" and "new federalism" policies of the "new right." It also gave us a greater number of rich, whose children tend not to attend urban public schools, and a greater number of people living below the poverty level whose children do. Often these latter children are children of single-parent households and minority groups living in urban cities. Even Peterson admits that it is in the central cities where poverty has increased in the last twenty years.[59] It increased by 778,000 children between 1980 and 1989. More than half of all households headed by a female (no husband present) make under $10,000, and three-quarters make less than $20,000.[60]

As socioeconomic class is a major correlate of school success, is it any wonder that urban schools are failing, based on achievement indicators? "Education 2000" is more rhetoric. What is the chance, if we keep 90 percent of all children in America's schools (given the same schools, the same programs, the same governance) that those 90 percent will score higher in science and math than the 10–20 percent of the children who graduate from the schools of Germany and Japan? Rhetoric may change presidential approval ratings, but it will not change the percentage of failure in urban schools.

CONCLUSION

We have shown that it is unlikely that urban schools, governed and structured as they have been for more than a half century, will suddenly begin to succeed. We have further demonstrated that the problems faced by urban schools—poverty, breakdown of the family, drugs, and violence—are not problems created by the public schools but ones the schools (as governed and structured) have been unable to solve. Additionally, those problems have exacerbated in the last twenty years and create a condition where urban public schools cannot succeed. It might be added that these problems, where they exist in rural America, are as likely to create school failure as they do in urban schools.

There are two solutions, which are probably interdependent; one will not succeed without the other. First, return the urban schools to the people they serve. Create a system that challenges and destroys governance by an oligarchy of a few, seldom of the same socioeconomic class or ethnic/racial composition of the child/family units served by the urban schools. In doing this, wrest policy power from the professional bureaucracy that delivers more rewards to its members than it does to its clients. This is not to recommend that the undereducated and poor can make better decisions about teaching/learning and curriculum structure. They cannot and, therefore, ought not try. They can, however, make political decisions about allocation of values and resources. They are in a position to know whether or not the schools are delivering the goods in a "material and specific" way. When the schools do "deliver," the schools will "make friends" of the people they serve, and those "friends" will support the schools and the professionals who work in them.

Some grass roots decentralization in the form of community/site-based management is to be recommended. We do not mean simply a reshuffle of power among the old enemies within the school bureaucratic machine (i.e., teachers, administrators, and the school board oligarchy). We are not recommending "tinkering" with the old system. We suggest school governance restructuring providing for real school/community input by elected community members. Elected community councils, excluding education professionals, but certainly not dominated by them numerically or in terms of rights and privileges, need to be given real decision-making power.

Second, once this new governance system is in place—not before—a different funding system for the nation's public schools should prove successful. Given the old governance trend of increasing state centralization and of local control by the bureaucratic professional machine, the money would likely be of no avail. One cannot fix education by throwing dollars at it, to use the new right rhetoric. But given a responsive school governance system, more money can usefully be invested in (rather than thrown at) our children. Upward bound programs throw money at the problem by paying the poor to sit in classrooms on Saturdays, with the old governance system in control. These programs have not helped much.

The regressive ad valorem tax must go as a means of basic funding for our nation's schools, particularly urban schools. It permits the rich publicly to fund their elite enclaves of excellence while ignoring the problems of the inner-city poor. It has created "poor schools" for the children of poor people, while requiring the poor to pay for them. A system of state/federal funding based on the least regressive and most effectively collected tax (probably some type of income tax) must replace the ad valorem tax for funding public education. The basic funding guarantee to every child should likely be three or four times today's national average and distributed among a set of local public agencies constituted and governed in a fashion so as to serve the needs of the child/family unit. P. G. Tweeddale has demonstrated how a "transagency" system can serve the pre-natally afflicted by drug children in schools.[61] Other problems for other children would also be effectively addressed through the transagency process. The schools should probably be the lead agency in this process, guaranteeing the child/family unit services that could change the face of central cities of America.

The major focus of urban school reform must be, however, the political process and the target of that process must be control and governance of local schools. M. R. Williams has shown that community does exist in inner-city neighbor-hoods. When speaking of changing urban cities, he emphasizes the key role that urban school reform must play. He concludes, "Throughout its campaign to improve the local public school, the neighborhood organization must keep before its collective eye above all else the vision of becoming part of the governance of its school in order to assure that parents' and students' voices will be heard and heeded."[62]

Whether or not one agrees with the "holistic critique" of education, few thoughtful individuals would disagree with R. Miller that "changes in schools do not produce changes in society, but are doomed to failure unless society itself is transformed. . . . We are approaching a critical point in history! Humankind *must* soon choose between total destruction . . . or a new world view that strives for peace, cooperation and justice."[63] Surely the fact that the events that took place in Watts in the 1960s could repeat themselves so vividly in the 1990s must tell us how little we have learned and how slowly we have moved. Our urban schools are the classrooms, in more ways than one, for the political views and behaviors of tomorrow's urban citizens. How many times will we let our cities burn before we learn that lesson? We neglect our urban schools only at a major cost to our total society.

NOTES

1. P. E. Peterson, *The Politics of School Reform 1870–1940* (Chicago: University of Chicago Press, 1985).

2. R. E. Callahan, *Education and the Cult of Efficiency* (Chicago: University of Chicago Press, 1962).

3. Peterson, 203.

4. Peterson, 207.

5. Peterson, 209.

6. United States. National Commission of Excellence in Education, *A Nation at Risk: The Implications for Educational Reform: A Report to the Nation and the Secretary of Education* (Washington, DC: U.S. Department of Education, 1983).

7. W. Wilson, "The Study of Public Administration," *Political Science Quarterly* 51, no. 4 (1983), 481–506 (reprinted from an 1887 issue).

8. R. E. Callahan, "The American Board of Education, 1789–1960," in P. J. Cistone, ed., *Understanding School Boards* (Lexington, VT: D. C. Heath, 1975).

9. J. M. Cronin, *The Control of Urban Schools: Perspective on the Power of Educational Reformers* (New York: Free Press, 1973).

10. D. Rogers, *110 Livingston Street: Politics and Bureaucracy in the New York City School System* (New York: Random House, 1968), 212–13.

11. E. E. Schattschneider, *The Semisovereign People* (Hindsdale, IL: Dryden Press, 1975), 34–35.

12. Peterson.

13. P. A. Cusick, *The Educational System: Its Nature and Logic* (New York: McGraw-Hill, 1992), 213.

14. Ibid., 213.

15. Ibid., 219.

16. Ibid., 227–29.

17. R. Michels, *Political Parties* (New York: Free Press, 1966).

18. F. H. Johnson, "Assigning Type of Local Codes to the 1987–88 C.C.D.," (paper presented at the American Educational Research Association, San Francisco, CA, 21 March 1989).

19. U.S. Department of Education, *Elementary and Secondary Schools: Common Care Data Survey* (Washington, DC: National Center for Education Statistics, 1989).

20. *Texas School Directory* (Austin: Texas Education Agency, 1991–1992).

21. L. H. Zeigler and M. K. Jennings, with G. W. Peak, *Governing American Schools: Political Interaction in Local School Districts* (North Sciluate, ME: Durbury Press, 1974).

22. Ibid., 36.

23. Ibid., 52.

24. Ibid., 71.

25. Ibid., 92–93.

26. Ibid., 250–51.

27. F. M. Wirt and M. W. Kirst, *The Politics of Education: Schools in Conflict* (Berkeley, CA: McCutchen, 1989).

28. D. Easton, *A Framework for Political Analysis* (New York: Prentice-Hall, 1965).

29. Wirt and Kirst, 222–23.

30. Ibid., 2.

31. Ibid., 392–93.

32. Ibid.

33. F. W. Lutz and L. Iannaccone, *Public Participation in Local School Districts: The Dissatisfaction Theory of American Democracy* (Lexington, MA: D. C. Heath, 1978).

34. R. Dahl, *Who Governs?* (New Haven, CT: Yale University Press, 1961).

35. Lutz and Iannaccone, 129.

36. F. W. Lutz and C. Merz, *The Politics of School Community Relations* (New York: Teachers College Press, 1992).

37. C. L. Marburger, *One School at a Time: School-Based Management—A Process for Change* (Columbia, MD: National Committee for Citizens in Education, 1985).

38. R. K. Merton, *Social Theory and Social Structure* (Glencoe, IL: Free Press, 1965).

39. G. Ritzer, *Sociological Theory* (New York: Knopf, 1988).

40. Merton, 114.

41. E. C. Banfield and J. Q. Wilson, *City Politics* (New York: Vintage Books, 1963), 117.

42. Ibid., 127.

43. Lutz and Merz.

44. L. Iannaccone, "Norms Governing Urban State Politics of Education," in F. W. Lutz, ed., *Toward Improved Urban Education* (Columbus, OH: Charles Merrell, 1970).

45. H. J. Walbert et al., "Reconstructing the Nations Worst Schools," *Phi Delta Kappan* 70, no. 10 (1981) 802–5.

46. T. N. Clark, "Fiscal Strain: How Different Are SnowBelt and SunBelt Cities," in P. E. Peterson, ed., *The New Urban Reality* (Washington, DC: Brookings Institute, 1985).

47. T. N. Clark, "Fiscal Management of American Cities: Funds Flow Indicators," *Journal of Accounting Research* 15 (1977 supplement): 54–106.

48. Clark, 254.

49. P. A. Jargowsky and M. J. Boon, "Ghetto Poverty in the United States, 1970–1980," in C. Jencks and P. E. Peterson, eds., *The Urban Underclass* (Washington, DC: Brookings Institute, 1991).

50. Youth Indicators, *Trends in the Well-Being of American Youth* (Washington, DC: Office of Educational Research and Improvement, U.S. Office of Education, 1991).

51. J. V. Greer, "The Drug Babies," *Exceptional Children* 56 (5): 382–84.

52. Youth Indicators.

53. T. Box, "Juvenile Crime in Area Takes Sharp Turn Up," *Dallas Morning News*, 17 May 1992, A1, A6.

54. Youth Indicators.

55. J. W. Guthrie, "City Schools in a Federal Vice," In F. W. Lutz, *Toward Improved Urban Education* (Worthington, OH: Charles A. Jones, 1970).

56. P. E. Peterson, "The Urban Underclass and the Poverty Paradox," in C. Jencks and P. E. Peterson, eds., *The Urban Underclass* (Washington, DC: Brookings Institute, 1991).

57. P. E. Peterson, *The Urban Reality* (Washington, DC: Brookings Institute, 1985), 25.

58. Peterson, 25.

59. Ibid.

60. Youth Indicators.

61. P. G. Tweeddale, "Crack-Afflicted Children: Implications for Public School Policy" (Ph.D. diss., East Texas State University, Commerce, TX).

62. M. R. Williams, *Neighborhood Organizing for Urban School Reform* (New York: Teachers College Press, 1989).

63. R. Miller, *What Are Schools For? Holistic Education in American Culture* (Brandon, VT: Holistic Education Press, 1990), 158–59.

6

Curriculum Politics in Urban Schooling

Louise Adler and Kip Tellez

There are as many definitions of curriculum as there are commentators; and, significantly for this discussion, defining curriculum is itself a political act that serves the value interests of the person positing the definition. A definition quoted by Tony Becher and Stuart Maclure will serve for the purposes of this discussion: "A curriculum is the offering of socially valued knowledge, skills and attitudes made available to students through a variety of arrangements during the time they are at school."[1] H. D. Lasswell described politics as "who gets what."[2] Three questions arise when discussing curriculum politics in urban schooling: (1) who decides what will be in the curriculum?, (2) whose interests are served by the curriculum?, and (3) what are the consequences of the choices?

This chapter begins with a definition of the scope of academic comment on curriculum politics in general. It then focuses briefly on two issues that override all others in curriculum in urban schools: (1) the connection between jobs and the willingness of students to be engaged with the curriculum and (2) the impact of waves of migration to cities by both voluntary immigrants and castelike minority groups. With this framework in place, the chapter then moves into a discussion of specific curricular political issues.

THE COMPLEX CURRICULUM GAME

What students are taught and what they learn in urban schools are determined by a complex interplay between the forces that determine curriculum content in general and the political, economic, and social forces that impact the urban setting (especially racial, class, and cultural issues). Capturing this complexity in a single model is very difficult. Many of the issues involved can be understood as debates between opposing views, which are frequently stated in terms of black-and-white issues. It is as if a five-level chess game is being played by an ever-changing number of players, some of whom can play on more than one level at a time. As in chess, the "whites" get to take the first turn.

One level of the game represents the dichotomy between reproduction and transformation as the underlying purpose of curriculum. This debate has special meaning for the players interested in urban schools who, by their own definition, may represent special interests of racial or cultural minority groups that have a greater political stake in transformation, though it should not be assumed that all members of racial or cultural minorities support transformation.

Second, players must also contend with the debate about the nature of knowledge. Are there truths that exist separate and apart from our cultural understandings, or is all knowledge socially constructed? Should the curriculum focus on an exclusive body of core knowledge that is to be passed to each new generation, or should the curriculum stress emerging perspectives that give access to divergent points of view? John Eggleston described two models of curriculum: received (knowledge is received as given and nonnegotiable) and reflexive (knowledge is negotiable and can be criticized and revised).[3] The received perspective supports the existing social order while the reflexive perspective sees knowledge and curriculum as artifacts that are socially constructed and amenable to change. Thomas Carroll and Jean Schensul describe this debate as a contest between "proponents of critical scholarship and . . . defenders of the 'great white Western male' tradition, including Bloom and Hirsch."[4] Part of this debate has been initiated by those who argue that what passes for "truth" or "scientific" has more to do with who is creating such axioms than the accurate representation of the world.[5]

A third level in this game is the debate about the proper locus of decision making—national, state, district, or school. It is further complicated by the potential for a debate about who should have the greater voice in decision making in restructured schools—community members, teachers, students, or administrators.

On the fourth level, but also influencing the play on other boards, is the debate about how we conceive the role of immigration, race, and culture. It is a debate between integration (the melting pot) and separation. The game is made more complex by the changing demographics of our nation. Rather than being a game with two players—the dominant culture and a single minority group—the game is now played between groups that represent various cultural and racial groups, only one of which is European-Americans.

On the fifth level, play proceeds to deal with economic issues and how they impact on urban areas. Will the focus be on providing a number of low-wage, usually "temporary" jobs to move people off welfare quickly, or will the focus be on education to provide access to jobs that will support stable families? The play on this level has important implications for curriculum decisions made on other levels of the game.

The underlying assumption of this discussion is expressed by Catherine Cornbleth: curriculum is a contextualized social process in contrast to technocratic conceptions of curriculum as a product. She argues against the notion that curriculum can be developed in one sphere and implemented largely as intended in another. "Conceptual decontextualization has meant separating curriculum as a product (e.g., a document . . .) from curriculum policy-making, design, and practice. Operational decontextualization has meant treating curriculum, however defined, apart from its structural and sociocultural contexts as if it were independent of its location in an education system, society and history."[6] Cornbleth notes that John Bobbitt and William Tyler promoted a decontextualized, technocratic system of curriculum development based on scientific learning theory. By contrast, she maintains that curriculum construction "is an ongoing social activity that is shaped by various contextual influences with and beyond the classroom and accomplished interactively, primarily by teachers and students."[7]

Thus, we argue that cultural, political, and economic conflicts described above are significant contextual influences on curriculum in urban schools. We reject the decontextualization of the curriculum because it is a subtle and very powerful means of antidemocratic social control. The notion that curriculum is separate from any cultural, political, or economic effects and has no consequences beyond the knowledge presented is false.

HISTORY OF CURRICULUM AS POLITICS

For most of twentieth-century history of education in the United States, the dominating paradigm has been that educational decision making is (and should be) apolitical. Elisabeth Hansot and David Tyack chronicled the rise of the professional superintendent as a reform of the patronage-driven political systems in urban schools in the early part of the century.[8] Likewise, the progressive era reforms that created school boards that were nonpartisan and elected to act as trustees rather than representatives were designed to save education from the "political morass."[9] Thus, the entire school enterprise was to rise above politics.

It was not until the 1970s that scholars began to use the word *politics* to describe their work in the study of schools. The Politics of Education Association was formed as a special interest group in the American Education Research Association twenty-three years ago. The notion that "curriculum politics" existed is a much more recent development. Dennis Carlson points out:

The analysis of the process by which the curriculum is planned, which at first glance might appear to involve a quite narrow, insulated, and technical field of inquiry, actually illuminates fundamental questions that are political in nature. They entail deep conflict over institutional control and direction among divergent social groups.

That these highly politicized questions have not generally been raised in the literature on curriculum planning is only indicative of the pervasiveness of dominant world views in the culture generally, and more particularly in the public schools, that serve to depoliticize issues by treating them as merely exercises in administrative rationality.[10]

Michael Apple has made a similar argument throughout his writing: "Not to recognize the inherently political nature of curriculum and teaching is to cut ourselves off from an understanding of how and why schools—especially urban schools—work the way they do and may prevent us from seeing what is required to alter them in progressive ways."[11]

Locus of Government Decision Making

One political perspective of recent studies has been to explore which levels of governance—federal, state, local, or school site—have or should have the greatest influence in curriculum decision making.[12] A similar issue about locus of power is raised in the debate about teacher empowerment, particularly as it refers to control of the curriculum.[13] Presumably, increasing teacher control of the curriculum would shift control to the local school away from more centralized district or state controls. Others have discussed the necessity for local community control of the schools, which has been the guiding principle underlying efforts to decentralize control of schools to community-based governance, illustrated by the efforts under way to reform the Chicago public schools. However, greater attention should be paid to the potential for conflict between teachers and local communities when the decisions and values of teachers and local citizens may be in conflict, as they were in New York City's 1960 reform efforts.[14]

Critical Approaches

Another perspective is provided by the scholars of critical theory and critical pedagogy who raise questions about whose purposes are served by the current curriculum and organization of schools.[15] Their critique of the schools as replicators of a dominant culture that disenfranchises outside groups moves the issue of curriculum politics beyond the question of which level of government official should have control of the curriculum and asks which curriculum should be taught and which pedagogy is empowering for those groups served by the schools.[16]

Similar questions have been raised by scholars whose work arises out of the study of black history and Chicano studies and addresses the place of multicultural issues in the mainstream curriculum.[17] Geoff Whitty, from Great Britain, raises the concern that "officially sponsored" multicultural education may be a way to "divert attention away from broader structural issues. There is also a growing recognition that sponsoring of progressive multi-racial, multi-ethnic or multi-cultural policies in schools is not, by itself, going to alter the power relations that sustain racial inequalities."[18]

Language and Curriculum

Related issues are raised about bilingual education's purposes and content. Should the curriculum focus on the earliest possible use of English, or should it support and maintain the native language at the same time English is taught? Some writers are beginning to focus on the variable outcomes of bilingual programs and the impact of the programs on various subgroups of Hispanics and other language minorities. Further, scholars such as Frances Montano-Harmon are beginning to investigate the impact of the use of culturally based dialects of English on the school performance of students of color.

Jim Cummins argued that education for minority students is often disempowering. By focusing on subtracting the students' home culture and language, the school tells students that their culture and life-style are somehow wrong and that they must learn to behave and think like dominant-culture students. For example, students whose native language is not standard English are often urged to "forget" their home language. The fullest expression of this stance is illustrated when teachers punish children who speak their home language at school. Cummins also pointed out that the cognitive advantages of bilingualism should compel teachers to help students to become better speakers of their native language while they learn functional and academic English, and he described several bilingual programs that accomplish this goal.[19]

While some people question the value of bilingual education for poor, urban students, the 1980 President's Commission on Foreign Languages and International Studies expressed concern about ignorance of foreign languages by U.S. citizens and suggested a need for this skill to conduct an adequate national defense and be competitive in international business.[20] The multicultural and bilingual debates are subsets of the integration versus separation debate that is taking place in our society.

School Reform

A voluminous literature has developed around the issues of school reform, much of which focuses on curriculum reform. "Hard content," which stresses higher-order thinking and problem solving, has been promoted to replace the "basic skills" approach of the 1960s and 1970s. A. Harry Passow argued that "a watered-down, diluted curriculum, limited to instruction aimed at success on tests of minimum skills, does not constitute an appropriate curriculum for the disadvantaged any more than it does for other students. . . . The remediation services of compensatory education should not impede access to this general education curriculum."[21]

The second wave of recent reforms has focused on teacher empowerment and restructuring the control of schooling. Many scholars have written about the political aspects of these reforms.[22] The questions raised by these scholars focus on which reform strategies result in more learning and which methods of implementation are most likely to bring about actual change in what happens in classrooms. The interplay of state mandates and local adaptation has been a continuing concern.[23] A more recent development in the reform movement has been the development of a national curriculum that is assessed by national tests.

Textbooks

The political nature of textbook development and use in the United States has been fertile ground for scholars such as Apple and Joel Spring, who focus on how text content reflects the dominant ideological trends and acts as a pervasive means of social control to replicate the dominant ideology. They point to the central role of textbooks in defining and delivering curriculum in the United States. They also discuss the tension between the movement for teacher empowerment and investments in all-encompassing text packages, which, if fully implemented, leave little time for teachers to exercise power over the curriculum provided for students.[24] Kenneth Wong and Tom Loveless point out that most of the political negotiations regarding textbooks take place within the institutionalized education network made up of experts from the universities, curriculum developers, and publishers. The decisions made by these groups are legitimated by state governments in those states that do statewide adoptions. They discuss the potential to ''de-institutionalize'' politics when organized interest groups that are not part of education take action to change the content of textbooks.[25] Specific examples of ''deinstitutionalized'' politics are provided by the research on citizen challenges to the content of texts and school library books that often occur in urban settings.[26]

URBAN SCHOOLING AND JOBS

Earlier in this volume Rothstein described urban schooling as predominantly affecting the poorer and dispossessed members of American society. Urban settings in America are characterized by high concentrations of populations from diverse racial and ethnic groups. They are also characterized by a highly stratified economic system that provides many rewards for those who are well educated and able to amass capital. Conversely, those who lack education are severely limited in their ability to participate in an economic system that is increasingly dependent on information management and service industries.

The number of jobs available for low-skilled workers, particularly in manufacturing, has been shrinking.[27] The military was also once an employer of low-skilled workers, but this too has shifted because of the increasing use of sophisticated military technology and the decrease in the necessity for military deployment. In the last century new immigrant groups were able to capture control of big-city political machines and provide, through patronage, low-skill jobs working for city governments. Both the civil service reforms and the deteriorating tax support for urban infrastructure have severely limited the availability of low-skill positions for the urban poor.

Economic dislocations are intensified for the urban poor because of a set of business practices identified as the creation of a ''job ceiling.'' John Ogbu points out that ''informal practices used to limit the minorities' access to desirable occupations, truncate their opportunities, and narrowly channel the potential returns they could expect to get from their education."[28] Thus, in addition to a decreasing pool of potential job openings, many students leaving urban schools face a "job ceiling" that limits their options to lower status and lower-pay jobs.

Social structures in an urban setting are highly interdependent. The connection between jobs and education is critical. Urban students must receive enough education to be prepared to move beyond low-wage, temporary jobs that will not support a family. Without sufficient income both to support current needs and to save for future improvement, there is no chance of escaping poverty. Even those students who become part of the "working poor" are only one crisis away from dependency on the welfare system. Most low-paying jobs do not provide the security of health insurance and other benefits that protect middle-class families.[29] Equally as important, access to jobs is a powerful motivator to stay in school. If sufficient entry-level jobs with real promise of advancement are not available,[30] a powerful message goes to children in school that there is little purpose in sacrificing to remain in school. William J. Wilson argued that African-American youth from urban areas face substantial barriers: "Poorly trained and educationally limited blacks of the inner city, including that growing number of black teenagers and young adults, see their job prospects increasingly restricted to the low-wage sector, their unemployment rates soaring to record levels (which remain high despite swings in the business cycle), their labor-force participation rates declining, their movement out of poverty slowing and their welfare roles increasing."[31]

The argument can be made that students from urban schools who drop out of school before graduation may be maximizing their lifetime earnings because even if they complete high school, they will not have access to jobs that will move them up the ladder of success. At least by dropping out and beginning to work earlier, they can maximize their lifetime earnings. Jonathan Kozol makes a similar argument in discussing the depressing conditions found in many urban schools: "For many, many students at Chicago's nonselective high schools, it is hard to know if a decision to drop out of school, no matter how much we discourage it, is not, in fact, a logical decision.[32]

RACE AND CULTURE

During the last great wave of immigration that ended early in this century, immigrants tended to settle in common neighborhoods within the urban setting for a variety of social reasons, including discrimination in housing and employment. For example, Italian neighborhoods and Irish neighborhoods were commonplace. In a similar manner, African-Americans displaced by economic depression and discrimination in the South also migrated to specific neighborhoods in northern cities. Using these segregated neighborhood patterns, urban schools tended to be segregated both by lack of concern about these patterns and by overt actions of school officials.

Some benign accommodations in the operations of these schools were made in response to the needs of specific immigrant groups, such as serving fish for Friday lunches and the secularization of the public schools in response to demands by Catholics to change the Protestant domination of schools. More perverse were the efforts to accommodate the needs of poor and working-class students by changing the curriculum to suit their perceived needs. Thus the curriculum of the high school was broadened to include vocational education and home arts to train poor and working-class students. It was assumed that forcing these children to take college preparatory courses would be not only impractical but inhumane.

Eggleston pointed to the important distinction between the elite curriculum, which assists some students in attaining high status, and curriculum for the masses, which is "predominantly concerned with basic skills of numeracy and literacy. . . . Its definition sprang from an appraisal of the knowledge regarded as appropriate for the new occupational roles of an industrial society. . . . It reinforced and re-emphasized the lower status of vocational and utilitarian knowledge and skills."[33] The existence of class-differentiated curricula was also noted by Kozol: "The evolution of two parallel curricula, one for urban and one for suburban schools, has also underlined the differences in what is felt to be appropriate to different kinds of children and to socially distinct communities.[34] Urban settings today are also characterized by poverty and high concentrations of minority groups, but the experiences and perceptions of many (though not all) of today's urban "minority" groups are quite different from those of the earlier waves of migrants. Involuntary immigrant or castelike minority groups such as African-Americans, who were first brought to America as slaves, and Mexican-Americans and Native Americans, who were conquered in war, have not fared as well as the waves of voluntary immigrants such as the Irish, Italians, and Chinese. Ogbu points out that voluntary immigrants "tend to respond differently from caste-like minorities to similar treatment. For example, immigrants are not highly influenced by the dominant group's denigration and rationalization of their subordination and exploitation."[35] Other minority groups seem to be "stuck" in the cycle of poverty and low educational attainment, with little hope of escape except for the most tenacious members of the minority group who attain middle-class status in spite of the difficulty of "breaking out" and who then are viewed by both the larger society and their former peers as the exceptions that prove the rule. The dominant Anglo culture says, "See, they just have to want to do it," and the other minority group members say, "See, they just let a few of us out as tokens." Both approaches lead to the achievement of very negative self-fulfilling prophecies.

These problems of how to provide real opportunity for urban minority groups without demanding that they "assimilate" and how to provide adequate entry-level jobs that have the potential for advancement and self-sufficiency are compounded and multiplied by the interactions among various minority groups that now occupy the same neighborhoods. Thus if one minority group seems to advance at a more rapid pace than another group, the potential for intergroup conflict is greatly enhanced. For example, in Los Angeles a young African-American explained why Korean businesses were burned during the 1992 riots: "We spend our money in their store, and they send their kids to college when we can't even get jobs." Schools are expected to be sensitive to the needs and cultural values of all groups, but this can be very difficult when cultural activities of one group are seen as affronts to another group. Gail Martinez suggests the importance of the intergroup dynamics in urban schools in her review of *The Politics of Hispanic Education*:

First, Black student discrimination relates to Hispanic student discrimination. By applying the authors' theory of the "power thesis" in a mixed population district and classroom, discriminatory educational practices will often be applied first to Black students and then to Hispanics. Consequently, Hispanics will experience less discrimination in the presence of Black students.

Second, the "power thesis" manifests itself by the "white flight" phenomenon. With a reduced middle-class Anglo enrollment, Hispanics gain greater access to "gifted" classes and become less subjected to . . . discrimination. One step gained for Hispanics becomes a two-step loss for Blacks and lower-class Anglos.[36]

As new waves of immigrants flow through the cities and into the middle class, those groups that are "stuck" in urban poverty may well come to demand more forcefully, "It's our turn now!"

UNINTENDED OUTCOMES

Scholars of policy-making have long recognized that because we live in incredibly complex social and economic environments, even the most carefully crafted and implemented public policy may have unintended outcomes, some of which are positive but more likely are negative. Curriculum decision making is a form of public policy-making. The decisions are made by public employees or representatives, with varying amounts of input from citizens, who may act with the best of intentions to improve the curriculum delivered to children; but these decisions can also have unintended outcomes. These unintended outcomes of well-intentioned curriculum designs must be recognized in the urban setting because the potential for racial and cultural conflict is inherent in the volatile mix of poverty and intergroup competition.

Unintended outcomes as discussed in this chapter should not be equated with the term *hidden curriculum*, which, in the field of curriculum studies, refers to the fact that "students seem to learn much that is not publicly set forth in official statements of school philosophy or purpose, or in course guides, syllabi and other curriculum documents."[37] In fact, we would argue that when the political and economic context of the curriculum of urban schools is examined, the hidden aspects of the urban curriculum become more obvious. Clearly there is much blame to be attributed to willful and uncaring public policymakers and educators, and many of the critics of urban schooling have used this concept of the hidden curriculum to fix that blame. What we argue here is that even the best-intentioned reform efforts may have unintended outcomes that were not perceived because of the complexity of the urban settings where the reforms are implemented. This is an argument drawn from studies of policy development rather than curriculum development.

For example, overt segregation and discrimination have been banned from public schools by law and court decisions, but as Kenneth Meier and Joseph Stewart, Jr. suggest, this has not ended practices that disadvantage minority students. They use the term *second-generation educational discrimination* to define the more subtle practices that are characteristic of today's urban schools.[38] This process, which begins in kindergarten, is called by Lorri Shepard "backdoor reinstitution of tracking."[39] She points out that the use of kindergarten readiness tests results in placement of a disproportionate number of poor and minority children in two-year kindergarten programs, where they may receive a curriculum that "stresses regimentation and drill on prerequisite skills."[40] Jean Anyon made a similar argument about the curriculum found in schools with working-class students who believe that they acquire knowledge by "doing pages in our books and things."[41] The same students steadfastly held that they could not create knowledge.

Once past kindergarten's "protected environment," urban children are influenced by all of the various trends and reforms that flow through the curriculum development process. However, they may experience these reforms very differently than do children in the dominant Anglo culture.

While segregation according to race or culture is against the law and tracking students by academic achievement that results in similar patterns of segregation is discredited, other curricular practices may have unintended results that appear to be very similar to segregation or tracking. There is strong support for bilingual education programs within the Hispanic community and among Hispanic educators, but the programs are largely segregated by culture. The fact that Hispanic students are more likely to attend schools that are racially isolated from other groups may obscure the impact of bilingual programs on racial-cultural isolation.[42]

Educators have also observed that non-Hispanic parents of students who do not speak English seem to put pressure on schools to move their children out of bilingual programs before the educators judge that they are well prepared for regular classes. This may occur because of a desire by some parents to have their children "excel," but it may also be caused by intergroup perceptions of the racial-cultural status of the largest group of students in the bilingual classes.

Another example of an unintended outcome is provided by research of face-to-face interactions between teachers and students in desegregated schools. McCarthy reported that "desegregated education at the elementary schools she studied had unintended negative (racial) costs for all black children."[43] She argued that this had an especially negative impact on African-American girls, who seemed to be urged toward stereotypical roles as service givers rather than stressing their academic skills.

Over the last twenty years the gap in the achievement test results between African-American and white students has been decreasing. Marshall Smith and Jennifer O'Day argue that "the basic skills curriculum has contributed both to the lack of change in white achievement and to the important gains of black students."[44] They suggest that the next wave of reforms toward intensification and challenge in curriculum may widen the gap again because wealthier suburban schools, which also tend to have fewer minority students, are better equipped to implement these curricular changes because of advantageous financing, which results in difference in staffs, curriculum development efforts, and curriculum supplies. Thus the curricular reforms that seek to present a fuller, more challenging curriculum raise important equity issues in how they are to be implemented.

University scholars and public school educators have been grappling with issues of how properly to address the contributions of all of the various ethnic and racial groups that are part of the American experience. Understandably there is a need to move away from past practice that presented history as the history of Europeans and European-Americans. "Students should . . . understand that history is not limited to the study of dominant political, social, and economic elites," according to a 1991 statement issued by the Organization of American Historians.[45]

The debate about multiculturalism is rooted in a larger struggle between integration versus separatist perspectives, which has important implications when dealing with race and ethnicity in urban settings, including schools. Extremists on both sides see the arguments as an either-or proposition: whether education should focus primarily on a "common" core of knowledge, or whether students should be taught to have pride in the accomplishments of their race or culture. Curricula that are either totally Eurocentric or, for example, Afrocentric represent these extremes. The point here is not to plow this ground again but to point out the often-overlooked impact of this curriculum debate on intergroup politics and the implications for public schools.

To the extent that public schools are funded by state or city governments, they must attend to the expectations of the political constituency beyond their immediate community. If the wider community perceives the curriculum of the school as hostile to the history, values, and contributions of the wider community, it will erode political and, eventually, financial support for the school. When this happens, political movements, such as the effort to take over control of the curriculum by creating a national curriculum or efforts to decrease the importance of public schools through the use of choice and vouchers, will find favor with the electorate, further reducing the ability of schools at the urban core to meet the needs of their students, however those needs are defined. Peter Edelman suggests a formulation that recognizes the importance of both poles in the multicultural debate: "Our vision should be of a single, unified, diverse society in which diversity is a value to be respected and encouraged."[46] Steven Arvizu and Marietta Saravia-Shore suggest a similar formulation: "Short-term unity through an ethnocentric curriculum could lead to long-term disunity, given reasonable predication of our future, technological change, and diversity. The basic institutions of our society do need to provide clear guidance to our diverse populations so that we are able to communicate and interact with order, mutual respect, and understanding."[47]

CASES OF URBAN CURRICULUM POLITICS

Wesley Elementary School Returns to the Phonics Approach to Reading

Recent national media attention has focused on the success of Wesley Elementary School in the Houston Independent School District.[48] The ABC television network's program, "Prime Time Live," recently did a segment on the school and its principal, Thaddeus Lott. Lott is known in Houston as a principal who is popular with a local tax watchdog group, some business leaders, and many of his teachers. Shortly after he was appointed to Wesley, fifteen teachers left the school; he is also known as a very demanding taskmaster. His style is autocratic—lines at the school are straight, and students are disciplined. He is not popular with some administrators "downtown" at the district office. He supports academic kindergartens, use of drill in instruction, and mastery learning. A reporter for the *Houston Chronicle* spent a week at the school, and a constant parade of dignitaries visits his school.

Houston, like most other large American cities, has vast areas where poor families reside. Most of these families are either African-American or Latino; many are recent immigrants from Latin America. Wesley Elmentary School is located in a very poor, primarily African-American section of Houston. Almost all of the children are eligible for free or reduced-price meals at school.

Called a model program for urban schools whose populations are composed primarily of students of color, Lott promotes the reading program known as Direct Instruction Teaching Arithmetic and Reading (DISTAR), an intensive, phonics-based reading program. In the mid-1980s the district ordered schools not to use Chapter 1 funds to buy DISTAR and encouraged use of the whole-language approach, which relies on the authentic use of language for social purposes. The district has set up a pilot program using DISTAR in seven schools, two of which have predominantly Hispanic students and five of which are predominantly African-American.

The whole-language approach assumes that learning to read is a natural process; therefore, students are exposed to quality literature, they are read to, and they learn to talk about the texts they read. Many whole-language approaches also use some phonics instruction, though it is not the central focus.

Whole-language instruction stands in stark contrast to the curriculum at Wesley, where teaching is based on a return to presenting "facts." On a nationally televised program, the principal proudly showed the media and the nation that many of Wesley's kindergartners were able to name all the state capitals. The excessive attention to a curriculum of "facticity" is a paradox in a contemporary educational environment that encourages teachers to help students be critical thinkers. Yet, this paradox is clearly understood when the population and social class of Wesley's students are understood. Parents of dominant-culture students would never accept such an education for their children. The phonics approach to reading is criticized as hopelessly boring and not giving students enough contact with outstanding literature. Furthermore, while knowing the state capitals may have somehow contributed to success in the modern United States, middle- to upper-class parents want much more for their children—to engage in meaningful dialogue with teachers and other students. The differences between the curriculum offered to the children at Wesley school and suburban schools have the characteristics of parallel curricula described by Kozol and Eggleson (see previous discussion).

A curriculum of facts is often allowed for poor children of color because these students are thought of as not having the requisite skills to think critically. It is also argued that kindergarten children come to poor urban schools without many of the skills taught in middle- and upper-class families during the preschool years. Another assumption seems to be that the curriculum for the urban poor must mirror the kind of work they will perform, that is, the menial, unthinking tasks that the dominant culture will not do. While there is nothing wrong with teaching children facts, many poor, urban students of color are never exposed to the critical, "upper-class" education they need to be successful in modern culture. Completing worksheets (a noticeable feature of the DISTAR program and other fact-based curricula) has the rhythm and feel of factory labor, a point made clear by Marie LeCompte and others.[49] Of course, many factory jobs have vanished from urban areas.

There are perhaps other, more devastating consequences for the children in urban schools like Wesley. Corporal punishment of students, allowed in Texas, has been reported at Wesley. The dreary curriculum offered to many urban students of color would suggest that corporal punishment is necessary to keep them "in line." In addition, it has been suggested by former teachers at the school that the high standardized test scores, which serve to support the curriculum, are the result of teachers' assisting students during examinations.[50] Some district officials were reported to be convinced that the high scores at the school were the result of wrongdoing, but an investigation by district officials did not support this belief. Others criticized the investigation as being motivated by the inability to believe that minority students could achieve high test scores.

Reports about this shift back to phonics instruction have raised interesting implications about restructuring as a reform process. Some of the same education critics who have supported restructuring as a way to make progressive reforms in schools would also support the use of a whole-language approach as a means to give all children access to what has been in the past the elite curriculum. In contrast, Principal Lott, who is African-American, has used the district's willingness to support site-based decision making to support phonics instruction rather than use a whole-language approach. Lott has recently been promoted to a position of lead principal, in which he will help to coordinate the efforts of the elementary, middle, and high schools in a neighborhood-based approach.

There are also important issues to be raised about the use of standarized tests to evaluate the success of curriculum changes, such as the move to the whole-language approach. Lott and other principals complained that scores on these tests dropped when the whole-language approach was used. Left unanswered are questions such as (1) whether the approach was fully implemented, particularly by principals who supported the phonics approach; (2) whether other intervening variables caused the drop in scores; (3) whether the test and the curriculum were aligned (none of the nationally normed referenced tests that have been used in Texas ask students to produce writing samples); and (4) most important, how literacy should be defined—as the ability to say words from a text or the ability to use text material as part of a larger dialogue.

When examined in context, a curriculum praised in urban schools while derided in suburban schools is not surprising. Indeed, a curriculum can never be examined outside its contextual sphere. In one school, the implementation of a phonics-based curriculum might be used as a fun exercise in which to engage when students have finished their other work. In a suburban school, a phonics-only curriculum could easily be supplemented by parents who can provide their children with literature to read. In a poor urban school, a phonics-only curriculum cuts off access to the richness of literature and story that is requisite for success in the mainstream culture.

A district official of the Houston Independent School District explained that the controversy over which approach to use in teaching literacy skills was resolved by the district's giving schools the right to make their own decision, using a site-based approach. The official made what seemed quite a significant point: "It wasn't a curriculum decision. It was a political decision!" This official demonstrates here the reluctance of many educators to recognize that all curriculum decisions are political.

California 1990 Social Studies Textbook Adoption

In 1990 the California State Board of Education adopted the Houghton Mifflin kindergarten to eighth grade books and the Holt, Rinehart, and Winston eighth grade U.S. history text. This adoption process could be viewed as a routine bureaucratic exercise in following established procedures that result in making new textbooks available to students in California. But, as many commentators have reported, this process has become part of a larger reform effort to change the curriculum in California by using state-level initiatives to present a more complex curriculum to students, to purchase "quality" textbooks, and to use these in conjunction with the reformed assessment system to drive curriculum reform.[51]

Some teachers in California objected to the 1988 history/social science framework on which the new books are based because of its emphasis on history and geography and the division of historical periods between various grades rather than repetition of U.S. history at three grade levels. The framework and the adopted textbooks have more extensive discussions of religion, and the textbooks were supposed to have a more interesting prose style and more primary source materials. It was also specified that there should be an effort to focus attention on the contributions of a wide range of cultural and racial groups.[52]

During the adoption process there were apparently some concerns raised about the treatment of multicultural issues in the text. The *New York Times* reported that Joyce King, director of teacher education at Santa Clara University who was a member of the State Curriculum Development and Supplemental Materials Commission that approved the textbooks, had objected to what she considered racist aspects of the books.[53] Gloria Ladson-Billings from the University of Wisconsin-Madison served on one of the instructional Materials Evaluation panels that reviewed the books for the commission. She also reported that she and other panel members raised issues about the treatmennt of multicultural issues in the books.[54]

After the adoption, when the textbooks were reviewed in local districts, a good deal of criticism was aired in predominantly urban districts in California.[55] Two lines of attack were made on the textbook. The books were attacked by representatives of Jewish and Muslim religious groups who objected to what they considered insensitive treatments of their religions in the books. A second line of attack was based on how the books dealt with multicultural issues. A Ravenswood school board trustee said that the books are "an insult to almost every ethnic group in this world."[56]

While those who had religious objections considered opposing the local purchase of the textbooks, they later decided to attempt to work with local districts to assure a more sensitive presentation by teachers as they used the textbooks. The debate about multicultural issues focused on urban districts. The Los Angeles Unified School District Board of Education and the San Francisco School Board heard strong challenges to the books but eventually adopted them. Oakland Unified, Hayward, Ravenswood City, and Berryessa school districts, all in northern California, all rejected the textbooks. The debate exposed in a public arena a controversy that has been simmering in academic journals and professional associations for some time about the best way to present history to students. It was described by one commentator as a " 'rather sad event' that pits white liberals against black and Indian scholars. 'People who thought they were good guys found themselves bad guys, called racists or separatists.' "[57]

The argument of the opponents to the textbooks was not that the books ignored various racial and cultural groups but that the basic premise of the series "marginalized'' their experiences in America. Sylvia Wynter from Stanford University, in a paper presented at the 1992 American Education Research Association (AERA) Conference, made a strong attack on the books because they use the ''immigrant'' model of assimilation. McCarthy made a similar argument: ''For minorities such as blacks and Native Americans, assimilation meant a special kind of cultural incorporation into a racial order in which they were accorded a secondary status. The ideology of assimilation clearly benefited white Americans.''[58]

Wynter argued that African-Americans and Native Americans are not immigrants, echoing Ogbu's distinction between voluntary and castelike minorities. On the panel with her at AERA were two other scholars, a chairperson, and a discussant, all of whom were African-Americans and voiced concerns about the textbooks. The textbook adoption process used to select the book was attacked by another presenter two days later at AERA, Ladson-Billings from the University of Wisconsin-Madison.[59]

At the San Francisco board's hearing on the possible adoption of the textbooks, Mary Hoover, professor of black studies at San Francisco State University, spoke against the books because they distorted black history. A lecturer from San Francisco State also spoke against the books because they did a poor job of presenting Native American history.[60] Kitty Epstein, professor of education at Holy Name College in Oakland, called the books ''racist and disrespectful, especially in their treatment of blacks.''[61] ''The whole notion behind the series is sort of a sense of a nation of immigrants who had problems and ultimately come together and had a better life. That excludes Native Americans, Latinos, and African-Americans.''[62] Jean Quan and Wilma Chan, both Oakland School Board members, also objected to the books because their four principal authors were white. The principal author is a University of California–Los Angeles (UCLA) professor of history, Gary B. Nash, who is reported to be an advocate of using multicultural materials in public schools.

After the debate the Oakland board voted along racial lines to reject the books. None of the black members voted for the books. Earlier the district's teachers had voted to recommend the books. The district was able to purchase other books, using a waver from the state for all of the grades except four, five, and seven. The district held a training session for teachers of these grades to help them develop their own materials. About 100 volunteers worked over the summer to develop curricula for the schools. District administrators have praised some of this material but found other material developed by the community volunteers troublesome. '' 'We are concerned that some of this material is biased and doctrinaire,' Newell [associate superintendent of schools for instruction] said, 'It is trying to indoctrinate students to a particular point of view.' ''[63] Some parents at one school tried to buy the Houghton Mifflin books for their children, and teachers have been quoted in the press as expressing their frustration with the lack of materials. '' 'This whole thing is a farce,' said Pam Johnson, a seventh-grade teacher. . . . 'You have 500 teachers desperately trying to put together materials in their spare time, each with a different program. There's no standard.' ''[64]

It is clear from the actions of the Oakland School Board that they wanted books that presented a more transformational view of history. They overrode the recommendations of the district teachers and were willing to open school the following fall without textbooks in three grades to achieve this goal. This case also illustrates the conflict over the locus of curriculum decision making. The teachers voted to use the Houghton Mifflin series so they were not ''empowered'' by the board's decision. Clearly, in this case community control took precedence. The board rejected the books adopted by the State Board of Education that were the culmination of an intensive effort by the State Department of Education and the state superintendent, Bill Honig, to acquire a better quality history-social studies textbook series. Thus, the local level asserted itself in the face of strong pressure from state-level policymakers.

The Oakland board also made explicit statements about their notion of how the issues of integration versus separation should be resolved. They clearly favored a curriculum that stressed the separate contributions of various cultural groups over what they saw as an attempt to ''dress up'' a Eurocentric presentation with the insertion of material about various ethnic and racial groups. Oakland is also an example of intergroup cooperation: African-Americans and Asian-Americans on the school board agreed about the need for a better treatment of multicultural issues in the textbooks. These board members were political players who do not usually assert themselves in the textbook policy game. They were very much influenced by African-American players who were part of the institutionalized politics of textbooks—members of the Curriculum Commission, the Instructional Media Review Panels, and university-based specialists. These players from inside the institutionalized field of education found allies in the Oakland community who came forward to support rejection of the textbooks. Thus the decision in Oakland was based on a combination of institutionalized and deinstitutionalized politics, using the Wong and Loveless model.[65]

Even the critics of these books admit that they are an improvement over the textbooks that have been available in the past. They are being used in about 600 school districts in California and in at least five other states. The books represent a very large investment by the publisher to respond to the dramatic changes in the California history-social science framework. The state approval process and local adoption process in Oakland are a vivid demonstration of the various levels in the game of curriculum politics outlined earlier in this chapter.

IMPLICATIONS

The issues raised in this chapter have implications on several levels. First, a situated, contextualized, urban curriculum must rely on the teacher and the students to negotiate together the particulars of what is taught and how it will be taught. We suggest that when teachers see their instruction as ever-changing, they view teaching as inquiry. This view is also held by those who argue for the "teacher as researcher."[66] When it is argued that curriculum is context-specific, the person who should know the context best is the teacher. We would argue that teachers have always made curriculum contextual but have not always understood this fact overtly. When teachers are exposed to a new curriculum, they examine it and immediately begin internally negotiating how they will implement it—what parts they will use, how they will teach it. This process must be made explicit, especially for urban teachers whose students change daily (the fringes of any culture are always those with the most movement; those who are successful in a society usually promote the status quo). This new view of curriculum construction applauds the teacher who reports, "This stuff is nice, but it won't work with my kids."

Second and equally necessary, we also applaud the school staff that understand the political context of their work with children and therefore, avoid reliance on stereotypical assumptions that disenfranchise poor and minority students. There are strong institutional norms that endorse a standard curriculum in public education.[67] Unless educators examine critically the curriculum to be used, they abdicate their responsibility as advocates for the children in their schools and cannot be said to be professionals—those who by definition exercise self-control over their work product. This line of argument is at odds with the efforts to define a nationally controlled standard curriculum. The assumption on which our argument is based is that pluralism and a recognition that diversity is to be valued require flexibility in curriculum content and pedagogical style.

Third, the success of urban schooling may well rest on reconceptualizing the term *curriculum* so that it is seen as a social process based on bargaining and negotiation rather than an empirical search for the "one best curriculum." Do urban students of color require a qualitatively different curriculum? We must make explicit the degree to which we will affirm the student's home culture and what portion of the curriculum is represented by dominant-culture knowledge. How will the curriculum take into account the different cultural responses of various groups to public education? Curriculum can no longer be considered a scientific, decontextualized process but rather must be recognized as a political engagement of compromise.

NOTES

1. Tony Becher and Stuart Maclure, *The Politics of Curriculum Change* (London: Hutchinson, 1978), 12.

2. H. D. Lasswell, *A Preview of Policy Science* (NY: American Elsevier Publishing Co. 1971), 25.

3. John Eggleston, *The Sociology of the School Curriculum* (London: Routledge and Kegan Paul, 1977), 52–55.

4. Thomas Carroll and Jean Schensul, "Cultural Diversity and American Education: Visions of the Future" *Education and Urban Society* 22 (4), August 1990, 344.

5. Jean Francois Lyotard, *The Postmodern Condition: A Report on Knowledge* (Minneapolis: University of Minnesota Press, 1984).

6. Catherine Cornbleth, *Curriculum in Context* (London: Falmer Press, 1990), 7.

7. Cornbleth, *Curriculum in Context*, 24.

8. Elisabeth Hansot and David Tyack, *Managers of Virtue* (New York: Oxford University Press, 1992).

9. Frederick Wirt and Michael Kirst, *Politics of Education: Schools in Conflict* (Berkeley, CA: McCutchan, 1989), 6–10.

10. Dennis Carlson, "Curriculum Planning and the State: The Dynamics of Control in Education," in Landon Beyer and Michael Apple (Eds.), *The Curriculum: Problems, Politics, and Possibilities* (Albany, NY: State University of New York Press, 1988), 98–118.

11. Michael Apple, "Conservative Agendas and Progressive Possibilities: Understanding the Wider Politics of Curriculum and Teaching," *Education and Urban Society* 23 (8), May 1991, 279.

12. Frances Kline, *The Politics of Curriculum Decision-Making: Issues in Centralizing the Curriculum* (Albany, NY: State University of New York Press, 1991).

13. A. S. Carson, "Control of the Curriculum: A Case for Teachers," *Journal of Curriculum Studies*, 1984 (16)1, 19–28.

14. F. W. Lutz and C. Mertz, *The Politics of School/Community Relations* (New York: Teachers College Press, 1992), chapter 7.

15. See, for example, the work of Arronowitz, Giroux, Shore, Freire.

16. Eggleston, *The Sociology of the School Curriculum*, 31.

17. Cameron McCarthy, *Race and Curriculum: Social Inequality and the Theories and Politics of Difference in Contemporary Research on Schooling* (London: Falmer Press, 1990), 38.

18. Geoff Whitty, *Sociology and School Knowledge: Curriculum Theory, Research and Politics* (London: Methuen, 1985), 54.

19. Jim Cummins, "Empowering Minority Students: A Framework for Intervention," *Harvard Educational Review* 56 (1), February 1986, 18–36.

20. Steven Arvizu and Marietta Saravia-Shore, "Cross-Cultural Literacy: An Anthropological Approach to Dealing with Diversity," *Education and Urban Society* 22 (4), August 1990, 373.

21. A. Harry Passow, "Urban Schools a Second (?) or Third (?) Time Around: Priorities for Curricular and Instructional Reform," *Education and Urban Society* 23 (8), May 1991, 253.

22. See Thomas Timar, "The Politics of School Restructuring," in Douglas Mitchell and Margaret Goertz (Eds.), *Education Politics for the New Century* (London: Falmer Press, 1990), 55–74; Susan H. Fuhrman and Betty Malen, *The Politics of Curriculum and Testing* (London: Falmer Press, 1991).

23. Milbre McLaughlin, "Learning from Experience: Lessons from Policy Implementation," *Educational Evaluation and Policy Analysis* 9 (2), 1987, 171–78.

24. See Michael W. Apple, "Regulating the Text: The Socio-Historical Roots of State Control," in Philip G. Atbech (Ed.), *Textbooks in American Society* (Albany, NY: State University of New York Press, 1991); Joel Spring, "Ideological Management in Textbooks: An Analysis of Political and Economic Forces That Shape the Ideological Content of American Textbooks" (San Francisco: American Education Research Association Presentation, 1992).

25. Kenneth Wong and Tom Loveless, "The Politics of Textbook Policy: Proposing a Framework," in *Textbooks in American Society* (Albany, NY: State University of New York Press, 1991), 27–42.

26. See Louise Adler and Kip Tellez, "Curriculum Challenge from the Religious Right: The Impressions Reading Series," *Urban Education* 27 (2), July 1992, 153–73; Martha M. McCarthy, "Curriculum Censorship: Values in Conflict," *Educational Horizons*, Fall/Winter 1989, 26–34.

27. McCarthy, *Race and Curriculum*, 102.

28. John Ogbu and Maria Eguenia Matute-Bianchi, "Understanding Sociocultural Factors: Knowledge, Identity, and School Adjustment," in Bilingual Education Office, California State Department of Education (Ed.), *Beyond Language: Social and Cultural Factors in Schooling Language Minority Students* (California State University, Los Angeles: Evaluation, Dissemination and Assessment Center), 91.

29. *The Forgotten Half: Non-College Youth in America* (Washington, DC: William T. Grant Foundation Commission on Work, Family and Citizenship, January 1988).

30. Dena Swanson and Margaret Spencer, "Youth Policy, Poverty, and African-Americans: Implications for Resilience," *Education and Urban Society* 24 (1), November 1991, 148–61.

31. William J. Wilson, *The Declining Significance of Race: Blacks and Changing American Institutions* (Chicago: University of Chicago Press, 1980), 151.

32. Jonathan Kozol, *Savage Inequalities: Children in America's Schools* (New York: Harper Perennial, 1991), 59.

33. Eggleston, *The Sociology of the School Curriculum*, 31.

34. Kozol, *Savage Inequalities*, 75.

35. Ogbu and Matute-Bianchi, *Understanding Sociocultural Factors*, 87–88.

36. Gail Martinez, a review of *The Politics of Hispanic Education: Un paso palante y dos patras* by Kenneth Meier and Joseph Stewart, Jr. in *Thought & Action* 8 (1), Spring 1992, 101.

37. Cornbleth, *Curriculum in Context*, 42.

38. Kenneth Meier and Joseph Stewart, Jr., *The Politics of Hispanic Education; Un paso palante y dos patras* (Albany, NY: State University of New York Press, 1991).

39. Lorri Shepard, "Readiness Testing in Local School Districts: An Analysis of Backdoor Policies," in Susan Fuhrman and Betty Malen (Eds.), *Politics of Curriculum and Testing*, (London: Falmer Press, 1991), 159–79.

40. Shepard, "Readiness Testing in Local School Districts," 173.

41. Jean Anyon, "Social Class and the Hidden Curriculum of Work," *Journal of Education* 162 (1), 1980, 67–92.

42. Martinez, a review of *The Politics of Hispanic Education*, 101.

43. McCarthy, *Race and Curriculum*, 94.

44. Marshall Smith and Jennifer O'Day, "Systemic School Reform," in Susan Fuhrman and Betty Malen (Eds.), *The Politics of Curriculum and Testing* (London: Falmer Press, 1991), 263.

45. Debra Viadero, "American Historians Enter Multiculturalism Debate," *Education Week*, 20 February 1991, 8.

46. Peter B. Edelman, "Dealing with Race and Ethnicity in Urban Change Strategies," paper prepared for the conference on Building Strong Communities: Strategies for Social Change, Cleveland, OH, 13–15 May 1992, 5–6.

47. Steven Arvizu and Marietta Saravia-Shore, "Cross-Cultural Literacy: An Anthro-

pological Approach to Dealing with Diversity,'' *Education and Urban Society* 22 (4), August 1990, 367–68.

48. Debra Viadero, "Opposed to Whole Language, Houston Schools Revert to Phonics," *Education Week*, 20 November 1991, 5.

49. M. LeCompte, "Learning to Work: The Hidden Curriculum of the Classroom," *Anthropology and Education Quarterly* 9 (1), 1978, 23–37.

50. Both former teachers from Wesley Elementary and district officials provided data discussed in this section of the chapter, but because of the politically sensitive nature of the data, they are not individually identified.

51. Bill Honig, "California's Experience with Textbook Improvement," in Philip Altbach et al. (Eds.), *Textbooks in American Society* (Albany, NY: State University of New York Press, 1991, 105–16.

52. "California Adopts History Texts," *AERA/SIG on Textbooks, Textbook Publishing, and Schools Newsletter*, December 1990, 1.

53. Robert Reinhold, "Class Struggle," *New York Times Magazine*, 29 September 1991, 26–29, 46–47, 52.

54. Gloria Ladson-Billings, "Distorting Democracy: An Ethnographic View of the California History-Social Science Textbook Adoption Process," paper presented at American Education Research Association Convention in San Francisco, 24 April 1992.

55. See "School Trustees Reject History Textbooks," *EDCAL* 3, 5 August 1991, 2; Debra Viadero, "Oakland Scrambles to Make Do Without Rejected Textbooks," *Education Week*, 26 November 1991, 1, 15; William Trombley, "In Oakland, a Textbook Case of Trouble," *Los Angeles Times*, 4 November 1991, A3, A25.

56. "School Trustees Reject History Textbooks," 2.

57. Reinhold, "Class Struggle," 52.

58. McCarthy, *Race and Curriculum*, 40.

59. Sylvia Wynter, "The Challenge to Our Episteme: The Case of the California Textbook Controversy," American Education Research Association Convention in San Francisco, 22 April 1992; Gloria Ladson-Billings, "Distorting Democracy: An Ethnographic View of the California History-Social Science Textbook Adoption Process," American Education Research Association Convention in San Francisco, 24 April 1992.

60. Reinhold, "Class Struggle."

61. Trombley, "In Oakland, a Textbook Case of Trouble," A25.

62. Viadero, "Oakland Scrambles to Make Do Without Rejected Textbooks," 15.

63. Trombley, "In Oakland, a Textbook Case of Trouble," A25.

64. Trombley, "In Oakland, a Textbook Case of Trouble," A25.

65. Wong and Loveless, "The Politics of Textbook Policy," 34–37.

66. Dixie Goswami and Peter Stillman (Eds.), *Reclaiming the Classroom: Teacher Research as an Agency for Change* (Upper Montclair, NJ: Boynton Cook, 1987).

67. Paul DiMaggio and Walter Powell, "The Iron Cage Revisited: Institutional Isomorphism and Collective Rationality in Organizational Fields," *American Sociological Review* 48, 1992, 147–60.

7

The Organizational Structure of Urban Educational Systems: Bureaucratic Practices in Mass Societies

Joseph G. Weeres

This chapter traces the evolution of the organizational structure of urban education over the past seventy-five years. During this period, urban school systems possessed two different forms of organizational structure: a unitary one that arose at the turn of the century and lasted until approximately the mid-1960s and an institutionalized form that still exists in most urban school districts today.

Each of these structures emerged from changes in the political economy of urban school districts. At the turn of the century, industrialization gave rise to a rapidly expanding, largely insular, city economy and a political system dominated by pro-growth urban elites. The demands of these elites for organizational practices and procedures that emphasized uniformity, standardization, and efficiency resulted in the establishment of the unitary form of organizational structure. This form closely resembled Max Weber's description of bureaucracy and was characterized by a functional division of labor, tightly integrated pyramidal structure, and strong unity of command. It was a structure that required strong, central control at the apex of the organization and that, in turn, depended on a governance system capable of identifying and legitimating a unitary school system interest.

By the end of World War II, however, the insularity of the city economy was being challenged by competition arising from suburbanization and a national economy. Most big cities fared poorly in this competitive arena and consequently became increasingly dependent on fiscal resources from state and federal governments. The resulting fiscal and political interdependencies fragmented school governance, making it necessary for school administrators to respond to the demands of many different interests. The institutionalized form of structure emerged out of these political and fiscal conditions. It is a form characterized by more loosely coupled subunits, accommodation to diverse centers of organizational power, and authority dependent on multiple, often contradictory, external sources of legitimation.

The organizational consequence of this form has been control loss—the inability of urban school systems efficiently to deliver coherent, consistent educational services. This structural failure cannot be resolved simply by organizational reform, because the roots of the problem lie in the political economy of urban school systems. Addressing these larger issues of political economy requires an institutional transformation of public education perhaps greater in scope than what took place at the beginning of this century.

THE POLITICAL ECONOMY OF THE UNITARY FORM

The unitary form of urban school organizational structure arose at the turn of the century after a coalition of municipal reformers succeeded in wresting political control of big cities away from the political machines that had dominated urban government since the Civil War. These political machines had structured a governance system characterized by the formal decentralization of authority to neighborhood units and local community politicians (e.g., ward committee persons) and by the corresponding informal acquisition of power by party bosses through the exchange of city contracts and favorable governmental decisions for financial kickbacks and other forms of political support. Municipal reformers argued that this system of organized bribery was not the way to run a modern industrialized city.

Although the dominant political actors in the municipal reform movement were usually business leaders, the movement drew support from a broad spectrum of the electorate. Its essential appeal was economic growth and the robust set of benefits that growth would bring to the community (e.g., jobs for ordinary, working people). It successfully argued that machine rule was inhibiting the city from taking advantage of the opportunities provided by industrialization and that to nurture industrial growth, cities needed efficient, centralized governmental services. By the early 1920s, the press of these arguments had shifted governmental control in most big cities to the municipal reformers.

A Unitary Interest

Long before there was such a doctrine as political correctness, Edward Banfield and James Wilson argued that the political beliefs espoused by these municipal reformers evolved from white, Anglo-Saxon Protestantism.[1] Reformers assumed that the practice of good government was essentially a technical enterprise rather than a political one. Government, they argued, should seek to realize the collective (citywide) interest, not competing private interests.

The task of identifying the collective, unitary interest was to be left to a small elite who, presumably because of wealth and education, would not be tempted to use government for selfish purposes and instead would enact policies beneficial to the city and school system as a whole (the white, Anglo-Saxon, Protestant notion of public-regard). Once these elites formulated policies reflective of the unitary interest, then these were to be turned over to professionals for implementation. Schools were to be scientifically managed: authority was to be centralized in the office of the general superintendent and a hierarchically arranged division of labor (bureaucracy) established to implement efficiently the district's unitary interest.

Governance

The governance structures that municipal reformers designed to achieve these goals included nonpartisan, at-large election of school board members, the separation of school and city governments, and the transfer of formal political authority from neighborhoods to the central policy-making body. Using the slogan "Let's keep politics out of education," reformers abolished neighborhood community councils and lodged most authority for school governance in a small central school board. These boards were kept purposively small in numbers so that they wouldn't be able to represent adequately the diverse political, social, economic, and ethnic interests that existed within the city.

Indeed, the logic of governance denied the legitimacy of competing interests, and therefore it was not designed as a system of adversarial democracy, where bargaining rules are established to protect the rights of competing interests. Rather, the system embodied an elite notion of democracy, where blue-ribbon boards served as stewards for the community and where school administrators became managers of virtue.[2]

Funding and Legitimacy

The primary agents for funding and legitimating the policies of this governance system were the business leaders, heads of citywide civic associations, and other elites who had access to the media and who could thereby most effectively promulgate an understanding of the unitary interest.[3] These elites generally identified the city economic interest with economic growth and focused on creating conditions conducive to that growth—a favorable business regulatory environment, a publicly financed economic infrastructure, and efficient public services. Public education was presented to the public as a developmental good, charitable, too, but mainly an investment in the future economic growth of the city.

These expressions of the unitary interest were reinforced by the dependence of local urban governments on primarily a single source of funding—local property taxes. The logic was straightforward: economic growth produced higher valuations of city land and property, tax revenues from these higher valuations allowed for the extension of schooling, and that, in turn, contributed to economic development.

Elites also were influential in school board affairs. Through the devices of nominating committees, good government endorsements, blue-ribbon commission recommendations, and old-fashioned politics, they helped shape the incumbency of boards and influenced the policies these boards enacted. They also used their connections at state levels to secure state regulations (e.g., in the area of teacher and administrator credential requirements) that buttressed local board-enacted policies. All of these actions helped create for urban school systems an environment in which a unitary interest could be implemented.

THE UNITARY ORGANIZATIONAL STRUCTURE

When municipal reformers gained control over urban educational systems at the turn of the century,, the administrative organization of urban school systems was already bureaucratized. Bureaucracy had emerged in the 1800s in response to the increasing size of the student population and the larger number of school employees required to provide services to this growing population. As the size of the organization increased, it was necessary to divide labor functionally, for example, separating the tasks of teaching from administration and school site administration from central office administration. Span of control limits led to vertical layering, and this, coupled with geographically dispersed school sites, magnified problems of organizational communication, coordination, and control over production. It was an organizational structure that demanded the exercise of strong central leadership in order to integrate effectively the functionally and geographically separated parts.

But under machine political regimes, superintendents could not exercise this kind of control because political power was formally dispersed. Neighborhood ward bosses influenced the hiring and selection of school site administrators and teachers. The spoils system dictated who received school contracts and services. Municipal reformers saw a need for greater educational standardization, higher standards of academic achievement, and greater efficiency in resource allocation. Organizationally, they created what David Tyack labeled "the one best system."[4]

Functional Integration

Creating a governance system that placed funding, legitimating power, and formal authority at the apex of the system allowed municipal reformers to pull together a unitary organizational structure in which the organization's subunits were bound together by hierarchically defined values. Much of the work of schools was standardized through the application of formal procedures and practices. Allocation formulas were developed to routinize resource allocation, including schedules for such mundane maintenance tasks as the painting of buildings. Accreditation of teachers and administrators facilitated centralized personnel practices connected to the hiring, promotion, and assignment of personnel. School principals were rotated among school sites to lessen the possibility that they would form political attachments to neighborhood constituencies. Structurally, reformers sought to create a monolithic organizational structure responsive to demands emanating from the top of the organizational hierarchy.

To combat the decentralizing tendencies of a functional division of labor (e.g., divisions of business, personnel, and instruction) and the geographical dispersion of school sites, reformers strengthened the formal authority of the school superintendent by giving superintendents broad decision-making discretion to manage the operations of the system. Legitimacy for exercising this authority was made possible by the centralization of governing power in the hands of a relatively small, elite-influenced school board. The power relationships between boards and superintendents were not zero sum. Both gained by the strengthening of formal authority in each.

Unity of Command

For the knowledge of how to exercise their authority effectively, superintendents turned to the new administrative theory of scientific management. Richard Callahan suggests that business interests in the city foisted scientific management on the schools.[5] However, Michael Katz's contention that school superintendents readily embraced scientific management seems more convincing.[6] Business leaders wanted greater efficiency in schools. But so did superintendents and most of the public. The logic of schools as an investment good depended on efficient management—on maximizing the effect of governmental expenditures on economic growth. Frederick Taylor, Luther Gulick, Lyndall Urwick, Henry Fayol, and others developed theories that offered superintendents the expertise to make schools more efficient (see Elwood P. Cubberly for applications of these ideas to education[7]).

Scientific management was a theory about the division of labor and its relationship to organizational efficiency. The keys to achieving organizational efficiency were control and predictability. These, in turn, depended on scientifically breaking down complex tasks to their constituent parts, routinizing and standardizing the work related to these parts, and hierarchically ordering the parts to achieve the desired production targets. Superintendents learned how to specify job descriptions, how to select and train individuals for these job descriptions, how to measure performance, how to structure and coordinate interrelated tasks, how to control time and space, and how to standardize planning, record keeping, organizational conditions, schedules, and instruction.[8] These concepts were applied to all aspects of schooling, including treatment of students (e.g., the use of intelligence tests for academic tracking), the design of curricular materials, and the structuring of secondary schools.[9]

This process of centrally controlling the division of labor effectively lodged organizational power in the office of the superintendent. As complex tasks were subdivided, knowledge about the organization and its coordination and control migrated up the hierarchy to senior-level administrators. This centralization of knowledge allowed for a division of labor between the board (policy) and the superintendent (administration), because the superintendent possessed something the board could not easily acquire: knowledge about the interconnectedness of the organizational parts. (See Tyack and Elizabeth Hansot for documentation concerning the growth of management courses in schools of education and the influence of some of these schools on the placement of big-city school super-intendents.[10])

Accommodating Nonunitary Interests

Scientific management theory assumed that a unitary organizational structure would produce unitary organizational purposes—that all organizational members would share, or comply with, centrally determined goals and objectives. Municipal reformers made similar assumptions relative to the subordination of special political interests to the interest of the city as a whole. In the 1920s, however, an influential series of studies in the Hawthorne works of the Western Electric Company revealed that some acknowledgment of the worker's individual and group interests might result in increased productivity. Workers produced more when they were noticed and treated humanely. Later, Chester Barnard noted that some authority within organizations flows from the workers to the manager.[11] To gain control, managers need to attend to individual worker interests as well as to those of the organization as a whole.

This research provided an intellectual justification for acceding to some special interests by the unitary organization. Which interests got acknowledged, however, was more a function of politics.

William Gamson's notion of an inner and outer circle is useful for describing this selection process.[12] Most interests reside in the larger polity and, though theoretically recognized as distinct, are not accorded legitimacy by the political system, or in this case by the organizational structure. Those in the inner circle, however, have gained recognition as legitimate interests within political and organizational bargaining processes. The ideology of reform government and scientific management theory wanted to place all special interests in the larger circle. But the organization's dependency on the articulation of external resources allowed some interests, both within the organizational structure and outside it, to gain entry into the inner circle.

Secondary school principals are a case in point. Most revenue of funding big-city school systems came from local property tax. Tax and bond increases required voter approval. The municipal reform coalition usually played the major role in securing the passage of these referenda. But principals, particularly in the secondary schools, could also mobilize constituencies in support of these referenda. Their primary organized constituencies were the various booster clubs connected to sports activities. These groups constituted a reliable source of votes in these referenda. Athletic directors, who worked most closely with these groups, often acquired sufficient external power relative to that of the school principal that superintendents frequently promoted athletic directors to these positions rather than risk conflicts that might endanger the principle of unity of command at the school site level. These personnel practices conferred upon school administration a "jock" image that lasted well into the 1960s, when the power of secondary school principals diminished as big-city school districts became increasingly less dependent on local property taxes for revenues. However, up until then, these secondary school principals were members of the inner circle. In Los Angeles, for example, the Association of Los Angeles Unified Secondary School Principals Association was a major player in the organizational politics of the district, especially in administrative personnel selection and promotion, up until the late 1960s.

Senior administrative line officers also joined the inner circle as a result of their special knowledge about organizational interdependencies and their external contacts with board members and influential political actors. Vocational and adult education directors also worked their way in because of the external revenues their programs articulated. All of these internal interests negotiated to codify and formally legitimate, as much as politically possible, their property rights associated with their special interests. Most gained de facto and, in many instances, de jure tenure in their job titles through this process.

Parents and community groups in the most affluent neighborhoods also entered the inner circle through their connections with members of the board and other actors in the municipal reform coalition. These constituencies also contributed a higher amount of tax revenue to the district and, as suburbs formed outside the big cities, used the threat of exit as a way of gaining legitimacy for their special interests.

The resultant school system organization could still be characterized as mainly unitary in structure, because most interests, including generally those of teachers and most parents, were located outside the inner circle and therefore were subject to the imposition of hierarchically defined organizational controls. But there were important pockets of fragmentation. Big-city school systems accommodated interests in the inner circle, even if these created asymmetries and discontinuities in the unitary structure. On balance, the organizational structure of big-city school systems was remarkably cohesive, particularly given the intrinsic problem of exerting central control over hundreds of geographically dispersed school sites. The relative cohesiveness of the organizational structure over a period of several decades produced by the late 1940s and early 1950s an educational system that had much to be proud of.

THE POLITICAL ECONOMY OF INSTITUTIONALIZED STRUCTURE

The unitary organizational structure presupposed the presence of cohesive, strong central control at the apex of the organization. A united board legitimating the actions of the superintendent was essential for this organizational structure to function effectively. By the 1930s, however, signs were already evident that the economic conditions supporting a governance system capable of identifying a unitary interest were already changing. Big cities no longer were able to annex adjacent territory to the city jurisdictions, which, in effect, capped the possibilities for territorial growth. Suburbs began to emerge on the city periphery, and although the Great Depression and World War II slowed these developments, by the 1950s big cities increasingly found themselves in economic competition with other communities within the metropolitan area and with other regions of the country. The effects of this economic competition were to undercut the economic and political conditions supportive of the unitary structure of urban school systems. Urban school systems became increasingly dependent on federal and state funding, their governance systems became more fragmented, and by the late 1960s they evolved an institutionalized form of organizational structure, which persisted through the 1980s.

Market Competition

In 1956, Samuel Tiebout constructed an economic model to predict the distribution of urban communities that would develop as a consequence of suburbanization. He argued that economic competition among cities within metropolitan areas would result in their economic stratification based on the taxpaying capacity of their residents and businesses. Citizens would shop for communities that offered the most services for the least cost, and local governments would design governmental service delivery packages to attract businesses and residents with the greatest taxpaying capacity. The result would be that cities with the most affluent taxpayers would have the lowest tax rates and the highest level of services, whereas those with the least affluent residents would have high tax rates and comparatively low levels of services. Most cities would end up with relatively homogeneous populations based on taxpaying capacity.

Tiebout's theory turned out to be highly prescient. Although the market was not perfectly efficient, the overall pattern displayed the predicted pattern.[13] Big cities were particularly hard hit by this market competition. By the early 1960s, it was already manifestly evident that big cities were entering economic decline as a result of this economic competition. Many of their businesses and most affluent residents were migrating to suburban communities where their tax dollars could purchase higher levels of governmental services. Equal service delivery regulations made it difficult for them to fashion service delivery packages to hold their most affluent taxpayers.[14]

Big cities fought these market forces with urban renewal projects, urban redevelopment efforts, freeway and airport construction projects, enterprise zones, tax incentives to lure businesses, and private-public investment partnerships. In some respects, these efforts were successful. Central cities, by the mid-1980s, glistened with new office buildings and could boast of sports arenas, music centers, and international airports, but alongside these accomplishments were poverty growing among the residents and large areas of decaying neighborhood housing. Much of the middle class and almost all of the most affluent residents had emigrated to suburban enclaves. The job base also had deteriorated to the point where large numbers of remaining residents could no longer find adequate employment.

Effects on School Finances

The capacity of big cities to finance themselves through local property tax declined as competition with suburbs and other regions intensified. The bankruptcy of New York City in the 1970s signified the economic duress that many major cities faced. Attempting to secure voter approval for tax and bond referenda became counterproductive because high tax rates spurred those most capable of paying these higher taxes to move to the suburbs where their tax dollars could more directly be spent on services related to their needs rather than partly support those who did not have the taxpaying capacity to pay for the services they received in the big cities.

Although it became fashionable in the 1960s to characterize metropolitan areas as composed of economically declining central cities and economically viable suburbs, this depiction overlooked the communities at the bottom end of Tiebout's sorting machine and failed to grasp the larger significance of metropolitan economic competition. By the early 1980s, most of the inner ring of suburban communities already displayed most of the characteristics of the economically declining central cities. Moreover, this process of decay continues to spread outward as suburban infrastructures and housing stocks age and as affluent residents and job-creating businesses migrate farther to exurban locations, where the possibilities for capital appreciation are greater and where tax revenues can be spent on services directly related to their needs.

Overlaying these economic distribution patterns has been racial and ethnic segregation. The student populations of the big cities and older, inner ring of suburban communities in many metropolitan regions are now composed of a majority of who were once labeled "minority" students. This combination of racial and economic segregation, coupled with the inability of many of these districts, including most big-city school systems, to fund themselves adequately with local property tax revenues, has led federal and state governments to assume larger responsibility for local school district financing. This change from largely local funding to mainly state and federal financing has profoundly altered the distribution of political power within big-city school systems.

Effects on Governance

The primary consequence has been the fragmentation of governance into multiple centers of power. Although school boards remain legally at the apex of the system, they no longer are the sole providers of resources. A significant part of their capacity to legitimate local district policy stemmed from their capacity to articulate local property tax revenues. During the heyday of the municipal reform era, the business community supported and guided boards in these efforts. But by the early 1950s, business participation in urban school politics was already waning. Much of business' involvement had been associated with directing and benefiting by the economic growth of the city.[15] As central city growth ceased and suburbanization offered alternate investment opportunities, the incentive to tend the governance system diminished. Also contributing to the withdrawal of business participation were absentee ownership, the emergence of large, nationally focused corporations, and, during the 1970s and 1980s, foreign ownership of central city property. The reform separation of municipal and school governments allowed business leaders to focus their attention on governmental sectors most directly related to their business interests, often special private-public development partnerships insulated from normal city electoral politics.

Court-ordered busing also contributed to the sidelining of other key reform coalition members. Parent-Teacher Associations, League of Women Voters, and other citywide civic associations usually were unable to take a stand on such a politically controversial issue. Long-standing board members who represented the ideology of "Let's keep politics out of education" went down in fights with neighborhood community associations bitterly opposed to school busing. At the same time, rising ethnic and racial consciousness allowed previously underrepresented groups to secure representation on the board. Increasingly, board membership came to reflect the ethnic and neighborhood divisions of the city. Many big-city school districts even eliminated the reform device of at-large elections in favor of regional representation.

Federal funding also encouraged political fragmentation. As John David Greenstone and Paul Peterson[16] point out, federal compensatory educational programs and the War on Poverty had a twofold mission: to redress economic and educational inequalities and to give voice to the political interests of these politically underrepresented groups. Almost all of the categorical federal educational funding required the establishment of community-targeted advisory and governance committees. Although many of these structures withered with reductions in federal categorical funding during the 1980s, their influence persists through the constituencies they mobilized in support of redistributive and equity issues. New forms of federal funding in the cities redevelopment funding in the 1980s also strengthened the political influence of neighborhood development associations, both in city and in school politics.

Teachers' unions also emerged as important influentials in big-city school politics, partly through their organizational capacity to mobilize votes in board elections and partly through their ability to secure additional funding from state governments. Teachers' associations in many big-city school districts assign personnel to lobby state governments for these fiscal resources. They are also influential in shaping state regulations that impinge directly on the operations of big-city school systems.

The dissolution of the old municipal reform coalition and the shift in urban school system funding from local to state and federal sources opened the governance system to numerous other organized special interest groups capable of bridging these intergovernmental sectors (e.g., parents of special education and "gifted" students). Power within the governance system as a whole has become more diffuse and multipolar. Yet, not all interests are represented or equally represented. Large segments of the population, especially the economically poor, remain outside the inner circle of political bargaining. Moreover, the organized interest groups that dominate the governance system are usually not capable of collectively speaking with one voice.

INSTITUTIONALIZED ORGANIZATIONAL STRUCTURE

These changes in the political economy of urban school systems have transformed their organizational structures from a unitary to an institutionalized form.[17] Three properties characterize an institutionalized organizational structure: the organization develops multiple, often contradictory, sources of funding and external legitimation; subunits attach themselves to multiple centers of power; and core production activities become loosely coupled to the organization's administrative structure.

Multiple Sources of Funding and Legitimacy

The organizational structure of urban school systems depends on external sources for its legitimacy. The unitary form emerged out of, and was sustained by, a system that was controlled by local urban elites and largely funded by local property taxes. By the mid-1960s this system was in disarray, and urban school systems increasingly came to depend on multiple providers of funding and political legitimacy. Initially, state and federal funding constituted a relatively small percentage of total district revenues, but it was the fastest growing source, and today these governments provide more than half of the funding for urban school systems.

Much of the central administrative bureaucracies that had been built up under reform rule were in support of standardized curriculum and instruction in the school sites. But as urban school systems developed diverse and often divergent relationships with external funding sources, other organizational units designed around the demands of external funding agencies have displayed the unitary structures. During the height of federal funding in the 1960s and 1970s, urban school systems tried to distinguish between programs with hard (local property tax and unrestricted state grant) and soft (categorical) funding, pushing those with soft funding to the periphery of the organizational structure and incorporating those with hard funding into the core. As long as the mix of categorical programs was changing, these tactics worked. Units that had been categorically funded were clipped off when the funded ended. Districts also attempt to subvent categorical monies, using the subvented funds to support programs designed to hold residents capable of paying local property taxes, while at the same time complying as much as necessary with the demands of the external agencies for compensatory and redistributive programs. But as districts draw less revenue from local sources and more from external governments, these efforts become counterproductive because some of the most stably funded programs are not fully integrated into core educational activities (e.g., Head Start and Chapter I).

In addition to the demands attached to funding, urban school systems have had to respond to court decisions and injunctions, regulatory decisions by various governmental agencies, state education codes, legislative actions, changing college and university requirements—all involving a host of diverse demands, not easily prioritized because each institutional actor can apply sanctions or withdraw support. Federal and state governments, for example, encourage districts to provide high levels of math and science education to all students but at the same time urge advanced placement courses, which result in virtually all of the math and science resources available in the high schools going to the smaller number of students enrolled in these classes.

Much of the attention of senior administrative officers of urban school districts is devoted to mediating these intergovernmental and institutional relationships. Legal advising and governmental lobbying are now important functions in the organizational structures of urban school systems. Linking these efforts to coordinated organizational processes from the superintendent down to the classroom, however, is an impossible task, given the complexity and diversity of external institutional constraints and demands. Instead of trying to maintain the kind of monolithic cohesion associated with the unitary form, the institutionalized structure proliferates horizontal and vertical differentiation, overlapping jurisdictions, and multiple lines of authority. It seeks to tolerate ambiguity by allowing different organizational subunits to respond separately to conflicting external institutional demands.

Multiple Centers of Power

These centrifugal tendencies are reinforced by the claims of special interest groups, many of which encourage and articulate relationships with external agencies. Some groups, such as parents of special education and ''gifted'' students, attach themselves to the subunits that mediate funds for these programs or administratively are responsible for compliance. These linkages compromise the unity-of-command principle characteristic of the unitary organizations. In order to survive in the position, administrators must strike a balance between the need to maintain political support from these interest groups and the imperative of being organizationally loyal and compliant.

Other groups, such as neighborhood community associations, seek general influence over educational services in their area. In the late 1960s, many urban school districts responded to angry neighborhood community demands, especially those coming from underrepresented racial and ethnic groups, with administrative decentralization, which, in effect, created an additional administrative layer between central administrative office services and the local school sites. This strategy for managing conflict legitimated the claim that urban school systems needed to attend to diverse neighborhood interests. Although many of the expectations of advocates for school decentralization were never realized, the restructuring did seem to tighten connections between administrators in the various areas and neighborhood constituents, thereby limiting to some extent the kind of central control exercised under the unitary form. Decentralization also encouraged regional representation on the school boards. Today, these same processes are moving forward through the devices of site-based management and school restructuring.

Almost all special interest groups have tried to secure property rights guaranteeing their participation and the legitimacy of their interests. The most successful of these groups has clearly been teachers' unions. The encoding of their property rights in formal labor contracts, state legislative actions, and board policies may surpass that of school administrators. Teachers' associations have become important claimants on the expenditure of the school purse and, through formalization of property rights, constrain administrative action and policies relative to teacher behavior. Numerous other groups (e.g., special education parents) have used courts, legislatures, and federal and state regulatory agencies to gain rights to school services.

Loosely Coupled Structures

These multiple centers of power and complex interrelationships to external sources of funding and legitimation have created loosely coupled urban school system organizational structures. The attention of administrators is drawn to issues of turf and power associated with managing these relationships and away from the efficient production of educational services. Trying to coordinate and bring cohesion to the patchwork of structural units, programs, and policies is an almost impossible task. Many superintendents focus their energies and discretionary financial resources on new ventures, trying to mobilize political coalitions strong enough to combat the disaggregating tendencies associated with the institutional form of organizational structure. In one sense, they are constrained by the political power that accrues to subunits and special interests, but in another, the complexity and fragmentation afford them opportunities to declare a crisis and seize the initiative.[18] Most of these efforts turn out to be fads, either because the new program idea isn't sound or because the imperatives of political economy eventually pull apart the integrity of the program design.

The organizational structure has a strong tendency toward disaggregation. The pull and tug of interest groups, their alignment to subunits of the organizations, and the complex sets of linkages among the interest groups, the organizational subunits, and the external legitimating and funding agencies make command-oriented leadership almost impossible to exercise. It's a bit like trying to push a string. The loosely coupled structures move and shift, but they don't necessarily move forward or go in the direction intended.

The salience of these realities is reflected in the curriculum provided to administrators in graduate educational administration programs. Whereas an earlier generation of school administrators were taught the principles of administering an efficient organization, today the curriculum focuses on negotiating an institutionalized organizational structure and managing its relationships to a diverse set of external environments. Courses teach students the property rights of special interest groups, the structure of intergovernmental relationships, the managerial imperatives of striking a balance between organizational purposes and the needs of individuals and groups. They are taught how to mobilize coalitions, how to read organizational environments, how to deal with diverse interest groups.

Many of the urban chiefs who had been steeped in the ideology of municipal reform failed to learn these lessons and went down in fights with teachers' unions, neighborhood redevelopment groups, antibusing activists, and other special interests seeking entry into the inner circle of bargaining.[19] During the late 1970s and early 1980s, the average length of incumbency for big-city school superintendents was only approximately 2.5 years. There is now some indication that the number of superintendents with longer incumbency terms may be increasing.[20] This new generation of superintendents may comprehend more fully the nature of leadership demanded by the institutionalized form—namely, that its defining elements are resource articulation and negotiation.

CONCLUSION

It is almost an axiom in the organizational literature in educational administration that urban school systems are highly successful in adapting to changes in their environment. The evolution of the organizational structures of urban school systems that we have examined in this chapter certainly supports this contention. Over the past century, urban school systems have managed to alter the structure of their administrative organizations in quite fundamental ways, moving from a unitary to an institutionalized form of organizational structure.

Yet today the viability of the existing organizational structure is being called in question. Even privatization, which was once a concept discussed solely by academic economists, has become part of the political discourse concerning the future of urban schools. Many are now demanding that urban school systems regain the academic excellence with which they were associated fifty years ago.[21]

Urban school systems appear to be responding to these demands by devolving the institutionalized form of organizational structure down to the school site level. Under the rubric of restructuring, the school sites are being asked to connect themselves to the array of external constituencies that exist locally. As more responsibility is passed to the school sites and central office administration supervision is trimmed, school principals will find that, like superintendents, their survival depends upon negotiation and resource articulation. Once local school site constituents realize that principals are unable to pass the buck up the organizational hierarchy, they will demand a greater share in school site decision making. Principals will need to learn how to exercise authority in an environment where the distribution of power is multipolar, where the legitimacy of their decisions depends upon multiple external sources, and where the overall structure of local school programs may become more loosely coupled. Giving more constituents a larger say in what schools do may help mute demands for excellence—for a while.

The quality issue, however, may run deeper than accountability. Just because local publics have a determinative voice in deciding what schools do does not necessarily mean that they, therefore, will conclude that schools are doing a good job. International student achievement comparisons, employment levels and wage rates, access to college and university admission—all may influence the public's definition of, and expectations for, academic excellence. Urban school systems already have lost a significant number of students to private schools because their parents no longer perceive the public schools as providing quality education.

Devolving the institutionalized form of organizational structure down to the school site level is more of an expression of the needs of the system to make itself accountable to diverse political interests than one designed to address interinstitutional issues of excellence and purpose. The answer to these issues lies beyond organizational structure, for as we have seen in this chapter, structure follows political economy. To transform the political economy of urban school systems would require an institutional redesign of public education perhaps greater in scope than what took place at the beginning of this century—one involving federalism (the respective roles of federal, state, and local governments), funding, governance, and, finally, organizational structure. Achieving that kind of transformation must come from outside urban public school systems, because today, unlike nearly 200 years ago, big cities occupy the periphery rather than the center of our economic and political institutions.

NOTES

1. Edward Banfield and James Wilson, *City Politics* (Cambridge: Harvard University Press and the Massachusetts Institute of Technology Press, 1963), chapter 1.

2. David Tyack and Elizabeth Hansot, *Managers of Virtue: Public School Leadership in America, 1820–1980* (New York: Basic Books, 1982).

3. Joel Spring, *The American School, 1642–1983: Varieties of Historical Interpretation of the Foundations and Development of American Education* (New York: Longman, 1986).

4. David Tyack, *The One Best System* (Cambridge: Harvard University Press, 1971).

5. Richard Callahan, *Education and the Cult of Efficiency* (Chicago: University of Chicago Press, 1962).

6. Michael Katz, *Class, Bureaucracy and Schools: The Illusion of Educational Change in America* (New York: Praeger, 1971).

7. For applications of these ideas see Elwood P. Cubberly, *Public Education in the United States* (Cambridge: Houghton Mifflin Company, 1934), 120–26.

8. Callahan, *Education and the Cult of Efficiency*.

9. Stanley W. Rothstein, *The Power to Punish* (New York: University Press of America, 1984).

10. Tyack and Hansot, *Managers of Virtue*.

11. Chester Barnard, *The Functions of the Executive* (Cambridge: Harvard University Press, 1938).

12. William Gamson, *The Strategy of Protest* (Homewood, IL: Dorsey, 1975).

13. Bruce Hamilton,, "Is the Property Tax a Benefit Tax?" in George Zodrow, ed., *Local Provision of Public Services: The Tiebout Model After Twenty-Five Years* (New York: Academic Press, 1983).

14. Paul Peterson, *City Limits* (Chicago: University of Chicago Press, 1981).

15. John Logan and Harvey Molotch, *Urban Fortunes: The Political Economy of Place* (Berkeley: University of California Press, 1981).

16. John David Greenstone and Paul Peterson, *Race and Authority on Urban Politics: Community Participation and the War on Poverty* (New York: Russell Sage, 1973).

17. John Meyer and Brian Rowan, "Institutionalized Organizations: Formal Structure as Myth and Ceremony," *American Journal of Sociology* 83 (September 1977): 340–63.

18. Robert Crowson and William Boyd, "Urban Schools as Organizations: Political Perspectives," in William Boyd and Charles Kerchner, ed., *The Politics of Excellence and Choice* (London: Falmer Press, 1988).

19. Larry Cuban, *Urban School Chiefs Under Fire* (Chicago: University of Chicago Press, 1976).

20. Barbara Jackson and James Cibulka, "Leadership Turnover and Business Mobilization: The Changing Political Ecology of Urban School Systems," in James Cibulka, Rodney Reed, and Kenneth Wong, eds., *The Politics of Urban Education in the United States* (London: Falmer Press, 1992).

21. Laurence Iannaccone, "Excellence: An Emergent Educational Issue," *Politics of Education Bulletin* 12 (1985): 1, 3–8.

SELECTED BIBLIOGRAPHY

Banfield, Edward, and Wilson, James. *City Politics*. Cambridge: Harvard University Press and the Massachusetts Institute of Technology Press, 1963.

Barnard, Chester. *The Functions of the Executive*. Cambridge: Harvard University Press, 1938.

Boyd, William, and Kerchner, Charles, eds. *The Politics of Excellence and Choice*. London: Falmer Press, 1988.

Callahan, Richard. *Education and the Cult of Efficiency*. Chicago: University of Chicago Press, 1962.

Crowson, Robert, and Boyd, William. "Urban Schools as Organizations: Political Perspectives." In William Boyd and Charles Kerchner, eds., *The Politics of Excellence and Choice*. London: Falmer Press, 1988.

Cuban, Larry. *Urban School Chiefs Under Fire*. Chicago: University of Chicago Press, 1976.

Gramson, William. *The Strategy of Protest*. Homewood, IL: Dorsey, 1975.

Greenstone, J. David, and Peterson, Paul. *Race and Authority in Urban Politics: Community Participation and the War on Poverty*. New York: Russell Sage, 1973.

Hamilton, Bruce. "Is the Property Tax a Benefit Tax?" In George Zodrow, ed., *Local*

Provision of Public Services: The Tiebout Model After Twenty-five Years. New York: Academic Press, 1983.

Iannaccone, Laurence. "Excellence: An Emergent Educational Issue." *Politics of Education Bulletin* 12 (1985): 1, 3–8.

Jackson, Barbara, and Cibulka, James. "Leadership Turnover and Business Mobilization: The Changing Political Ecology of Urban School Systems." In James Cibulka, Rodney Reed, and Kenneth Wong, eds., *The Politics of Urban Education in the United States*. London: Falmer Press, 1992.

Katz, Michael. *Class, Bureaucracy and Schools: The Illusion of Educational Change in America*. New York: Praeger, 1971.

Logan, John, and Molotch, Harvey. *Urban Fortunes: The Political Economy of Place*. Berkeley: University of California Press, 1987.

Meyer, John, and Rowan, Brian. "Institutionalized Organizations: Formal Structure as Myth and Ceremony." *American Journal of Sociology* 83 (September 1977): 340–63.

Peterson, Paul. *City Limits*. Chicago: University of Chicago Press, 1981.

Rothstein, Stan. *The Power to Punish*. New York: University Press of America, 1984.

Spring, Joel. *The American School, 1642–1983: Varieties of Historical Interpretation of the Foundations and Development of American Education*. New York: Longman, 1986.

Tyack, David. *The One Best System*. Cambridge: Harvard University Press, 1971.

Tyack, David, and Hansot, Elizabeth. *Managers of Virtue: Public School Leadership in America, 1820–1980*. New York: Basic Books, 1982.

Weeres, Joseph. "Economic Choice and the Dissolution of Community." In William Boyd and Charles Kerchner, eds., *The Politics of Excellence and Choice in Education*. London: Falmer Press, 1988.

8

Teacher Competency in New York City Schools: Administrator and Supervisory Perceptions

Laurence J. Newman

INTRODUCTION

Schools have recently been under attack for the quality of education that students receive. Looking for causes, teacher competency has been singled out as one explanation of the decline in academic achievement by our nation's students. Among the factors that have contributed to this scrutiny of teacher performance are the advent of student minimum competency tests, numerous reports of students who have been granted high school diplomas and cannot read, inadequate teacher applicants who fail to pass basic skills tests, and the tottering general confidence in our public schools.[1]

Of all the reasons given for the dismissal of a tenured teacher, incompetence is most often cited by school administrators and supervisors.[2] Incompetence is a term that is vague and usually applied to those teachers who have displayed less than desirable professional and personal characteristics in their overall classroom performance. Unfortunately, there are no objective standards by which teacher competence can be assessed.[3] School officials in individual schools rarely agree upon a definition of incompetence that can be universally applied to all teachers in all cases. Incompetence is a concept that does not contain a precise technical meaning.[4] For instance, in section 3012 of the New York State Education Law, incompetence is enumerated as one of the three major reasons for teacher dismissal; however, within the law, there are no guidelines to determine what type of teacher behavior specifically constitutes incompetence. Even in the smallest school districts throughout the United States, the lack of an exact definition of incompetence severely restricts the number of tenured teachers who can be successfully removed from their teaching position.

In legal cases that have involved incompetence, the courts have been establishing definitions of incompetence based on the specific situations that have been present in each individual case.[5] Michael C. Nolte claims that incompetency has no legal definition.[6] Therefore, a jury would have to be instructed as to what to look for concerning the facts of a particular case that would assist them in rendering an impartial verdict. An additional impediment in arriving at a verdict of incompetence is the legal presumption that the teacher's service was satisfactory because he or she held a valid teaching certificate.[7] Success in the dismissal of a tenured teacher for incompetency ultimately depends upon an administrator's ability to convince an impartial hearing committee that he or she has provided sufficient proof relating to the teacher's incompetence.[8] Because of this lack of a precise definition of incompetence, removing a tenured teacher from his or her job on the grounds of incompetency generally becomes such a herculean task that administrators and supervisors are extremely reluctant even to initiate formal dismissal proceedings.

COMPETENCY IN URBAN SCHOOLS

This chapter reports on a study of how teacher competency is defined in the largest school district in the United States, the New York City Board of Education. This city school district contains over 60,000 teachers, over 1 million students, and over 1,000 school buildings.

In order to discover how teacher competency is perceived and defined in the New York City school system, personal interviews were conducted with twenty administrators and supervisors at various levels in the New York City school system. Individuals who were in administrative positions and have retired from the school system within the last three years were also included in these interviews. To give some kind of balance to the opinions articulated by these administrators and supervisors, two representatives from the United Federation of Teachers were interviewed as well.

Sample selection involved the snowball sampling technique. Robert C. Bogdan and Steven K. Biklen described this technique as asking the first person who has been interviewed to recommend a second person to be interviewed.[9] This process is repeated over and over at the end of each interview until a theoretical saturation point is reached in the research. Andrew Strauss and James Corbin[10] contend that theoretical saturation is reached when "(1) no new or relevant data seem to emerge regarding a category; (2) the category development is dense, insofar as all of the paradigm elements are accounted for, along with variation and process; (3) the relationships between categories are well established and validated."

Initial entry was made by invitation from individuals who volunteered to participate in this study. In some instances, entry was made by an introduction through a third party who had a particular interest in the topic that was being studied. Formal requests for entry were made to other individuals who were not accessible through the first two channels but who were essential to the study.

Data collection procedures consisted of in-depth interviews with individuals who are or have been involved in the evaluation of a teacher's classroom performance. Individuals who were interviewed included high school principals, middle school principals, elementary school principals, assistant principals on all levels, high school department chairpeople, superintendents and assistant superintendents employed by the local community school districts, and representatives from the teacher's union who are involved in the remediation of less than competent teachers.

What is a competent or effective teacher? According to Benjamin Gudridge, "Research into teacher effectiveness often attempts to separate the sentimental ('loves children') from the scientific ('gets results')."[11] However, according to the individuals interviewed in this study, loving children and getting results were only some of the elements that go into making a competent teacher. It therefore should come as no surprise that all of the administrators and supervisors who were interviewed sought to define teacher competence in terms of their own observations and perceptions of how teachers should perform in the classroom. In some instances, the perceptions of teacher competence differed by varying degrees depending upon what grade level the administrator or supervisor was responsible for. Yet in other instances, there was no difference as to what grade level was involved in deciding upon a definition of incompetence. However, there were certain characteristics that transcended all grade levels of the school system. The one constant that was evident throughout all of these interviews was that each respondent found it impossible to come up with an all-encompassing statement that would provide a concrete or absolute definition of teacher competence.

ATTENDANCE

A common characteristic of teacher competence cited by administrators and supervisors who were interviewed was a good attendance record. An elementary school principal who has been in his position for over five years said that "a competent teacher is defined as someone who . . . arrives on time and has excellent superior attendance." Another elementary school principal who has been in his position for about the same period of time stated, "One who has excellent attendance." A high school principal who has been in the city school system for over twenty years stated that "it is extremely difficult to run a school effectively when 10 to 15 percent of your staff is absent on any given day." When questioned why so many teachers in their schools were absent on a given day, their reply was that some of these teachers were legitimately ill but that there was another group of teachers who, for one reason or another, had either lost interest in teaching or were frustrated with how the school system operates. This concern with teacher attendance is indicative of a principal's constant effort to provide adequate teacher coverage for all of his or her classes on a daily basis during the school year. Teacher attendance is a major concern to school principals in New York City because, according to the principals who were interviewed, it is extremely difficult to attract qualified substitute teachers to teach on a day-to-day basis in the city school system.

KNOWLEDGE OF SUBJECT MATTER

In their definitions of teacher competence, some administrators and supervisors seemed to be extremely concerned with a teacher's scholarship and mastery of the curriculum of a particular grade level. A high school principal claimed that one of the criteria he uses in determining teacher competence is the teacher's knowledge of his or her subject matter: "A competent teacher is one who has scholarship." When the principal was asked to define what he meant by scholarship, he believed that, to be effective in the classroom, the teacher should have an extensive background in the subject that he or she is teaching.

An elementary school principal also felt that in order for a teacher to be considered competent, he or she should be "well versed in his or her content area whether it be in elementary or secondary curriculum." Another elementary school principal also believes that a competent teacher is one "who is well prepared, is taking course work to improve his or her understanding of a particular area." Thus, scholarship is an important component of teacher competency that pervades all grade levels from elementary to high school.

MOTIVATE TO LEARN (TEACHING ABILITY)

One of the most mentioned criteria included in the definition of a competent teacher is the teacher's ability successfully to motivate students to learn. One high school principal believed that "a competent teacher is one who is able to motivate young people so they want to be there [in class] and want to learn." A retired high school principal said that teacher competency is "the ability to motivate youngsters to learn the knowledge, skills, concepts, and values that society has accepted as the standards to live by."

Another retired high school principal saw a competent teacher as "one who is able to accomplish learning objectives with whatever students he or she has in front of them." The principal pointed out that there are various levels of competence, as well as a multitude of different teaching styles. In his words, "No two teachers operate the same, and yet, each can be effective in his or her own way." Nevertheless, this distinction concerning different teaching styles was not addressed by a retired community school superintendent when he was asked to provide his definition of what, in his opinion, constituted a competent teacher: "A competent teacher is one who is able to, and has the ability to, motivate kids to learn." In this superintendent's view, the fact that teachers have different teaching styles should have little or no effect on the ability of an individual teacher to motivate students.

One of the high school principals interviewed believes that student motivation and student learning are the only important things to consider when you are defining teacher competence: ''A competent teacher is one who can transmit subject matter to students in such a manner that they want to learn the subject. They are [the students] interested in what they are doing and hopefully will be able to retain what they have learned.''

Another high school principal, who by her own admission, is somewhat of an idealist, also described teacher competency in terms of student motivation, but she placed a greater emphasis on teaching students how to think. This principal, who has been in her position for only one year, comes to her position with over twenty years in the school system. She was a department chairperson and was given a promotion to work in the offices of the central board of education. In defining teacher competence, she stated: ''A competent teacher is one who makes the most use of instructional time. Involves the kids in problem-solving situations, teaches the kids how to think, not just their own subject matter, but how to think and how to solve their own problems.''

It was evident that all the administrators and supervisors interviewed believed, to some degree, that teaching and motivating students to think were very important. However, to many of these administrators and supervisors, motivating and teaching students how to think were just one facet of the broader educational picture that encompasses meeting the needs of all types of students.

An elementary school principal believes that one of the characteristics of a competent teacher is that the teacher is able consistently to meet the needs of his or her students: ''A competent teacher is one who is able to meet the needs of the children, is able to provide the children with an education that is current.'' The ability of a teacher to empower students to learn is a major concern of almost all of the administrators and supervisors who were interviewed. According to these administrators and supervisors, it is not enough for a teacher to be able to teach; a teacher must be able to demonstrate that his or her students are learning. As one community district administrator stated, ''A teacher who is competent asks him or herself, 'What have my students learned?' A competent teacher is concerned with learning, not just teaching.'' When asked to define teacher competence, another elementary school principal posed the question, ''Is the teacher actively getting the children involved in their own learning and becoming a facilitator?'' This principal went on to say that ''competence is when you become a facilitator of learning.''

In an interview with an official of the United Federation of Teachers, she seemed annoyed that she was being asked to put some kind of generic label on a teacher that would imply that this teacher was competent. After pursuing the issue for some time, this person reluctantly went on to say:

Teacher competency is subjectively defined by the needs of the individuals whom you are teaching. Competency depends on who you are teaching, and one had better not decide what is needed without knowing the population. A competent teacher is the person who meets the needs of his or her clients, and his or her ability to meet those needs shouldn't be determined without knowing who the client body is. We should be talking about relationships with kids, we should talk about needs, and we should talk about being a teacher by itself.

What seems to be the most important factor in determining teacher competence to this individual from the teacher's union is knowing who your students are and what their needs are that you as the teacher should be there to fulfill. In this teacher's union official's definition, there seem to be two areas of concern about the factors that constitute a competent teacher. One area of concern in this definition seeks to define what a competent teacher should be in relationship to the needs of his or her students. According to this teacher's union official, students may have many needs that may not be obvious to the teacher, such as language problems faced by new immigrant students, hunger problems faced by impoverished families, racial inequities, violence in the schools, and the rising tide of drug abuse, which are all matters of immediate concern to all school-children. The other area of concern to this union official addresses the notion that we should be aware of who the teacher is in terms of himself or herself and his or her ability to deal effectively with these needs of the students.

In one way or another, all of the respondents believed that being able to meet the needs of the students is one of the strongest qualities in a competent teacher. Not being capable of meeting the needs of the students in the classroom on a day-to-day basis, a teacher fails to inculcate students with a sense of self and who they are. Every administrator and supervisor agreed that it is fairly difficult for a teacher to assess the individual needs of all the students in his or her classes. One elementary school principal characterized some of the difficulties in meeting the needs of the students by saying:

We work under conditions which are overcrowded classrooms, and I don't say it just to find an excuse, and you could go to any one of my classrooms today, and you will find thirty-seven children in a third grade class. . . . We work under conditions in which children come from many, many backgrounds. Many students are newly arrived to this country. We are also asking our teachers to act as interpreters, act as social workers, act as mom and dad in order for the children to survive.

Meeting the needs of the students was a frustrated concern that confounded all of the administrators and supervisors in this study. All of these individuals found great difficulty dealing with this problem and attributed much of this difficulty to the changing demographics of the student population in the city during the last twenty years. However, all of the individuals interviewed were in strong agreement that meeting the needs of the students begins with good classroom management and student control.

MAINTAINING DISCIPLINE/CONTROL IN THE CLASSROOM

Classroom management and student control are areas of critical concern to administrators and supervisors in this study. Each of these individuals made reference to the incidents of crime and violence in the New York City schools, which they felt were increasing at an alarming rate each year. Almost all of the administrators and supervisors interviewed said that these incidents are becoming more and more frequent both inside and outside the classroom. As one high school principal stated: ''All you have to do is look at the television and read the newspapers to see all of the violence that is going on in our schools. You rarely read about anything good that is taking place in the schools.'' All of those individuals interviewed agreed that there is also an acute awareness on the part of the Board of Education that more and more teachers are feeling threatened for their own personal safety. All of the administrators and supervisors interviewed believed that one of the most desirable characteristics of a competent teacher is the ability to maintain discipline in the classroom. According to one intermediate school principal, keeping student discipline problems to a minimum in any school begins with a teacher who has good classroom control. ''Can the teacher control the class? Does the teacher have management skills?'' are just some of the questions that this principal asked as he was trying to define teacher competence. Although this principal seemed overly concerned with student discipline and class control, he stated that when compared with other schools in the city, his school was about average in the number of disciplinary infractions committed by students in the school.

Another assistant principal stated: ''There are many things that go into making a teacher competent. First of all, is the ability to have control in the classroom where something can be taught.'' Yet, teachers working to maintain classroom discipline may go too far, as illustrated by what one high school principal had to say:

You don't want to have a person who works with kids because there is a certain amount of control factor, where there is a captive audience, where they [the teachers] have very little control in their own life, very little ego gratification and very little self-esteem. So when they go into a classroom, they have a captive audience, and they can expound, and they can talk, and they can carry on, and the kids have to listen, and if the kids don't listen, it is the kids' problem.

PSYCHOLOGICALLY/MORALLY HEALTHY

The teacher's ego is another area that was addressed by other administrators and supervisors in this study. In conjunction with class control and student discipline, many administrators and supervisors who were interviewed believe that the teacher has to exhibit superior personal qualities as well. A teacher needs to have a good image of himself or herself and have a positive attitude toward educating students. One high school principal explained it this way: ''Attitude is very important. Teachers have to have respect for people, not just children, but respect for people and the understanding of the human psyche, and how people [students] need to be treated if they are going to react in a positive way.''

An intermediate school principal went further and said, "Not only is it important for a teacher to understand the psyche of a child, but it was equally important that the teacher himself or herself be a person who is well integrated psychologically." Equally important in this definition of competence was that a teacher is, as an elementary school principal stated, "fairly well organized in his or her own life, or in his or her capacity to handle a body of work, a body of children, and all the other peripherals that come along that you are not prepared for every day." Relating to the idea of a teacher's being organized, this elementary school principal went on to say that "a competent teacher is one who sets examples daily for his or her students that one can be proud of."

A high school principal probably stated the obvious when she said, "If a person is first graduating from college and they are young, you hope that they like kids. You hope that anyone who works with kids likes kids." An intermediate school principal also addressed the issue of liking children and asked, "Does the teacher have a feel for children, does he or she like children?" Concern with teachers' being prepared, liking children, and having a positive attitude toward their job as an indication of competence were qualities that, remarkably, almost all of the administrators and supervisors agreed upon.

WELL ORGANIZED/RESPONSIBLE TO BUREAUCRATIC CLERICAL PAPER DEMANDS

To some of the administrators and supervisors, being flexible to deal effectively with matters that did not directly pertain to the classroom was also a sign of a competent teacher. Referring to this issue, a high school principal believed that, "a competent teacher is one who is able to deal with the gaggle of clerical chores and tasks as well as the housekeeping responsibilities that unfortunately pertain to each classroom setting." All of the administrators and supervisors interviewed agreed that in New York City today, teachers not only have to be proficient in teaching their classes but must be equally proficient in dealing with school administrators, local communities, and, in many cases, parents. An elementary school principal explained it this way: "A competent teacher must be able to deal with irate parents, someone who basically gets along with the administration, who is willing to work in a system that what is said on Monday, is changed on Tuesday and is back on Wednesday, and at the same time, be their own person and respect their own individuality." This principal agreed that these are not everyday occurrences, and what he meant by this statement was that a competent teacher should be flexible in both thinking and actions to be able to handle all of the nonteaching activities that may occur within the school on a day-to-day basis.

RELATIONSHIP TO ADMINISTRATOR AND SUPERVISOR STATUS

Teachers are subjectively defined by their administrators and supervisors in terms of how well they perform in their classroom. As one elementary school principal stated: "I never base competency on standardized test scores. I base competency on what I see happening in a classroom when I walk in there. Are all the children enthusiastic, is the teacher enthusiastic, is there a give-and-take between the students and the teacher, or is the teacher a lecturer, a drill-and-kill type of person?" Thus, teacher competency is based on the perceptions of the administrator or supervisor who is observing a particular teacher during the teaching of a lesson.

Many of the administrators and supervisors who were interviewed agreed that a teacher may be considered less than competent teaching a class one day and be considered competent teaching a different class another day. This only adds to the dilemma in securing a realistic definition of competence or incompetence that would apply to all teachers at all times. Referring to reaching a definition of teacher competence, a teacher's union official said:

One of the reasons why we get into trouble is we develop checklists of teacher competencies away from the classroom. In fact, they frequently come from the universities, and we take them into the classroom and we say, "These are the criteria that we have established for teacher competence. Now we will apply them to you. Oh, by the way, the kids are here, oh fine," and we check all of the items. That is the problem. We are constantly looking for a definition of teacher competency where we shouldn't be.

Where should we be looking for a definition of teacher competence? From these interviews, it would seem that there are many teachers whose proclivity for teaching is overtly evident. On the other hand, there seems to be a wide range of definitions of competency concerning those teachers who, at one time or another, may have varying degrees of difficulty in the classroom.

PERCENTAGE OF COMPETENT TEACHERS

The consensus among the administrators and supervisors in the New York City school system who were interviewed for this study seems to be that 15 to 20 percent (some individuals feel that this figure is significantly higher in their own schools) of the teachers presently teaching in the New York City school system could be considered to be less than competent. However, all of the respondents in this study agreed that within this range of 15 to 20 percent, there are various degrees of incompetency. If we are to believe these numbers, this would suggest that out of approximately 60,000 teachers, 9,000 to 12,000 teachers are performing their teaching duties at less than a competent level. Considering that there are approximately 1 million students attending the New York City schools, this would imply that 15 to 20 percent of all students are believed by administrators and supervisors in this study to be receiving an education that may be inferior to the education that is being received by the majority of the students in the city system. If we divide the number of students by the number of teachers in the school system, the pupil-teacher ratio would be approximately

16.67 to 1. If we multiply this figure by the number of teachers who are considered to be less than competent, there would be approximately 150,000 to 200,000 students in the city school system who are assumed to be taught by teachers who are performing at a level that is deemed by their administrators and supervisors to be less than competent.

In this study, administrators and supervisors were asked to give a percentage of the number of teachers whom they consider to be competent in their own school. Some respondents who were not working in a school gave percentages based on their experience within the New York City school system. For example, a retired community school superintendent, referring to his total experience in the city system, believed that

the percentage [of competent teachers] is quite small. I would say only 25 to 30 percent are what I would consider truly competent. I would say that about 80 percent are focused, and I don't mean that only 25 to 30 percent are competent; I mean that those figures represent the incompetent teachers that I have come into contact with. Most teachers do an adequate job, but working in this system makes their job more difficult.

When asked about the percentage of teachers in his school that he considered competent, an elementary school principal said, "Off the top of my head, 85 percent." Another elementary school principal, responding to the same question, said: "In my overall experience, I must say that it is probably closer to 75 percent of the staff who are competent teachers. The other 25 percent present more of a challenge, and my work is set up for me to try and improve the attitude of those teachers." A recently retired high school principal replied to the percentage of competent teachers who were present in his school: "Well, let me answer it two ways: on the first level, the teacher that I came in contact with when I was an intermediate administrator, a chairperson, I'd say 50 to 80 percent were competent. As a principal, it is more difficult to come up with percentages for the school." An intermediate school principal said that "90 percent of the teachers that I am able to evaluate" are competent.

A high school department chairperson made this assessment: "About 10 to 15 percent of your teachers are superstars. The broad range of 70 to 80 percent, say 70 percent, are adequate. Fifteen percent are less than competent on an advanced level and need improvement." An intermediate school department chairperson believed that "80 percent in my department" are competent.

Probably the most interesting assessment made concerning the percentage of competent teachers present in a particular school came from an intermediate school principal:

The percentage now, would probably be . . . I have to give you demographics. . . . Teachers who basically trained in the manner in which I was, by having role models who were competent teachers, . . . the percentage would be better than 60 percent. With teachers who are in the profession now, who have had role models which are not on the level of what I defined as competent teaching or competent training, the percentage would probably be less than 40 percent.

An elementary school principal who has been employed in the same district since she entered the city school system gave this percentage analysis: "I would say that 75 to 80 percent of the teachers in this school have always been competent. . . . If you wanted to rank the competence, I would say that probably 15 to 20 percent are really superior and could be master teachers. Whereas, at the other end of the curve, there are 5 to 10 percent who barely make it, or shouldn't have been here at all and still are."

A more pessimistic percentage was offered by another elementary school principal, who said, "Percentage-wise, I would say I come across 50 percent of those kind of people [competent teachers]." Echoing this pessimistic point of view, a high school principal believed that "very, very few" teachers in the school system were competent. However, in response to the question of percentage of teacher competence in his school, another elementary school principal said, "I guess 75 percent of them are able to meet children's or partially meet children's needs." Two other high school principals believed that the majority of teachers in the high schools were competent. One high school principal believed that "75 to 85 percent of the teachers are competent." "The majority, in terms of percent, 75 to 80 percent" was the reply of another high school principal. Another high school principal said that "today, the overwhelming majority of teachers are competent."

NOTES

1. Benjamin Gudridge, *Teacher Competency: Problems and Solutions* (Arlington, VA: American Association of School Administrators, 1980), 4–8.

2. Edward Bridges, *The Incompetent Teacher* (London: Falmer Press, 1992), 14–17.

3. James A. Gross, *Teachers on Trial: Values, Standards, and Equity in Judging Conduct and Competency* (New York: Cornell University Press, 1988), 21–23.

4. David Rosenberger and Robert A. Plimpton, "Teacher Incompetence and the Courts," in *Journal of Law and Education* 4 (1975): 468–86.

5. Stephen B. Neill and John Custis, *Staff Dismissals: Problems and Solutions* (Arlington, VA: American Association of School Administrators, 1978), 41–43.

6. Michael C. Nolte, *Guide to School Law* (West Nyack, NY: Parker, 1969).

7. Edward E. Reutter and George Hamilton, *The Law of Public Education* (Mineola, NY: Foundation Press, 1976).

8. Bridges.

9. Robert C. Bogdan and Steven K. Biklen, *Qualitative Research for Education: An Introduction to Theory and Methods* (Boston: Allyn and Bacon, 1982).

10. Andrew Strauss and James Corbin, *Basics of Qualitative Research* (Newbury Park, CA: Sage, 1990), 187–89.

11. Gudridge, 8–10.

III

MINORITY PERSPECTIVES

9

Multiculturalism in Urban Schools: A Puerto Rican Perspective

Antonio Nadal and Milga Morales-Nadal

INTRODUCTION

The celebration of the American bicentennial in Philadelphia and elsewhere throughout the country in 1976 provided a watershed for the debate surrounding the nation's treatment of its marginalized racial and ethnic communities. The debate surrounding the "Encounter" or the so-called Discovery of America some sixteen years later is no less controversial. However, the difference is that the bicentennial counterdemonstrations were from marginalized U.S. schools. Schoolchildren were unaware of the significance of the slogan "a bicentennial without colonies," referring to the oppressed and indigenous minorities both in the United States and in Puerto Rico. In 1992, however, teachers and students wrestled with Christopher Columbus's status as hero or villain. In New York City, public school teachers are being confronted by parents suggesting that "Ten Little Indians" is an inappropriate, if not racist, song and should not be the centerpiece of a Thanksgiving Day play. On the other hand, some parents are also demonstrating against any references to gays and lesbians in New York City's "Children of the Rainbow" multicultural curriculum.[1] While differences in perceptions abound regarding these issues, the fact is that multiculturalism is itself an issue and at issue today in U.S. urban public schools.

In this chapter we seek to provide a context for this development from our position as Puerto Rican educators working with teachers in urban schools and to suggest that the problems with the acceptance of multiculturalism that are surfacing are endemic to this society and should not prevent those of us interested in pursuing ways of assuring the inclusion of all children in our schools from doing so. To assure that this happens, it should be noted that we must be critical and evaluative of the concept while developing acceptance and respect into our schools. We attempt to address the concept as it relates to the Puerto Rican community and the strategies for its implementation.

THE MULTICULTURAL DEBATE IN AMERICAN PUBLIC SCHOOLS

While the New York State Education Department deliberated for several years to review the social studies curriculum for its public schools so that it would more equitably reflect the diversity of the school population, from the very panel doing so there arose at least one voice that countered these initiatives. In his book, *The Disuniting of America*, Arthur M. Schlesinger, Jr., warns against a culturally pluralistic view that does not, in the end, contribute to the "common American culture."[2]

In his view, the underpinnings of a dominant Anglo culture in American society have served the country well, and rumblings to the contrary have come from ethnic intellectuals that constitute a small, academic elite. What Professor Schlesinger fails to point out is that these elites were once nonexistent and that their very presence as an identifiable, dissident force, product of a militant movement for self-determination and cultural reaffirmation in the American academy, hears testament to the failed ethic of his common American culture. From other quarters, E. D. Hirsch's *Cultural Literacy* posits that knowledge of a highly selective laundry list of concepts and literary works is the key to success in American education.[3] Albeit a well-intentioned attempt to address the informational shortcomings inherent to the schooling process in America, Hirsch's book is notably skewed toward the Eurocentric, Anglo tradition.

In large measure, the fuel igniting the multicultural debate was provided by the Portland, Oregon, African-American Baseline Essays. In these writings, intended for use in Portland schools, the authors sought to "re-discover and reconstruct" some of the lost history of the African disaspora.[4] Asa Hilliard, one of the most prominent of these writers, was the object of inordinate criticism for his contention that Africa was the true birthplace of scientific inquiry and artistic expression. The validation of this thesis would certainly entail an overhaul of the conventional wisdom and, therefore, a reexamination of the premises on which traditional public and urban school curricula are based.

No less an object of vituperation and ire is Dr. Leonard Jeffries of the City College of New York. Dr. Jeffries, for many years a professor of African history, incurred the wrath of some of his colleagues when several comments from his lectures were taken out of context. He was then portrayed as a supporter of an Afrocentric curriculum model that sought to debase the Western and Eurocentric tradition. Most of Jeffries's detractors do not negate that there indeed is a Eurocentricity in U.S. school curricula, but they defend this focus and suggest only that "in the past our history has been taught as a drama in which white men had all the good roles . . . but the picture was incomplete, and it was not honest."[5] This moderate view accommodates a curriculum that is more expansive and inclusive but continues to assume an assimilationist posture suggesting that there is a common "smelting pot," as Schlesinger calls it.

In June 1991, the New York State Social Studies Review and Development

Committee published *One Nation, Many Peoples: A Declaration of Cultural Interdependence*. In addition to Schlesinger, who acted as consultant to the committee, many notable educators, sociologists, and historians, as well as teachers, constituted the working group that was commissioned by Thomas Sobol, commissioner of education of New York State, to examine the existing social studies curriculum and make recommendations designed to increase the understanding of students with regard to American culture and its history, the history of diverse groups that comprise American society, and the culture, identity, and history of people throughout the world.[6] What is truly innovative about this document is its stress on multiple perspectives in the presentation of the nation's historiography. Multicultural knowledge is proposed as a vehicle, and the goal is the development of learners with the capacity to view the world and understand it from multiple perspectives.

From our perspective as Puerto Ricans and as teacher-educators, we may suggest that without multicultural education, people of color will continue to prevail. In fact, sometimes our ghettoization and socioeconomic marginalization have contributed to the maintenance of our cultural, linguistic identity and our survival as a people. We, therefore, do not need multicultural education if it in fact does not lead to empowerment. We will consider the kind of multicultural agenda that includes a sharing of power and not just a sharing of cultural artifacts. James Banks of the University of Washington at Seattle and a leading author in the field of multiethnic teaching, has articulated a model that includes just such an agenda. He suggests that "the shared power model, if successfully implemented, would result in the redistribution of power so that excluded ethnic groups in Western societies would control such institutions as schools, courts, industries, health facilities, and the mass media. They would not necessarily control all institutions within their society, but would control those in which they participated and that are needed to fulfill their individual and group needs."[7] Banks, on the other hand, cautions that groups in power, in schools, or in society at large may not be eager to participate in such a model and, therefore, the challenge remains for us to encourage power sharing with disempowered minority/ethnic groups while attending to the maintenance of a socially cohesive society. While Alan Sleeter and Lee Grant and many others have since supported this notion, using a multicultural and social reconstructionist model, the inclusion of class issues in the discourse on multicultural education has not filtered through to many "multiculturalists." Nonetheless, many political conservatives understand the significance of this power sharing. Reactions to multicultural curricula throughout the country are often based on the feeling of insecurity and a perceived threat to the status quo as a result of the possible changes in the institutional structures and in the design of those structures. Banks appears to agree when he states that "the resistance to multicultural content in curriculum is basically ideological."[8] He posits that this ideology may be reflected in the assimilationist philosophy often envisioned as the American melting pot and promoted as a tool to foster patriotism and loyalty to the nation-state. The difficulty has been that the melting pot has not included all those it purports to represent. More to the point, many minority/ethnic groups, particularly people of color, have been excluded to a large degree from the economic structures that allow them to achieve economic equality and prosperity. Multicultural curricula continue to pose a challenge to mainstream Americans who may view them as too inclusive and too empowering of ethnic groups.

Those of us who have witnessed what happens to our children in the traditional urban public school systems in this country are searching for ways to restructure the system. The "savage inequalities" of which Jonathan Kozol writes—the unequal distribution even in public urban institutions—are not surprising to those of us who work in or visit these schools daily. It is clear to us that imposed changes from the top, even by the most forceful and caring school managers, cannot fully address these inequalities. We suggest that allowing the recalcitrant strain to continue to feed on the system is promoting the notion of two parallel school systems—one for the poor and most people of color and one for the upper middle class, one black and one white.

Puerto Ricans, as a people of color, continue to remind the Anglo-dominated society that race, as well as class, is the mischief-maker for the assimilationist philosophy. As American citizens—a citizenship imposed in 1917 through the Jones Act in order to draft Puerto Ricans into the military—we should have, over the last several decades, assimilated and partaken of the common "American dream" as envisioned by Anglo society. In the next section we attempt to address the myths about Puerto Rican assimilation and suggest related theories that may provide an explanation for the derailment of the assimilation process.

THE PUERTO RICAN STRUGGLE FOR SELF-DETERMINATION AND DEFINITION IN THE UNITED STATES

In *Minority Education and Caste*, John Ogbu refers to American-Indians, Mexican-Americans, and Puerto Ricans as castelike minorities within the framework of the U.S. socioeconomic order. He posits that along with American blacks these groups share "the experience of having been brought into United States society against their will and then relegated to subordinate status."[9] Paradoxically, these groups did not have to "earn" American citizenship as a passport to ascend the ladder of social mobility, but their subjugation and conquest relegated them to an inferior status and an adaptation to a sociocultural environment that negated their language and culture. As such, in the case of Puerto Ricans, there is no reward for discarding a native language and culture that are both a product of our castelike existence and a reaction to the society that has created it. The sociocultural and political ambivalence that characterizes the relationship between the United States and Puerto Rico celebrates, on one hand, the free association and commonwealth status that bind the two nations and denounces, on the other hand, any attempt to impose English as the official language of Puerto Rico. This issue has a long history dating to the colonial policies of American administrations immediately after the conclusion of the Spanish-American-Cuban War of 1898 and resolved somewhat ambiguously shortly before the creation of the Commonwealth in 1952, when Spanish was established as the official language of instruction in Puerto Rican schools, with English as a required second language. That struggle has had its counterpart in the United States as Puerto Rican communities fought for and obtained the right to bilingual education as a way to counteract the unconscionable failure rates of Puerto Rican children coming from communities where their native language was being maintained in spite of school efforts to the contrary. Within the multicultural discourse it is crucial to understand that Puerto Ricans may be included among what Ogbu calls "involuntary minorities," that is, "groups incorporated to the host society involuntarily, most frequently by means of colonization, conquest or slavery."[10] Moreover, as racially heterogeneous people, Puerto Ricans do not readily fit into the fixed typologies of race in America. The consequences of this are readily seen in curricular materials that present images of Anglo children in cultural situations and environments that are totally alien to the reality of the Puerto Rican child's racially and culturally diverse background. The dilemma for the Puerto Rican is exacerbated by what Clara Rodriguez calls "a primary point of contrast." She suggests that "in Puerto Rico, racial identification is subordinate to cultural identification, while in the U.S., racial identification, to a large extent, determines cultural identification."[11] Thus, when Puerto Ricans are asked the very sensitive and possibly divisive question, "What are you?", Puerto Ricans of all colors and ancestry answer, "Puerto Rican." This should be construed not as a negation of one's blackness or whiteness but as an affirmation of one's ethnic identification. Similarly, in what may seem to be a contradiction, Puerto Ricans are more readily identifying themselves with the more inclusive term *Latino*. This indicates our concern and heightened level of awareness of a heritage that includes the African and indigenous cultures in addition to the European. The term *Hispanic* has traditionally reflected only the European heritage. The term *Latino* is also an empowering and enabling label allowing an identification with other groups, such as Mexican-Americans, and fostering the recognition of Latinos as a major "minority" group in this country. Given the class status of Puerto Ricans, more than half of whom live under the federally designated poverty level, the castelike relationship to the U.S. socioeconomic order, and the persistence of racism in American society, it is not surprising that Puerto Ricans have become a non-meldable minority. These conditions have contributed to a brand of militancy that originated in the civil rights movement of the 1960s but continues as Puerto Ricans strive to realize our political potential for the enfranchisement of the broad masses of the community. Since so little has been documented with regard to this relatively recent movement, the following seeks to describe some of the more salient aspects of its development, with particular emphasis on those struggles related to Puerto Ricans and education.

¡DESPIERTA BORICUA! ¡DEFIENDE LO TUYO!

In order to comprehend fully the significance of this slogan, "Arise, Puerto Ricans! Claim what is yours!", we must explore some of the issues that generated so much controversy and militancy during the 1960s, with a focus on the Puerto Rican community, that had in fact been the most active of the Latino groups in the Northeast at the time and also the largest in number.

The appointment of Luis Fuentes in the late 1960s, as the first Puerto Rican principal of the New York City public schools, is an important point of departure. His appointment was viewed as a milestone by those Puerto Ricans, such as ourselves, who had gone through an educational system that had exposed them to no people of color, from kindergarten through high school, and to very few, if any, positive images of Puerto Ricans residing in the United States.

Dreaming the American dream but finding a "thatched roof" up above gave rise to a generation of young, militant, and ideologically diverse Puerto Ricans. Pablo "Yoruba" Guzman, a former member of the Young Lords, a militant organization led by young Puerto Ricans in the 1960s, characterizes this generation by stating that "two characteristics are of prime importance to distinguish itself: 1) it has been a most radical generation, at least during the period in which it came to adolescence, between 1965 and 1973; and 2) it is the group realizing America's 'upward mobility' promise in greatest numbers (thus far)."[12] Guzman comments on the organizations that led the movement for civil rights, against the colonization of Puerto Rico, and for political empowerment in the Puerto Rican community, citing the Young Lords, the Puerto Rican Socialist Party (PSP), El Comite, and the Puerto Rican Student Union. We would like to add that Puerto Ricans, then and now, were also organized and organizing in their churches, in the school yards, in hometown organizations, such as Los Hijos de Guayanilla or other towns in Puerto Rico, and in local, community-based organizations for presumably social activities. In addition, ASPIRA, an educational youth advocacy and nationally recognized organization, and El Desfile Puertorriqueño, were groups into which other sectors of the community were organized. Unfortunately, some sectors viewed others suspiciously, and it was sometimes assumed that the other were not working in one's own interests. Many of the members of these groups and of other Puerto Rican "professional" organizations, however, were in the thick of the struggle for community control of schools in the late 1960s. Diana Caballero, the director of the Puerto Rican/Latino Roundtable, has written:

The struggles in the late 1960's by African American and Puerto Rican parents for community control came as a direct response to the continued failure of the school system to provide quality education to the urban poor. . . . Issues raised by parents included an irrelevant and racist curriculum and teachers and a hostile bureaucracy with professional power exercised through strong teachers' and administrators' unions, particularly the

United Federation of Teachers (UFT) and the Council of Supervisors and Administrators (CSA).[13]

Luis Fuentes's appointment must be viewed within the context of this struggle for community control versus centralization. Other Puerto Ricans, such as the first Puerto Rican president of the New York City Board of Education, Joseph Monserrate, and his special assistant, Professor Carmen Dinos, were also involved in this initiative. Yet community control and decentralization, the plan to create thirty-two school districts, each with a nine-member board in New York City, were not viewed in the same way by the Puerto Rican community. Many community activists anticipated that the teachers' union would control the school boards and few, if any, people of color would be elected to serve on those school boards.

Luis Fuentes states in *The Puerto Rican Struggle: Essays on Survival in the U.S,* "By combining the racial fears of . . . two populations (Jewish and ethnic Catholics) the UFT has hand-picked and financed six virtually lily-white slates of community school-board candidates since 1970."[14] The Puerto Rican community throughout the late 1960s and the early 1970s participated in dozens of demonstrations and even more militant actions in an attempt to become participants in the education of their children and to change the face of the school boards.

During the late 1960s, the Latino community was also fighting for bilingual education, and it was expected that the natural allies would be African-Americans, as was the case in the struggle for community control. But, at times, the language issue did not allow for that kind of communication to take place, and Puerto Ricans were seen as segregating themselves in programs designed to heighten their cultural identification and awareness. As was suggested above, while Puerto Ricans came from a strong tradition of militant unionism, they did not find allies that they could identify with among the United Federation of Teachers. The strong teachers' union appeared to be supporting the teachers and not the community. Demonstrations of Puerto Ricans were organized, and they found themselves at the doors of the UFT, city hall, and, eventually, Washington, DC. The scorecard, at the close of the 1960s, indicated that many teachers still believed Puerto Rican children to be inferior academically. The drop-out rate for Puerto Ricans between their junior and senior year in high school in 1969–1970 was 58.2 percent.[15] Criteria for the evaluation of potential educational attainment and intelligence were designed primarily for the white middle class. Not surprisingly, college admission rates for Puerto Ricans at the publically funded City University of New York (CUNY) were 4 percent in 1971, whereas almost 23 percent of all schoolchildren in the New York public school system were of Puerto Rican background.[16] At that time neither the broad working-class masses nor the minuscule population of militant Puerto Rican college students clearly understood the underlying sociocultural, economic, and political factors that fashioned the Puerto Rican reality alluded to earlier in this chapter. On the coattails of the civil rights and black power movements of the late 1960s and early 1970s, second-generation Puerto Rican college students in CUNY and elsewhere came of age in the demand for programs of study and revised curricula that would include the history, culture, and language of the Puerto Rican people. The creation of Puerto Rican Studies departments and programs predominantly in urban, public universities of the Northeast was a major victory in opening the public academy to the demands of the children of working-class minorities and people of color toward the recognition of ethnic diversity.[17] In the evolution of their pedagogy, the more successful and enduring programs were those that Josephine Nieves cited as structured around four primary principles: autonomy, methodology, theoretical framework, and community involvement.[18] For these programs to survive, they had to attain departmental status in the university and develop a tenured faculty that would pioneer in inter- and multidisciplinary teaching approaches. Their research would have to revise and create new paradigms in the humanities and the social sciences for the study of the Puerto Rican reality in all of its manifestations, both in the United States and in Puerto Rico. A natural extension for the acquisition of the new knowledge would be the laboratory of our communities. Via the study and analysis of the colonial condition under which our people live in Puerto Rico and the internal colonies of the United States, the Puerto Rican scholar-activist may effectively combine theory and praxis. The university, then, is not the ivory tower for empty, intellectual discourse but a broker between the Puerto Rican intellectual community and the broader communities that nurture our academic work, while both are involved in resource sharing.[19] In this context, Puerto Rican Studies was poised to address the burning issues in our communities and schools. More importantly, the nexus between the university and community provided fertile ground for us to recruit faculty with diverse academic backgrounds to educate our students in the "multiple perspectives" that are now a part of the new state curriculum for multicultural education. In addition to the teaching of history, culture, language and literature, society, politics and economics, Puerto Rican Studies departments became involved in offering course sequences for the education and training of prospective bilingual teachers. Noting the almost total disregard of urban school districts and schools of education for the recruitment and training of Spanish-speaking teachers even when, as in New York City, large percentages of (im)migrant children were of limited English proficiency, Puerto Rican Studies programs began to recruit a cadre of Latino teacher-educators who would bridge and supplement the offerings of traditional education departments in early childhood and elementary education divisions. This collaboration, by its very nature, employed a multicultural, interdisciplinary approach while developing the broader philosophical framework of bilingual education. Puerto Rican/Latino educators brought new insights and perspectives in areas such as first and second language acquisition, language variety, bilingualism and diglossia, inter- and intragroup differences among Latinos(as), learning styles, and new approaches to the assessment and evaluation of children from culturally and linguistically diverse backgrounds.

The fact that bilingual education has not been a focus in all Puerto Rican Studies departments, particularly in the Northeast, is unfortunate. Sonia Nieto suggests that given the interdisciplinary nature of these departments and their commitment to an education for liberation, it would make sense to unite these two perspectives, thereby "joining a philosophical and political awareness to the acquisition of concrete educational skills."[20] A larger issue, perhaps, is the reluctance of departments and schools of education to house and support bilingual teacher education programs. Conveniently perceiving them to be the "turf" of ethnic studies programs and perceiving the overwhelming reliance of students on these departments for counseling, school placement, future employment, and overall ethnic affiliation, departments of education do not see a need to fulfill their responsibilities to Puerto Rican/Latino education majors.[21]

At no time has the need been greater than at the present time to forge an educational agenda for our communities that cements the collaboration and co-operation between Puerto Rican faculty and administrators in the university and community-based organizations, local civic and political leaders, and parents. Drastic cutbacks at all levels of the educational establishment, product of the current economic recession, have savaged the support and outreach work in the universities and communities. Inner-city schools have disproportionately suffered most as young teachers with the least seniority and minority group background have been retrenched. With the paring of teaching faculties in the elementary and secondary schools, class sizes have ballooned, special programs (special education, bilingual education) have been slashed, and support services have been vastly diminished. For the Puerto Rican and other Latino communities this may signal the need to regroup and concentrate our efforts on the education of our children and adolescents for the twenty-first century. Our agenda, as outlined in what follows, will be multifaceted and multicultural.

INCLUDING PUERTO RICANS IN THE MULTICULTURAL CURRICULUM

In a recent interview, Dr. Virginia Sanchez-Korrol, a member of the New York State Social Studies Review and Development Committee, when asked about the difference between a multicultural curriculum and ethnic studies, responded that the two were related concepts with an important distinction. She suggested that multiculturalism, as it relates to education, is an approach whereas ethnic studies is the content.[22] Her statement serves as a reminder that multiculturalism ought not be used to obfuscate the diversity that is essential to, and representative of, ethnic studies. Neither should it be utilized as a neoassimilationist scheme focused on the submersion of ethnically related culture and language issues.

In her recent study on the sociopolitical context of bilingual education, Nieto further cautions that multicultural education is not a panacea for all things gone wrong in American education. Only when multicultural education is conceptualized as broad-based school reform with an underlying philosophy and focus on knowledge, reflection, and action (praxis) can it truly permeate the curriculum and extend into the lived realities of individual students and their communities.[23] The seven basic characteristics of multicultural education as suggested by Nieto include antiracist education, basic education (including multicultural literacy), education for the majority as well as the minority, education that is pervasive and comprehensive, education that promotes social justice, education that is process-oriented, and education that includes critical pedagogy.[24] In effect, it is an education that is transformative and inclusive.

Much of the debate to date surrounding multicultural education has centered on the seven characteristics previously mentioned. While those of us in ethnic studies and related disciplines have embraced the concept of an education that is multicultural and social-reconstructionist and continue to reject the "piñata syndrome" (the most common celebration of diversity found in public schools is the display of cultural artifacts devoid of social context), we are cognizant that the empowerment of many voices may be disconnecting for those who believe that the nation should speak with only one voice. The debate has crystallized in the discussion of cultural studies versus ethnoreligious programs, institutes, or centers in higher education. In the public schools the polemic has taken the form of multicultural curricula versus an ethnically infused curriculum stressing a common American culture. The following is an attempt by the authors to provide some guidelines for an implementation of a multicultural curriculum that recognizes, tolerates, and respects a diversity of voices while acknowledging the empowering effect of what Paulo Freire has called *"concientizacao,"* or the liberating of an individual's potential to contribute to society. It behooves us to state that in line with our thesis throughout this chapter, we now suggest how this topic may be concretely approached with regard to Puerto Rican/Latino children and adolescents in urban public schools.

PUERTO RICANS IN URBAN PUBLIC SCHOOLS: THE CHALLENGE OF INCLUSION

In order to empower our Puerto Rican/Latino students, we must demonstrate to them the successes and achievements of our community as it has historically struggled to overcome the barriers of prejudice, racism, and linguistic bias. We should, however, also consider what has yet to be done and how it must be accomplished. Puerto Rican/Latino students alone cannot eradicate the persistent poverty rates identified by the Institute for Puerto Rican Policy. It notes that of 2.5 million Puerto Ricans living in the United States, 41 percent are living at or below poverty level. Most of the families living under these conditions are headed by single parents, the majority of whom are female. In New York City the poverty figure for Puerto Rican/Latinos grows to 55 percent.

Nor can the Puerto Rican/Latino students alone address the impact of racism on their self-identity and self-worth or the effect of language bias on their cultural identification. The latter is especially relevant in New York City, where more than one-fifth of the population five years of age and over reported speaking Spanish at home. Puerto Rican/Latinos are often isolated in the colleges and in government offices as well since there are few in either place. The high drop-out rates from high school (of persons twenty-five years and older, Puerto Ricans had the lowest proportion with a high school diploma—45 percent in 1991) often preclude college accessibility and/or retention. While government service in New York City appears to be becoming more inclusive, Latinos make up only 12 percent of the city government work force. While our young people may not be aware of such specific statistics, this is the reality they "know" intuitively. It is going to take a strong, well-developed partnership including home, school, and community to attack the cynicism developed by some of our most promising young people with regard to the resolution of all the issues cited above. The following is a minimal set of recommendations based on the issues identified in this chapter and is meant to complement the wonderful work of other authors, such as the Latino Commission on Reform in Education, of the New York City Board of Education, spear-headed by Dr. Luis Reyes, member of the board.

RECOMMENDATIONS

1. Develop an ethnically based curriculum. Several documents mentioned in this chapter have already incorporated Nieto's ideas regarding the comprehensive and transformative nature of a multicultural curriculum (see Children of the Rainbow—New York City Board of Education and state-revised state curricula for California and New York[25]). These resources could be supplemented by the work of ethnic studies departments in the colleges throughout the United States. We suggest that, in addition, boards of education could commission ethnic studies programs to develop historical and cultural resources to be used in:

a. teacher preparation programs

b. in-service staff development

c. supervisors' training seminars

d. parental empowerment workshops

e. first and second language literacy classes

f. development of assessment and evaluation instruments

g. basic education and civics training sponsored by community-based organizations

2. Institutionalize ethnically identifiable student support networks. The drastic cuts in school budgets, particularly in the public sector and reflected in the lack

of counselors in schools with the most need, suggest that we must pull together all of our resources to build in a student support network that is comprehensive and stable. In preparing the multicultural agenda that truly advocates for the student, the following groups must be involved:

a. parent associations

b. community-based organizations, for example, ASPIRA clubs

c. churches/religious institutions

d. school-based support personnel, for example, counselors

e. Puerto Rican/Latino mentors, for example, school alumni

3. Provide avenues for leadership training and development. While in this chapter several Puerto Rican/Latino academics and educational activists have been identified, few students have access to these leaders and, therefore, to their organizational experience and wisdom. In order to prepare students for a leadership role in their communities and in preparation for higher education and careers, we recommend the development of social action teams involving students in preparing projects of benefit to the community as a whole. The following includes groups to be contacted and proposed projects (ASPIRA has such a model, which the Latino Leadership School is adapting in New York City):

a. Puerto Rican/Latino government officials

b. local civic and educational leaders, for example, Antonia Pantoja, founder of ASPIRA

c. civil rights activists, including advocates of community control and decentralization

d. union organizers, for example, Local 1199's Dennis Rivera

e. city-sponsored internships in community service areas

f. Puerto Rican/Latino role models from the worlds of business and industry, sports and entertainment

g. classroom-based opportunities for leadership and responsibility, election of class officers

4. Strengthen ethnic identification. As suggested in this chapter, we have, as a community, struggled for the right to learn in our native language. Originally, this was acceptable since it was promoted as a way to help our students achieve academic success. However, we are now at the point that global interdependence demands a recasting of bilingual education in order to promote intercultural understanding and to enhance the self-worth of our students. Moreover, our cultural institutions and our cultural workers (entertainers, artists, and so on) have so enriched our literary tradition that not to include the work of this new generation with the contributions of our ancestors is a form of cultural omission. We are, therefore, recommending that cultural workers become part of the school and contribute to the development of dual-language enrichment programs that

contain a strong component emphasizing intercultural exchange. In order to carry out this recommendation, we must assure a collaboration with:

a. the Association of Hispanic Arts (AHA)

b. the Puerto Rican Traveling Theatre

c. El Repertorio Espanol (Spanish Repertory Theater)

d. Latinos in media, for example, broadcasters David Diaz, Ana Carbonell

e. artists associated with colleges, galleries, and advertising

f. interns from Puerto Rico, Latin America, and the Caribbean

5. Promote intercultural communication. Our recent history has taught us what we can achieve in collaboration with other ethnic groups. We are proposing that in order to develop the multicultural agenda, we must promote collaborative projects that focus on the successes of groups that have come together to learn about each other and to develop collaborative programs. In order for this to take place, we are recommending the inclusion of the history, art, and culture of other ethnic/cultural groups with whom we are in contact in our communities:

a. Native American nations

b. African-Americans

c. Haitians

d. Asians and Pacific Islanders

e. ethnic Catholic and Jewish organizations

f. other Latinos

CONCLUSION

In this chapter we have sought to review some of the recent history of our community without which we, as Puerto Rican educators, could not begin to discuss a multicultural agenda. We have presented the debates surrounding the issues as we perceived them. Additionally, we have sought to supplement the reader's background with information related to the past and present conditions of Puerto Ricans/Latinos in the United States. It is our intention that the aforementioned provide a context for the development of a multicultural agenda that is broad and inclusive and promotes ethnic awareness and global understanding while addressing the lived realities of our children and adolescents.

NOTES

1. Steven Lee Myers, "In curriculum fight, an unlikely catalyst," (The *New York Times*, 27 November 1992), B1.

2. Arthur M. Schlesinger, Jr., *The Disuniting of America* (New York: W. W. Norton, 1992), 90.

3. E. D. Hirsch, Jr., *Cultural Literacy: What Every American Needs to Know* (Boston: Houghton Mifflin, 1987), 152–215.

4. Portland Baseline Essays, "Social studies African-American Baseline essay" (Portland, 1987), 4, 8–11, 59, 60.

5. Albert M. Shanker, "Promoting dishonesty and divisiveness: 'Multiple perspectives,' " (The *New York Times*, 24 November 1991, feature column "Where we stand"), E7.

6. New York State Social Studies Review and Development Committee, *One Nation, Many Peoples: A Declaration of Cultural Interdependence* (June 1991), vii–x.

7. James A. Banks, *Multiethnic Education: Theory and Practice* (Boston: Allyn & Bacon, 1988), 183–185.

8. Ibid., 163.

9. John U. Ogbu, *Minority Education and Caste* (New York: Academic Press, 1978), 221–27.

10. Margaret A. Gibson, "Immigrant minority school performance: Some implications for ethnographic research and educational policy," paper presented at "Recent Contributions to the Study of Culture, Society and Schooling in Plural Settings," Division of Education, University of California, Davis, 12 October 1990, 2.

11. Clara E. Rodriguez, "Puerto Ricans: Between black and white," in Clara E. Rodriguez, Virginia Sanchez-Korrol, and Jose Oscar Alers (eds.), *The Puerto Rican Struggle* (New York: Waterfront Press, 1980), 21.

12. Pablo Y. Guzman, "Puerto Rican barrio politics in the United States," in Clara E. Rodriguez, Virginia Sanchez-Korrol, and Jose Oscar Alers (eds.), *The Puerto Rican Struggle* (New York: Waterfront Press, 1980), 121–23.

13. Diana Caballero, "School board elections: Parents against the odds," *Bulletin of the Centro de Estudios Puertorriqueños*, 2(5): 87.

14. Luis Fuentes, "The struggle for local political control," in Clara E. Rodriguez, Virginia Sanchez-Korrol, and Jose Oscar Alers (eds.), *The Puerto Rican Struggle* (New York: Waterfront Press, 1980), 115.

15. Adalberto Lopez, "The Puerto Rican diaspora: A survey," in Adalberto Lopez and James Petras (eds.), *Puerto Rico and Puerto Ricans: Studies in History and Society* (New York: John Wiley, 1974), 334–35.

16. Ibid., 332.

17. Antonio Nadal and Maria E. Sanchez, "Preface," in Maria E. Sanchez and Antonio M. Stevens-Arroyo (eds.), *Toward a Renaissance of Puerto Rican Studies: Ethnic and Area Studies in University Education* (Highland Lakes, NJ: Atlantic Research and Publications, 1987), ix–x.

18. Josephine Nieves et al., "Puerto Rican studies: Roots and challenges," in Sanchez and Stevens-Arroyo, *Toward a Renaissance of Puerto Rican Studies*, 3–12.

19. James Jennings, "Puerto Rican Studies and community activism in the 1980's," in Sanchez and Stevens-Arroyo, *Toward a Renaissance of Puerto Rican Studies*, 117–18.

20. Sonia Nieto, "Puerto Rican Studies and bilingual education," in Sanchez and Stevens-Arroyo, *Toward a Renaissance of Puerto Rican Studies*, 37–38.

21. Ibid., 39.

22. Interview with Prof. Virginia Sanchez-Korrol at Brooklyn College of CUNY, 10 November 1992.

23. Sonia Nieto, *Affirming Diversity: The Sociopolitical Context of Multicultural Education* (New York: Longman Publishing Group, 1992), 208.

24. Ibid., 207–22.

25. *Children of the Rainbow* (New York: New York City Board of Education, 1991).

SELECTED BIBLIOGRAPHY

Freire, Paulo. *Pedagogy of the Oppressed*. New York: Seabury Press, 1970.

Institute for Puerto Rican Policy. "Puerto Ricans and Other Latinos in New York City Today: A Statistical Profile," pamphlet based on meeting held at the Rockefeller Foundation 20 June 1992.

Kozol, Jonathan. *Savage Inequalities*. New York: Harper Perennial, 1991.

Latino Commission on Educational Reform. *Toward a Vision for the Education of Latino Students: Community Voices, Student Voices*. New York: New York City Board of Education, 1992.

Ogbu, John U. *Minority Education and Caste*. New York: Academic Press, 1978.

Simonson, Rick, and Scott Walker. *Multicultural Literacy*. Saint Paul, MN: Graywolf Press, 1988.

Sleeter, Christine E., and Carl A. Grant. "Race, Class, Gender and Disability in Current Textbooks." In *The Politics of the Textbook*, ed. Michael W Apple and Linda K. Christian-Smith. New York: Routledge & Chapman Hall, 1991.

10

Teacher Perspectives: Why Do African-American, Hispanic, and Vietnamese Students Fail?

Jacqueline Jordan Irvine and
Darlene Eleanor York

INTRODUCTION

Students from every social class, every ethnic and cultural group, and every geographic region experience academic success and failure in schools. However, when particular racial or ethnic groups of students achieve or fail at disproportionate rates, questions surface about differences in their educational experiences. For example, since 1975, Asian students have consistently scored higher on the mathematics section of the Scholastic Aptitude Test (SAT) than any other racial group in the United States. In the 1987–1988 school year, the difference in the mathematics score between Asian and white students (the second highest scoring group) was more than 30 points (College Entrance Examination Board, 1988). Conversely, during the same period, African-American and Hispanic students ranked at the bottom of the SAT verbal and mathematics sections, consistently scoring lower than all other ethnic groups, including American Indian and Puerto Rican students. During the 1987–1988 school year, the difference between Asian students (the highest scoring group) and African-American students (the lowest scoring group) was more than 50 points on the verbal section and more than 130 points in mathematics (College Entrance Examination Board, 1988). Similar low performance of minority students on standardized tests has also been found by the National Assessment of Educational Progress (NAEP, 1985).

To understand the reasons for school failure among minority students, researchers have examined many facets of minority education: poverty and deprivation (Coleman, 1966), lack of parental involvement (Clark, 1983), segregated schools, (Camburn, 1990; Hawley, 1989; Rist, 1985), and an irrelevant Eurocentric school curriculum (Asante, 1988; Viadero, 1990). Another body of research has focused on teachers: their expectations for students, their treatment of students, and their explanations of student academic performance. This final area—teacher explanations of student academic performance—is the focus of this chapter. How do teachers explain school failure among minority students? Do teachers explain school failure in the same way for all minorities, or do teachers believe different minority groups fail for reasons that are unique to themselves?

In previous research, J. J. Irvine (1990) reviewed thirty-six experimental studies, naturalistic setting studies, and teacher perception and attitude studies and found that teachers, particularly white teachers, have more negative expectations for black students than white students. This research, although informative, is limited because the teacher expectation measures included a wide array of variables such as teachers' verbal and nonverbal feedback, amount of touching and eye contact, and teacher perceptions of black students' personality traits, behavior, language, ability, and physical appearance, resulting in cumbersome and vague explanations of the phenomenon. In addition, previous studies do not address the causal issue of how teachers' explanations of student academic achievement inform and shape subsequent teacher behavior and expectations.

THEORIES AND MODELS OF ATTRIBUTION

Attribution theory is the study of the processes people use to link events to causes. This theory asserts that people collect information about their own and other's behavior to develop general explanations of behavior and to predict future behavior. By observing and interacting with students, teachers form attributions of student behavior. Teachers then use these attributions to predict future student behavior. An important element of attribution theory is the notion of consequent or subsequent behavior, that is, behavior that occurs as a consequence of the attributions made. Attribution theorists argue that, once an explanation has been given, the consequent behavior of the person making the attribution is influenced by the explanation. For example, a teacher who attributes minority academic failure to low ability will not, in future lessons, challenge and encourage minority students to learn difficult material. However, a teacher who attributes the failure of a minority student to materials that were too difficult or inappropriate will search for teaching methods and classroom materials that are appropriate for the student. Teachers' attributions influence their consequent teaching behavior.

Fritz Heider (1958) was the first to formulate a theory of causal attribution. He believed that all people develop explanations of cause and effect in order to make the world a predictable place. The significance of Heider's work was to place attributions within social contexts. He theorized that the formation of attributions was influenced by culture; hence, members of different cultural groups might after substantially different explanations of identical events (Heider, 1958).

E. E. Jones and E. Davis (1965) refined this idea further. They suggested that people speculate about options for the behavior of others and formulate generalizations or stereotypes based on these expectations. For example, a teacher might believe students may choose to do an assignment correctly or incorrectly or may choose not to do an assignment at all. Jones and Davis theorized that each of these options is linked to a constellation of culturally informed personality traits. For example, students who do the assignment correctly might be viewed as industrious, competitive, and ambitious. Students who do the assignment incorrectly might be viewed as flippant, rebellious, and defiant. Students' behaviors become explanations of students' personalities. Jones and Davis argue that these behaviors reflect cultural patterns and information: people believe the behavior of others always conforms to social definitions. For example, if teachers define African-Americans as flippant, rebellious, and defiant, then an African-American student who does an assignment incorrectly is seen as operating within a consistent, culturally defined norm.

A third important contribution to attribution theory was made by H. H. Kelley (1971). He suggested that three variables are present in attribution formation: (1) the person making the attribution, (2) the person about whom the attribution is made, and (3) the context in which the behavior occurs. Kelley believed the process of attribution involved the covariation of these variables. Researchers interested in refining the inferential process in attribution formation tested Kelley's work by attempting to hold two of the three variables constant while varying the other. For example, a teenage African-American male wearing gold jewelry, sunglasses, and a hat in class may be viewed by a white teacher as inappropriately dressed and resistant to learning. By manipulating one of these variables (teacher, student, the classroom context), the attribution may change. For example, a white student similarly dressed might be considered playful by a white teacher. On the other hand, an African-American teacher might consider jewelry, sunglasses, and a hat important adolescent symbols of an African-American male's identity and conclude that they do not interfere with student learning.

Taken together, these theories suggest that the process of attribution can be seen as follows:

1. Culture influences our understanding of the causes of human behavior.

2. Options for behavior are linked to inferences about underlying personality traits.

3. Behavior reveals personality traits and confirms (or fails to confirm) our understanding of consistent cultural norms.

4. Attribution is the combination of three variables: the context of the behavior, the actor, and the observer. Varying one of these may alter the attribution.

ATTRIBUTION THEORY IN EDUCATION

Two significant adaptations of attribution theory have been made by educational researchers. The first was made by Weiner, Frieze, Kukla, Reed, Rest, and Rosenbaum (1971) who created four categories for teachers' attributions of student academic achievement. Listed below are the categories, using student failure as the event:

1. Students fail because they lack the internal ability to perform academically.

2. Students fail because they choose not to make the internal effort to succeed.

3. Students fail because the external task required was too difficult.

4. Students fail because the external outcome of an event (such as guessing how many jelly beans are in a jar) was tied to luck.

These four categories—ability, effort, task difficulty, and luck—were divided into further dimensions by Weiner (1979). Ability and effort, for example, are linked to internal locus of control: task difficulty and luck are linked to external locus of control. Furthermore, ability and task difficulty are considered stable dimensions; that is, they do not vary over time. Luck and effort, however, are unstable. Finally, the degree of control varies. For example, a student's ability level is uncontrollable, but a student may choose (control) the amount of effort directed toward a task. Luck and task difficulty are both perceived as out of the student's control. In summary, teachers' attributions to student ability are considered internal, stable over time, and uncontrollable. However, teachers' attributions to student effort are considered internal, unstable over time, and controllable by the student. Both luck and task difficulty are uncontrollable and external, but luck is unstable while task difficulty is stable.

The second significant adaptation of attribution theory within education centers on the notion of consequent behavior. Consequent behavior in teachers has been examined in two ways. First, theorists (Dweck, 1975) argue that, if an individual believes that the outcome of an event is divorced from his behavior, then the individual gradually ceases to make efforts to influence outcomes. For example, if a teacher believes that students fail because they refuse to make the effort (internal, unstable, controllable attributions), then the teacher will gradually feel less responsible for student failure, less willing to try to influence educational outcomes, and less involved in the activity of teaching. This process is called learned helplessness. Learned helplessness occurs when teachers believe that their actions will not influence student learning. In this way, the consequent behavior of teachers is influenced by their attributions of student failure. Second, Darley and Fazio (1980) have suggested that teachers' attributions inform expectations. Teachers engage students in different learning activities, expecting that students will respond in a variety of ways. When students fail, teachers may attribute the failure to a variety of causes such as ability, effort, task difficulty, or luck. These attributions then shape the teacher's view of the student's disposition and personality, providing a basis for teachers' expectations of future student achievement and influencing teachers' behavior toward students who are expected to fail. Thus, teacher attributions, by shaping teacher expectations, influence the consequent behavior of teachers.

ATTRIBUTION THEORY AND MINORITY STUDENTS

Are there differences in teachers' attributions of student achievement when the cultural backgrounds of teachers and students are dissimilar? Recently, Irvine (1990) suggested that school failure for minority students was caused by a "lack of cultural synchronization" (p. 23) between the traditional, mainstream culture of schools and the cultures of ethnically and racially diverse students who attend them. Teachers whose training has prepared them to teach students with similar values, attitudes, and behaviors experience a form of culture shock when they encounter students whose languages, dress, behaviors, attitudes, and values are different (LeCompte, 1985). If minority students do not match a teacher's mainstream cultural stereotypes for school success, their failure might be attributed to "cultural deficits" rather than to academic factors.

Culturally based differences in teacher attributions may result in subsequent teaching behaviors that reinforce these attributions. For example, teachers who attribute academic success among Asians to ability and effort may reinforce that success by sharpening teaching skills and providing even more challenging classroom assignments. Conversely, teachers who attribute academic failure among African-American and Hispanic students to a lack of ability coupled with task difficulty may reinforce that failure with learned helplessness, that is, by withdrawing from active teaching and assigning easy learning tasks.

THE EFFECT OF STUDENT RACE ON TEACHER ATTRIBUTIONS

Reviews by Dusek and Joseph (1983) and by Moore and Johnson (1983) underscore the importance of student race in the formation of teacher expectations. Moore and Johnson (1983), examining the literature on elementary school teachers' expectations, found that Asian children, regardless of academic grades and socioeconomic levels, were expected to achieve higher occupational status than African-American or white children. However, lower-class African-American students were not expected to achieve high occupational status even when their grades were high. Similarly, Dusek and Joseph (1983) comparing seventy-seven studies of teacher expectations, found that cumulative folder information, social class, and student race were highly correlated with teacher expectations. This research suggests that membership in certain minority groups leads to teacher expectations of academic failure; however, this connection is mediated by social-class level.

Teachers may expect minority students to fail, but to what do they attribute academic failure? If tall students were experiencing academic failure at disproportionate rates, and if teachers expected tall students to fail and short students to succeed, it would be important to understand what teachers believed caused tall students to fail. It is important to understand what teachers believe causes minority students to fail. However, little research has been done in this area.

In an early study by Cooper, Baron, and Lowe (1975), education and psychology majors completed the Intellectual Achievement Responsibility Scale (a locus of control measure) for a student who was described as either middle- or lower-class and as either African-American or white. Attributions for academic success did not vary across the four combinations. However, attributions for academic failure were attributed to internal causes (ability or effort) only for middle-class whites. Lower-class whites and African-Americans of both classes were believed to fail because of external causes (task difficulty or luck).

In a similar study, Domingo-Llacuna (1976) asked preservice teachers to complete the same scale (Intellectual Achievement Responsibility Scale) but divided the score into average ability and average effort measures. Using these measures to assess the effects of social class and student race, she found that social class had no significant effect on teacher attributions of academic success or failure. However, teachers attributed African-American students' academic performance (both success and failure) to effort; white students' performance was attributed to ability.

Somewhat contradictory results were obtained by Wiley and Eskilson (1978). They asked elementary teachers to rate a fictional student who was described as either performing well in the classroom and on standardized tests or performing poorly in the classroom and on standardized tests. Teachers were asked to explain which of four factors contributed most to the student's performance: teachers, parents, individual effort, or luck. Teachers attributed African-American academic performance to internal causes while white academic performance was attributed to external causes. However, no measure of social class was included in the study.

In a later study, Fequay (1979) also found that external attributions were more often cited as reasons for academic failure for minority students. Fequay (1979) asked preservice teachers to evaluate six fictitious students—two African-American, two Native American, and two white. One student from each race was failing; one was succeeding. No significant differences were found among the races for students who were succeeding. However, academic failure was attributed to bad luck for African-American and Native Indian students significantly more often than for white students.

Using a sample of twenty-five white, elementary school teachers, Tom (1983) asked them their expectations of fictitious white and Asian children's academic performance and their attributions of success or failure. Asian males were expected to attain higher occupational status than white males, while white females were expected to attain higher status than Asian females. Teachers attributed Asian male success primarily to internal causes, but family and peer support were believed to have a strong impact as well.

One of the limitations of these studies is that of Weiner's (1979) three dimensions of attribution (locus, stability, and controllability), only locus (internal-external) was examined as a variable in attribution patterns. A recent study has included both stability and controllability as well.

Tom and Cooper (1984) asked elementary teachers to suggest causes for academic success or failure for fictitious students of different races (white, Asian), social classes (lower, middle), and genders. They found that, in general, teachers attributed academic success to internal factors (such as ability and effort) and academic failure to external factors (such as task difficulty and luck). Middle-class white students' success was attributed to consistent effort and high ability significantly more frequently than for Asians and lower-class students. In terms of controllability, teachers took greater responsibility for Asian student academic failure than for white academic failure.

Taken together, this research suggests that teachers consistently explain white and Asian academic success as a function of high ability and consistent effort. For these groups, academic failure is frequently attributed to bad luck or task difficulty. However, academic failure among African-American and Hispanic students is attributed to low ability and inconsistent effort. Of course, other factors impact these results. Student social class obviously influences teachers' attributions; however, the measures of the construct, the age of the children studied, and the level and kind of teaching experience may also affect the results. Thus, the simplistic dichotomy attributing minority student failure to internal causes and white failure to external causes is unsatisfactory. Furthermore, each study has compared minority groups with white students. No research has compared teacher attributions of various minority groups. This reliance upon white student populations as a sole comparison group fails to elucidate and refine minority intergroup comparisons.

A RESEARCH STUDY

In order to address this void in the research, the authors investigated the distinctions teachers make in explaining academic failure among three minority student groups—African-Americans, Vietnamese, and Hispanic students. Specifically, the researchers asked, What attributions do teachers form to explain the school failure of African-Americans, Vietnamese, and Hispanic students? What are the similarities and differences in teachers' attributions among different minority groups?

Methodology

The researchers administered a questionnaire to 474 elementary teachers, requesting three separate rank orderings (from 1, most important, to 11, least important) of the following factors that contribute to the school failure of African-American, Vietnamese, and Hispanic students: language difficulty, negative teacher expectations, negative peer influences, lack of motivation, irrelevant school curriculum, inadequately trained teachers, societal racism, poverty, student's negative self-concept, lack of parental support, student's lack of personal discipline, and a blank space for each teacher's comments.

Table 10.1
Mean Rankings of Teachers' Attributions of School Failure for African American, Vietnamese, and Hispanic Elementary Students

Attribution	African American		Vietnamese		Hispanic	
	Mean	Rank	Mean	Rank	Mean	Rank
Language	6.30	7	1.89	1	2.58	1
Neg.Teacher Expectations	7.55	9	7.25	10	7.63	11
Peer Influence	5.87	6	6.08	5	6.42	7
Motivation	4.12	2	6.86	9	5.84	5
Curriculum	8.53	10	6.30	6	6.95	9
Teachers' Training	9.56	11	6.47	8	7.15	10
Racism	6.36	8	6.03	4	6.32	6
Poverty	5.18	5	5.45	2	5.60	4
Self-Concept	4.29	3	5.46	3	4.99	2
Parents	3.25	1	6.36	7	5.33	3
lack of discipline	4.63	4	7.49	11	6.55	8

Respondents

The respondents were 474 teachers in all of the twenty-six elementary schools in a metropolitan school system in the Southeast. Ninety percent of the teachers were white, and 10 percent were African-American; a vast majority (96 percent) were women. In the last decade, this metropolitan area experienced dramatic growth of its minority populations. The African-American population increased by 314 percent, Asian (mostly Southeast Asian) by 437 percent, and Hispanic by 132 percent.

Results

Table 10.1 illustrates the mean ranking and the rank order of the eleven factors on the questionnaire. The results indicate that teachers attributed African-American students' school failure to lack of parental support. Other reasons that ranked high included African-American students' lack of motivation, their negative self-concept, and lack of discipline. The teachers in the sample did not think that their preservice or in-service training, negative teacher expectations, or the school's curriculum contributed to the lack of achievement of these students.

There were very different attributions for Vietnamese students. The teachers thought that the primary reason for Vietnamese students' school failure was their inability to speak English. The second and third highest-ranking variables were poverty and students' negative self-concept. It should be noted that a 3.5-point spread between the first and second reason indicates the strength of the teachers' conviction about their primary reason. Unlike for African-American students, the teachers did not believe that Vietnamese students' lack of discipline and motivation were significant contributory factors to school failure. Furthermore, the teachers failed to connect negative teacher expectations to school failure for either African-American or Vietnamese students.

In examining the teachers' attribution of school failure for Hispanic students, the data indicate that, as for Vietnamese students, teachers believed that Hispanic students' lack of achievement stems from their language difficulties. Secondarily, they indicated that Hispanic students' negative self-concept and lack of parental support were also important factors in school failure. These two factors were also considered operative for African-American students.

Discussion

The data suggest that there are very different attributions of school failure for African-American, Vietnamese, and Hispanic students. The teachers in the study did not take any personal responsibility for the school failure of the minority students in this district. Teachers explained African-American students' academic failure as a function of their parents' inadequacies and deficiencies in the students' personal traits and characteristics—lack of motivation and discipline and negative self-concept. For the Vietnamese and Hispanic students, teachers explained academic failure as a function primarily of language difficulties.

Another way to examine that data presented in Table 10.1 is to group the failure variables into three categories: variables related to teachers and schools (expectations, training, and curriculum), sociocultural variables (poverty and racism), and student, parent, and peer characteristics (language, peer influence, motivation, self-concept, parents, and lack of discipline). For all three minority groups, particularly the African-American and Hispanic groups, the teachers did not perceive these teacher- and school-related factors to be important causes of school failure. Instead, they focused on student and family variables. It is interesting to note that the teachers perceived that racism and poverty were more salient variables in explaining the school failure of Vietnamese students than African-American and Hispanic students.

These data have serious implications for minority students. Hawley and Rosenholtz (1984) suggest that "differential teacher behavior can be conceptualized as a response to patterned attributions" (p. 33). This suggests that differences in teaching behaviors may generate from teachers' beliefs that the success of high-achieving students can be attributed to the skills and competence of the teacher while failure among low-achieving students is unrelated to the teacher variables but rooted in students' lack of ability and deficit in the home environment.

These data imply that the teachers in this study lacked a sense of efficacy or empowerment. In other words, they perceived that there were few factors within their personal or professional control that might reverse the cycle of school failure for minority youngsters. A teacher's sense of role efficacy appears to be a critical element for effective instruction of minority students. Irvine (1990) stated that a sense of efficacy among effective teachers prevents them from stereotyping or categorizing minority students based on standardized test scores, social class, or behavior. When minority pupils do not initially master learning materials, effective teachers who have a sense of professional efficacy do not ascribe blame to external factors, nor do they impute negative characteristics to the child or family. Instead, they restructure the learning activities, assuming that the child has not yet mastered the instructional objectives, not that the child is incapable or unwilling to learn. "If something is not learned the first time through, they teach it again." (Brophy (1982), p. 527)

Although a common attribution for the three minority groups was that teachers did not assume personal responsibility for a student's failure, there are differences among the groups. For the Vietnamese and Hispanic students, the teacher attributed language difficulty as the primary reason for failure; lack of parental support was the primary reason given for African-American students. The findings have significant negative and endurable implications for the African-American population. If Vietnamese and Hispanic students master the English language, it can be assumed that teacher attributions will change and consequent teacher behavior will facilitate higher levels of academic achievement among students in these groups. However, there is little that African-American students can do to lessen the negative attributions that teachers make about their parents. Teachers who internalize these beliefs about African-American students and their parents will succumb to learned helplessness (Dweck, 1975) characterized by negative expectations, ineffective teaching behaviors, and reinforced racial stereotypes.

When the teachers in this study were asked to respond to an open-ended question (What is your most difficult problem in teaching minority children?), their responses reflected these negative perceptions of African-American parents. The following are representative of the teachers' responses:

• It is difficult to secure parental support; therefore it is hard to motivate the children to work to their fullest potential.

• There are no motivation at home and no concern shown to the child.

• The biggest problems are no parental support and poverty. How can you teach a child who has been ignored for five years and comes to you with no academic background?

When the child does get to you, he's hungry, tired, dirty, and wants only love and affection. There's too much to give in 180 days!

- Typically the minority parent bears children for welfare purposes and offers no parental support or guidance.

- Black parents won't cooperate! They will not come for conferences, send forms or notes back, and so on.

The attitudes expressed in the above statements indicate the degree of alienation between teachers and minority parents in some school communities. Yet this area of school improvement is a critical one because the need for minority parental involvement in schools is well documented in the research. (Chavkin, 1989; Comer, 1986; Irvine, 1990). There is growing evidence that the problems of minority parents and teachers are related more to educators' inability to establish meaningful collaboratives and home-school partnerships than to minority parents' lack of concern and neglect of their children.

IMPLICATIONS FOR TEACHER TRAINING

Kelley's (1971) work suggested that there are three variables that can be manipulated to change the nature of attributions: (1) the person making the attribution (the teacher), (2) the person about whom the attribution is made (the student), and (3) the context in which the behavior occurs (the school). Previous efforts directed at changing minority students were grounded in a cultural deficit theory that assumed that minority children, because of cultural, biological, environmental, and social differences, lacked the necessary traits, behaviors, attitudes, and knowledge necessary for school achievement. Predictably, interventions designed to remedy "deficits" did not work. Presently, educators are implementing programs aimed at restructuring schools. However, these programs rarely incorporate substantive reforms that would dramatically change the context of schooling, such as organizational structures, roles, and teaching and learning processes.

The third area, the person making the attribution (the teacher), may be the most promising and powerful focus for change. However, the traditional approaches used in teacher education and staff development have not been effective. Yao (1985), for example, found that Texas teachers who had some multicultural course work were still unprepared to teach culturally diverse students. Inadequate or cursory knowledge can lead to more, not less, hostility and stereotyping toward culturally different students (LeCompte, 1985).

York (1991) has suggested that successful training for teachers of culturally diverse students requires three departures from traditional teacher training methods. First, training institutions must become more sensitive to the specific cultural mix of the school districts in which their teachers are most likely to be placed. Colleges of education and state departments of education must establish partnerships with local schools based on an understanding and acceptance of the culture and educational aspirations of the parents and their community and on the best research information available on teaching the cultural minorities present in those schools. Second, school officials, leaders in minority communities, and community agency administrators must take an aggressive role in recruiting and training teachers for the specific needs of schools they serve. Teacher training institutions must relinquish their exclusive grip on the training process of teachers, allowing these para-educational groups more direction and management. Finally, cross-cultural teacher training should be hierarchical. Two levels of training should be created. As a minimum standard, all preservice candidates should receive sustained training using a variety of methods. That is, all candidates should be able to demonstrate cultural knowledge and awareness, and they should have the opportunity for some cross-cultural experiential and interactive learning. This training can be accomplished in university classrooms. However, for teachers who wish to teach in cultural enclaves, a field-based cultural immersion experience should be available for them. Training for those who select that option will necessarily be more focused on the educational needs of that particular culture and will be a joint training venture with community leaders and educators from within the enclave.

In summary, this chapter suggests that teacher attributions for school failure are related to membership in certain minority groups, and these attributions are associated with negative perceptions of minority students and their parents. Unless significant changes are made in the manner in which we recruit, select, and train teachers, the continuing cycle of minority students' school failure will escalate.

BIBLIOGRAPHY

Asante, M. K. (1988). *Afrocentricity*. Trenton, NJ: Africa World Press.

Brophy, J. E. (1982). Successful teaching strategies for the inner-city child. *Phi Delta Kappan, 63*, 527–30.

Camburn, E. M. (1990). College comparison among students from high schools located in large metropolitan area. *American Journal of Education, 98*(4), 551–69.

Chavkin, N. F. (1989). Debunking the myth about minority parents. *Educational Horizons, 67*, 119–23.

Clark, R. M. (1983). *Family life and school achievement: Why poor black children succeed or fail*. Chicago: University of Chicago Press.

Coleman, J.S., (1966). *Equality of educational opportunity*. Washington, DC: Government Printing Office.

College Entrance Examination Board. (1988). *National report on college-bound seniors, 1988*. New York: Princeton Educational Services.

Comer, J. P. (1986). Parent participation in the schools. *Phi Delta Kappan, 167*, 442–46.

Darley, J. M., & Fazio, R. H. (1980). Expectancy confirmation processes arising in the social interaction sequence. *American Psychologist, 35*, 867–81.

Domingo-Llacuna, E. A. (1976). The effect of pupil race, social class, speech and ability on teacher stereotypes and attributions. *Dissertation Abstracts International, 37*, 2737–38. (University Microfilms No. 76–24, 072).

Dweck, C. S. (1975). The role of expectations and attributions in the alleviation of learned helplessness. *Journal of Personality and Social Psychology, 31*, 674–85.

Fequay, J. P. (1979). Teachers' self-attributions and their projections of student attributions under varying conditions. *Dissertation Abstracts International, 40*, 4487. (University Microfilms No. 8003570)

Hawley, W. (1989). The importance of minority teachers to the racial and ethnic integration of American society. *Equity and Choice, 5*(1), 31–36.

Hawley, W. D., & Rosenholtz, S. J. (1984). Effective teaching. *Peabody Journal of Education, 61*, 15–52.

Heider, F. (1958). *The psychology of interpersonal relations.* New York: Wiley.

Irvine, J. J. (1990). *Black students and school failure: Policies, practices, and prescriptions.* Westport, CT: Greenwood Press.

Jones, E. E., & Davis, E. (1965). From acts to dispositions: The attribution process in person perception. In L. Berkowitz (Ed.), *Advances in experimental social psychology* (pp. 219–65). New York: Academic Press.

Kelley, H. H. (1971). *Attribution in social interaction.* Morristown, NJ: General Learning Press.

LeCompte, M. D. (1985). Defining the differences: Cultural subgroups within the educational mainstream. *Urban Review, 17*, 111–27.

Rist, R. C. (1985). Sorting out the issues and trends in school desegregation. In J. H. Ballantine (Ed.), *Schools and society* (pp. 330–37). Palo Alto, CA: Mayfield.

Tom, D. (1983). *Teacher cognitive style, expectations, and attributions for student performance.* Paper presented at the Annual Convention of the American Psychological Association, Anaheim, CA, August 1983. (ERIC Document Reproduction Service No. 239 178)

Tom, D., & Cooper, H. (1984). *Academic attributions for success and failure among Asian Americans.* Paper presented at the Annual Meeting of the American Educational Research Association, New Orleans, LA, April 1984. (ERIC Document Reproduction Service No. ED 246 145)

Viadero, D. (1990, 14 November). Afro-centric study boosts performance by black students, researcher finds. *Education Week*, p. 6.

Weiner, B. (1979). A theory of motivation for some classroom experiences. *Journal of Educational Psychology, 71*, 3–25.

Weiner, M. G., Frieze, I. H., Kukla, A., Reed, L., Rest, S., & Rosenbaum, R. M. (1971). *Perceiving the causes of success and failure.* Morristown, NJ: General Learning Press.

Yao, E. L. (1985). *Implementation of multicultural education in Texas public schools.* (Report No. RC–015–560). Paper presented at the Annual Meeting of the American Educational Research Association, Chicago. (ERIC Document Reproduction Service ED 264 995)

York, D. E. (1991). *Teachers for tomorrow's children: Cross-cultural training for teachers.* Unpublished comprehensive review paper. Atlanta, GA: Emory University.

11

Meeting the Needs of Girls in Urban Schools

Charol Shakeshaft

INTRODUCTION

Girls enter kindergarten sure of themselves and their abilities. More developmentally advanced, they outdistance boys in both academic and physical tasks. Yet, by the time they become seniors in high school, females have fallen behind. They are no longer confident, nor do they value themselves. Between kindergarten and graduation, females have been bested by males on every physical, mental, and psychological measure of achievement and well-being. What is it about schools that puts females at risk?

Despite more than a decade of research and hundreds of studies that document the harmful effects of schools on girls, few educators have questioned a system that at best ignores females and at worst attacks them. Far from being teachers' pets, females are at risk every day in classrooms, in hallways, on playgrounds, and in extracurricular activities.

In the classroom, girls learn that they aren't important. Because teachers spend most of their time with boys—answering their questions, encouraging them to do a good job, and trying to shape their behavior so that it is acceptable for school—girls become invisible. Boys receive the majority of all kinds of attention from teachers and peers, both positive and negative. Girls are ignored. The message to girls is that they are worthless.

When girls aren't being ignored, they are being excluded or harassed. In math, science, and computer classes, females learn they don't belong. Even in the traditionally female academic subjects, they learn that the stuff of instruction is not about their lives, since women's history and literature are the exceptions rather than the rule. Females still read about the lives of males and learn that these lives are what made America great. Although females are told over and over that "he" means everyone and mankind includes them, what they internalize is that they are not the main event, only a sideshow.

Sexual, physical, and verbal abuse of females in schools is widespread. Studies of peer and teacher/administrator abuse document that a female in American schools has at least a one-in-three chance of being sexually abused by either a male classmate or a male teacher. Her chances of being verbally abused because she is female are even higher. Thus, a day in school for most girls is a day in which she can expect to be ignored by her teachers, excluded from important academic events, and physically and sexually abused by male students and staff.

Most data on girls in schools have not been specifically analyzed for urban differences. Thus, we have very little data that are specifically urban-focused. However, the studies we do have would indicate that if there are differences, conditions are probably worse for girls in urban settings if they are minority girls and/or girls from lower socioeconomic status (SES) backgrounds. Thus, although this chapter focuses on meeting the needs of girls in urban schools, the research presented could be about any school and any girl and probably understates the conditions for urban females.

GOALS OF EDUCATION

The goals of schooling, which are fundamental, have been built upon the needs of males. Most of the time, educators are unaware that a choice is being made and even less aware that they are choosing to perpetuate a male model of schooling. These choices are reflected in everything, from what is taught in the classroom to the goals of education in general. For example, an analysis of the purposes of schooling by Jane Roland Martin concludes that schools were created to serve the public purposes of men's lives, not the private purposes of women's lives (1985). Martin suggests that education should serve both the public and private needs of all individuals, rather than merely the traditional public needs of men. Because schools began in response to what males needed to know in order to become public people, the very nature of schooling is shaped in the male and public image. Reimagining what other legitimate goals schools might serve for a healthy society helps all people.

STRUCTURE OF SCHOOLS

Not only are the goals of schooling primarily male and public, but the process by which knowledge is transferred in schools is based upon male development. Although females mature earlier, are ready for verbal and math skills at a younger age, and have control of small motor skills sooner than males, the curriculum has been constructed to mirror the development of males (Greenberg, 1978). The result is that girls are often ahead of the game in some areas and never in the game in others. Some grow bored, others give up, but most learn to hold back, be quiet, and smile.

A good way to understand this point is to examine the formal curriculum in schools and the informal curriculum. For instance, boys come to school less developed than girls in small motor skills, as well as with less ability to sit and focus. Early childhood and primary curricula put these skills at the center of classroom learning and thus help boys learn small motor skills, sitting and listening, and appropriate ways to interact in the classroom. Most girls come to school with the development of these skills well under way. On the other hand, girls generally begin school with weak large motor skills and a reluctance to be aggressive. Girls are also more likely than boys to be self-conscious about themselves and hold back, playing the role of observer to the boy participants. Schools rarely address these deficits as part of the formal curriculum, leaving them for free play. Not surprisingly, girls do not incorporate these activities into their free playtime and thus are left only partially served by the schools they attend (Greenberg, 1978).

Developmentally, adolescence seems to be a particularly difficult time for females. Studies indicate that when girls reach eleven or twelve, they begin to dissociate from themselves and not know who they are (Brown and Gilligan, 1992). L. M. Brown and C. Gilligan believe that this crisis is in proportion to the oedipal stage in early childhood for boys. In their work, they found that girls move from being outspoken and aware to suppressing their own feelings in order to be "nice." Brown and Gilligan were able to isolate behavior by teachers and administrators that contributed to this silencing of adolescent girls.

Other work (AAUW, 1991) points to a tremendous loss in self esteem for adolescent girls. Understanding that something happens to girls at age eleven that affects achievement and participation in classroom learning might lead not only to what is taught but to how it is taught. However, we have not incorporated what we know about female development into curricula, counseling, or practice. Rather, we have based much of what we do on male development, having wrongly assumed that the issues are the same for females.

Even the very composition of schools shows more concern for male development. There is strong evidence that girls learn and grow better in all-female environments, while for boys the opposite is true (Lee and Bryk, 1986; Riordan, 1982). Academically, boys do equally well in single-sex and coeducational schools, but coeducational schools provide a secondary curriculum in social behavior for boys. Thus, the best environment for a boy is one in which both male and female students are represented. For girls, a single-sex school provides more positive academic and growth experiences. In single-sex schools, girls exhibit higher self-esteem, more involvement with academic life, and increased participation in a range of social and leadership activities. Yet, when decisions about coeducation are made, one seldom hears the question, How will this affect female students? Coeducation is a good thing for males and not for females. Nevertheless, it is what we have in most public schools.

Interestingly, when the issue of single-sex schools has been entertained, it has been considered for male needs. For instance, despite research that would caution against such policy, single-sex schools are being tried in several urban cities for black males as a way to help them succeed in a system that has not been kind to them. However good or bad a policy of offering single-sex and single-race schools for black males may be, single-sex schools have not been considered for females, despite evidence that indicates a positive effect for them.

INSTRUCTIONAL TECHNIQUES

Teaching techniques also reflect the pattern of male needs. An examination of the use of competition as a learning style provides an illustration of the ways in which male development guides instructional style. From the Bluebirds against the Cardinals in a spelling bee to the boys against the girls in a game of math facts, pitting student against student in a win/lose contest is a common and accepted means of instruction in our schools. Students learn not only how to compete but that competition is a worthy endeavor. The ''I win, you lose'' philosophy is seldom questioned, is constantly reinforced in classrooms and on playing fields, and, according to some (Gilligan, Lyons, & Hammer, 1989) is not the best environment for girls.

Unfortunately, educators not only cling to a model that is difficult for girls but fail to realize that if this model is to be used, girls will need help adjusting to it. Thus, we have imposed a competitive model on females but have not given girls the tools to feel comfortable with competition. Because girls tend to have a relational approach to life and learning, they often find direct competition threatening. Rather than helping girls work through the threat to relationships that competition is seen to hold, schools expect girls to compete without adequate support.

TEACHER-STUDENT INTERACTIONS

If instructional methods aren't enough to alienate female students, then the interactions between teachers and students trumpet the message that girls are not as important as boys. A number of researchers (see, for instance, Sadker and Sadker, 1986; Grayson, 1988) have studied teacher-student interaction patterns and have found gender inequity, which is directly related to student learning and achievement. These studies indicate that males receive two to three times as much teacher time as females in the classroom and that teacher-student inter-actions disproportionately favor males in the following areas: response, acknowl-edgment and feedback, grouping and organization, classroom management and discipline, probing and listening, and evaluation of performance.

Response Opportunities

Teachers allow more opportunities for boys to respond—to answer questions, engage in activities, give opinions, help out, and so on. Teachers call on males more often than on females for two reasons. Males are more likely to call out and interrupt the classroom dialogue, therefore demanding and getting the teacher's attention and classroom time. However, even if males do not demand attention, teachers are more likely to call on males and to spend more time in that interaction than in a female interaction.

Acknowledgment and Feedback

Patterns of praise differ by sex. For instance, males are more likely to be praised when they give a right answer than are females. The effect on girls of a neutral response tends to be negative. For instance, neutral feedback was found to have a discouraging effect on female math achievement (Fennema and Peterson, 1986). Boys are more likely to be praised for the content of their work or their abilities. Girls are more likely to be praised for the appearance of their work. Thus, a boy is more likely to hear, "The essay you wrote was a creative and well-crafted approach to this issue," while a girl will more likely be told, "Your work looks good." If they do well, males get the message that they are smart, and if they don't do well, they get the message that they are smart, but not trying hard enough. Girls who do well get the message that they have worked hard or that they are lucky, and girls who don't do well believe they lack ability.

Grouping and Organization

Classrooms still tend to be grouped by sex. Males and females are put into separate lines and pitted against each other in classroom activities such as spelling bees and kickball games. Studies indicate that teachers still use "sitting with the girls" as a threat and punishment for boys. Despite their attitudes toward race or religion, most teachers would never think of dividing the class into the Hispanics and the whites or the Jews and the Gentiles. However, most teachers don't think twice about male-female divisions.

Despite increased awareness, teachers still assign classroom tasks by sex, asking boys to carry and run audiovisual equipment and girls to water plants and take care of the emotional work of the group.

Classroom Management and Discipline

Males receive more disciplinary action than females in all areas. Studies (Grayson, 1989; Sadker and Sadker, 1986) indicate that if males and females misbehave in the same way, males are more likely to be disciplined more strongly. However, when males are disciplined, the responses tend to be more instructive. For females, the same learning opportunity is not the norm. While disciplinary action needs to be more uniform across sexes, one of the unintended consequences for males is that from the early school years onward, they are more likely to get practice in learning to take criticism and to respond in appropriate ways. Studies indicate that this early practice has implications for adult achievement and risk taking (Shakeshaft, 1987).

Probing and Listening

Teachers talk more to males than to females and spend more time listening to their answers. Additionally, teachers are more likely to ask males questions that require intellectual knowledge and thought (Grayson, 1989) and to encourage and reward creative responses in males.

Evaluation of Performance

Three patterns emerge in the research on gender differences in evaluation. The first is that males are given more feedback related to performance, while females are more likely evaluated on the appearance of their work. Males hear they are smart and have done good work; females hear that their work looks nice.

Second, effort statements are used with males to encourage more effort, while with females effort statements are commentary. For instance, the teacher is more likely to say to a boy, "You can do this, just try harder" and to a girl, "Well, you tried."

The third pattern encourages learned helplessness in females. Teachers are much more likely to require males to do the work themselves, while with females they do the work for them. A common practice is that if males and females are doing a task such as cutting out an object, the teacher is more likely to demonstrate the task to a boy who asks for help and then urge him to keep trying. On the other hand, the teacher usually cuts out the object for the girl who asks for help. The result is that given the same problem (wanting something cut out), boys learn to solve the problem by doing it, and girls learn to solve the problem by asking for help and getting someone else to do it.

The result of all of the above behaviors (response opportunities, classroom management and discipline, probing and listening, evaluation of performance) is a classroom in which boys dominate. They talk more, interact more, receive more teacher time, and have more opportunities to learn. Boys learn to handle criticism because they have opportunities to respond that allow them to grow. Boys also have more opportunities to build self-esteem because they speak more and are more often praised and told they have ability.

The average female is ignored—neither reprimanded nor praised—and the high-achieving female receives the least attention of all students. Both majority and minority girls learn that their opinions are not valued, that their responses to questions are not worthy of attention. Consequently, female students come to believe that they are not smart or important. They learn that if they do well in school, it is because they are lucky or work hard, not because they are smart or capable. The interactions of teachers with students reinforce the societal message that girls don't belong.

CURRICULUM MATERIALS

Girls are further distanced from school life through the curriculum materials they encounter. Bias in books, movies, and handouts takes many forms, including the invisibility of female characters, blatant or subtle stereotyping, selectivity, unreality, fragmentation, and male-exclusive language. Whether it is the portrayal of doctors as males or the assignment of *A Portrait of an Artist as a Young Man*, female students are told repeatedly that their identities and experiences are not the stuff of literature or history.

Although a unit on women's history in a social studies class may deliver the message that women have a place in history too, it also announces that there are two kinds of history: American history, which is important and about men, and women's history, which is peripheral. Female students are also ignored in textbooks and instructional materials through the use of male-exclusive language—language that is also used by most educators. Studies of language demonstrate that the generic "he" and other kinds of male-exclusive language (i.e., mankind) are coded by both males and females to mean males only.

GIRLS AT RISK

At-risk issues are often different both in kind and in appearance for girls than for boys. For instance, pregnancy is solely a female risk, sexual harassment is more often experienced by females than by males, and dropping out and suicide are risks to both females and males, but the patterns are different by sex.

Sexual Abuse and Harassment

Schools are not safe places for females, and school life for a girl often includes many kinds of abuse. Girls are much more likely than boys to be victims of sexual abuse at the hands of both school staff and male peers. In a recent study of allegations of sexual abuse of students by faculty and staff in 184 school districts in New York, of the 300 reported incidents in elementary, middle/junior high, and high schools, 97 percent of the faculty/staff abusers were heterosexual males and 74 percent of the victims were female students. (Shakeshaft & Cohan, 1990; Shakeshaft, Cohan, & Greenberg, In press). While these studies probably underreport abuse of students by school staff, it alerts us to the severity of the problem.

Although sexual abuse of students by school employees is a serious concern, there are many reasons to believe that sexual harassment by peers is an even greater threat. K. Bogart and N. Stein (1987/89) began to document this abuse, and Stein is continuing this work by analyzing the self-reports of girls who responded to a survey published in the September 1992 issue of *Seventeen Magazine* asking about sexual harassment in schools. Both of these studies of peer sexual harassment document that in all kinds of schools, girls are the focus of a great deal of verbal and physical, hostile sexual attention.

The following is representative of the kinds of physical abuse reported by Bogart and Stein:

A young woman who had been cheerleader at our school received threatening notes and phone calls with sexual innuendoes, in school and at home. After football season was over, this young woman was told, after track practice one day, that her mother had gotten into an accident right near the school. The young woman, tricked into believing it was true, ran outside and was knocked out and assaulted, but not raped. The female student suffered terrible fear after the situation and missed a lot of school due to both physical and emotional reactions to this incident. (152–53)

In analyzing letters sent by readers of *Seventeen Magazine*, Stein reports the following:

Teenage girls representing almost every major racial and linguistic group . . . tell stories that reveal the tenacity and pervasiveness of sexual harassment in our schools. . . . Most of the harassment the girls write about happens in full and plain view of others—in public places such as hallways, lunchrooms, physical-education playing fields, on school buses, school playgrounds, in classrooms, and at school-sponsored concerts and assemblies. Usually there are witnesses and bystanders.

Girls describe attempts to snap their bras, lift their skirts, and grope at their bodies; nasty, personalized graffiti and sexual jokes and taunts; unwanted physical attention. They also related outright physical assaults, even rape. (Stein, November 4, 1992, *Education Week*, p. 37)

In a study under way now of peer sexual abuse, we have found that girls in middle and high school are subjected to sexual harassment from morning to night (Shakeshaft and Sawyer, unpublished data). We have also found that this harassment affects behavior in the classrooms. Girls report that the reality of the fear of sexual harassment influences their actions and silences them. For instance, several girls report that one of the consequences of verbal sexual abuse by male peers is that they keep quiet in class, hoping not to call attention to themselves. They also report that boys tease them about their periods: "The boys say they know when we are having our periods because they can smell us." As a result, these girls report that while they are menstruating they don't want to stand up in front of the class or get too close to boys.

This harassing behavior toward girls is tolerated by teachers and administrators, who view these sexual comments, jokes, and "come-ons" as an inevitable part of male development, thereby creating and condoning an environment hostile to female students. In other words, they support a culture of "Boys will be boys," and, not surprisingly, these educators do not stop behavior that puts down females. They allow boys to rate girls on their anatomy and to call girls such names as "bitch" and "cunt." As one girl phrased it, "I was told to learn to deal with it because that's the way males are."

These teachers also consent to an environment that is sexually abusive to males, using female-identified words to insult both males and females. Male homophobic language such as "pussy," "pussy-whipped," "pansy," and "sissy" are used to humiliate males by equating them with females and to trivialize females.

When a sexist word is scrawled across a locker or when a male student or teacher uses sexist language, the silence can be deafening. Few teachers even code such behavior as a problem, and many of the insults and put-downs of girls come from teachers and administrators themselves. Thus, the school environment is not a safe one for female students, making schools inhospitable places for girls; environments that threat them neither equitably nor kindly.

When schools do respond to sexual abuse, it is to teach children how to stop it. Most programs about sexual abuse teach children how to say no and the difference between good touch and bad touch. While these are important skills that may help children, especially girls, live safer lives, they don't focus the responsibility for change on the abuser. Until schools begin to identify male sexual abuse as a problem that needs to be addressed, it won't matter how skillful females are at just saying no.

Pregnancy

The possibility or the reality of teenage pregnancy is a risk that only girls face. Studies of the antecedents to teenage pregnancy indicate that those most likely to become pregnant are girls who are victims of incest and sexual abuse, girls with a traditional sex-role orientation, girls with low self-esteem (often caused by sexual abuse), girls who abuse drugs and alcohol, girls who don't come to school regularly and, once there, don't achieve (AAUW, 1992).

The response of schools to the prevention of teenage pregnancy and to teen mothers themselves has not been uniformly exemplary. While there are some pregnancy prevention programs and while some schools have school-based health clinics and programs for teenage mothers, most schools don't. Few schools work with males to help them understand the problems that are connected with early sexual behavior.

Dropouts

While many of the reasons for male and female dropping out are the same (low SES, minority status, parents with little education), females have an additional set of reasons for dropping out of school. Although it is commonly believed that pregnancy is the major reason girls drop out, studies indicate that 50 to 60 percent of girls drop out for other reasons (Morgan, 1984). R. Ekstrom and her colleagues report that 37 percent of female dropouts (as opposed to 5 percent of males) say they left school for family reasons (1986). Girls with the most traditional sex-role stereotypes are more likely to drop out to care for younger siblings. If these girls have a mother who has little or no education, they are not likely to stay in school. Girls who have low self-esteem or who have been left back a grade are also likely to drop out.

Depression and Suicide

Girls more often than boys report suffering from depression and are four to five times more likely to attempt suicide. The relationship of low self-esteem and sexual abuse to depression and suicide is a direct link for females. Yet, schools rarely attend to the issues that have the most impact for girls (Reinherz, Frost, and Pakiz, 1990; Gans and Blyth, 1990).

CONCLUSION

Schools are not kind to girls. From classroom practices to extracurricular activities, it is clear that girls are being shortchanged by schools. Many of the problems that females face in later life—poverty, single parenthood, physical abuse, underachievement, depression, substance abuse, concentration in low-paying jobs—can be traced to practices that undermine female self-esteem and learning in schools.

Educators at every level have neglected the needs of girls and, thus, the welfare of our society. Improving the education of females should be a societal expectation since it will surely provide a societal benefit.

BIBLIOGRAPHY

AAUW. (1992). *How Schools Shortchange Girls*. New York: American Association of University Women Educational Foundation.

AAUW. (1991). *Shortchanging Girls, Shortchanging America*. New York: Association of University Women Educational Foundation.

Bogart, K., & N. Stein. (1987/1989). Breaking the silence: Sexual harassment in education. *Peabody Journal of Education, 64*(4), Summer, 146–63.

Brown, L. M., & C. Gilligan. (1992). *Meeting at the Crossroads: Women's Psychology and Girls' Development*. Cambridge: Harvard University Press.

Ekstrom, R. et al. (1986). Who drops out and why, findings from a national study. *Teachers College Record, 87*, 376.

Gans, J., & D. Blyth (1990). *America's Adolescents: How Healthy Are They?* Chicago: American Medical Association.

Gilligan, C., N. P. Lyons, & T. J. Hammer (Eds.). (1989). *Making Connections: The Relational Worlds of Adolescent Girls at Emma Willard School*. Troy, NY: Emma Willard School.

Grayson, D. (1988). *The Equity Principal: An Inclusive Approach to Excellence*. Earlhan, IA: Graymill.

Greenberg, S. (1978). *Right from the Start*. New York: Houghton-Mifflin.

Lee, V., A. S. Bryck. (1986). Effects of single-sex secondary schools on student achievement and attitudes. *Journal of Educational Psychology, 78*(5), 381–95.

Martin, J. R. (1985). *Reclaiming a Conversation: The Ideal of Educated Women*. New Haven, CT: Yale University Press.

Morgan, W. (1984). *The High School Dropout in an Overeducated Society*. Columbus: Ohio State University, Center for Human Resources Research.

Reinherz, H., A. Frost, & B. Pakiz. (1990). *Changing Faces: Correlates of Depressive Symptoms in Late Adolescence*. Boston: Simmons College School of Social Work.

Riordan, C. (1982). Public and Catholic schooling: The effects of gender context policy. *American Journal of Education*, August, 518–40.

Sadker, M., & D. Sadker. (1982). *Sex Equity Handbook for Schools*. New York: Longman.

Sadker, M., & D. Sadker. (1986). Sexism in the classroom: From grade school to graduate school. *Phi Delta Kappan*, March, 512–15.

Shakeshaft, C. (1987). *Women in Educational Administration*. Newbury Park, CA: Sage.

Shakeshaft, C. (1986). A gender at risk. *Phi Delta Kappan*, March, 499–503.

Shakeshaft, C., & A. Cohan. (1990). In locl-parentis: Sexual abuse of students in schools. Paper presented at the annual meeting of the American Educational Research Association. Boston.

Shakeshaft, C., A. Cohan, & S. Greenberg. (in press). *Sexual Abuse of Girls in Schools*. New York: Routledge.

Shakeshaft, C., & J. Sawyer. Unpublished data.

Stein, N. (1992). School harassment—An update. *Education Week*, 4, 27.

IV

TEACHER-PUPIL RELATIONS

12

Teachers and Students in Urban Schools

Stanley William Rothstein

The pedagogy of education does not function well in urban schools, where inculcation and correction are primary considerations.[1] Yet in these mass institutions, educational practice and curriculum do evolve. Sequential curricula are devised for youth who cannot speak the language and come from distant, exotic lands. Their aim is not so much to instruct as to correct by holding student's language and values up to those of the urban school. The student's presence is regarded as proof of his need for instruction—whence those disciplinary drills that deaden the mind and teach the young to obey at all costs.

There is in the pedagogical act, even in its most benign forms, an element of subjugation and submission. If in urban schools the students are subjected to constant surveillance, it is because they cannot be trusted to control themselves when they are unwatched; if schoolwork often results in ignorant looks and confusion, it is because the minds of students are too unformed, too given to idleness, or too sensitive to the baser pleasures: in any event, they lack the knowledge and understandings they will develop after years of urban education.[2] Beneath the overt arbitrariness of pedagogic work, which seems to entail endless assignments of meaningless work, there is the demand for obedience and submission to authority; students' idleness and ignorance are only passive forms of resistance to a process that seeks to change their personality and self-esteem. What is desired, then, is an educational process that will teach students the virtues of obedient labor and instill a willingness to persist in meaningless work long after reason would have told them to cease. More than the image of subordination and submission is desired, however. Youths must learn to accept the social relations that develop between them and their teachers during their educational experiences together.[3] A spirit must be founded within the children's nature that allows them to accept, without question, the authority relations that exist in schools and in the workplace.

The ideal urban educational process involves the transmission of a cultural arbitrary and a language that hide the powers supporting such training. To reproduce a stratified economic and social system, urban schooling attempts to represent the classroom and social world, misrecognizing the social relations of production that develop during the educational production process. Through language, an attempt is made to describe and understand the social world, without ever dealing with the distortions that develop in this movement from social reality to linguistic categories.[4] Since language is the essence of the urban schooling experience, Louis Althusser and others have labeled schools as ideological state apparatuses, that is, institutions that use ideological understandings and effects to represent themselves and their social systems. Amid these ideological and linguistic constructs, students are formed into socialized individuals who see the world through ideological sunglasses; political credos are seen as ongoing realities that require little thought or introspection. The teachings in state classrooms are accepted as valid knowledge by students who are being prepared to take their place in an employee society. Teachers present their materials in realistic and empirical terms, generating in youth an acceptance for what they have been taught by their parents and previous instructors. Finally, to assure their students' inculcation, teachers test and retest them on a variety of skills and factual materials that are learned by methods of rote remembrances.

When students have shown that they have accepted urban schools and their agents as the transmitters of valid knowledge, a final consequence of urban educational production becomes apparent: students are seen to have internalized the social relations of educational production as ahistorical, unchangeable givens that must be accommodated but never questioned. This final consequence of inculcation consolidates within the youth the essential elements connecting them to legitimate, natural structures in modern society.

But there is no better way of defining the institutional identities of teachers and students than the use of linguistic categories that are internally logical and superimposed on an essentially external and illogical social enterprise. Language divides and separates, in its speech and usage, all the variant classes that have developed in the social relations of economic production. Nothing defines an individual better, and nothing can better separate men from their betters; it is a complete system that has its own structure and reason for being. It is when children speak that the teacher is able to discern who they are and who their parents are in the scheme of things. The old example cited in George Bernard Shaw's *Pygmalion* comes readily to mind, in that a common flower girl is transformed into a cultured woman of rank when her ability to speak is radically altered by a speech professor. The power of correct usage and the assurance of proper diction combine to confer upon the well-spoken individual a sense of power and control. But the language of the poorer classes evokes a different response, condemning the speaker to a position that is inferior and undesirable.

The structure and meaning of language in classrooms can never be discovered through empirical research. Rather, the search should be for what lies beneath the surface of such communications. What is happening to teachers and students as they communicate with one another in classrooms?

Using a command voice, chastising children in front of their peers, separating students according to their deportment and attainments, violence, humiliation of the spirit—instruction in urban schools elicits an entire series of debasements, each of which has a part in preparing youth for the workplaces that await them in the adult world.

The ideal training is an institutional, linguistic communication that unconsciously disseminates the structures and intentions of forces that are outside the classroom walls. It consists of grammatical laws teachers use without consciousness. In classes where immigrants or urban poor predominate, there is a particular language of devaluation that is spoken without conscious recognition or intent. Attempts to study these linguistic structures have been ahistorical, with certain communication processes being seen as invariant and ever-present givens in all urban schooling enterprises. Yet language cannot be successfully isolated from the social and economic system within which it flourishes, nor can its historical effects be ignored. An unmasking of the communications and curriculum of urban schools necessarily involves an unmasking of the symbolic violence inherent in pedagogical actions.[5]

Such unmasking could be done only if pedagogic actions were studied as ideological communications, helping teachers and students to see the true nature of educational production in capitalist society. The production of educational knowledge has, as its historical and social function, the reaffirmation of class divisions through the dissemination of ideology. This, in turn, teaches the poorer classes their inferior condition and prepares them to accept the successes of others as deserved in the fair competition of universal urban schooling.

THE TEACHER'S DILEMMA

The preferred methods of teacher communication forestall disobedience and encourage subordination. We know that effective teachers must use the approved methods and curriculum and must be linguistically correct even when their children cannot understand their words. We know that students suffer trauma when they give up their personal fronts and assume institutional identities. Are not the teacher's constant evaluations of students the same as those that workers experience in the workplace? Then nothing would be more reasonable than that such practices suffuse the urban schooling experiences of children, the replacement workers of the future.[6] From this situation comes the curriculum that attacks the culture and language of the immigrant and lower classes, seeking either to shame or to make students aware of the shortcomings of their heritages: linguistic portrayals that underline the social and economic differences that segregate in the name of equity and the social norms of order and safety.

To the language of devaluation belong all the disciplinary actions that seek to create urban students' persona, controlling their bodily movements during every moment of the school day. To the structures of the synthesized workplace belong all the disciplinary aspects of worker subordination and the internalization of the language of legitimate authority. Thus researchers explain the meaningless work of the urban classroom as a constant; in schooling, the animal spirits of children are beaten back through a constant application of words and symbols; children are thus deprived of their needs and desires; they submit to the demands of the student role under penalty of excommunication or failure, becoming deeply troubled and confused in the process. Classroom discipline has the advantage of regimenting their thoughts and behaviors; they are bombarded with a cascade of words that construct the social reality of their classroom experiences so that the practices of the past may be continued into the present. But controlling the bodily movements and thoughts of children produces a stultifying effect. It forces children to regress into the behaviors of an earlier, less-developed period of their lives; the impositional behaviors of teachers force students to respond to the all-powerful and demanding adult, to adopt transferences that they were able to use in past situations. By the end of the primary grades, these practices have apparently triumphed, although the repressions of students assure an adversarial relationship between students and teachers.

But the principal task of teachers is to inculcate the values and ideologies of the state and society, giving rise to the schooled individual. To accomplish this, the chief methodology is a constant correction. Correction has all the immediate virtues of a constant discipline; it achieves its aims by wearing away resistances; it works its will on everything that is idle, unfriendly, uncooperative, and un-yielding in the child's personality. Constant and demanding, it is useful for establishing the order and control that are essential to the learning situation in mass institutions; it establishes the status system through a series of traditional practices, for it is the prerogative of teachers and adults to order about and control youngsters in every walk of life. There is in corrective discipline coercion without concern, a purifying and socializing power that needs little justification. Corrective discipline reduces negative student responses to adult authority: those who experience it feel that it is legitimate for teachers and adults to guide students and children, fulfilling responsibilities that have their origin in the prehistory of the human species. Corrective discipline is demanding, but also necessary if youth are to see things from the perspective of their parents and teachers; it is effective in pointing the way for those children whose family lives are disrupted and depressed; several years of elementary school usually eliminate complaints and cause students to assume a compliant and respectful demeanor toward their mentors. For those who do not conform, corrective discipline must be associated with unpleasant consequences; but if students are able to internalize the discipline of urban schools, their acceptance of the social and economic relations of the larger society is assured.

Quite naturally, rewards and punishments enjoy a central place in these disciplinary practices. Some believe that the reward system causes students to strive more energetically and that it helps teachers to identify disruptive and failing students at an early age. But more often it is merely the preferred, traditional method of doing things in urban schools. Of course, there are difficult children whose behavioral infractions are so serious that they must be separated from the main body of students. Special punitive schools are often recommended once the normal processes of appeal have been exhausted.

These, then, are the relational and structural processes that govern relations between teachers and their students, between the paid agents of the state and the children who must be trained for their future roles in modern society.

NOTES

1. Pierre Bourdieu, with Jacques Passeron, "Reproduction" in *Education, Society and Culture* (London: Sage, 1977), 31–35.

2. Stanley W. Rothstein, *The Power to Punish* (Lanham, MD: University Press of America, 1984), 3–9.

3. Alfred Schutz, *Collected Papers, vol. 1* (The Hague: Martinus Nijhoff, 1962).

4. Steven Smith, *Reading Althusser: An Essay on Structural Marxism* (Ithaca, NY: Cornell University Press, 1984), 43–45.

5. Pierre Bourdieu, *The Inheritors: French Students and Their Relation to Culture* (Chicago: University of Chicago Press, 1979), 1–28.

6. Herbert Gintis and Samuel Bowles, *Schooling in Capitalist Society: Educational Reform and the Contradictions of Economic Life* (New York: Basic Books, 1976), 18–24.

13

How Does the Culture of the Teacher Shape the Classroom Experience of Latino Students?: The Unexamined Question in Critical Pedagogy

Antonia Darder

Much has been written during the last three decades regarding the conditions that Latino students face in public schools. A variety of studies have explored issues related to culture, cognition, learning styles, language differences, bicultural development, multicultural curriculum, and various educational approaches and their impact upon these students. But despite all the talk about cultural differences and the need to develop educational strategies that will ensure the educational achievement of Latino students, no research has specifically examined the manner in which the teacher's culture might impact the academic development and social empowerment of students in the Latino community.

The question of the teacher's culture is a particularly salient one, given the current rapid shifts in demographics sweeping this country. School districts in all major urban centers in the United States are experiencing dramatic changes in the cultural composition of their student populations. As a consequence, students of color now constitute the majority population in twenty-three of the nation's twenty-five largest school districts. Despite this reality, the majority of the teachers in these school districts are still white (Gay, 1989).

Even more disturbing are studies that show a decline in the number of teachers of color entering the field. In a report entitled *Education That Works: An Action Plan for the Education of Minorities* (1990) prepared by the Quality Education for Minorities Project at the Massachusetts Institute of Technology, the current situation was described in the following manner:

Over the next decade, when minority student population [nationally] in schools will exceed the present 30 percent and will approach 50 percent in most urban areas, minority teachers are expected to decline from the current 10 percent of the overall teacher workforce to just 5 percent. Fewer than 8 percent of the students in teacher preparation programs are minority, and this pool is likely to be cut in half by the candidate's subsequent failure to pass teacher competency tests required for licensing in most states. To achieve parity between the teaching force and the student population would require the licensing and certification of 450,000 minority teachers among the 1.5 million teachers needed for our schools during the next five years. Of the 700,000 new teachers who are expected to be trained in this period, only about 35,000 are estimated to be minority (p. 41).

The low percentage of Latino teachers in the public schools must also be considered in terms of what Lisa Delpit (1986) terms the "dilemma" faced by teachers of color even in progressive school environments: being silenced and "left out of the dialogue about how to best educate children of color." Delpit describes the consequences of this phenomenon: "Too often minority teachers' voices have been hushed: a certain paternalism creeps into the speech of some of our liberal colleagues as they explain that our children must be "given voices." As difficult as it is for our colleagues to hear our children's voices, it is often equally difficult for them to hear our own. The consequence is that all too often minority teachers retreat from these . . . settings (p. 384)."

Even when Latino educators do manage to enter the field, they are often forced to contend with conditions that disregard, marginalize, and delegitimize the cultural knowledge they bring about themselves and their communities, while being expected to conform and assimilate (as are their students) to the Eurocentric cultural system that informs the practices, preparation, and certification requirements of the profession.

Delpit's work suggest that although many well-intentioned white educators might readily admit that there exist cultural differences between Latino students and white students in how they see themselves, produce knowledge, and think about their world, seldom are the differences between white teachers and Latino teachers given serious consideration. There continues to exist an unexpressed and hidden expectation that by the time all teachers of color move through the traditional teacher formation process, they should have become no different from their white counterparts. Despite the troubling, unrealistic, and unjust nature of such an expectation, this liberal assimilationist ideal is echoed loudly in the perspectives held by the majority of white educators, educational theorists, and researchers irrespective of where they fall along the ideological spectrum.

Due to the fierce expectations placed upon Latino teachers to conform, many do succumb to the professional pressure to assimilate. Nonetheless, many resist such assimilation and struggle together to examine the impact of such standards on their work and on their Latino students. By so doing, these Latino educators have waged major campaigns to maintain and nurture the cultural values, history, communication styles, and language of the children in their communities.

Yet, it is also necessary to recognize that there are effective white critical educators who have also worked for the development of multicultural curriculum and made real efforts to engage questions of bias and discrimination so prevalent in the educational experience of students of color. Despite the worthy efforts of teachers of the dominant culture, their contributions to the education of Latino students are not sufficient. The limitations that arise are best understood from the standpoint of their social subject position as members of the dominant culture, a position that entitles them to a host of generally unexamined or unacknowledged social privileges and teaches them to perceive all nonwhite people as "other."

Even progressive white teachers still approach students of color from outside their cultural context. The consequence of this type of relationship can bring about many moments of cultural conflict and dissonance, which create much stress for students of color and, more often than not, go unrecognized or misperceived by their teachers. Nevertheless, white critical educators have much to contribute to Latino students who attend public schools, particularly when they are willing genuinely to grapple with the impact of racism on their own lives, as much as the lives of their Latino students. Many white critical educators in public schools have accepted such a challenge.

DIFFICULTIES FACED BY LATINO STUDENTS

Despite a multitude of educational reforms and compensatory programs, Latino students in the United States continue to experience much difficulty in adjusting to the traditional expectations of the public schools. For many of these students, cultural, class, and linguistic barriers prevent their active participation and successful movement through the educational system. These barriers persist in students' lives in a variety of ways. Whether overtly or covertly, intentionally or unintentionally, the cultural standards and norms of the English-speaking mainstream culture greatly shape, mold, and influence teacher-student interactions, parent-teacher communication, teacher demands and expectations, the curriculum, instructional approaches, achievement testing, and the system of meritocracy utilized to evaluate and track Latino students through the system. As a consequence, these students are forced to contend with environmental conditions of social injustice, social inconsistency, and denied personal efficacy (Spencer, 1991).

It should not be surprising then to discover that in a variety of studies (Cardenas & First, 1985; Cummins, 1986; Fernandez & Velez; 1989, Darder & Upshur, 1991) that focus on the academic development of Latino students in public schools, there are a number of barriers and environmental conditions directly related to teacher competency, curriculum, instructional practices, and the classroom environment that are consistently identified as contributing dramatically to their underachievement. Some of these include

- cultural conflicts between the school and home
- language differences
- stereotypical attitudes that persist despite all the talk about diversity and multicultural education
- teachers who are ignorant about the realities faced by their students
- insufficient role models for students of color

- lack of knowledge by teachers regarding the pedagogical needs of bilingual/bicultural students
- inconsistent and too infrequent communication between the school and parents
- curriculum that is not connected to the students' lives or reflective of their cultural values, beliefs, and practices
- lack of adequate curriculum materials and technological equipment to enhance the student's learning opportunities
- texts and educational materials that reflect inaccuracies and distortions or completely ignore the historical contributions of Latinos to U.S. and world history
- bilingual programs that fail to support the development of genuine bilingualism
- incompetent teachers teaching in bilingual programs
- testing that reflects cultural and class biases
- homework policies that are inconsistent with the realities of students' lives
- overcrowded and uncomfortable classroom conditions
- questionable use of expulsion and other disciplinary actions

The impact of these persistent conditions is quite evident in the high retention and drop-out rates of Latino students across the country. In large urban school districts such as Los Angeles, San Francisco, Chicago, New York, Boston, and Miami, attrition and dropout rates for Latino students can range anywhere from 40 to 70 percent. In addition, the retention rates for many Latino students far surpass those of their white counterparts. This is particularly troubling since studies indicate that Latino students who have been delayed in their schooling as a result of retention are far more likely to drop out of high school (Velez, 1989). Even when Latino students manage to graduate from high school, this does not guarantee that they will readily have access to a college education or that they will achieve success in their pursuit of a degree.

WHAT LATINO STUDENTS NEED

Unfortunately, it is not unusual for some educators to negate the values of studies that focus on Latino students and insist that what Latino students need is what all students need—namely, competent teachers who care; adequate textbooks, materials, and equipment; clean and safe environments; parents who are involved in their education; and opportunities for the future.

While, on one hand, I wholeheartedly agree, on the other hand, I adamantly challenge the assimilationist intent to obscure the cultural conflicts and subordination faced by Latino students in the United States and the particular educational needs derived from this subject position—educational needs that must be addressed by public schools if we are to move toward a culturally democratic society.

Historical Identity and Collective Consciousness

Recently, one of my white colleagues was examining a poster in my office with a collage of Chicano/Mexicano historical figures. He was trying to identify their photographs based on a recent Mexican history class he had taken in Mexico. As he moved through this task, he commented that despite the fact that he had been a history major in college and a real history buff all his life, he knew very little about Mexican history. As he said this, I thought about what it had been like to grow up as a Latina child in U.S. public schools, never hearing anything substantial about my own history or the contributions of Latinos to this country or the world.

Such an educational reality subjects and conditions Latino students to a realm of historical amnesia and to a perpetual foreign identity of otherness in their own country. It means to grow up without a firm grasp of their collective historical identity; without a sense of how Latinos as a group have survived; without a sense of their collective historical movement as a people; without the knowledge that would help us to understand better and accurately the struggles of Latinos on this land that we call America. More specifically, what I am suggesting is that Latino students cannot undergo a process of genuine empowerment without the opportunity to come to know who they are as historical beings.

For Latinos, as for other subordinate cultures in the United States, the development and cultivation of a collective consciousness are an essential component to the formation of bicultural identity and the development of voice in Latino students who attend public schools. As has been defined by a variety of sociologists, psychologists, and educators of color in the field (Valentine, 1971; Ramirez & Castañeda, 1974; Red Horse, et al., 1981; Solis, 1980; Rashid, 1981; de Anda, 1984; and Darder, 1991), *biculturalism* is a term that is used to describe a phenomenon experienced by people of color who must survive in the midst of societal institutions that, more often than not, are defined by a system of both affective and behavioral standards that are in conflict with those of subordinate groups.

To understand ourselves as cultural beings requires that we understand the manner in which social power and control function to structure the world in which we exist and to define our place within that world. Hence, to speak of biculturalism in the United States solely from the standpoint of an individual psychological phenomenon without addressing the impact of social, political, and economic contexts that have historically sustained the cultural subordination of people of color would constitute a fraudulent act. It is impossible to ignore that every group in this country perceived outside the English-speaking (Anglocentric) mainstream shares a history of what Iris Marion Young terms "the five faces of oppression": marginalization, exploitation, cultural invasion, powerlessness, and violence. It is also significant to note that this has been the case even when a large majority of the members of a particular subordinate cultural group have become predominantly English speakers (i.e., Chicanos, Japanese-Americans, African-Americans, and so on).

The overt struggles by Chicanos and Latinos to resist subordination and retain a cultural identity over assimilation to a national (homogeneous) identity have long been viewed as divisive and un-American acts by the U.S. mainstream. To counter such ethnic and cultural "divisions" in the population, the conservative "melting pot" ideology was combined with the liberal doctrine of individualism to fuel the "Americanization" movements of this century—movements that were driven as much by politically naive and well-meaning intellectuals as by politically astute intellectuals concerned primarily with preserving the dominant interests of the status quo.

One of the most pervasive impacts of these movements was the systematic erosion of the collective identity of non-English-speaking cultural and ethnic communities, including Latinos. In its place was substituted a national or "American" identity reinforced by the institutionalization of the cultural standards and norms of the English-speaking mainstream. This institutionalization of an English-speaking worldview in the United States ensured that those already in power would not only perpetuate but maximize their control over the country's political system and economic wealth. Camouflaged by a rhetoric of national unity and prosperity, "American democracy" flourished, while all other cultural and ethnic groups were systematically repressed and relegated to a subordinate status.

The systematic subordination of those groups perceived as threatening to the core values of "American democracy" has been carried out (even today) by implicit (or hegemonic), rather than explicit, mechanisms of social control. Hence, the country's institutions have championed conformity to "common" values, in the face of rampant capitalism, an obsession with an ever-changing "modernity," and a doctrine of rugged individualism.

This hegemonic rhetoric has been nowhere more alive and well than in the discourse of public schooling. To be good U.S. citizens, Latinos have been expected to assimilate to "American" standards and values and, in so doing, discard the values of their primary culture, breaking free of all bonds to a cultural or ethnic identity. Just as schooling has been deemed apolitical and neutral by the mainstream, so, too, has embracing values of "American democracy" been principally deemed and portrayed as a matter of individual choice and personal freedom, rather than political exigency. In both cases, the great rhetoric of "American democracy" was flawed, for it in fact functioned to veil the social processes of power and deny the existence of an institutionalized system of subordination at work—a system that rigorously perpetuated the Anglocentric values inherent in the predominant colonizing culture of the United States.

Bicultural Identity

In the midst of institutional practices driven by such hegemonic rhetoric, subordinate cultural groups have struggled to retain their cultural identity and find a voice in this country. Thus, it is no wonder that there exist diverse and contradictory patterns or responses among people of color with respect to questions of cultural identity.

In *Culture and Power in the Classroom* (1991), I present a framework to describe generalized patterns of response prevalent among bicultural students. In an effort to shed light on our understanding of bicultural development, four primary patterns are examined: alienated, dualistic, separatist, and negotiated cultural responses. Within this bicultural framework, there also are responses that might best be described within the scope of bicultural affirmation. These responses are less fixed than those that fall into the four categories. Instead, a greater flexibility exists in responding to the social environment, without the necessity to abandon the reality of one's experience as a bicultural human being. In considering bicultural identity, these five positions can also reflect predominant categories for determining the strength of cultural identity experienced by students of color.

In addition to students' consistent participation (or nonparticipation) in their cultural community of origin, it is important to understand that their cultural identity and predominant bicultural responses are also influenced by their efforts to contend with the social tensions that are inherent in conditions of cultural subordination. As a consequence, students from subordinate groups must interact with societal structures that consistently produce varying levels of cultural conflict and dissonance. Their responses to the power differential and consequent inferior social status play an important role in the development of bicultural identity. For example, does a Latino student primarily respond to the social tensions of cultural subordination by accommodating to domination or does the student respond with resistance? In accommodating, the student may attempt to move completely away from identification with the Latino culture or, instead, function with two faces without engaging the conflict or contradiction in values that exist between the two worldviews. On the other hand, when Latino students respond with resistance, they may choose to separate from the dominant culture and segregate themselves within their own primary cultural community, or they may struggle to negotiate between the dominant and subordinate structure of values in an effort to actualize some degree of social change. When Latino students are functioning from a greater sense of affirmation with respect to their bicultural existence, their responses reflect greater flexibility and movement. This is clearly evidenced with a student's particular interaction at any given moment, more likely than not, emanates from a critical assessment of the actual power relations at work and when the student, based on his or her assessment, responds accordingly. This type of cognitive, physical, emotional, and spiritual flexibility requires a greater sense of consciousness related to cultural identity as both an individual and social being—a consciousness that supports and nurtures both personal and collective empowerment.

The Bicultural Voice

In his writings on the nature of voice, Henry Giroux describes voice in the following terms: ''Voice refers to the principles of dialogue as they are enunciated and enacted within particular social settings. The concept of voice represents the unique instances of self-expression through which students affirm their own class, culture, racial, and gender identities. . . . The category of voice, then, refers to the means at our disposal—the discourses available to use—to make ourselves understood and listened to and to define ourselves as active participants in the world (Giroux, 1988, p. 199).''

In more specific terms, the bicultural voice points to a discourse that incorporates the worldviews, histories, and lived experiences of subordinate cultural groups in the United States. From this standpoint, Latino students have at their disposal the consciousness to reflect critically upon collective and individual interactions with mainstream institutions, affirm the knowledge they possess, given their particular subject position in U.S. society, resist domination through explicitly challenging the implicit mechanisms of cultural subordination that dehumanize, disempower, and obstruct their democratic rights, and enter into relationships of solidarity as equal participants.

From my observations of Latino students, it is quite apparent that a strong relationship exists among bicultural identity, critical social consciousness, and the development of the bicultural voice. For example, Latino students who principally exhibit responses of cultural alienation are least likely to possess a strong critical consciousness and, hence, also least likely to reflect a bicultural voice. Most of these students resist adamantly any differentiation between themselves and the dominant culture, with a greater tendency to identify with, and conform to, the ''American'' culture or hold conflicting, dualistic perceptions of themselves. On the other hand, Latino students who possess a strong bicultural identity tend to display a greater critical understanding of social contexts and a greater proficiency for giving voice to their experience as bicultural human beings.

Classroom Conditions that Support the Development of Bicultural Identity and Voice

Culture is an enacted phenomenon. Therefore, in order for Latino students to develop fully their understanding of, and participation in, their culture, they must have consistent opportunities to engage actively with members of their cultural group. Gloria Johnson Powell's (1970) work suggests that there is a significant correlation between positive self-concept and a student's opportunity to learn and develop academically within a school setting that respects, reinforces, and enacts their cultural worldview. This supports the notion that Latino students require people in their environment who can serve as active cultural agents, translators of the bicultural experience, and examples of critically conscious adults with whom students can directly identify and consistently interact. Further, it has been observed that many bilingual Latino students are more likely to give voice to the bicultural discourse when there are bilingual Latino adults in their classroom environments who legitimate their perceptions, insights, and concerns than when these adults are not present (Darder & Upshur, 1991).

In structuring classroom life to affirm and encourage the development of student voices, teachers must

organize classroom relationships so that students can draw on and confirm those dimensions of their histories and experiences that are deeply rooted in the surrounding community . . . assume pedagogical responsibility for attempting to understand the relationships and forces that influence students outside the immediate context of the classroom, . . . develop curricula and pedagogical practices around those community traditions, histories, and forms of knowledge that are often ignored with the dominant school culture, . . . create the conditions where students come together to speak, to engage in dialogue, to share their stories, and to struggle together within social relations that strengthen rather than weaken possibilities for active citizenship (Giroux, 1988; pp. 199–201).

Herein lies the foundation for creating the conditions for a culturally democratic critical education environment where Latino students may come to know themselves and the world in relation to their own conditions, rather than based upon contrived notions of life that are often completely foreign to their own existence. The bicultural voice is awakened through a critical process of dialogue and reflection where Latino students have the opportunity to reflect together on their common lived experiences, their personal perceptions of the bicultural process, and their common responses to issues of cultural resistance, alienation, negotiation, affirmation, and domination.

Most importantly, Latino students require teachers in their environments who understand the dynamics of cultural subordination and the impact that this has on students, their families, and their cultural communities. Latino students also need critically conscious teachers who come from their own cultural communities, who can speak and instruct them in their native language, who can serve as translators of the bicultural experience, and who can reinforce an identity grounded in the cultural integrity of their own people. Latino students also require classroom relationships that make explicit social injustice and that reinforce their inalienable rights to participate and have a voice within and outside the classroom environment. Further, they require dialogical approaches and curricular materials that will assist them in knowing themselves as historical beings and empowered subjects in the world.

CRITICAL PEDAGOGY AND THE EDUCATION OF LATINO STUDENTS

Without question, critical pedagogy has provided all educators of Latino students with a viable foundation for their practice. This foundation is strongly anchored by philosophical principles that function in the enactment of an emancipatory classroom culture. Moreover, these educational principles are intimately linked to a paradigm or way of thinking about human beings, culture, knowledge, social power, and the world that supports notions of social justice and self-determination. To understand education in this way means to deinstrumentalize the practice of teaching and infuse it with the possibilities of passion and creativity that are informed by the vibrant critical presence of both teachers and students. To support an educational environment that can sustain the complexity and diversity of such a reality requires educators who are theoretically well grounded in principles of democratic schooling.

The fundamental commitment of critical educators to create conditions that support the empowerment of students and the transformation of those conditions that perpetuate human injustice is a purpose inextricably linked to Paulo Freire's (1970) notion of our "vocation"—to be truly humanized social agents in the world. A major function then is to critique, expose, and challenge those conditions within schools that thwart the formation of critically thinking and socially active individuals.

Through its direct engagement with cultural politics, economics, history, the production of knowledge, ideology, hegemony, resistance, praxis, critical discourse, dialogue and the development of critical social consciousness, critical pedagogy provides the solid ground from which to consider the needs of students from subordinate cultures based on their actual histories and experience.[1] Education begins with the knowledge that students bring with them, placing them at the center as subjects of their own destinies and cocreators of knowledge within the context of the classroom.

Informed by critical educational principles, all teachers can pose questions that can be helpful in the assessment of existing educational conditions and practices and their potential impact to Latino students. Some of these questions include:

- Does the curriculum reflect the cognitive, motivational, and relational styles of Latino students?
- Who is involved in the development of curriculum and the selection of materials?
- Are the everyday lives and community realities of Latino students integrated into the daily life of the classroom? If so, how is this done?
- Are there consistent and ongoing opportunities for Latino students to engage together in dialogue that centers upon their own experiences and daily lives? If so, what are some examples of this practice?
- Are there adults in the classroom environment who are able consistently to engage Latino students in their native tongue and who address students' issues related to both their primary cultural and bicultural experiences?
- Are there sufficient opportunities for Latino students to engage their personal cultural histories and to develop their consciousness with respect to their subject position in the United States? If so, what are some examples?
- Are Latino parents and community members involved in the students' educational process and school governance? If so, in what ways does this take place, and what roles do they play?
- Are classroom relations and curricular activities designed to stimulate and nurture the

ongoing development of cultural identity, voice, participation, solidarity, and individual and collective empowerment? If so, give some examples.

- Does the teacher make explicit relations of power at work in the classroom, school, community, and society, with respect to the students' lives? If so, give examples of how this is done.

- Does the teacher struggle with Latino students to overcome limiting and debilitating forms of resistance, while at the same time supporting resistance to cultural subordination and human injustice? If so, how is this undertaken?

- Does the teacher understand the relationship between theory and practice? If so, how is this apparent in the manner in which the teacher perceives her or his role, relates to Latino students, their parents, and community, defines student expectations, creates and establishes new curriculum, acknowledges personal limitations, and perceives the production of knowledge and the development of literacy and bilingual proficiency?

Unfortunately many of these questions fail to be asked within traditional educational environments where knowledge is perceived as neutral and education resembles what Freire (1970) describes as a "banking system"—namely, a system where students are passive objects who come to school in order to be filled with the knowledge of the teacher. Instead of making explicit the power relations and elitist interests that shape institutional life (including schools) in the United States, these remain forever veiled in the hidden curriculum of conformity to idealized "American democratic values" that perpetuate class, race, gender, and cultural oppression and language domination—a subordination of identity, consciousness, and voice carried out, in part, by the best-intentioned and well-meaning teachers and educational leaders of our time.

Yet, despite its liberatory foundations, critical pedagogy engages the practice of teaching from a Eurocentric, albeit radical, definition of cultural politics. Hence, it falls short to the extent that it fails to grapple fully with a dynamic notion of cultural integrity[2] as part of a socially enacted phenomenon, particularly as this pertains to the collective, subordinate identities and realities of bicultural communities. More specifically, there is a persistent failure to recognize fully the extent to which a non–Euro-American cultural identity and the phenomenon of biculturalism are experienced by students of color who live in disenfranchised conditions of social, political, and cultural subordination. Instead, the critical discourse is shaped by radical theories of culture based on a class analysis that, more often than not, subsumes questions of race and cultural oppression beneath those of class. While there is significant discussion the dominant/subordinant cultural experience within the context of schools, this often conflates and similarly equates cultural subordination with experiences that arise from race, class, or gender discrimination. This perception of subordinate cultures unwittingly obscures, distorts, and minimalizes significantly the actual impact of cultural invasion on the lives of black, Latino, Chicano, Asian, American Indian, and other communities outside the English-speaking dominant group—communities in which the majority of their populations continue to suffer the historical legacy of slavery, colonization, and genocide.

Hence, seldom in the writing of major critical education theorists is the culture of the teacher specifically and substantively addressed as a significant variable in the shaping of classroom experience. Yet, this constitutes a significant question, given the continued failure of schools successfully to educate bicultural students and the failure of teacher education programs to prepare effective white teachers and to recruit and retain student teachers of color.

CRITICAL EDUCATORS AND THE QUESTION OF CULTURE

Few educational researchers have been willing to venture into the danger zone of controversy that is generated when one proposes to examine how the culture of the teacher influences what takes place in the classroom. In fact, I venture to say that this publicly uncontested arena is a profoundly oppressive one, particularly in the manner in which the traditional discourse conceals its assimilationist expectations. Generally, when the question of the teacher's culture is raised, it immediately sparks concerns about essentialism, along with a myriad of horror stories about teachers of color who treated their students of color even worse than the white teachers did. What is hidden beneath this discourse generally reflects the unacknowledged fear of displacement by white teachers and the unexamined contextual issues that shape the conditions of assimilation under which teachers of color are educated and expected to survive professionally. As a consequence, important pedagogical questions are neglected in order to quell the possible conflicts and tensions that these questions might elicit. An effort to introduce and stimulate greater consideration of this factor into the dialogue of critical educators in public schools motivates this study. It represents an effort to identify how the culture of the teacher influences the classroom practices of Latino critical educators in contrast to white critical educators and to consider the implications of this knowledge for teacher education programs in the United States.

Latino Critical Educators

The cultural perspective held by Latino educators clearly impacts upon the manner in which they teach. Some of the ways in which this is evident are through their direct interactions with students. For example, their knowledge of the culture assists Latino teachers to gain a better grasp on the reality from which their students come. As a consequence, these teachers can relate to their students on concrete terms to enhance their ability to establish trusting relationships with their students. These teachers often draw on their own experiences of survival to help their students engage issues related to the language and cultural differences that their students must face daily.

Latino teachers also exhibit an enhanced capacity to recognize and empathize with the academic and social needs of their students. These teachers strongly believe that Latino students require a greater level of encouragement, affirmation, and recognition of their worth by their teachers. By the same token, they are able to understand the expressed concerns of their students, particularly with respect to dealing with problems they encounter in society (racism, resistance, and so on). One teacher writes: "I distinguish between the realities of White children and children of color, in general, and between the various realities of different cultural groups. . . . I consciously and overtly support Chicano, Latino, African American and other students of color."

Immigrant Latino teachers are able to work with newly arrived students in ways that validate and affirm the struggle these students face in acclimatizing to a new cultural and linguistic environment. In this way, they are able to offer concrete support and encouragement, utilizing anecdotes that are familiar or at least seem plausible given the conditions immigrant Latino students are currently facing. Immigrant Latino teachers are effective in moving their students through a transitional program that is based on concrete knowledge of the experience. As a result, they are able to set goals for their students that are more realistic and that enhance and promote their success, rather than hindering the difficult process of transition into a new linguistic academic and social setting.

Latino educators strongly support the development of language and literacy skills in the primary language. Often these teachers promote bilingualism among their students and encourage parents to maintain the primary language in the home, unlike the traditional mandate given to parents, which generally discourages them from perpetuating the use of their primary language.

Latino educators are acutely aware that all students can learn, but many Latino students may not learn as well by traditional means. Hence, they acknowledge responsibility for carefully reflecting upon their own cultural learning experiences, observing the students' struggles to learn, and, together with their students, develop alternative strategies for approaching the learning process. It is interesting to note that teachers believe that this requires a greater sense of openness and creativity on their part, as well as extra time with their students. But they identify this process as ultimately setting the groundwork for greater participation by students in their learning and production of knowledge.

Latino educators express a strong commitment to making explicit the students' cultural worldview and histories, not just from books but in the living experience of the classroom environment. The colloquial expressions they use with their students, the way in which they construct humor, the style of classroom management they employ, how they plan and prepare for the day, and how they interact with parents all are driven by the forces of an enacted culture that defies explicit articulation and goes beyond what can be specifically reduced to definition. Instead, they speak of the heart and soul of the cultural experience, which is comprised of the shared collective history and common knowing that extends itself across generational spaces within particular cultural communities. One teacher writes, "I am constantly looking for ways to incorporate the culture into the lessons: through music, art, language, literature and by connecting with them through discussion of everyday occurrences."

Latino teachers also function as translators of the culture of power. They believe that part of their responsibility is to make explicit the power relations at work in the lives of their students. Through dialogue, journals, and classroom projects, they create the conditions that give Latino students an opportunity to understand their current conditions and to consider ways in which they might re-create them.

Latino Educators as Role Models and Advocates

One of the most significant contributions that Latino educators make to Latino students is to provide them with positive role models—people with whom their students can relate and with whom they feel comfortable expressing their views. One teacher describes his thoughts about this issue:

I am constantly conscious of the significance of being a positive role model for all Latino youth. I have a strong identification with their struggle in the acculturation process as recent immigrants to this country. Helping them to understand themselves, helping them to express their voice, to appreciate their rich cultural heritage and to never forsake it and their language are very important goals I communicate to them. I frequently speak to my Latino students on campus in Spanish both in the classroom and informally during lunch and class breaks.

Through the teacher's modeling, Latino students obtain greater confidence in their own ability and see the teacher as a person who has gone through the system, yet maintained his or her cultural integrity. In this way, Latino teachers affirm their students' linguistic and cultural experiences, share their own life struggles, and encourage their students with clear messages that they, too, are capable of learning and achieving academically. In addition, these teachers not only take the time to listen to their students' problems, frustrations, and struggles but also assist them to identify possible solutions.

When Latino educators express pride and identification with their culture, this reinforces the legitimacy of the Latino cultural experience and helps to generate a sense of rapport and connection with their students. As teachers are in a position of authority, their respect for the culture and language communicates a strong message of acceptance, respect, honor, and dignity, and hence, Latino students experience a greater opportunity to develop their voices and participation in classroom life. One teacher writes: "I have found that as I give culture a place in the classroom, the students begin to light up in a variety of ways. They begin to talk about themselves more often, they bring things from home, they speak [Spanish]. . . . It adds a very rich dimension to the environment for everyone. It provides the children with more opportunities to learn about themselves—in their own way."

In addition to affirming the worldview and realities that Latino students face, these teachers see themselves in a good position to challenge their students in ways that will cause them to reconsider many of their unexamined notions and ideas about themselves and their own cultural community, as well as the dominant culture, particularly those views that can lead to actions of injustice against others and the perpetuation of their own oppression.

Many Latino educators openly admit to feeling a greater affinity with Latino students. This affinity functions to enhance their ability to communicate not only with their students but with Latino parents—a factor that has been shown to improve the academic achievement of students (Cummins, 1968; Rivera, 1990). In addition, many also express a greater sense of urgency to be an advocate for Latino students to succeed. One teacher described it as experiencing a "vested interest" in the educational success of children in our community.

The Pedagogical Approach

One of the major similarities in the pedagogical approach of Latino teachers is the strong emphasis on a variety of alternative methods that stress student involvement and participation in the process of their learning. These include the use of cooperative learning strategies and collaborative group work that provide many opportunities for student dialogue and the development of students' voices. These teachers also identify the development of critical thought, personal responsibility, discipline, and positive self-concept as important goals in the education of Latino students.

Latino educators strongly share the view that everyone in the classroom is both teacher and student. One teacher explains her perspective in the following way: "My relationship with my students is based on authenticity and sincerity. I view everyone in the room as both teacher and student, including myself. All experiences are learning ones, however silly, fun, spontaneous, profound, or painful they may be. I want to instill a love of learning in a very dynamic, critical and personal way within the social/cultural experience of the children."

Latino educators encourage student participation in the development of curriculum activities and decisions about reading, writing, and other classroom assignments. This participation is significant to the process of student empowerment. As students become involved in making group decisions about their learning, they also develop both critical thinking and social skills. Self-selected reading programs, writing workshops and journals, songs and performance activities are all utilized by the teachers to enhance language skills and the development of bilingualism and biliteracy.

The creation of a positive and accepting environment is another significant factor in the education of Latino students. Latino educators consistently voice their desire for students to learn, and these educators express a real faith in their students' capabilities. They stress that it is important that Latino students feel enthusiastic and enjoy coming to school. As a consequence, Latino educators make efforts to create an educational setting where disciplines are integrated as much as possible and where the culture of their students can serve as the basis for their learning. In this way, Latino students gain a better sense of their own place in the world and experience themselves as effective and competent.

A most significant factor related to pedagogy is addressing questions of bias in the classroom and the society at large. Latino educators stress the need for Latino students to understand the existence of bias and the manner in which it affects their life and the world. These teachers actively engage issues related to bias, prejudice, and discrimination, particularly when these arise within the course of school life. In their handling of such issues, Latino teachers attempt to deconstruct with their students their current understanding of biases and prejudices and to examine the consequences of attitudes and behaviors that reflect injustice. Through such dialogues, the teacher and students reconstruct a deeper understanding of their world and their own participation with respect to differences among people.

Classroom Management Style

Although Latino teachers express a warmth and openness in describing their classroom management style, they clearly believe that it is important to maintain a sense of their authority as the teacher and to behave in a firm and direct manner when disciplining their students. They stress that Latino students need to know what is expected of them and that this must be communicated clearly and un-ambiguously. This knowledge then serves to define the boundaries that determine the criteria for respect between students and teachers. This is particularly important since the student offense cited as most serious by Latino educators was disrespect—for the teacher, fellow students, or self.

The disciplinary action taken by Latino teachers varies, depending on the degree of the problem. Generally, most teachers begin with calling attention to the behavior immediately. If it continues, the next step is an individual conversation with the student in an effort to explore together what is happening with the student and to determine the consequences if the behavior persists. If the behavior persists, many of the teachers invite the parent to assist them in handling the situation. This is generally a last resort. It is interesting to note that the majority of the Latino teachers in the study appear to experience a real sense of efficacy with their classroom management and report few problems with Latino students.

Although Latino educators seem to exhibit little difference in how they approach classroom management problems with Latino students or white students, what seems a bit different is their understanding of the motivations that can drive Latino students to act up in the classroom. Most of the teachers are quite conscious of the manner in which resistance works among students of color who have experienced difficulties achieving in public schools. They are also aware that Latino students often collide head-on with dominant cultural values that go contrary to their own. As a consequence, they are more likely to engage students' frustrations within the classroom concretely and to consider with their Latino students the possible consequences of their behavior in the future. In this way, Latino educators are able to relate in a more connected manner to their Latino students and to assist them in developing more constructive approaches to dealing with their frustrations and more effective strategies for resisting what they experience as oppression in their daily lives.

Teacher Expectations

Latino educators hold a steadfast expectation that Latino students can and will succeed. They begin with a faith in the Latino student's ability to master the material and to be able to apply what is learned in the world. Also associated with this perception of their students is a clear sense that all their students possess knowledge that they bring with them into the classroom. Therefore, an expectation exists that the students will build upon the knowledge they already possess.

Much of the expectations held by Latino educators for their students are centered not only on successful academic achievement but also on the students' development as human beings. In light of this, Latino teacher expectations often focus strongly on the notions of respect, personal discipline, social responsibility, and an understanding of the manner in which the students' bicultural reality impacts upon their view of themselves and their world.

These teachers challenge their students to grow and to struggle within the classroom environment, while providing them with the support and encouragement necessary for students to succeed with their academic tasks. Although many Latino educators express their expectations in a humorous and personable manner, there is no question that they also express a very serious desire to see Latino students succeed. Hence, these teachers not only cultivate and stress the development of language and math skills, group communication, critical problem-solving abilities, and a knowledge of history and culture but also nurture in Latino students a willingness to challenge and be challenged, the expression of creativity, their active classroom participation, a deep respect for differences, and a love for justice and freedom.

Parent Involvement

Latino educators express a strong belief in the importance of parent participation in the education of their children. They support Latino parents and engage them directly regarding their concerns over their children's education. Although more time-consuming, most of these teachers utilize a very personal and direct approach in their communication with parents. In addition to notes that are written in the parents' primary language, they also frequently converse with parents over the telephone and personally invite them to make room visits, to assist them in particular classroom activities, or to attend school meetings. This personal approach communicates to Latino parents that they are welcome and valuable.

Forming a sense of partnership or coalition with parents is another strategy utilized by Latino teachers. Here teachers seek consistently to involve Latino parents in the education of their children through receiving their input, while addressing the concerns they share regarding the children. Teachers who establish such a partnership with parents find that they are able to teach more effectively because they experience greater cooperation from both their students and the parents. Another benefit is that Latino teachers are able to develop a variety of ways for parents to get involved, since they become more knowledgeable of parents' strengths and abilities and, thus, what they can concretely bring to the educational setting.

Another issue concerning parent involvement that is stressed by many Latino educators is related to the nature of the interaction. These teachers stress that they make efforts to communicate consistently with parents about the positive progress their children are making in school, rather than to contact a parent only when there is a problem with their child. They found that this practice enhances the sense of community between the parents and the school and leads to more conducive interaction when problems do arise.

WHITE CRITICAL EDUCATORS

White critical educators embrace the principles of critical pedagogy in their work, particularly as these relate to notions of social justice and the enactment of a democratic classroom. In general these teachers share a commitment to a culturally diverse society and consider themselves open to discovering new knowledge and new ways of thinking about the world. White critical educators also express real concern with conditions of social oppression associated with race, class, gender, and other forms of group discrimination.

More specifically, these teachers express an understanding of racism and its impact on both individuals and society. Many clearly recognize some of the limitations inherent in their subject position as members of the dominant culture. One teacher explains this aspect in the following way:

It is so important that white teachers understand the way that our institutions are racist. We need to understand the depth of this racism—not just the more overt things, like the lack of teachers and administrators of color, but like the fact that the curriculum is racist, the narrow view of "intelligence" is racist, etc. We need to understand that we will never really know what it is like to be oppressed. We need to listen, really listen, to students of color. We need to respect who these children are and all their talents and strengths—and if we don't think we see them, we need to look harder to find them—we have to believe they are there.

White teachers also speak to the importance of knowing themselves as cultural beings, that is, they recognize the privileges and entitlement they receive as members of the dominant culture, even when they themselves may experience gender, class, or other forms of discrimination. One teacher speaks to this issue in the following way: "White teachers must be aware of our own culture and the inherently oppressive values of traditional pedagogy. We must be aware of our own face and how children who idolize us as white and think they must imitate us might be hurt in the development of their cultural identity." Another teacher writes: "White teachers must constantly assess their own values and cultural dominance. They must develop a consciousness of and sensitivity toward values and differences of children of color."

To improve their effectiveness with Latino students and other students of color, white critical educators struggle to develop a greater sense of competency and efficacy with respect to Latino students through reading, attending courses and professional development seminars, and engaging actively with their Latino colleagues. Their educational views and practices reflect concerted efforts to incorporate values of respect, openness, humility, caring and concern, and sensitivity to cultural differences, with love for both their students and teaching. This is most apparent in the manner in which they listen, communicate, and are willing to learn from Latino students and their parents, promote open dialogue in their classrooms, confront acts of racism and other forms of oppression, make efforts to learn Spanish, and involve themselves in the community.

Contributions of White Critical Educators

White critical educators make significant contributions to Latino students and the schools they attend. Many of these teachers help to bridge the differences that exist between the school culture and the home culture of their students. In many ways, their efforts assist Latino students to understand better the "culture of power" at work in their lives (Delpit, 1986). They explicitly orient Latino students and their parents to the set of codes and expectations that are at work within the school culture and that will ultimately impact upon the achievement of Latino students. Along the same lines, they recognize that the best way to transform a system is to know it well. In this way, they not only advocate for Latino students but work with them to develop new strategies and approaches for challenging those conditions of power within schools that prevent their development and empowerment. One teacher writes: "I find myself translating alot. . . . I can assist parents and students by helping them break the code of white society, because I'm part of it. I can assist in alleviating a good amount to stress that people encounter in negotiating two cultural worlds by my participation with them."

Most important, white critical educators work to create the conditions within their classroom that will enable Latino students to develop their voice, participate in their own learning, value their culture, learn about their history, accept their language as valuable, and actively involve themselves in educational activities that will stimulate their sense of self-empowerment. Through their interactions with Latino students and their parents, these teachers also model emancipatory approaches for meaningful cross-cultural relationships—knowing full well that for some of these students, they are among the few white adults with whom the students experience a concrete, day-to-day relationship.

The Pedagogical Approach

The pedagogical approach of white critical educators is grounded in both an emancipatory and participatory view of education: "Students and teachers in the classroom are both learners and teachers. Learning is a process of participation. Learners are to be recognized, understood, and affirmed for their work. They must also be challenged to think about what they believe and how this might work against their own well-being." As such, these teachers clearly see their role as linked to creating student-centered environments that involve the whole class as both individuals and members of their cultural communities. They consider schools as places that should function as a community with families, students, teachers, and other community members sharing in the educational process of the children.

Great importance is placed on "starting where the students is." The teacher is perceived as having the primary responsibility for establishing a classroom process and incorporating curricular materials that assist students to discover themselves as cultural beings and fully entitled members of American society. In this way, the teacher provides both support and direction as students critically engage textbooks and other materials in order to make them relevant to their own lives. Most concretely, these teachers utilize activity-based learning, collaborative approaches, group projects, and writing assignments that stimulate and reinforce ongoing dialogue and classroom interaction among culturally diverse students.

Classroom Management Style

What appears to be most common among the white critical educators who participated in this study is to handle classroom management issues on a one-to-one basis. Generally, they do not use one absolute set of consequences but rather tend to deal with problems according to the actual situation. Some teachers talk with the student immediately, others temporarily separate the student from the group and talk later, some ask students to stay after school, while still others give writing assignments related to the misconduct. Calling parents is generally used as a last resort.

A number of teachers express having very little problem with classroom management. These teachers attribute their success to the establishment of an open classroom environment in which students have many choices and opportunities to move around freely. Another effective measure that is widely used is speaking to students with humor and warmth.

The offense most often cited by white critical teachers as an example of student misbehavior in their classroom is abusive verbal or physical behavior toward other students. Other identified offenses include speaking at inappropriate times, touching another's property without the owner's permission, not completing assignments, and failing to pay attention in class when others are speaking.

Teacher Expectations

The expectations held by white critical educators for Latino students place an important emphasis on the students' ability to learn, that is, they generally approach their students with faith and believe in their capacity to learn. In more specific terms, white educators expect their students to participate actively in their own learning and in activities that can assist them to develop greater academic proficiency, self-confidence, and critical thinking abilities. From a purely academic standpoint, most of these teachers express real concern that Latino students learn to speak, read, and write English proficiently. This expectation is strongly associated with their expressed desire to see all their students succeed in school.

White critical educators also expect their students to develop values of compassion, trust, tolerance, cooperation, and self-respect, as well as respect for others. A number of the teachers also establish specific expectations in their classrooms related to diversity. Students are expected to participate actively in the making of a democratic environment by challenging and engaging racism and other forms of bias when they surface in the classroom.

It is interesting to note that, for the most part, white critical educators do not readily differentiate their expectations for students based on cultural background, with the exception of English language proficiency for students of color. In general, there is a set of classroom expectations that are considered at work for all their students, while efforts are made to support the fulfillment of these expectations.

Parent Involvement

In order to encourage the participation of parents in the classroom, white critical educators often establish open-door policies. Parents are welcome to come in and visit or talk at their convenience and to assist in classroom activities. Many teachers design homework projects that involve parents or other family members. Some write weekly letters or make monthly phone calls in an effort to maintain some contact with the home. One teacher describes her parent involvement strategies: "The most effective strategy I've found is direct communication with the parents—either a home visitation or a telephone call. Generally, the first step is to build trust—often this takes awhile. An assessment by the teacher of the parents' time limitations is important (many work long hours). Placing value on their efforts, such as listening to their children read at home, is a beginning step to greater parent involvement. Also, soliciting and using the input from parents regarding their children's needs and expectations is important.''

White critical educators also recognize that making the classroom a welcoming environment is an important consideration. To do this, cultural representations of Latino culture are made visibly present, and Spanish is used in songs, lessons, and stories whenever possible. The teacher's involvement in the community also heightens parents' sense of comfort in the classroom and eases their participation in parent-teacher conferences.

These teachers create meaningful ways for parents to participate in their classroom. This educational strategy enhances the parents' involvement as community resource persons who can assist and orient the white educators to values and practices that are a common part of the Latino community experience. In this way, the parents and teacher work as a team in diversifying the culture within the classroom. Further, this collaborative effort between the teacher and the parents provides teachers with an ideal opportunity to learn more about the actual lives and histories of their students. As one teacher describes it, this opportunity allows her to ''develop an individual and personal relationship with each parent from the beginning, before any problems or misunderstandings occur; to encourage each parent to add something of themselves to the classroom, whether donating time, materials, talent, culture, or whatever is appropriate. This helps parents to see the strength of their children and of themselves as parents.''

Although the teachers readily agree that parent involvement is an important element in the academic success of Latino students, it nonetheless constitutes an area of some difficulty for many white teachers. Language and cultural differences, as well as parents' work schedules, are most often cited as contributing to this difficulty.

THE MAJOR DIFFERENCE BETWEEN LATINO AND WHITE CRITICAL EDUCATORS

It is not difficult to see that many similarities exist in the educational practices of both Latino and white critical educators. Without question, both groups serve to create powerfully effective learning environments that positively impact the development and empowerment of Latino students. But on closer observation, it is clearly evident that the quality of cultural interaction constitutes the most significant difference in their actual classroom practice.

While white educators can utilize their knowledge to construct classroom experiences that enhance academic achievement, produce opportunities for democratic participation, and affirm cultural differences, they are, nonetheless, unable to participate in the consistent and implicit affirmation and reinforcement of the Latino cultural experience. The primary reason for this is that ''members of any culture transmit information implicitly to co-members . . . [but] when implicit codes are attempted across cultures, communication frequently breaks down (Delpit, 1988; p. 283)."

Latino critical educators, on the other hand, who have grown up within the cultural community, possess a well-formed bicultural identity, are committed to cultural integrity, and teach by emancipatory principles serve as ideal role models of empowered subjects for Latino students in the public schools. These teachers are conscious of their cultural values and the contextual realities that inform them. Their leadership in the classroom is strongly shaped by their implicit participation with their students in the enactment of Latino culture. In the course of their everyday interactions with their students they support the development of cultural understanding. Through the very nature of their existence and participation with their students, Latino teachers serve to reinforce and perpetuate those collective values that support Latino community survival and integrity.

The deep structural consciousness that emerges is fluid, sensitive, and filled with the recognition and comfort of continuity. More specifically, the culture is shared and experienced through a myriad of mannerisms, gestures, nuances, and particular linguistic styles, including tone, inflection, and pitch of their speech, as well as the shared meaning of both the affective and behavioral world that teachers and students create together. As a consequence, there is a greater possibility of understanding and responding more effectively to their students. This serves to reduce the discontinuity and dissonance so often experienced by Latino students in public schools. In other words, the teacher's implicit familiarity with the cultural codes and realities of their students reduces school stress and anxiety and opens the door to greater possibilities for creativity and learning to take place. This heightened sense of familiarity is not only felt and heard but sensed and experienced at the deeper levels of consciousness shared by the student and the teacher.

Further, knowledge of the histories and differences among Latino ethnic groups and the living history of these cultural communities provides the teacher with the necessary information to respond to Latino students with genuine recognition and acknowledgment of their strengths and limitations. This facilitates their social development and provides them with opportunities to further their ideas and maximize their participation in the creation of knowledge by eliminating the constant need for students of color to rehash, reinterpret, or translate for the teacher in order to explain what they are trying to say or to explain and justify the source or basis of their thoughts, concepts, and ideas.

The cultural familiarity in values, behavior styles, and even physical characteristics between Latino students and their teachers serves to enhance the student's ability to identify more fully with the teacher as a viable role model. Hence, students experience more concretely the belief that they too can gain the knowledge held by those in positions of authority. This is particularly important, given the small numbers of visible academic models available to Latino students in their world.

In addition, Latino educators who reinforce a spirit of cultural integrity respond to students according to the actual needs that exist for their students, rather than according to their cross-cultural inferences, which often inadvertently distort the meaning and intentions behind students' words or actions. All in all, Latino critical educators bring to Latino students a unique educational experience that actively and very concretely reinforces their cultural identity, makes meaningful use of their language in every aspect of daily activities, and supports an active collaboration with parents—characteristics that have been shown powerfully to enhance the academic achievement of Latino students (Cummins, 1986).

IMPLICATIONS FOR TEACHER EDUCATION

When both Latino and white critical educators are asked about the quality of teacher education programs, they overwhelmingly agree that these programs are not adequately preparing teachers to contend with the realities they will find in public schools. For the most part they point to the failure of these programs to engage critically and substantially issues related to race, class, and gender. Instead, what is found is a smattering of superficial and simplistic presentations related to these issues. In addition, the faculty of these programs are predominantly white and very inexperienced with respect to differences in cultural worldviews, differences in cognitive, learning, and motivational styles, understanding of second language acquisition skills, and critical principles of education.

In addition, Latino critical educators express much distress over the deficient manner in which students of color continue to be portrayed within many teacher education programs. As one teacher describes this: "The programs focus on children of color as appendages to "normal" white children. The education of children of color is seen as no different, just slightly exotic. The political and social implications of biculturalism are rarely addressed."

These concerns obviously point to the necessity drastically to re-create teacher education programs in this country, particularly those that are preparing their students to enter public schools with large Latino populations. Some of the ways in which these programs must change are implicitly echoed in the frustrations and concerns of educators who find themselves ill prepared to contend with the needs of Latino students. Some of these changes include courses and practical experiences that will "normalize the experience of biculturalism . . . and place the issues of bicultural development at the center of the educational agenda." More specifically, this means the establishment of a curriculum that will assist all educators in understanding the developmental process by which Latino students become bicultural, bilingual, and biliterate.

In addition these programs must establish culturally democratic educational environments where issues related to culture, race, class, gender, and other social differences are engaged critically, with respect to the development not only of curriculum and instructional approaches but of student teachers' abilities to position themselves contextually as cultural beings. More often than not, this is an important missing element. One white teacher describes the consequences: "We are taught white ways to teach white students and this doesn't translate into bicultural communities. Most of us are not required to search our own souls for our racial identity. We are taught to be agents for the educational system which has a stake in reproducing people who fit into the society as it currently exists."

Lastly, teacher education programs must move beyond diversity in the abstract and recognize that in order to live diversity in the concrete there must exist diversity in the population to enact such an environment. These programs must seriously contend with the unique contributions that Latino educators make to students in Latino communities. Hence, this requires that teacher education programs value, nurture, and support the recruitment and development of Latino faculty and student teachers.

CONCLUSION

This study represents an effort to address an issue that, for the most part, has gone unaddressed and unexamined within the mainstream discourse of public schools—namely, the impact of the teacher's culture on the classroom experience of Latino students. More specifically, the focus has been to consider the contributions of both Latino and white critical educators in creating the conditions within their classrooms that nurture and support the academic achievement, social development, and empowerment of Latino students.

Without question, the quality of the cultural interaction and its impact on classroom practice must be recognized as a powerful variable that cannot be ignored in the educational process of Latino students and other students of color. In addition, it is of tremendous importance to stress that the effectiveness of both Latino and white critical educators with Latino students is founded on a set of critical education principles that support democratic schooling. Hence, what cannot be overlooked here is the manner in which both the quality of cultural interaction and the principles of critical pedagogy function together to create an educational environment that stimulates greater creativity, voice, and participation of Latino students.

Although I firmly believe that all critical educators and all Latino educators can contribute positively to the education of Latino students, it is the powerful combination of an emancipatory educational approach and the ability to enact and participate implicitly and in vivo in the cultural milieu of the student that fundamentally potentiates the social development and empowerment of Latino students. In light of this reality, critical pedagogy can no longer afford to ignore the impact of the teacher's culture nor continue to deny the powerful influence of cultural integrity on the daily lives of students from subordinate cultures in the United States.

NOTES

Portions of this chapter first appeared in "Buscando America: The Contributions of Latino Critical Educators to the Development and Empowerment of Latino Students," a paper presented at The Education of Latino Students: Challenges and Opportunities, a Latina Research Seminar sponsored by the Tomas Rivera Center in Los Angeles, California, on 27 October 1992.

1. For an excellent introduction to critical pedagogy see Peter McLaren, *Life in Schools: An Introduction to Critical Pedagogy in the Foundations of American Education* (New York: Longman, 1988).

2. Integrity here is strongly associated with the notion described by Lawrence Rosen, "The Integrity of Cultures" (*American Behavioral Scientist* 34, no. 5 (May–June 1991):611: "It can . . . refer primarily to some sense of coherence, an appearance of orderliness to the constituent experiences of those who entwine their lives with the precepts of their culture. But integrity may also refer to a coherence even when the facts of everyday life do not correspond, in logic or in elegance, to the set of conceptualizations that inform a people's life." This poses a view of culture that is always in process and inherently amorphous and ambiguous, despite particular sets of rituals, a common language, and the customary practices of a cultural group. This notion encompasses a dialectical view of culture that respects its elements of coherence at the same time as it recognizes the historical process of change that persists, given the manner in which subordinate groups must survive within an often hostile environment.

BIBLIOGRAPHY

Cardenas, J., and First, J. M. (1985). "Children at Risk." *Educational Leadership*, (September).

Chestang, L. W. (1972). *Character Development in a Hostile Environment*. (Occasional Paper No. 3). Chicago: University of Chicago Press.

Cummins, J. (1986). "Empowering Minority Students: A Framework for Intervention." *Harvard Educational Review*, 56:18–36.

Cushner, K., McClelland, A., and Stafford, P. (1992). *Human Diversity in Education*. New York: McGraw-Hill.

Darder, A. (1991). *Culture and Power in the Classroom*. New York: Bergin and Garvey.

———. (1992). "Buscando America: The Contribution of Latino Critical Educators to the Academic Development and Social Empowerment of Latino Students in the U.S." Paper presented at the Education of Latino Children: Challenges and Opportunities, a Latina Researchers Seminar sponsored by the Tomas Rivera Center, Los Angeles.

———. and Upshur, C. (1991). *What Do Latino Children Need to Succeed in School?: A Study of Four Boston Public Schools*. Boston: Mauricio Gaston Institute for Latino Community Development and Public Policy.

de Anda, D. (1984). "Bicultural Socialization: Factors Affecting the Minority Experience." *Social Work* 2:101–7.

Delpit, L. (1986). "Skills and Other Dilemmas of a Progressive Black Educator." *Harvard Educational Review* 56, no. 4 (November): 379–83.

―――. (1988). "The Silenced Dialogue: Power and Pedagogy in Educating Other People's Children." *Harvard Educational Review* 58, no. 3 (August): 280–98.

Fernandez, R., and Velez, W. (1989). *Who Stays? Who Leaves? Findings from the Aspira Five Cities High School Study*. Washington, DC: Aspira Association.

Freire, P. (1970). *Pedagogy of the Oppressed*. New York: Seabury Press.

Gay, G. (1989). "Ethnic Minorities and Educational Equality." In *Multicultural Education: Issues and Perspectives*, ed. J. Banks and C. McGee Banks. Boston: Allyn and Bacon.

Giroux, H. (1988). *Teachers as Intellectuals*. New York: Bergin and Garvey.

McLaren, P. (1988). *Life in Schools: An Introduction to Critical Pedagogy in the Foundations of Education*. New York: Longman.

Powell, G. J. (1970). *Black Monday's Children*. New York: Appleton-Century-Crofts.

Quality Education for Minorities Project. (1990). *Education That Works: An Action Plan for the Education of Minorities*. Cambridge: Massachusetts Institute of Technology.

Ramirez, M., and Castañeda, A. (1974). *Cultural Democracy: Bicognitive Development and Education*. New York: Academic Press.

Rashid, H. (1981). "Early Childhood Education as a Cultural Transition for African-American Children." *Educational Research Quarterly* 6: 55–63.

Red Horse, J. (1981). "Family Behavior of Urban American Indians." In *Human Services for Cultural Minorities*, ed. R. Dana. Baltimore: University Park Press.

Rosen, L. (1991). "The Integrity of Cultures." *American Behavioral Scientist* 34, no. 5 (May–June): 594–617.

Solis, A. (1980). "Theory of Biculturality." *Calmecac de Aztlan en Los* 2:36–41.

Spencer, M. B., Swanson, D. P., and Cunningham, M. (1991). "Ethnicity, Ethnic Identity, and Competence Formation: Adolescent Transition and Cultural Transformation." *Journal of Negro Education* 60, no.3.

Valentine, C. (1971). "Deficit, Difference, and Bicultural Models of Afro-American Behavior." *Harvard Educational Review* 41: 137–57.

Velez, W. (1989). "High School Attrition Among Hispanics and Non-Hispanic White Youth." *Sociology of Education* 62:119–33.

Wheelock, A. (1990). *The Status of Latino Students in Massachusetts Public Schools: Directions for Policy Research in the 1990's*. Boston: University of Massachusetts, Mauricio Gaston Institute for Latino Community Development and Public Policy.

Young, I. M. (1990). *Justice and the Politics of Difference*. Princeton, NJ: Princeton University Press.

14

The Special Needs Child and the Role of the Urban School

Andrew E. Dubin and Jane Wheeler-Dubin

Urban schools have an increasing responsibility to serve the needs of the exceptional child. In the light of recent legislation and restructuring efforts, there has been a growing emphasis on the placement of children with physical and intellectual handicaps within the educational mainstream.[1] Who are these children? What histories do they bring to the urban school environment? What history does the urban school bring to the treatment of special needs children? How able is the urban school to accommodate their complex needs? The answers to these questions will help us define the role of the urban school in dealing with these multi-faceted issues.

THE EXCEPTIONAL CHILD

Exceptional children can be defined in many ways. Definitions generally assigned to the exceptional child focus on the following developmental characteristics: (1) cognitive, (2) physical, (3) communicative, (4) sensory, and (5) emotional/behavioral. Although this chapter addresses the ways in which the urban school organization processes and ultimately affects these children, an understanding, first, of the family histories will shed considerable light on the type of child with whom the educational system must contend and the likelihood of the system to treat this population of students adequately.

MEDICAL HISTORY: THE CHILD AND FAMILY BACKGROUND

In Erik Erickson's framework for normal childhood development, the need to evolve basic trust in infancy relies on certain physical features: the sameness and continuity of outer providers and the ability of the child to trust himself or herself and his or her own capabilities. For example, the healthy infant demonstrates these mastery characteristics through ease of feeding and depth of sleep and in other areas. These masteries depend largely on the support system provided to the child.[2] Steps necessary for the child to develop this sound foundation depend on the availability of the primary caretaker (in most cases, the mother) to provide nurturing and care and the ability for the child to be satisfied with his or her own ability to meet his or her needs (e.g., grasping and biting). It is clear how the child with various disabling features is unable to develop the grounding necessary to function in a complete way. Superimposed on this "affected" child's developmental process are the nuclear family members, who significantly impact this process by their ability to accept and traverse this extremely difficult path. This involves their ability to support and care for their family member. Other factors that are particularly significant in the nuclear family's ability to treat the child's development include family history, prior exposure to children with disabilities, socioeconomic status, culture, medical care, and environment.

At birth, when a child is diagnosed as developmentally impaired or delayed, the family is impacted by a range of decisions that bring them into contact with health and educational professionals with whom they, in most cases, had little or no contact before. Prebirth preparation and experience are almost entirely focused on the healthy child. The entire family and societal environment stress the joy and fulfillment of this exciting and positive life experience. The literal shock, then, of this unanticipated and grievous birthing event shatters the image families psychologically and physically assign to the moment. As a result, they are brought into an emotional world beyond what they have ever experienced. Navigating these turbulent waters on every conceivable front is a monumental and personal upheaval for each family member and ultimately has considerable import for the special needs child. Since chronically ill children learn strategies of coping and adaptation to treatment regimens from their interaction with family members, the quality of intrafamilial coping is a critical component of the child's ability to negotiate the stressful demands of disease-related regimens, socialize with physically healthy peers, and function effectively in school and at work.[3] Later in this chapter, when the role of the urban school is explored regarding the interaction between school officials and the family members, the importance of that interaction on the family members and the resultant impact it bears on the disabled child will be clear. Some families are fortunate to have opportunities to interact with other families of similar circumstances in support groups in order to learn effective coping and living strategies. In those instances, families are better able to relate to the school officials because they've explored some of the confounding and upsetting issues involved with their children and because they're more likely to have been given information from other parents regarding the school processes. Other less "educated" or "informed" families grapple with these life issues in a vacuum and have a far more difficult experience when they interact with the school organization.

THE ROLE OF THE PHYSICIAN

Physicians play the most significant role in the initial phases parents undergo in learning about the specific disability of their children. They are the supreme authority and the primary information sources. Parents rely almost entirely on the physicians' expertise to determine the most appropriate care for their children. While parents do engage and interact with their children on a daily basis and often have more instinctive understandings regarding their children, they look to the medical practitioners to interpret that information. They also expect them to provide medical guidance and psychological support to help them through their life crises. There is a constant transfer of information and decision making from the practitioners to the families throughout the physician-family interaction.

Interestingly, practitioners find themselves in the awkward position of being asked to provide services for which they are, most often, not trained. Physicians, however well intentioned, vary considerably in their psychosocial care of chronically ill children and their families. Techniques for pain control, guided fantasy, hypnosis, and relaxation therapy are not often found in the repertoire of the pediatric clinician. Even if residency or fellowship training programs emphasized these skills, the demands for psychosocial care for chronically ill children would outstrip the time and energy of the physician.[4] This interface between the family and the medical provider becomes quite complex for both parties because of the demands being made by the family, which most often are greater than the delivery system or ability of the physician.

On the basis of personal interviews with physicians and feedback from parents, physicians find the task of conveying grim news both arduous and extremely awkward and often rely on ancillary personnel to perform that task.[5] Many accounts from parents indicate that physicians assume that role most inadequately. In addition, physicians often indicate that they don't see themselves as trained to perform that role. Rather, they see their medical role as providing support and treatment in a more objective, rational, and scientific way. Perhaps the first step in providing appropriate intervention for the family with a seriously ill or disabled member is recognition by involved professionals of the often profound, pervasive, and far-ranging consequences that the disability may have for the family. It is not unusual for professionals confronted with severe disease to use denial or other protective devices in regard to the consequences of disability lest they themselves feel overwhelmed and powerless.[6] This reflects the endemic conflict between the professional medical school socialization and practical need. Obviously, it is extremely important for a practitioner to be skilled in analyzing and diagnosing health problems in order to prescribe the appropriate treatments, but the range of alternatives must be broadened to encompass not only the clinical problems but the other less apparent aspects of the disability. These other aspects fall into categories that address the social-psychological or ''soft sciences'' areas, for which the clinicians often do not have the training or inclination.

In the film documentary *Lives in Transition*, a physician states, "In medical school, we are taught to effect cure."[7] Still another physician indicates, "We're simply human beings who have chosen to take this path."[8] Soon after the birth of his child with Downs syndrome, one parent comments: "The doctor approached our bed where both I and my wife were, right after the birth, and said that our baby was healthy but there appeared to be some chromosomal abnormalities. He didn't draw the curtain. There were at least 4 other mothers in the room having just given birth so that this information was not delivered confidentially. And, well, I just don't know what he said after that. I guess I was in shock."

In other interviews with physicians who were not part of the study but had viewed the documentary, they indicated that there were organizational problems that prevented them from providing a more nurturing, supportive, and private environment to interact with these parents. Others appeared unaware that the transmission of this information had such an impact on the family and should be approached in an entirely different manner.

SUPPORT GROUPS

A nonprofit support group in San Francisco, Support for Parents of Special Needs Children, focuses on providing a communication network and forum for other families of children with special needs. Parents of affected children are invited to participate in discussions with other parents in order to help them better manage their unique and challenging situations. These groups are particularly important for these parents because they provide the support, sensitivity, understanding, and information that are virtually impossible to find in any other setting. The following are parents' responses excerpted from the video documentary entitled *Lives in Transition:*[9]

It was a world I didn't know existed. I felt that I was in a dream that I would eventually wake up from. It was unbelievable pain. I kept on asking myself the question, Why me? I'm still asking myself the question.

This may sound strange and somewhat uncaring but I feel that I am in a better place in my life now, after the birth of my child, than I was before.

I don't know what I would have done without this support group. I mean, I know my friends care and everything, but, they can listen to my problems only up to a point. Here, I know I can talk about it in a safe and appropriate place.

While each personal trauma has enormous life consequences, family members bring to the situation characteristics that allow them to operate and respond differently, as evidenced by the prior remarks. Through these exchanges, parents learn to cope with these issues by hearing how others confront their situations. The honesty and information exchanges offer unusual relief for these parents.

Thus far, the personal and medical accounts alluded to in this chapter have focused on the chronically ill child, whose medical histories and situations were of a more extreme nature. The authors presented these cases in order to highlight the need to identify these children. Their needs are different, and the school system must have the capability of dealing with these differences. With children with more manageable disabilities or limitations, the family perspectives obviously present other types of issues, although they are still quite complex. Regardless of the degree of the disability, the families bring to the urban school a perspective that departs from the "norm." In order to understand these families and offer appropriate and meaningful recommendations regarding placement and instruction, schools must be aware of these histories and offer effective training to the faculty and staff.

THE URBAN SCHOOL

Free and appropriate public education must be available to all handicapped students between the ages of three and twenty-one. There is an exception for providing services to the preschool, handicapped age group (ages three to five) or to high school students (ages eighteen to twenty-one) if this is inconsistent with state law or practice regarding public education to these age groups. The educational implication of this legal requirement is that school systems must admit handicapped students into educational programs.[10]

This statement reflects Public Law 94–142, which had enormous impact regarding the treatment of children with disabilities. Beyond the law is its implementation, which focuses more on both the process and the outcome. A close examination of the implementation component will help determine the effectiveness of the urban school in its ability to serve this unusual student and parent population.

The scope of special education at any time and place is determined by at least the following factors: (1) terminology, (2) philosophical beliefs, (3) history, (4) local tradition, (5) legal foundations, and (6) fiscal constraints.[11] Each category requires a clear definition in order to understand how the school approaches its treatment of these children. It is particularly important to understand these terms and their implications because exceptional children are addressed in different ways in the urban school environment, depending on the school's perspective of this type of child.

Terminology

We've purposely used the term *exceptional* child because the term is more objective and less pejorative than much of the lexicon of the profession. The term *exceptional* carries more positive connotations than the negative ones generally associated with the term *handicapped*.[12] *Special needs* is another term assigned to these children that is often viewed as essentially synonymous with *exceptional*. Yet in certain districts (e.g., New York State), specific legal classifications of pupils with special educational needs (PSED) are established to define and authorize services distinct from those for pupils with handicapping conditions (PHC).[13]

Furthermore, distinctions between *handicapped* and *disability* are quite interesting and particularly important. Social psychologists are clear to separate the two terms. While both terms suggest limitation of some kind of personal physical function, the term *handicapped* has greater stereotyping and negative features to it than the term *disability*, which is perceived and interpreted as more objective. Douglas Biklen and Robert Bogdan quote one activist as saying, "Our bodies make us disabled, but society makes us handicapped."[14] It is believed that this type of stereotyping contributes to the perception that people so affected are less able to function in more ways than would be derived from the disability alone. The function and application of terminology are a significant aspect to the treatment of these children in the urban school environment. Obviously, if the school is sensitive to these distinctions and communicates information that reflects attitudes and belief systems consistent with these understandings, children, families, and all school personnel would relate to these children in a far more nurturing, supportive, and constructive manner.

Philosophical Beliefs

The philosophy of the school in large part determines the ways in which special education children are treated. Whether a child requires remediation because of a learning disability or whether there are significant physical limitations so that the child requires more support at the school site will be treated in different ways, depending on the philosophy of the school. By philosophy, we mean the compartmentalization of approach the school takes as determined by its viewpoint of the problem. In other words, to what extent is the disability at variance with the school population so as to require a specific type of segregation from the mainstream population? One administrator might view children with dyslexia as requiring special classroom settings somewhat apart from the mainstream, while another administration may include those students in far more traditional programs within the school context. It is important to note that the general administrative approach of separation is institutional, since the administration of the children in terms of instruction and personnel is controlled by the centralized operation, although the placement of the children is at sites that are overseen by the site principals, thus creating a precondition of separation. Efforts to change this arrangement have been made in some districts so that the decision-making power is vested in the localities and the conflict of authority is avoided.

History

The historical patterns for serving special needs children are worthy of a more extensive review since the mind-set of urban school officials is often affected by the historical context that spawned the specific school precedents under which they operate. As we know, for every exceptional case, e.g., Helen Keller, for which there have been considerable notoriety and support, there are literally thousands of others who have not been treated in an adequate manner. The late nineteenth century is clear testimony to the limited perception, understanding, and support of the greater society, let alone our urban school system, in working with exceptional children. Only the most severe cases were supported. Maynard C. Reynolds and Jack W. Birch cite four major time periods:[15]

Late nineteenth century: Residential model, with most states accepting public responsibility for the blind, deaf, and mentally retarded

Early twentieth century: Community-based special classes and schools, begun within local school systems

Ca. 1945–1970: Proliferation of the special class model for a greater variety of pupils, with legislative support as a result of political action by organized parents

Ca. 1970—: More inclusive arrangements as a result of parent and professional pressure through courts and comprehensive legislation, based on civil rights principles

Prior to the nineteenth century, people with virtually any type of disability were treated as an economic liability; that is, the history of disabled people was the history of poverty.[16] People who were incapable of maintaining themselves, regardless of reason, were treated similarly. Using the terms of the times, whether a person was an idiot, lame, an alcoholic, an orphan, an unwed mother, or a feeble widow made little difference. Distinctions of pathology and etiology were understood but were approached as irrelevant. If these deviants were not able to be maintained by their immediate families or those who could care for them, they were assigned to local "almshouses," which became a part of nearly all major cities. These were the repositories for those who were not capable of maintaining themselves.

Although the Jacksonian period of the nineteenth century brought about significant reform efforts and attitudes, the focus and strategy of separation were the driving force behind such reform. This population was still seen as dangerous pathologies that must be excluded from the mainstream. With business interests underscoring the political and social mind-set of an evolving capitalist system, any deviation from the norm that could adversely affect this machinery must be extracted and isolated. Residential schools for deaf and blind, asylums for those identified as idiotic, large state prisons for the incorrigibles were all derived from the same institutional blueprint. Although there were initial efforts to relate to these people in a more humane and rational way, alms houses ultimately served as the custodians for society's deviant members.

Poverty underscored the perception of the masses toward these people. The wealthy saw poverty as the cause of their problems and pathologies rather than the result of them. The overriding societal perspective was to remove these deviants, these social and physical defectives, from society in order to safeguard the population from irreparable harm. Again, separation, isolation, sequestration were always the driving strategies utilized by society's decision-making agencies. Public education was founded on similar perspectives. Any behavior considered deviant and not following the preestablished norm was treated by removal. Any disruption from the institution's ability to process its population, this causing a lack of predictability, was isolated and removed. In large part, we find this perspective and operational procedures functioning today.

At the turn of the century, compulsory education had a significant impact on public education and its treatment of special needs children. The newly forming industrialized America required places whereby workers' children could be placed while they served the American industrial machinery. At that early time, a large number of children identified as problematic because they couldn't be handled in the regular classes were from Southern European background (mostly Italian). They were almost always poor and seen as lazy or recalcitrant. A large pool of deviants, with institutional definition and from within our educational system, were labeled as "incorrigible boys, defective children, and children who speak no English."[17]

Another important historical event that affected public education as to its treatment of special needs children were the intelligence tests, specifically, the Binet Intelligence Test, which was brought to the United States by H. H. Goddard. Terms such as *moral defective* and *moron* were used clinically to describe children and were legitimated by these newly applied tests. Most school systems excluded any children from regular classes who performed three years below their chronological level. Considering that approximately 70 percent of the children in New York City schools, for example, were immigrant children, one can appreciate the staggering implications these tests had on the system and children. It was also clear to see the political and social implications and control mechanisms derived from the use of these tests on cultures and ethnic groups attempting to integrate themselves into the system.

Another important historical development that impacted the rationale for segregation practices for special needs populations was social Darwinism. Here, the well-reasoned linkages between biological history and variation with social evolution were established. The poor and defective members of society were simply atavistic throwbacks to less developed cultures and societies. For example, *Mongolian idiocy* and *Mongolism* were racist terms derived from the belief that such people with Down's syndrome were deviants from the less advanced Oriental racial group. Microcephalic people (with small heads) were said to be evolutionary deviants and were called "Aztecs."[18] Again, the result of this perspective and treatment of these various populations of "deviants" was removal and separation. Tracking became a systematic procedure to deal with these populations that oftentimes led to their placement in institutions and asylums. Although much has changed within this century socially and politically that addresses the special needs population in a more rational and legal manner, it is clear that the school system still operates with the vestiges of its historical baggage.

Local Tradition

More recently, the power of local control through influence groups within communities has made considerable impact on the school enterprise. The family involved, an influential educator, a community support group, the political configuration of a local school board, a business organization—each can exert enough pressure to influence the ways in which urban schools relate to their special needs children. The argument offered in the middle of the nineteenth century by proponents and supporters of special needs concerns has considerable resonance today. They felt, as do many more today, that segregation was a violation of children's rights and that the integration of both classes would be beneficial to everyone. This inclusion strategy would develop deeper understandings and sensitivities in those whose exposure to these groups was quite limited. By a similar token, those special needs populations would benefit by having the opportunities to engage and interact with "able" companions. It would be challenging and quickly improve their mental development. This decision-making influence of local control could be the most penetrating aspect to overcoming barriers that have traditionally existed in school systems dealing with the special needs population.

Legal Foundations and Fiscal Constraints

The legal foundations are, to a large extent, determined by these aforementioned characteristics. Although there are explicit constitutional laws requiring urban schools to provide various services to special needs children, each locality defines its needs rather specifically. In short, the areas involved in such definitions include, but are limited to, financial considerations, personnel, clients served, services provided, the organizational body and process.

PROCESSING SPECIAL NEEDS CHILDREN

As indicated in the beginning of this chapter, the background of a child requiring special services is quite complex. Depending on the extent to which a child needs services, the school must determine whether it is equipped to provide those service. Schools generally utilize a special conference involving the school administrator, a special education teacher, the school counselor, a resource specialist, the parents, outside experts, (e.g., doctors), and therapists (parent's request) in order to identify the child's special needs and establish the appropriate Individualized Education Program (IEP) for the child. Legal counselors representing either the school system or the parents are legally able to attend. Under the Education for All Handicapped Children Act (20 U.S.C. Section 1401 et seq.) and under California law, all special needs children are entitled to a "free appropriate public education" tailored to meet their unique needs. Such needs are identified in the IEP. Theoretically, these meetings should be nonadversarial, comprehensive, and honest, with the primary mission to determine the most appropriate educational decisions for the child.[19]

A more typical special education referral should follow the outlined procedures, so that a special education referral is initiated by:

• parent

• agency

• SEIU (Special Education Intake Unit)

• SST (Student Study Team)

Based upon the information contained in the referral, an assessment plan is developed within a fifteen-day period whose intent is to identify the type and degree of problem the student is experiencing, relate that information to the parent, convey to them their legal rights and responsibilities, and obtain consent for assessment. Should the child already be enrolled in special education and a request made from the parents for an IEP, the school district has thirty days from receipt of the written request to schedule an IEP. These guidelines are applicable to transfer students as well. It is important to note that the referral for assessment does not necessarily mean a special education placement, rather, it allows the school to pursue the search for more information.

At this juncture, if the parents reject the plan or do not return it, authorizing this procedure, the process is stopped. If the assessment plan is returned and signed, the assessment must be conducted and the IEP meeting scheduled within fifty days of the district's receipt of the signed assessment plan, according to state (California) time lines (Education Code Sec. 56344).[20]

Several aspects to the IEP are particularly important for the parents to understand prior to their attendance: there may be more than one meeting; there may be a variety of personnel involved in the meeting; the assessment should be accurate and thorough and provide a complete analysis of the child's strengths and weaknesses; it must be provided in the child's primary language and cannot be racially, culturally or sexually discriminatory; the assessor must be cognizant of the child's disability and competent in both the oral and written skills of the child's primary language or mode of communication and if not, translators must be available for this service.[21]

Parents may wish to review the IEP prior to the actual conference. This request must be made in writing prior to the meeting. Lastly, if there is a discrepancy between the IEP school personnel and the parents, for example, regarding its thoroughness, an independent assessment can be requested and performed. In the event there is a different assessment from that of the district, the parents can be reimbursed for the cost, if the district is in agreement with the independent assessment.

Thus far, we have provided information focused on the histories of special needs children, their interaction with the primary care providers, the ways in which schools are charged to accommodate them, and the organizational processes that affect them. Let's turn to some actual cases that further illuminate in more realistic and dramatic terms the life events by which these children are impacted.

CASE STUDIES

The ways in which the legal and bureaucratic systems, school sites, families, and school personnel approach specific cases vary considerably from situation from situation. The following cases are examples of how urban schools and the principal players have dealt with some of these complex issues.

In late 1991 a court case was reported in the Sacramento Bee, in Sacramento, California (December 17, 1991) that had important consequences throughout California. At issue was the question of whether a moderately mentally disabled nine-year old child had been retarded in her development because she had not been enrolled in a special education class. Arguments were presented about whether developmentally disabled children should or should not spend their school days in regular classrooms for all or part of their school day. Rachel Holland, the focus of this litigation, was a second-grader in a private school. Her mother and father wanted to enroll her in a regular class in the Sacramento public school system, but educators argued that she needed to spend at least half of her school day in special education classes. An administrative judge had ruled previously that Rachel would best be served by spending all of her school day in a regular classroom with the help of a part-time aide. The teacher of the aforementioned class would be provided with help from a special educational specialist. The decision was appealed by California school bureaucrats because it might set a precedent. These bureaucrats argued that such an arrangement would not be in the best interests of the child. They felt Rachel should spend most of her school day in a special education class, and a couple of hours of non-academic time with non-disabled children. Rachel's academic achievements were also disputed. She had been enrolled in a regular second grade class in her private school during the appeal, and had assistance from an aide. Legally the question was put as follows: Did she benefit educationally and did her presence in a regular classroom harm the educational experiences of children who were more advanced than she? Rachel's lawyer said that the curriculum of other students had not been affected by her presence, and her academic achievement had improved about one year. Witnesses and attorneys for the school district disputed these claims arguing that the gains were insignificant and subject to regression. Other experts believed Rachel had been harmed by being in a regular class because she had no access to a person trained in special education. The practice of putting Rachel in a regular classroom was deemed as experimental and harmful.

Analysis. There are a number of critical issues being raised in this case. Initially, if the district is concerned about the financial implications of the inclusion strategy, to the extent that the thrust of its decision is predicated on this, the specific educational goals and objectives regarding Rachel's plan are being undermined. While the financial consideration is an organizational factor that can't be ignored, it cannot be the critical mechanism for making the decision regarding student placement and individual program design. It clearly violates the sabotages the plans to help the child progress and grow in a meaningful way. It is counterproductive to the very intent of the IEP.

Indeed, if there is no clear-cut research that supports full inclusion as making a significant impact on the development of the child and if the specific documented case does not justify inclusion as the optimal strategy for this child's growth and development, then the philosophy and political force of the parents and administration will be the key variables in determining which course of action the school will take. The issue of priorities, perspective, and overall perception of the special needs population ultimately will characterize the decisions regarding these controversial cases. It is the opinion of these authors that full inclusion is supported by the research and that it does make a meaningful contribution to the growth and development of the child. As well, the inclusion strategy also develops sensitivity to, and greater awareness of, the special needs student by the greater student population.

Clearly, these values and belief systems that are transmitted through administrative and programmatic decisions underlie the treatment of special needs children. How often are these values discussed and analyzed by administrators, educators, and parents? How able is the system in furnishing the type of environment through procedures, rules, and staff development opportunities in fostering such growth? Who benefits from the programs that theoretically are designed to accommodate the child? There are a multitude of other issues that are more subtly involved when one asks the question, Whom does the program serve?

Special needs programs provide employment opportunities for special education professionals, allow for the highly sought-after respite for the parents, and involve various additional sources of money for school functioning, to mention a few of the additional, less obvious aspects associated with these programs. As a result, it is not unusual for there to be a number of "interests" at stake when decisions are taken in the treatment of the special needs child.

Judy

It was nearing the end of the second semester of school. Judy's parents were scheduled to meet with her teacher, Mr. Roberts, at 3:00 P.M. Mr. Roberts was looking forward to this appointment. He felt he had some very good news to report. Judy was finally learning to differentiate the primary colors. He had been working with her on this for some time.

Three o'clock arrived. The parents said: "Mr. Roberts, it's real nice that Judy knows red from blue. It's not that we don't care. It's just that it doesn't seem very important when you see her dripping food down her chin and blouse at dinner or when she screams bloody murder in the department store because she can't have a toy. Can't you work with her on some of these things, instead of red, blue, or green?"[22]

Analysis. In this particular case, the objectives and priorities of the parents and the teacher were in conflict. Objectives regarding short- and long-term goals and the types of specific behavioral changes between these parties were not consonant. These issues and expectations would likely have been resolved if the initial meeting and interaction were focused on agreed-upon outcomes. Often, this dialogue does not take place, and when it does, agreement is difficult to achieve. Generally, areas such as learning potential, safe and productive environment, personal contentment and happiness, economic independence, and societal acceptance are vitally important focal points for discussion.

David

Ruth and Michael Burnstein had placed their severely retarded son, David, in a state institution for the mentally retarded when he was five years old. They had been told this was the best thing to do by their family, friends, and professionals in the field. Years passed by; they visited their son when they could. It was always a sad experience, but they were faithful.

It had been eleven years since David had entered the institution. A letter arrived at their home. Ruth read it first. She couldn't believe it. Her heart started pounding against her rib cage. David was ready to come home. The evaluation team at the institution felt he was prepared for a home-community life-style. They wanted the parents to take him back home.

Ruth couldn't understand her feelings. She knew she should be happy that David was able to come home. But all she felt were anxiety and even a slight tinge of dread. She and Michael were comfortable in their life together. They had their careers and commitments in the community, and they were older. What would they do with David, a sixteen-year-old, severely retarded young man— a stranger?

Michael and Ruth panicked. They called the institution that evening to see if there had been some mistake. Was the evaluation team certain that its decision was in David's best interest? Wouldn't he be lost in the community? Surely, it would be better for him to be around others who were more like him. The institution's official was a young man who didn't seem very sympathetic to their concerns. He even seemed to be angered by their questions. As far as he was concerned, David should come home.

Analysis. In this situation, the process to deal with the needs of the parents and child was central to resolving this matter. The reactions of the parents were perfectly reasonable, based on their current life circumstance, albeit painful and complex. The perception of the administrator seemed to lack a deeper understanding as to the reaction of the parents. What types of parent education programs were available to assist parents to make the transition to accept their children back into the home? What process of transitioning these parents, over time, was part of the strategic planning of the institutions that served these children? What alternatives were available to meet the complex and conflicting needs of all those family members involved in these life-affecting decisions. These issues require careful consideration when reviewing these critical life decisions. Which options are viable and why?

Billy

"I don't know why you're having so much trouble with Billy at school, Ms. Dickens. I've had him toilet trained at home for some time now," boasted Mrs. Jennings.

Mr. Jennings began to feel a little uncomfortable. He knew that Lillia had worked very hard with Billy at home and with some success. He usually had three accidents a day. So why was she coming on so strong with the teacher?

"Well, I can't understand it either, Mrs. Jennings. For Billy to be doing so well at home and yet be only partially successful at school is puzzling, to say the least. Are you sure that he isn't having a few accidents now and then? He has about one a day at school."

Mrs. Jennings replied confidently, "He is doing fine at home."

Mr. Jennings was really disturbed now. Billy wasn't doing as well at home as he was in school, if what Ms. Dickens said was true. So, why was Lillia implying that he was? Why was she being so defensive?

Analysis. Oftentimes, parents and educators unconsciously compete and, as a result, distort the situation in order to accommodate their own interests. In this case, the parent could have been threatened by the success being realized by the teacher. For a "stranger" to experience greater success than the parent is not a reflection of the ability of the parent to help her child, although this apparently was her reaction. Understanding that the child's success could be realized in a number of different situations and initiated by a variety of sources is extremely important. Both professionals and parents must be cognizant of this and open enough to work through their own personal feelings associated with these possibilities.

Julie

Mrs. Clark began the planning meeting with Julie's parents by asking them if they had disagreed with any learning objectives listed in the plans.

"Yes," said Mr. Ross, "we don't like those items you've listed concerned with sex education."

"May I ask why, sir?"

Mr. Ross shifted in his chair. "We are facing more immediate problems with Julie right now."

Mrs. Ross interjected: "Quite frankly, we aren't convinced that she ever really needs to have a lot of knowledge about sex. She will live with us most of her life, and we don't think there will be any occasions when someone would try to take advantage of her. I mean, after all, she's severely retarded, Mrs. Clark. We doubt that she will ever even date, much less get married."

Mrs. Clark really couldn't understand the Rosses' viewpoint. Julie was fourteen years old and developing into a very attractive young woman. Older boys at school were already noticing her in the hallways. Besides, Julie was progressing well enough in school to be able eventually to live in a semisheltered environment in her adult years. Why were her parents being so short-sighted?[23]

Analysis. There are two issues here: values clarification, (i.e., sex education) and long-term planning. From the standpoint of the sex education, parents of "normal" children often have to approach this topic with deep understanding and sensitivity. Parents of children with special needs might not even accept this developmental possibility for their children, let alone know how to approach it should it become something with which they must contend. In addition, this is the type of long-term planning that is so important in considering the child's future. Complex matter such as these must be viewed and planned within a long-term context. Should this type of information be deemed appropriate, then specific counseling and information should be presented in a meaningful and timely way.

The previous case studies dealt with a variety of issues concerning special needs children. Although these cases focused on more severe special needs children, the issues of treatment by our urban school system remain constant. The special education field accommodates a staggering range of children with disabilities, most notably with learning disabilities. The range of disabilities, both learning and physical, will grow in the future because the technology in the medical field is advancing at such a pace that more children are surviving with disabilities and will be a part of our school system. In addition, advocacy groups continue to gain strength in their legal victories and by their funding efforts to support special needs children's inclusion in the school system. It is clear that our urban school environment has not yet progressed to the point where it can adequately treat the myriad of demands required by these children.

RECOMMENDATIONS

The following list represents some of the effective strategies that we feel can be utilized in the public school environment that can help address the complex needs of the special needs child:

- Sensitize the facility, staff, and parents to the special needs population in the school through workshops, staff development, and other information conduits.
- Develop a matrix organization within the school that would involve different educational and health professionals and parents to plan for the inclusion of these children in the "normal" school functions.
- Plan regular and special education teachers' schedules so that they can interact with each other, to share teaching and philosophical approaches regarding their studies.
- Schedule regular and special education classrooms in close proximity within the school building.
- Provide integration opportunities for both the "normal" segment of the student population as well as the special needs population.
- Adjust the regular curriculum to include information about children with disabilities: values, attitudes, and so on.
- Consider the language and terms utilized in all the communication outlets to students and community when alluding to special needs children.

CONCLUSIONS

Public schools have moral and legal responsibilities to provide a nurturing and educationally sound environment for all segments of our student population. The special needs child requires, and is entitled to, such an environment. The historic backdrop, which has traditionally viewed this population as highly problematic and dysfunctional beyond what should be approximately assigned, is being changed dramatically due to the tireless efforts of parents, parent organizations, and enlightened and committed health and educational officials. The challenge is an endless one and requires constant vigilance.

NOTES

1. Robert H. A. Haslam and Peter J. Vallentutti Haslam, *Medical Problems in the Classroom: The Teacher's Role in Diagnosis & Management* (Austin, TX: Pro-Ed, 1985).
2. E. H. Erickson, *Identity and Crisis* (New York: Norton, 1968).
3. Dennis Drotar, Peggy Crawford, and Marcy Bush, "The Family Context of Childhood Chronic Illness: Implications for Psychosocial Intervention," in Myron G. Eisenberg, LaFaye C. Sutkin, and Mary A. Jansen, *Chronic Illness and Disability Through the Life Span: Effects on Self and Family* (New York: Springer, 1984), 103.
4. E. J. Anthony. *The Child and His Family: The Impact of Disease and Death* (New York: Wiley, 1973).
5. Andrew E. Dubin et al., *Lives in Transition. Support for Parents of Special Needs Children*, Original videotape: nonprofit organization. (San Francisco, 1989).
6. L. C. Rustad, "Facilitating Communications: An Aid to Effective Treatment on the Renal Dialysis Unit," in M. G. Eisenberg, J. Falconer, and L. Sutkin (Eds.), *Communications in a Health Care Setting* (Springfield, IL: Charles C. Thomas, 1980).
7. Dubin, et al. *Lives in Transition.*
8. Ibid.

9. Ibid.

10. Ann P. Turnbull and Jane B. Schulz, *Mainstreaming Handicapped Students: A Guide for the Classroom Teacher* (Boston: Allyn and Bacon, 1979), 63.

11. Daniel D. Sage and Leonard C. Burrello, *Policy and Management in Special Education* (Englewood: Prentice-Hall, 1986), 1.

12. Ibid.

13. Ibid.

14. Douglas Bilken and Robert Bogdan, "Media Portrayals of Disabled People: A Study in Stereotypes," *Interracial Books for Children Bulletin* 8, nos. 6, 7 (1977): Also in Sage and Burrello, *Policy and Management in Special Education*, 2.

15. Maynard C. Reynolds and Jack W. Birch, *Teaching Exceptional Children in All America's Schools* (Reston, VA: Council for Exceptional Children (1982), 18. Also in Sage and Burrello, *Policy and Management in Special Education*, 4.

16. D. J. Rothman, *The Discovery of the Asylum: Social Order and Disorder in the New Republic* (Boston: Little, Brown, 1971).

17. E. Hoffman, "The American Public School and the Deviant Child: The Origins of Their Involvement," *Journal of Special Education* 9 (1975): 415–35.

18. Diane L. Ferguson, Philip M. Ferguson, and Robert C. Bogdan, "If Mainstreaming Is the Answer, What Is the Question?" in Virginia Richardson-Koehler (Sr. Ed.), *Educator's Handbook: A Research Perspective* (New York: Longman Press, 1987).

19. Katrina Abel, "For the Record," p. 24, in *Thrust for Educational Leadership*. Association of California School Administrators (Burlingame, California. Vol. 20, No. 3. November/December 1990).

20. *Special Education Handbook: A Resource Guide for Parents and Guardians*, 9th ed. Community Advisory Committee for Special Education (San Francisco: Unified School District, 1991).

21. Ibid.

22. Philip Roos, a compilation of materials from several publications, uncited, presented in a booklet, *The Partnership: How To Make It Work*, (Sacramento, CA: Special Education Resource Network, 1992).

23. Ibid.

V

THE URBAN BATTLEGROUND

15

The Urban Crisis

Stanley William Rothstein

To those who live in the inner cities the dominant assumptions of American society no longer apply. It is discouraging to see the hopes of the 1960s dashed by the realities of the depressed 1990s. Even after a triumph in the political arena, things remain pretty awful for the minority and immigrant families forced to live and work in the reservations of our inner cities.

As unemployment rises, so do crime and the desperate voices inside the ghetto. Urban protest movements revive even in the current rocky soil, and the Los Angeles riots have had their echo in many other urban centers. Newspapers announce to the world that the drug culture has created a new and dangerous world of gangs, as if that explains or justifies the terrible neglect of our inner cities. Crime is rising, and the ability of the police to control the situation is faltering badly. Many minority people are convinced that their depressed conditions are a direct consequence of the system's neglect and deeply held prejudices. Many solve their everyday problems by joining a gang to secure themselves against assault while working in illegal trades to make ends meet. Many others are forced onto the dole, experiencing welfare and inflicting humiliation on themselves and their children. All assume, of course, that there are no political movements reflecting their interests and concerns. The schools and community groups are losing their influence and control over inner-city youngsters.

In response, community organizations, churches, and urban protest movements have taken more extreme positions. Confronted with the logic of an apartheid society in the United States, they are falling into despair and violent rhetoric. The rappers are the vehicle for the smoldering anger and frustration of minority communities that are living in conditions that rival those of Third World countries. Still the most important evidence of the breakdown of social order and control in our inner cities has been the riots, which are beginning to take on the coloration of a revolt against the penal system. As in the explosions that followed the hot summers of 1967 and 1968, the Rodney King verdict has ignited long-standing grievances and concerns. The concentration of African-Americans in inner-city reservations is comparable to the apartheid measures that were taken in South Africa. As in Soweto, there are no jobs for the racial and ethnic minorities living in isolation in America's inner cities. This is because of an expanding world trade and the exportation of production jobs overseas. High unemployment and underemployment have become widespread in our depressed urban areas. Just as serious have been the development of surburban areas and the deterioration of urban housing, public transport, and health and educational services.

An unfortunate legacy of this urban crisis has been a more intense socioeconomic and racial segregation and the collapse of the public school system in inner-city districts. Governmental policies have contributed to these difficult problems. Yet they are not alone in bearing responsibility. We must take note of the new global economy and the marginalization of unskilled and skilled American workers in the new order, developments that occurred with the encouragement and consent of the American government. Allowing multinational corporations to relocate to low-wage, low-tax countries in the less-developed parts of the world was wholly incompatible with any hope of maintaining high-wage jobs and an effective, assertive union movement. The failure to limit these practices accelerated the exportation of jobs and capital and further depressed the conditions of workers, especially in our inner cities.

Our ability to correct these problems is reduced because business now transcends national boundaries while, as yet, no international political government exists for regulating and controlling these modern-day robber barons. In short, the urban crisis has developed because of unwise and unrestrained economic policies, the flight of the middle classes to the suburbs, and the resulting inability of local governments to provide adequate services for their residents.

The urban crisis is worsening because so many unemployed people are migrating to our large cities and towns. With unemployment and under-employment running at increasingly high levels, it seems obvious that the tax base of urban governments will not increase. Adding to these problems are the further growth in crime, homelessness, and poverty and their savage consequences for racial minorities, women, and children. The more the urban crisis goes unchecked, the more family life is destroyed by single-parent homes and the pernicious welfare system. Unattended children are usually a factor in developing gang cultures and criminal activities.

Against this crisis and the holocaust that the drug culture has created, religion has played a role, as our next chapter by Anthony M. Stevens-Arroyo and Ana María Diaz-Stevens demonstrates. Then we end this section with a discussion of crack kids and their implications for urban schools.

16

Latino Churches and Schools as Urban Battlegrounds

Anthony M. Stevens-Arroyo and Ana María Diaz-Stevens

The rumors of the demise of religion have been greatly exaggerated. Certainly among Latinos, one of the salient characteristics of the barrios from Boston to San Diego is the omnipresence of religion. Whether in stately stone churches, ebullient storefront Pentecostal chapels, or the mysterious *bótanicas* filled with incense and African amulets, the Latino people of the United States surround themselves with vehicles of religious expression.[1]

But what is the schooling function of religion, especially in the midst of Latino urban poverty? Among African-Americans, the study of the permanent underclass led Jeffrey Wilson to consider this question. He viewed the educative role of religion skeptically and generally considered it to offer no remedy to the hope-lessness of the poverty cycle.[2] A study on black churches was more precise in analyzing the reason poverty and faith coexist with such little apparent mutual influence, pointing out that members of black urban churches tend to view themselves as different from the underclass around them.[3] These authors are more optimistic than Wilson, anticipating that part of the definition of an African-American Christian is to combat poverty and that education in moral values of the poor is within the future agenda of black churches.

It would be a mistake to consider that what is said about religion among African-Americans necessarily is also true for Latinos. Not only is the religious tradition different, but the culture and the social experiences also are essentially distinct. Thus, the urban experience of Latinos is colored by a religious factor that is as unique as it is pervasive. Like urban problems and poverty, religion seems never to fade away, despite the secularist premises of liberals and radicals alike.

As Marx testified in his celebrated phrase, religion may be "the opiate of the people," but it is also "the cry of the oppressed." Certainly no one familiar with the radical ideological role of liberation theology in Latin America can pretend that religion in each and every manifestation is antithetical to real change.[4] Thus, religion in the barrios is not easily dismissed as a font of consolation to uptight conservatives.

The forces that configure religion can be understood, however, only by making a distinction between the role of institutions and belief. Religious institutions provide ceremony, ritual, doctrine, and ethical norms. In addition to matters strictly religious, churches frequently offer services as varied as food for the homeless and a school for education. The members of a religious institution are believers, characterized by faith in God, in the saints and miracles, in prayers and providence. All of these kaleidoscope beliefs shape the idealized, moral world. Believers usually know that neither they nor the society they live in is perfect, but faith means that they hope for a transformation according to these ideals. When this hope is projected onto a transparent and invisible world (heaven) as an excuse for not getting involved in the present order, religion is the opiate Marx talked about. But when believers focus their collective efforts on changing the present order, religion acquires political ramifications. The institution with its management and employees—the bishops and clergy—often plays the decisive role of tipping collective action either toward the next world or in favor of change in the present order.[5]

The Venezuelan sociologist Otto Maduro has offered a key interpretive text for understanding religion from a political economy perspective.[6] He conceives religion as the producer of beliefs and sentiments about the values of life and human relationships. Masterfully, he shows how religion usually mirrors the existing sociopolitical order and harmonizes itself in a symbiotic relationship with power. Yet, at certain times of crisis and change in structures, religion is capable of defending its interests by attacking the status quo. Religious schooling is a prime vehicle for communicating the churches' view of the world.

Because leaders exercise such a key role in determining the direction of religion's social projection, Maduro has included some of Antonio Gramsci's thinking about leadership, which he applies to analysis of authority, both in church and in society. His focus is upon Catholicism, particularly since its watershed event of 1965, when world Catholicism adopted a reform plan that had been drafted in Rome during the Second Vatican Council. The far-reaching effects of this event—and reactions to it—still shape Catholicism.[7] Moreover, because Catholicism is the major denomination among Latin Americans and Latinos, changes within the Catholic church quickly demanded adjustment from many other religions as well. The council decentralized institutional Catholicism, delegating much decision making to regional groupings of bishops. Simultaneously, it switched from Latin as a pulverizing and univeralizing instrument of ritual conformity to a policy of encouraging the actual spoken language of people in religious services. Perhaps most important of all, the council redefined for the church a role of cooperation with, rather than opposition to, many modern social forces. Thus, for instance, Catholicism affirmed a need to coalesce with socialism for issues of social justice, embraced the goals of the United Nations as an instrument of world peace, and rejected policies that prohibited collaboration with nonbelievers, non-Catholics, or Communists.

In Latin America, these tendencies were fleshed out in specific policies fashioned at a two-year meeting (1967–1968) at Medellín in Colombia. At this meeting of bishops, through the prodding of progressive young clergy, Latin American Catholicism embraced its preferential option for the poor, incorporated Marxist analysis in the theology of liberation, and moved toward the grass roots ministries. In the wake of these benchmark policy changes, similar trends were evidenced in most Protestant denominations, except perhaps among Pentecostals of Latin America.[8]

Certain studies of Latin American clergy demonstrate several of the characteristics of the new role of religion.[9] These include:

1. The use of Marxist analysis in assessing church activity
2. A preferential option for the poor, that is, a favoritism to provide services to the impoverished even at the expense of society's ruling class
3. A shift away from clerical and centralized control toward grass roots communities (*communidades eclesiales de base*) in which local lay leaders, including women, assume key roles of leadership

While there has been much enthusiasm for the potential of liberation theology, a cautionary note is in order. Because it closely paralleled progressive social forces retreat beaten by socialism worldwide since 1990 has had its impact in church circles. Charles Hewlitt is probably unduly focused on his own conservative agenda, but there is a ring of truth to his assertion that the desire to shift responsibility to lay people at the grass roots had its origins more in a clerical initiative than in any spontaneous lay interest.[10] In other words, the idea of giving more power to the people came at the clergy's insistence. Hewlitt brashly categorizes the option for the poor as a subterfuge of church leaders win concessions from ruling military dictatorships. He asserts the option constituents elitist intent to distort the true faith that is inherently conservative. Notwithstanding such easy definitions, the transformation of religion in Latin America during the past decades is the single most important characteristic of its social relationships to people and the institutions of economic and political power.

In order to understand the role of religion among Latinos in the United States today, therefore, the dimensions of the changes instituted by the Second Vatican Council cannot be underestimated. In fact, because the abandonment of Latin and the adoption of the language of the people were mandated by the council, within the United States it quickly became apparent that there were two significant Catholic populations to be served. On one hand, there were the Euro-American Catholics, principally of Irish, German, French, Polish, and Italian background, who had now adopted English as their language at the expense of an earlier family tradition. On the other hand, there were the Spanish-speaking Catholics, largely those of Mexican, Puerto Rican, and Cuban heritage, who still identified themselves by a cultural tradition. These two groups, formerly juxtaposed in U.S. Catholicism under the apparent umbrella of a common Latin ritual, were now divided linguistically with separate services, clergy, religious books, hymns, and the like. In Maduro's concept, the religious production of the institutional church was now diversified, with two publics competing for attention and resources.

Several recent sociohistorical works have addressed the conflictive dimensions of the competition within different religions between the English-speaking and the Spanish-speaking.[11] This chapter focuses on one aspect of that process, namely, how religious schools and programs of religious education became urban battlegrounds between Latinos and other believers. Although the schooling aspect of this process offers only a partial view of this phenomenon, it is an important one because it is through education that churches recruit, indoctrinate, and legitimate their members. How did the changes in the United States and Latin America affect religious education among Latinos? What were the key instruments of change and institutional control that emerged in this process? What forms of cooperation with progressive political forces took shape, and what results became reactionary political opposition? Most importantly, how does religion affect schooling in the nation's large cities among the growing numbers of Latinos?

HISTORICAL BACKGROUND

In order to appreciate the changes in U.S. religion, particularly in Catholicism, a brief review of the status of religious schooling before the 1964–1965 council is in order. Since the founding of the republic, religious education for most Protestant denominations was primarily achieved through various forms of Sunday school. In other words, a specifically religious training was imparted in a voluntary weekly program meant to supplement public school education. Ostensibly, the Sunday school taught only religion, and the public schools taught only reading, writing, and arithmetic. In the tradition of separation of church and state, therefore, religious education and public education were two different realms from the time of the Founding Fathers.

Yet as far back as the second half of the nineteenth century, Catholic bishops felt that the separation of church and state worked against them. Protestant religious culture pervaded public school instruction, even if no particular Protestant denomination was favored. School celebrations such as Christmas, history texts about the Pilgrims, and civic and social studies courses were diagnosed as identifying the United States as a Protestant country and simultaneously reinforcing negative views of Catholics. In the twentieth century some Jewish leaders came to feel the same. This led to a desire to establish special schools for Catholics and observant Jews in order to ensure that their specific religious worldview would be preserved in education and not be affected by Protestantism.[12]

Accordingly, alongside the public school system, religious schools were founded in order not only to teach the dogmas of faith but also to provide the basic educational skills of the three Rs. The most numerous of religious schools in the United States are those in the Catholic parochial school system. Through the first half of the twentieth century, it was normal for every Catholic parish church to have its own school for the children of its members. Completely financed and run with the voluntary contributions of churchgoers, the parochial schools were nonetheless accredited by state and local governments. When joined to similar Catholic high schools, colleges, and universities, Catholic education was a complete system unto itself and many Catholics went on to advanced degrees without ever setting foot inside a publicly supported educational institution.[13]

The function of such a system was to provide United States' Catholicism with members who could compete in the general society in politics, economy, and education but without internalizing the premise that America is a Protestant country. Ironically, while the Catholic schools nourished a particularized identity as "non-Protestant," it also stressed a very pro-America set of values that extolled the United States as the most democratic, most peaceful, most just nation on earth. By the 1950s, most Catholics viewed their religious opposition to "atheistic Communism" as intrinsic support for virtually all policies of the United States during the cold war. It was the Catholic cardinal of New York, Francis Spellman who coined the phrase "My country, right or wrong" as a way of excusing misguided policies such as U.S. intervention in Vietnam.[14]

Catholic schools in the 1950s represented the incubator of a new generation of Catholics with this mentality. The schools provided a traditional set of both cultural and religious values and were relatively affordable. Because the teaching faculty was composed mostly of religious women (nuns and sisters) who worked with only minimal compensation, parish members were able to finance an entire year's education, both grammar and high school, for as little as thirty or forty dollars' tuition per child. Through investment portfolios, real estate holdings, and centralized banking, many of the costs of education were subsidized at a regional level by bishops. Yet Latinos were virtually invisible in the parochial schools of this prosperous and contented urban Catholicism before the Second Vatican Council.

LATINOS AND RELIGIOUS SCHOOLING BEFORE 1964

The first Catholic churches and schools in what is now the United States were founded under Spain in St. Augustine, Florida, in the second half of the sixteenth century—and that is without counting Puerto Rico, which was the first diocese in the New World to receive its bishop in 1511. Yet, as late as the 1950s, Latinos—principally Mexicans, Puerto Ricans, and Cubans—were treated as if they were immigrants and recent arrivals to the United States, bringing up the rear in a long line of Catholic ethnic groups that had settled in the United States.

The subterfuge used to turn the original inhabitants of Texas, New Mexico,

Arizona, Colorado, and California into "immigrants" was to lump third- and fourth-generation natives with Mexican immigrants on the basis of language. In other words, speaking Spanish made one "foreign," even if one's ancestors had intermarried with the Indians and built the first cities of Texas, the Southwest, and California. The English-speaking Catholic migrants to these areas, which had been wrested from Mexico by military conquest in 1836 and 1848, marginated the natives and established themselves as the ruling group in terms of power, even if they were not the majority group in demographic numbers.[15]

The U.S. Catholic church followed this pattern by building new parishes for the Irish, German, and French Catholics who poured into Texas, the Southwest, and California. These churches were for the English-speaking and segregated themselves and their financial resources from the already existing Spanish-speaking parishes that had been founded under Spanish and Mexican rule. These older parishes, often historic mission churches, did not follow the norm established in the urban Catholicism of the United States to build a Catholic school for every parish with its pro-America, assimilationist agenda. These parishes were staffed largely by members of religious orders, who were dependent on their own sources of funding, but yet subject to decrees of the bishops, and the financial resources of the Spanish-speaking parishes were usually inferior to those of the English-speaking churches that were aligned with the ruling classes.[16]

Even the increased migration of Mexicans to Texas and California during the upheavals of the revolution (1910–1917) and during the Cristero Revolt (1922–1927) did not significantly alter the pattern of assigning the Spanish-speaking to the inferior facilities on the basis of language. These institutions were called "national parishes," to distinguish them from the territorial parishes for the English-speaking, and were supported from the general treasury of the bishops. Thus Catholicism practiced its own version of Jim Crow for the Mexican-origin people, with separate and inferior facilities for the Spanish-speaking.[17]

In urban centers like New York and Chicago, these national parishes were constructed for the Spanish-speaking into the 1940s. But by the post–World War II period, it became evident that new parishes in the cities would be counter-productive. The white, non-Latino, Catholic population was on the move out of the cities and toward the suburbs. Latinos (along with African-Americans from the U.S. southland) were pouring into urban centers for manufacturing jobs. Rather than leave the already built churches empty in favor of building new national parishes for the Spanish-speaking, several bishops decided to supplant the departing English-speaking with the Spanish-speaking.[18] This decision was first articulated by Spellman in New York (1939) and later duplicated in Brooklyn, Chicago, Philadelphia, and other urban centers.[19]

Yet this move toward integration of the church was colored by the inferiorization of the Spanish-speaking within the territorial parishes. As had been inflicted on the Italian-speaking before them, the Spanish-speaking found themselves in the basement church, while the English-speaking enjoyed the advantages of the upper, more grandiose church. In New York, this meant that the Puerto Ricans were assigned the younger, less-experienced, less-influential clergy; they were forced into the inconvenient hours of early morning or pushed into the afternoon for their activities; they were given secondhand resources. Yet, this segregation ironically nourished a sense of independence among the Puerto Ricans and helped them re-create a Catholicism similar to what they had experienced in the rural areas of their native island.[20]

Spanish-speaking Catholic children managed to find their way into parochial schools before 1964. There are no reliable national statistics for judging how many Latinos were in Catholic schools at that time, but inasmuch as only 10 percent of Latino students are in Catholic schools today, it seems likely that the number of Latino Catholic pupils was relatively small.[21] Moreover, there was little, of any, consideration given in the Catholic schools toward preserving Latino culture and the Spanish language. The pro-America and assimilation norms were imposed on Latino students as the price of attendance, with more than frequent intimations of prejudice against Latino culture.

The vast majority of Latino students, however, remained outside the Catholic schools and had to rely on Sunday school—called "catechetical programs" within Catholicism—for any transmission of religious values outside the home. Often enrollment in such supplemental education was the price to be paid in order to receive the rites du passage, baptism, first Holy Communion, and matrimony.

Fortunately, as Latinos grew in numbers within the cities, some sympathetic religious leaders recognized that religious instruction was best carried out in the native tongue of the Spanish-speaking. Some pastors entrusted the transmission of this supplemental education to native Spanish-speaking teachers. Such native Latino catechists worked on a volunteer basis and conducted classes in Spanish in place of the sisters and the nuns who did not speak the language.[22]

This practical outreach to Latinos was not the case in each and every Catholic parish, however. The difficulties placed in the way of the practice of Catholicism by prejudiced clergy or parishioners often rendered it more attractive to the Spanish-speaking in urban centers to join Pentecostal and Evangelical churches. Less burdened by institutional interests, open to a married clergy, and able to adapt quickly to social conditions, these other religions experienced considerable success recruiting Latino members in virtually every urban center of the United States. Usually close-knit groups consisting of a few extended families, such churches offered Latinos an intensity of religious experience that was hard to come by in a segregated Catholicism.[23]

The drawback to membership in Pentecostal churches was the absence of the traditional cultural norm of Latino religion. Historically, this culture was derived from Catholic customs, and those who joined Pentecostal and Evangelical churches were often expected to jettison much of their Latino cultural identity in embracing a new faith.[24]

CRUSADES AND CONFLICTS

The impact of the Second Vatican Council on Catholic institutions and Catholic belief was magnified by the political events of the war on poverty, the civil rights movement, the change in the immigration law, and opposition to the war in Vietnam. Among the English-speaking, the simplistic identification of Catholicism and pro-American patriotism as infallible crusaders against communism withered. Catholic priests, such as Fathers Daniel and Philip Berrigan, became synonymous with radical religious opposition to the Vietnam War. In civil rights, welfare legislation, and immigration policy, there was a conspicuous Catholic presence that not only spoke in favor of a progressive agenda but exercised considerable political clout in implementing change.

There had always been Catholics sufficiently progressive to advance peace and social justice, of course, but previously, they had been more or less forced to march in lockstep behind the bishops. Now Catholic lay organizations mushroomed around the country, responding to the council's call for collaboration with political forces and not waiting for an imprimatur from above. Thus a specifically "Catholic" agenda was submerged in order to combine Catholics with larger national political movements.

Such swift and radical turnabouts had fallout. The Berrigans, for instance, fled as fugitives from generally Irish Catholic Federal Bureau of Investigation (FBI) agents by hiding in church convents. This delicious irony was duplicated on a host of other fronts as well. While some clerics marched in Selma, Alabama, with Martin Luther King, white, ethnic Catholics in blue-collar neighborhoods began a trek out of the Democratic party and toward a reactionary Republicanism.

The changes in church and society were not limited to the English-speaking believers. The council and the political milieu had profound effects upon the Latinos in the United States. The war on poverty and the civil rights movement combined to offer political and economic opportunities that Latinos had not enjoyed previously. African-Americans led the struggle for racial justice, culminating in the march on Washington led by Martin Luther King. The traditional black churches were instrumental in opening the way for passage of comprehensive civil rights legislation. Yet, although the framers of the law and the general public viewed the cause as largely as black-white racial issue, Latinos were included as parts of the "minority groups." Likewise, although the war on poverty targeted African-Americans trapped in the nation's inner cities, Latinos also benefited from the measures that directed money for social services directly to organizations headed by Latinos.[25]

Early on, Monsignor Robert Fox, head of New York's office for the Spanish-speaking, seized upon these opportunities to mobilize Puerto Ricans and other Latinos in his charge. From 1966 until 1971, when he resigned his position within the bureaucracy of the New York archdiocese, Fox initiated a series of innovative programs for the Puerto Ricans in New York.[26] The basic elements of these programs included the following:

1. Use of government funds, especially from the war on poverty, for church-initiated programs

2. Inclusion of native Latino laypersons as leaders in these programs, that is, membership on boards and paid workers, assistants, and staff

3. Shift away from centralized control under the bishop toward local parish initiative for innovation

4. Active collaboration and/or confrontation with existing political structures to achieve community power

While Fox was moving in this direction for Puerto Ricans, progressive Catholics were taking similar steps throughout the nation.[27] The road was not always smooth, as evidenced by the confrontation in Los Angeles during Christmas 1964 between Cardinal McIntyre and progressive Catholics called, Católicos por la Raza. This Chicano group demonstrated in support of César Chávez strikers and documented what they pictured as failures of the official institution in Los Angeles adequately to serve the needs of Chicano Catholics. But even in losing the confrontation, Católicos por la Raza eventually sensitized church leaders to the validity of the complaints.[28]

By the summer of 1972, the year of Richard Nixon's fated reelection campaign, Catholicism was divided into two opposing camps in virtually every phase of institutional and religious life. Catholic Latino leaders placed their interests squarely on the side of the progressives. Whether it was the cause of the Delano strike for migrant workers or the service to urban poor in the inner city, Latinos had found in the progressive church a fitting ally in advancing the welfare of Latino people by mobilizing resources from within Catholicism. Similar alliances developed among Latino Protestants, especially those of the more liberal denominations.

But sensing the impracticality of working as minority groups, dispersed throughout the nation, religious leaders of Latino Catholics adopted a national planning congress. Already used with great effect in Latin America, this meeting was held in June 1972 in Washington, D.C., in what became the First Hispano Pastoral Encounter. Serving as officially designated delegates of various dioceses, the participants of the encounter drew up a comprehensive agenda for using church resources to assist Latino religious and community development.[29] Thus, in less than seven year, Latinos had organized themselves as a distinct entity within U.S. Catholicism with their own language of worship, prayer, instruction, political agenda, and radical theology.[30] Rapidly, similar kinds of Latino caucuses, commissions, and boards sprang up within most Protestant denominations that repeated the paradigm successfully launched by the Catholic leadership.

While not neglecting Catholic parochial schools as a valued resource that should be opened up more widely to Latino participation, the First Encounter stressed, rather, what was called "leadership formation." This term more or less corresponds to what might be called in the secular world "adult" or "continuing education.'' Analysis of the trajectory of these projects, of their spotty implementation, and of the ideological struggles for control between progressives and conservatives demonstrates how battles fought elsewhere in the churches were likewise duplicated in schooling.

MORAL TRAINING AS YOUTH LEADERSHIP

The traditional or rural experience of many Latinos creates a problematic understanding of teenagers. In the traditionalist definition, a person is a child until marrying and moving out of their parents' house. The idea of teenagers— no longer children, but still only young adults—did not fit a pre–1950 Latino society in which schooling ended at high school graduation, if at all, and in which Latinos were more or less limited to the marginal farming of their parents and grandparents. Even after migration to the cities and the explosion of educational and career opportunities for Latinos in the latter part of this century, typical church organizations, both Catholic and Protestant, paid scant attention to the special needs of teenagers in an urban environment.[31] Within Latino Catholicism, for instance, teenage girls were segregated into an association called Hijas de María, which provided social activities and participation in church affairs that separated these young women from young men. In a sense, such organizations served the purpose of the chaperone system of Mediterranean culture in which young men and women were never left alone without the supervision of an adult.[32] The principal purpose of the such Catholic organizations and their Protestant and Pentecostal counterparts, such as the child choirs, was to combat sexual sin by inculcating piety.

Non-Latino Catholic teenagers, however, had the Catholic Youth Organization (CYO). Although this U.S. Catholic invention consisted mostly of sports leagues, the CYO allowed for some incidental forms of education in the faith, largely serving the function of sex education. Although the expenditure of parish resources was much greater—gyms, team uniforms, practice fields, coaches, and so on—in the CYO sports programs, the purpose was similar: combat sexual sin by dissipating youthful energies.

In neither system was there much evidence of the Catholic Action Movement, which was very important in Latin America and much of Europe from the middle 1930s until the 1960s.[33] Much more serious and politicized, the Catholic Action groups for young people focused on labor struggles, political voting rights, and ideological advancement of papal teachings for social justice. The main groups were the Juventud Obrera Católica (JOC) for unmarried youth working full-time and the Juventud Estudiantil Católica (JEC) for university students. In the United States, only the Newman Clubs on university campuses approximated the seriousness of these Latin American youth groups.

The supplemental education of Latino youth within U.S. churches, therefore, was largely modeled on a traditionalist conception of society. It is little surprise, then, that many Latino youth in U.S. cities after 1940 were attracted to juvenile gangs. The pachucos or zoot-suiters in Los Angeles and the New York gangs popularized by the Broadway hit show, *West Side Story*, represented an alternative society for Latino teenagers.[34] This function of youth gangs continues today, although seriously complicated by drug addiction and the escalation of violence brought about by easy acquisition of handguns.

Much of church supplemental schooling for youth has focused on the need to find ways to counter the appeal of these juvenile gangs. Together with the dramatic shift in Catholic teaching after the Second Vatican Council, organizations such as the Hijas de Maria or child choirs in Pentecostal churches have been eclipsed as the principal means of addressing the needs of teenagers.

What has been substituted is moral training as youth leadership. Through a host of programs with different names—Crusade for Youth, Jornada, Youth Retreats—the churches have attempted to create the environment for a conversion experience. Such a conversion is designed to include an ethical commitment to avoid the type of sins most common to young adults in urban centers. Thus the commitment to Christ involves renunciation of drug use, gang membership, sexual promiscuity, and even forms of fad dress and haircuts.

Such strategies are easier to install within a denomination that has a tradition of conversion as integral to church membership. On the face of it, this would seem to favor Pentecostals and Evangelicals over Catholics, since the former have a theology based on adult conversion, while membership in the Catholic church usually is imparted through infant baptism. But shortly before the Second Vatican Council, the Cursillo movement was popularized among Latino Catholics. The Cursillo originated in Spain and was designed for adults who had a cultural sense of Catholicism, but without much adult knowledge of, or commitment to, their traditional religion. Somewhat later, in the 1970s, a form of Catholic Pentecostalism also became common among Latino Catholics.[35] Thus, not only exuberant Evangelicals and Pentecostals but also staid Catholics were able to embrace pastoral strategies that utilized an emotional commitment to religion for young people.

The conversion experience is induced by a structured use of peer pressure and conditioned environment. Usually the Jornada or youth retreat involves leaving the neighborhood and spending a weekend in a rural or suburban setting that provides individual sleeping arrangements and communal dining. The retreat is directed by youth already initiated into the group and is under the supervision of a leader, who usually achieves this role in the basis of a demonstrated ability to provide charismatic inspiration in preaching and lecturing. Each stage of the retreat invites self-revelation to a sympathetic audience and structured activities that inculcate trust in the initiated peers.

It is expected that at the end of the process, the recruit will manifest the same commitment to the group as the peers have exhibited to the recruit. The commitment or conversion moment is recognized by some emotional feeling or outburst that legitimates and underscores the depth of conviction. Once committed, the recruit can now participate in the other activities of the initiated. In this way, conversion during the moral training bestows the status of leader upon the participant.

Described in this clinical way, the Jornada and its cognate movements take on the appearance of a cult, or even of brainwashing.[36] There is something of the same dynamics in these movements. But it would be a sad exaggeration to dismiss either the importance of such a religious experience or the sincerity of the leadership. From the Boy Scouts and marines to ACT-UP and NOW, virtually every important social movement depends on some emotional dynamic to build loyalty from its adherents.

Rather than emphasize the limitations of such emotion-based conversion experiences, however, it seems more appropriate here to stress their effectiveness. Just as Alcoholics Anonymous offers evidence that quasi-religious faith is virtually required for rehabilitation of alcoholics, these youth movements have enjoyed marked success in reforming youth surrounded by the drug culture.[37]

With some encouragement from Republican administrations in Washington, federally funded programs to serve minority youth have begun to incorporate many elements taken from the specifically religious programs for youth. Thus, for instance, the New York Center for Alternative Education, the Door, actively engages youth in discussion about their moral values and need for belief, even though the program is strictly non-sectarian. Likewise in New York, in May 1992, the Board of Education voted to stress sexual abstinence rather than the use of condoms as the principal mode of avoiding autoimmune deficiency syndrome (AIDS). While it may be difficult to view this or similar decisions in a nonideological way, the popularity of the decision, among minority parents in particular, is evidence that moral training can be considered to be a dimension of education. Put another way, if public education is interpreted as secular (i.e., no favoritism for religion) only when it excludes any sense of morality, it is no longer effective education.

It would be all too easy to allow the right wing of the Republican party to monopolize a moral education as equivalent to a fundamentalist concept of family values. This was attempted during the 1992 presidential campaign by Vice President Danforth Quayle in his notorious hectoring of the TV character Murphy Brown for having a child out of wedlock. But in the wake of the 1992 Los Angeles riots sparked by the decision to acquit white police officers accused of beating Rodney King, it has become clear that discussion of moral values in the public forum is far more complex than a simple liberal versus conservative dichotomy.

Religious programs of moral training for young people have thus entered into the public consciousness and have provided elements that are repeatable even by government. The blurring of the lines between what is religious and what is secular is addressed by scholars such as David Hayes Batista of the University of California, Los Angeles (UCLA) who views ethos as a vital dimension of Latino cultural identity. But whatever the academic assessment of moral training, its embrace by public society can be expected to continue.

On one hand, it is increasingly more common to find federal and local governments funding programs based within religious institutions. In some instances, such as in foster child care and centers for the elderly, the argument is advanced that the religious identity enhances the success rate of services.[38]

On the other hand, some churches must now compete for membership of Latinos and other minorities or face extinction within many major U.S. cities. The demographics of New York, Los Angeles, San Antonio, Chicago, and Washington are such that unless Latinos continue as Catholics, Evangelicals, or Pentecostals, those churches will be virtually memberless within a generation.[39]

SOCIAL JUSTICE AND POLITICAL REFORM AS MORALITY

But if it is important to attract Latino youth to church membership, to what kind of church do they belong: Is it the status quo, conservative religion of the upper classes or the revolutionary, progressive church that works for the poor? To date, these opposing ideologies still are locked in struggle for the heart of religion. While there may be a moment in which one side or the other appears to have triumphed because of a papal pronouncement or an elder's statement, it is likely that both interpretations will coexist. In the barrios where today's Latinos live, there is a measure of choice as to whether one belongs to a conservative or a progressive parish. One makes the decision by joining the church most favorable to a particular point of view. But the choices made when one is young are key to the future of religion. A brief review of this struggle for influence upon Latino youth in the northeastern part of the United States should serve as an example of the kind of small battles that take place.

The First Hispano Pastoral Encounter of 1972 in Washington paid little attention to youth, preferring instead to speak about Latinos in general. But since youth movements already existed before the First Encounter, the stipulation that all Latinos prepare for a Second Encounter by review of their goals necessarily included these movements as well.

In New York City, there are two Catholic administrative districts—the New York archdiocese, which includes Manhattan, Staten Island, and the Bronx; and the Brooklyn diocese, which covers Brooklyn and Queens. Both districts had CYO sports leagues, which served some Latinos but maintained their largely white, middle-class orientation. In the Bronx, for instance, the CYO league was divided into two divisions: one in the north for the mostly Euro-American parishes and one in the south for the Puerto Ricans and blacks. Moreover, as Puerto Ricans moved northward year by year, "adjustments" were made from time to time to segregate the two groups. Similar segregation could also be found in Brooklyn.

In 1971, the Catholic Bishops' Campaign for Human Development, which is a sort of Catholic foundation for deserving social projects, funded a proposal for Latinos in the New York archdiocese. This youth project was called Equipos

Unidos. Its leaders were young people, mostly in their twenties, from the Dominican Republic and Puerto Rico, who had extensive experience in the JOC or the JEC of those island nations. The idea of the project was to institute training sessions, or workshops, so that young Latinos could assess their own life goals within a support group of peers. But there were a de-emphasis of the role of emotion and a focus on follow-up in the local groups, or *equipos*. Imbued with a sense of social mission that derived from liberation theology, Equipos Unidos added the dimension of social justice to the moral training. At its peak moment in 1973, there were some thirteen local parish *equipos* of some fifty to seventy members in each of the areas of Manhattan and the Bronx, each cooperating with the central committee in coordinated leadership training and social justice projects.

In Brooklyn, there was a much larger youth movement called the Jornada, based on the Cursillo for adults and directed by one of the priests on the staff of those directing the Cursillo. The Jornada focused on conducting some eight to ten retreats each year. Local parish groups of those already initiated recruited new members. Weekly parish meetings planned activities as varied as raffles, car washes, clothing drives, and dances, when they were not engaged in staging the Jornada. Social justice issues, political education, and self-assessment for developing leadership abilities were virtually nonexistent. But what the Brooklyn Jornada lacked in intensity, it made up for in numbers. Whereas Equipos Unidos barely numbered more than a hundred or so young people, the *jornadistas* were in the thousands.

In 1973, the New York archdiocese disassociated itself from Equipos Unidos, depriving the group of its central office and salaried priest director. This rejection of its own creation by the archdiocese came among several reactionary measures taken in reprisal for Latino Catholic militancy.[40] But Equipos Unidos was itself internally divided along national lines. The leaders from the Dominican Republic had decided to focus on the largely Spanish-speaking, first-generation migrant youth in the organization of the movement. Since most of the Puerto Rican youth in New York had been born and raised in the city, they were less likely to prefer Spanish over English and had developed a teenage culture that differed significantly from most of the Dominicans. Faced with this internal decision to abandon Puerto Rican youth, the Puerto Rican leaders began to leave the central committee, and the initial balance between the two groups was destroyed.

This dynamic of intra-Latino rivalry is characteristic of multiple-nationality urban centers. Chicago has faced this since the 1950s and understandably developed a sense of "Latino" identity that served as an umbrella for the Mexican- and Puerto Rican–origin groups within the city.[41] New York, Miami, Los Angeles, and Detroit now face a similar reality after first developing a profile as a region where only one group predominated. Moreover, among Mexican-origin people, there is a profound difference between those who have been born and raised in the United States (the Chicanos and the Mexican-Americans[42]) and those who have migrated here (Mexicans). These differences are most pronounced among teenage youth, who are at an age most sensitive to questions of group identity and have little personal experience as adults to guide them. Thus in everything from dress, choice of music, sense of humor, food preference, and types and forms of social activities, the social distance between Latinos born here and those who have migrated from Latin America is considerable.[43]

Latino youth movements, then, are target groups where notions of cultural identity, group loyalty, linguistic preference, and social consciousness compete for acceptance. Despite attempts to bring first and subsequent generations together in the same groups, unity has often proven illusive. Ironically, as first-generation Latin Americans marry and have children, their offspring come to resemble culturally the Latinos whom their parents found difficult to understand. In other words, a second-generation Dominican in New York often finds himself or herself holding more in common with second- or third-generation Puerto Ricans than with his or her parents. The frequent intermarriage between Puerto Ricans and Dominicans in New York[44] may produce a generation of true "Latinos" who are a mixture of Puerto Rican and Dominican and experience little or none of the intra-Latino conflicts of earlier generations.

ESTABLISHING A NATIONAL PASTORAL PLAN FOR LATINO YOUTH

In 1974, in a parish in the Bronx, New York, a unique youth group was founded that was not only to help unify the Catholic youth of New York and Brooklyn but also to sow the seeds for a national Latino Catholic youth program. Called Naborí, after the native Taíno Indians of Puerto Rico, this group of a dozen university-age youth organized as a grass roots community.[45] Using cultural identity as the matrix for organization, Naborí's members came to view their social identity as based on a Catholic ethos. But at the same time, the study of Puerto Rico's history as a colony under Spain and then the United States imparted to them an awareness of social justice. The experience of a weekend retreat helped in this process, but as with Equipos Unidos, weekly meetings and self-assessment were intended to continue the process begun by the retreat experience by enhancing self-development without undue emphasis on the emotional dimension.

Naborí was successful with this notion of cultural identity as a window to both church loyalty and social commitment, largely because the City University of New York, which most members attended, had serious academic departments of Puerto Rican studies and various radical student groups that viewed a Puerto Rican identity as a commitment to work for radical social change and for the independence of Puerto Rico. Thus Naborí provided a bridge between the traditional religious identity of Catholicism and the social identity within the university as a radical or revolutionary leader of the people. Moreover, because it was a grass roots community rather than a parish activity club, Naborí drew a distinction between service to the church as institution, on one hand, and commitment to Catholic social justice, on the other.

Naborí's members prepared themselves after nearly a year's work to launch the idea of "cultural awareness retreats" for a wider audience of Latino youth who had not yet considered the issues of social identity. The retreat was so successful that Naborí was quickly declared "Communist" by the pastor, and both the priest leader and the group were expelled from the parish.

This expulsion permitted the group to widen its scope and focus on not just a parish, but the church itself. Securing participation in a regional pastoral encounter intended to prepare for a second national encounter, Naborí made a presentation in a workshop on youth that proved the first step in uniting movements from various cities of the Northeast. Rapidly, the different local movements, now organized regionally as the Consejo Pastoral Juvenil or CPJ, obtained legitimation from the adult committee that had been named to coordinate regional activities for Latinos. The CPJ managed to inherit the remaining funds of the now defunct Equipos Unidos and, over the summer of 1975, sponsored three weeks of the cultural awareness retreats, largely inspired by Naborí.

The cultural awareness retreats offered a week of university-style history and culture of Latino groups with a focus on the role of Catholic values and required a week's apprenticeship to a social justice cause. In the first summer and subsequent programs offered at St. Joseph's College in Hartford, Connecticut, in 1977 and 1978, the service was to the Puerto Rican migrant tobacco workers' union, ATA.

The superior vision, organizing skills, and personal gifts of the Naborí members gave them wide influence over youth groups, which generally followed the Jornada model, wherein a narrow church focus and once-in-a-lifetime emotional experience were the basis for organization. Yet as a general rule, Naborí members never accepted official roles as president or chair of the youth committees they helped organize. They maintained a goal of developing awareness (*concientización*) among the leaders of larger groups. This strategy of working with peers made it difficult for conservative church leaders to halt the growing influence of the cultural awareness approach to youth ministry. Adult church leaders were put into the uncomfortable role of taking on the young Naborí organizers themselves and thus appearing as the controllers rather than the guides of their own youth movement. If they left the young people to sort out their own affairs, Naborí generally shaped the agenda. Moreover, although Naborí readily surrendered positions of leadership to the other movements, they worked as a collective and always produced a document or an agenda that bound the elected leader to implement the decisions of the group rather than arbitrarily impose a leadership style from the top down.

The success of Naborí's organizational models was demonstrated during the preparations for the Eucharistic Congress to be held in Philadelphia in the summer of 1976. Because that meeting provided funds to include CYO members from all over the nation, the CPJ in the Northeast argued that similar funds should be provided for Latino youth to participate as equal members of the church. The Mexican-American bureaucrats who administered the national office for Latino Catholics were eager to collect as much money as they could as proof of their effectiveness, so they sided with the CPJ in securing the funds from the congress's organizers. But once they had the money, the Mexican-Americans in Washington became aware that there was no similar regional organization of Latino youth anywhere in Texas, the Southwest, or California. As in the Northeast prior to the CPJ, there were only local parish groups or an occasional diocesan movement. In an effort to "swamp" the CPJ with what was considered an overwhelming majority of Mexican-American youth in the nation, the Washington-based secretariat office provided for a planning session in San Antonio, Texas, prior to the congress.

This strategy of control backfired. Once again, the Naborí organizers won over the young people to their vision. When the Washington office sought to minimize Puerto Rican participation in favor of Mexican-American symbols like mariachi music, the middle-of-the-road Puerto Rican *jornadistas* moved closer to the politicized vision of Naborí. Eventually, the CPJ, now organized for Operation Understanding, threatened the adult Catholic leaders with busloads of picketers unless the original plans of the young people were respected.

A year later, at the 1977 Second Hispano Pastoral Encounter held in Washington, the secretariat organizers had made sure that there was a significant youth representation from regions where Cubans and Mexicans predominated. This was a kind of insurance policy against Puerto Ricans from the Northeast dominating issues on the youth apostolate. The organizers even proposed to eliminate a special workshop on the Latino youth and their needs, preferring to scatter the young people into a dozen or more adult-dominated sessions on other issues. This divide-and-conquer strategy was squelched by the personal intervention of Cardinal Cooke of New York. Despite his own conservative leanings and past history of the expulsion of Equipos Unidos, he came to view the Latino youth movement of the Northeast as a legitimate church group, albeit somewhat more liberal than his own views.

With this birthright, the National Hispanic Youth Task Force was formed as a result of the 1977 encounter, and Latino youth achieved a national presence at long last. This dynamic of organizing nationally with a specific set of goals and methods generated by youth leaders themselves is a protection against conservative reaction at the local level, which can easily deprive a youth group of its needed independence. By appeal to standards set by a national body, individual groups are protected and general goals are preserved.

The members of Naborí, however, never came to enjoy the fruits of their labor. Although one member was named as the first national task force,[46] Naborí had seen its organizers graduate, go on to professional schools, get married, and start families. Rather than destroy the continuity of the group by adding new members as old members left, Naborí had more or less stayed with the original organizers and was content to disband in 1978, considering that it had completed its mission.

The absence within the national task force of Naborí or similar groups, such as the Mexican youth at Casa Romero in San Diego, has diluted the political vision of Latino youth nationwide. But the legacy of this struggle has irrevocably combined concepts of cultural awareness and political involvement with the more traditional moral training focus of the youth apostolate. Curiously, during the 1980s, the CYO moved to a less sports-oriented format. This more serious direction for the CYO came from its own leadership and is not directly attributable to the Latino youth. Nonetheless, at a regional level, the superior vision of the meaning of a youth movement that is frequently found among the Latinos has served as a stimulus to Euro-American groups to do the same. Ironically, at the end of two decades the roles of the pace-setter and the following have been inverted, with Latinos leading the way in the 1990s where before they were expected to follow the example of the Euro-Americans in the church.

CATHOLIC SCHOOLS AND LATINO URBAN EDUCATION TODAY

Just as Latino movements must be understood in the light of social changes and the council, so, too, is it necessary to interject the same context for analyzing the changing role of the parochial schools. In fact, the suburban migration of Euro-Catholics and the council changes may have impacted more sharply on the schools than on other elements of U.S. Catholicism. As the notion of a separate Catholic society with its own institutions and school system withered after the Second Vatican Council, the medieval concept of convent life—isolation from the world—was fatally torpedoed. If the council urged involvement with secular and political movements of the day, what sense was there to devote one's whole life to a cloistered existence? In the fifteen years after the council, from 1965 to 1980, more than a third of all the sisters and nuns in the United States abandoned the religious life. But although the former nuns and resigned priests often worked enthusiastically for causes in which they fervently believed, their departure from traditional roles within Catholic education required major accommodation.

The problem for the institutional church was not only a loss of those already within the ministry. Recruitment of new nuns and sisters dropped drastically. Instead of a hundred or so newly professed each year, orders like the Dominican nuns of Amityville, Long Island, acquired only ten or twelve new members a year. Moreover, with the "graying" of those who chose to stay, by 1990 more than half of all religious women in the United States were over fifty years old.[47]

The impact of this mass exodus, the withering of recruits, and the aging of those who stayed have fallen particularly hard on Catholic schools. As parochial schools were forced to hire teachers who were not nuns or sisters, the labor costs of the schools skyrocketed. With the rise in such costs, tuition also rose, driving away many families who could no longer afford a Catholic education. In the vicious circle of capitalist economics, the fewer the students, the higher the tuition; the higher the tuition, the fewer the students. From 1970 to 1985, more Catholic schools were closed than were opened. Although there has been a leveling off, and even slight gain, in enrollments since 1985, the nature of Catholic parochial schools has been irrevocably altered.[48]

As already suggested, only about 10 percent of Latino youth attend Catholic schools in the United States today. That means that the overwhelming number of Catholic Latino youth are in the public school system. But the importance of Catholic schooling to the Latino community should not be minimized. The Catholic school system is not big enough to serve all Latino youth, even if questions of tuition—the principal barrier—could be resolved. But in Latino neighborhoods, it is not uncommon for the parochial school to have a nearly 100 percent enrollment of Latinos, besides a mixture of non-Catholics, often African-Americans. Thus, while Catholic schools can be criticized for not being open to more Latinos, they often are, in fact, virtually dedicated to Latino youth at the local level.[49]

The moral training imparted within Catholic school instruction, the discipline, and the parental involvement at every level are compelling characteristics of its success. Given the low wages of Catholic schoolteachers when compared with salaries in the public systems, Catholic school faculty generally exhibit a high degree of commitment. Without peripherals such as computers and art, dance, recreational, and science facilities, Catholic schools usually concentrate on the basic skills of education and generally produce high grades in the periodic testing within education today. Most importantly, the parochial school is a community school, where access to teachers and parents is woven together with similar cultural values.

Several of these elements of Catholic school education are now entering the realm of public school education. Faced with low performance levels, high absenteeism and drop-out rates, and lack of discipline, many public schools are now adopting policies long associated with parochial schools. In New York city, uniforms and dress and haircut codes are now standard in a growing number of public schools. Through the mechanism of target schools and specialized programs, discipline is imposed at the threat of expulsion—if not from school, from the chosen school. Moreover, faced with draconian cuts in funding due to a lost tax base, urban public schools often seek donations and fund-raising activities from parents, characterized the "cookie sales" familiar to Catholic school experience. In these circumstances, support for school choice, including a voucher system that would help finance a Catholic school education, is widening among segments of the Latino urban community. The issue is not viewed in the traditional terms of separation of church and state, but as a question of how best to provide a quality education in the face of a deteriorating public school system. Without pretending to take sides in what is clearly a complicated political debate, we should emphasize that among the Latinos it serves, Catholic schooling is hugely successful.

At the level of secondary education in the high schools, the superiority of Catholic school education is even more marked. While the national level of dropouts for Latinos fluctuates between 50 percent and 60 percent, the success rate of Catholic schools is over 90 percent.[50] Moreover, the number of Latino graduates entering colleges and universities stands at about 95 percent at a largely Latino Catholic high school like Cardinal Hayes High in New York. On the other hand, only about 10 percent of Latino public school graduates in New York finish college. We do not have national statistics to verify these patterns as a national trend, but it appears that once in college, the Catholic high school graduate is five times more likely to graduate with a four-year degree than the public school student. Thus, while Catholic schooling serves only about 10 percent of Latinos nationwide, about half of all Latino college graduates have attended Catholic schools.[51]

From this pool of college graduates come the professional leaders of the Latino communities. Doctors, lawyers, and successful business and community leaders are very much influenced by the value system of their education, even if they cease to practice their religion in a regular way.[52] The criticism that ought to be leveled at Catholic schooling is how poorly they inject elements of Latino cultural awareness into their curriculum. Often, Latino students are able to form extra-curricular clubs and associations to provide some minimal source of cultural identity within the larger community. But it remains to be seen how or if Catholic educators will provide civic or history texts that enhance the kind of cultural awareness so successfully utilized by Naborí simultaneously to develop personal pride in one's heritage and to stimulate a progressive sense of commitment to Catholic values.

CONCLUSIONS

Thus, with some modest successes and the various challenges opened up by a crisis in urban education, Catholic schools and churches remain battlegrounds. Recognizing the parallel between one's religious view of what the world should be and politics, opposing forces fight for control of the religious production that will shape the leaders of a generation to come. As Maduro points out, the control of religious production lies with the elites who manage the institution. But as religious consumers, the believers also influence the decisions of the church. Latinos can no longer be automatically presumed to be Catholics.

The continual hemorrhaging of Latino Catholics to Pentecostal and Evangelical churches is well documented during the last part of the 1980s.[53] While it is not certain what the factors are causing this switching of allegiance, it has not abated. Latinos are the crucial population that can ensure the difference between growth or shrinkage for many urban churches, both Catholic and Protestant. With a lower median age and higher birthrates, Latinos are increasing faster than the general U.S. population.[54] Thus, they are a target group for denominations seeking to grow and for Catholicism, which needs Latinos to preserve much of its influence in cities.

The need to ensure the loyalty of Latinos is likely to occasion policy adjustments within Catholicism. From a political economy point of view, urban churches need to target their religious production in much the same way that commerce and politics turn to bilingualism, biculturalism, and forms of local participation in order to entice Latino membership. Political issues that confront poverty, drug addiction, and inferior housing and community services require an ideological definition from the institution. Clearly, the more progressive the views adopted, the more likely is the institution to earn the loyalty of Latinos. In this, the mainline Protestant churches with their long-standing liberalism and the considerable resources of Catholicism would seem to favor these denominations in this battle for religious loyalty.

But although religion may be political, religion is not politics. The conflicts between liberal and conservative English-speaking Catholics in the United States after the Second Vatican Council are proof that progressives do not always win such battles within the church, even if their cause is just. The personal and psychological dimensions of religion affect individuals more deeply than politics. In many instances, the only way to avoid the pessimism of the underclass described by Wilson is to look for hope from some religious inspiration.[55] Without the psychological strength imparted to individuals and families through various forms of religious experience, it is difficult to imagine any reversal of the discouraging deadline in quality of life among Latino poor. Thus the battle for religious allegiance may also be the battle for Latino survival.

NOTES

1. For statistics on the incidence of religious identification see Kosmin; also see Moses in *Newsday* for a journalistic account.

2. Consider the listing of remedies that omit religion in Wilson, chapter 7.

3. Lincoln and Miamya, 334–36.

4. There is considerable important literature on Marx and religion. Consider the excerpts edited by Reinhold Niebuhr. Detailed commentaries on this point can also be found in Werner Post's *Kritik der Religion bei Karl Marx* and Helmut Gollwitzer's *The Christian Faith and the Marxist Criticism of Religion*; Gregory Baum offers a philosophic overview in *Religion and Alienation*. Marxist categories are explained as the basis for Latin American theology in Gustavo Gutiérrez's classic *A Theology of Liberation*, and Philip Berryman gives a layman's appraisal in his 1987 publication, *Liberation Theology*. See also the historical development in Samuel Silva Gotay.

5. The key works on this process among Latin American clergy are found in Vallier, who first analyzed religion as an agent of radical social change, and Levine, who updates the information and improves the theoretical underpinnings. See Adriance for the role of laity and women in Brazil for influencing policy. The connections with Gramsci are explored by Fulton and Cadena.

6. Maduro's contribution has been translated into three languages.

7. Maduro, 143–48; also see Cadena for an application to the Latinos in the United States.

8. Levine is a reliable sociological source on the effects of Vatican II and the meetings at Medellín and Puebla, while Beryman's *Religious Roots of Rebellion* (1984) adopts a sociohistorical reading; see Bonino for Protestant theology in Latin America in the wake of liberation theology. For Pentecostals, see Deck's chapter in the Cushwa Center's three-volume history (1994).

9. Vallier and Levine; Adriance develops the grass roots perspective in Brazil, while Cadena approaches the issue from a U.S. context.

10. Hewitt and Adriance report on the same phenomena, but with contrasting conclusions.

11. The first book is Stevnes-Arroyo's *Prophets Denied Honor* (1980); see also Alan Deck's *The Second Wave*, Moises Sandoval *On the Move*, and Ana María Díaz-Stevens's prize-winning *Oxcart Catholicism on Fifth Avenue*.

12. When public schools in the latter part of the twentieth century adhered to a strictly secularist premise, Seventh-Day Adventists, the Amish, and some fundamentalist churches viewed public education as antithetical to the Bible. In a sense, they wanted a restoration of the Protestant influence that had been objected to earlier by Catholics and some observant Jews. For a general assessment today see Gamoran; Davidman compares the different attitudes toward Jewish religious education.

13. Halsey, 155–61; Castelli and Gremillion, 6–17; see also O'Brien, 115–16, 144–45.

14. Gannon; O'Brien, 161–74.

15. Stevens-Arroyo and Díaz-Stevens in the article on religion in the *Handbook of Hispanic Cultures in the United States* (forthcoming in 1993).

16. See Stevens-Arroyo, 1987; see Tomasi for the pattern among Italian Catholics.

17. Fitzpatrick (1987); see also Deck (1989) and Vidal (1988).

18. Díaz-Stevens, 1993; chapter 4.

19. Vidal, in press.

20. Díaz-Stevens, 1991.

21. Moore and Pachon, 157, fn. 31; see Hall and Reck, 29, citing the Catholic bishops' 1989 pastoral letter, "The Hispanic Presence."

22. See the description in Díaz-Stevens, 1993: chapter 4.

23. González, 1990, 72–74 et passim; Deck, 1989, 138–41.

24. González, 1990, 55.

25. Haveman, 36–41, 241–78.

26. Díaz-Stevens, 1990.

27. Wills, 148–52.

28. Cited in Stevens-Arroyo, 1980, 123–33.

29. Sandoval, 79–84.

30. Stevens-Arroyo, 1993.

31. When there were programs for youth, they were usually intended to prevent involvement with gangs. See Fitzpatrick, 1971, 96–97, fn. 19.

32. See Fitzpatrick, 1971, 94–98; Piri Thomas in Stevens-Arroyo, 1980, 164–65.

33. This is not to deny that there were influential groups of young Catholic workers in the United States, only that their influence was less than in Europe and Latin America. See O'Brien, 45–50.

34. Stevens-Arroyo, 1980, 40–46 et passim.

35. Vidal, 1988, in *Nueva Presencia*.

36. See Garrison for a clinical analysis of the adult movement, the Cursillo.

37. Doyle et al., 40–42. The number of former addicts turned minister/preachers is large among Latinos, including Nicky Cruz and Piri Thomas.

38. Hayes Bautista's survey studies only California, but the theoretical basis of his analysis is applicable to all Latinos. For the moral renewal within culture, see Kavolis.

39. This is the argument made for black churches in Lincoln and Mamiya, 154–56, 334–38.

40. González, 1988; Sandoval.

41. See Díaz-Stevens, 1993, chapters 7–8.

42. Padilla; for the wider question in the nation, see Maldonado.

43. For the difference between these two terms see Stevens-Arroyo, 1980, 1–5, 251–57.

44. Hurtado studied Mexicans and Mexican-Americans, but the data seem applicable to most Latino groups, except for Puerto Ricans who have a special political arrangement with the United States that makes citizens of people both in the homeland and in the United States. See Stevens-Arroyo, 1993.

45. This opinion uses the evidence but not the conclusions of Fitzpatrick and Gurak. See also Doyle et al., 10–14, 50–51.

46. The original members included the authors of this article. For one of the documents from Naborí, see Stevens-Arroyo, 1980, 341–43. The history is analyzed in Díaz-Stevens, 1993.

47. See Stevens-Arroyo, 1980, 330–33; Díaz-Stevens, in press.

48. See Neal for a historical description of the two decades after 1960 and Wittenburg for a contemporary assessment.

49. Yeager et al., 37–47.

50. Fisher; Hall and Reck, 39–46.

51. For the national rates see Moore and Pachon, 68–69; Doyle et al., 3–4 offers information on Catholic school experience among Latinos.

52. These numbers have yet to be verified by a survey sample. The reasoning is that since less than half of Latinos at public schools finish high school and less than 20 percent of that number finish college, the higher college success rate of Catholic schooling makes them equal to the public system in producing professionals.

53. The role of Catholic education in the life choices of two Latinos who have produced significant literary attention is remarkably similar. See Edwin Rivera and Richard Rodriguez.

54. For a summary, see Deck, in press.

55. Moore and Pachon, 52–61.

BIBLIOGRAPHY

Adriance, Madeline. *Opting for the Poor: Brazilian Catholicism in Transition*. Kansas City: Sheed and Ward, 1986.

Baum, Gregory. *Religion and Alienation*. New York: Paulist Press, 1975.

Berryman, Philip. *Religious Roots of Rebellion*. Maryknoll: Orbi, 1984.

———. *Liberation Theology*. New York: Pantheon, 1987.

Bonino, José Miguez. *Doing Theology in a Revolutionary Situation*. Philadelphia: Fortress Press, 1975.

Cadena, Gilbert R. "Gramsci, Maduro and the Sociology of the Chicano/Latino Religious Experience." Paper read at the conference of the Society for the Scientific Study of Religion, 8 November 1922, Washington, DC.

Castelli, Jim, and Joseph Gremillion. *The Emerging Parish: The Notre Dame Study of Catholic Life Since Vatican II*. New York: Harper and Row, 1987.

Cervantes, Carmen María. *Cries of Hope*. Stockton, CA: St. Mary's Press, February 1993.

Davidman, Lynn. "Accommodation and Resistance to Modernity: A Comparison of Two Contemporary Orthodox Jewish Groups." *Sociological Analysis* 51:1 (Spring 1990): 35–51.

Deck, Alan Figueroa. *The Second Wave*. Mahwah, NJ: Paulist Press, 1989.

———. "Hispanic Catholics and Conversions." In *History of Hispanic Catholicism*, vol. 3, Jay Dolan, ed. Notre Dame: University of Notre Dame Press, in press.

Díaz-Stevens, Ana María. "From Puerto Rican to Hispanic: The Politics of the *Fiestas Patronales* in New York." *Latino Studies Journal* 1:1 (January 1990): 28–47.

———. "Social Distance and Religious Conflict in the Pre-Vatican Catholicism of Puerto Rico." *MACLAS Essays* (Journal of the Middle Atlantic Council for Latin American Studies) 4 (1991): 291–99.

———. *Oxcart Catholicism on Fifth Avenue: The Impact of the Puerto Rican Migration upon the Archdiocese of New York*. University of Notre Dame Press, forthcoming 1993.

———. "Hispanic Youth and Catholic Ministry." In *History of Hispanic Catholicism*, vol. 3, Jay Dolan, ed. Notre Dame Press, in press.

Doyle, Ruth, John Kuzloski, Thomas M. McDonald, and Olga Scarpetta. *Church-Related Hispanic Youth in New York: An Exploratory Study*. New York: Office of Pastoral Research, Archdiocese of New York, 1983.

Fisher, Ian. "A Struggling Tradition: Cardinal Hayes Changes with the Bronx." *New York Times*, 30 June 1992.

Fitzpatrick, Joseph P., S.J. *Puerto Rican Americans: The Meaning of Migration to the Mainland*. Englewood Cliffs, NJ: Prentice-Hall, 1971.

———. *One Church, Many Cultures: The Challenge of Diversity*. Kansas City: Sheed and Ward, 1987.

———, and Douglas T. Gurak. *Hispanic Intermarriage in New York City: 1975*. New York: Hispanic Research Center, Fordham University (monograph 2), 1979.

Fulton, John. "Religion as Politics in Gramsci: An Introduction." *Sociological Analysis* 48:3 (Fall 1987): 197–216.

Gamoran, Adam. "Civil Religion in American Schools." *Sociological Analysis* 51:3 (Fall 1990): 235–56.

Gannon, Robert Ignatius. *The Cardinal Spellman Story*. Garden City, NY: Doubleday, 1962.

Garrison, Vivian. "Sectarianism and Psychosocial Adjustment: A Controlled Comparison of Puerto Rican Pentecostals and Catholics." In *Religious Movements in Contemporary America*, Irving I. Zaretsky and Mark P. Leone, eds. Princeton, NJ: Princeton University Press, 1974, 298–329.

Gollwitzer, Helmut. *The Christian Faith and the Marxist Criticism of Religion*. Trans. David Cairns. New York: Charles Scribner's Sons, 1970.

González, Justo. *The Theological Education of Hispanics*. New York: Fund for Theological Education, 1988.

———. *Mañana: Christian Theology from a Hispanic Perspective*. Nashville: Abingdon, 1990.

Gutiérrez, Gustavo. *A Theology of Liberation*. Maryknoll: Orbis Books, 1973.

Hall, Suzanne, and Carleen Reck, eds. *Integral Education: A Response to the Hispanic Presence*. Washington, DC: National Catholic Educational Association, 1987.

Halsey, William M. *The Survival of American Innocence: Catholics in an Era of Disillusionment, 1920–1940*. Notre Dame: University of Notre Dame Press, 1980.

Haveman, Robert H., ed. *A Decade of Federal Antipoverty Programs: Achievements, Failures, and Lessons*. New York: Academic Press, 1977.

Hayes Bautista, David. *No Longer a Minority: Latinos and Social Policy in California*. Los Angeles: Chinao Studies Research Center, UCLA, 1992.

Hewitt, W. E. "Religion and the Consolidation of Democracy in Brazil: The Role of the CEBs." *Sociological Analysis* 51:2 (Summer 1990): 139–52.

Hurtado, Juan. *An Attitudinal Study of the Social Distance Between the Mexican-American and the Church*. San Antonio, TX: Mexican American Cultural Center, 1980.

Kavolis, Vytautus. "Contemporary Moral Cultures and the 'Return of the Sacred.' " *Sociological Analysis* 49:3 1 (Fall 1988): 203–16.

Kosmin, Barry A. *The National Survey of Religious Identification, 1989–1990*. New York: City University of New York, 1991.

Levine, Daniel H. *Religion and Politics in Latin America: The Catholic Church in Venezuela and Colombia*. Princeton, NJ: Princeton University Press, 1981.

Lincoln, C. Eric, and Lawrence H. Mamiya. *The Black Church in the African American Experience*. Durham, NC: Duke University Press, 1990.

Maduro, Otto. *Religion and Social Conflicts*. Maryknoll: Orbis Books, 1982.

Maldonado, Lionel A. "Latino Ethnicity: Increasing Diversity." *Latino Studies Journal* 2:3 (September 1991): 49–57.

Moore, Joan, and Harry Pachon. *Hispanics in the United States*. Englewood Cliffs, NJ: Prentice-Hall, 1985.

Neal, Marie Augusta. *Catholic Sisters in Transition: The 1960's to the 1980's*. Wilmington, DE: Michael Glazier, 1984.

Neibuhr, Reinhold, ed. *Marx and Engels on Religion*. New York: Schocken Books, 1964.

O'Brien, David J. *The Renewal of American Catholicism*. New York: Paulist Press, 1971.

Padilla, Felix. *Latino Ethnic Consciousness: The Case of Mexican Americans and Puerto Ricans in Chicago*. Notre Dame: University of Notre Dame Press, 1985.

Post, Werner. *Kritik der Religion bei Karl Marx*. Munich: Kösei-Verlag, 1969.

Rivera, Edward. *Family Installments: Memories of Growing Up Hispanic*. New York: William Morrow, 1982.

Rodriguez, Richard. *Hunger of Memory: The Education of Richard Rodriguez*. Boston: David R. Godine, 1982.

Sandoval, Moises. *On the Move*. Maryknoll: Orbis Books, 1990.

Silva Gotay, Samuel. *El pensamiento cristiano revolucionario en América Latina y el Caribe*. Salamanca: Ediciones Sígueme, 1981.

Stevens-Arroyo, Anthony M. *Prophets Denied Honor: An Anthology on the Hispanic Church*. Maryknoll: Orbis Books. 1980.

———. "Puerto Rican Struggles in the Catholic Church." In *The Puerto Rican Struggle:*

Essays on Survival in the United States, C. Rodríguez, V. Sánchez Korrol, and J. O. Alers, eds. Maplewood, NJ: Waterfront Press, 1980, 129–39.

———. "Cahensly Revisited?: The National Pastoral Encounter of America's Hispanic Catholics." *Migration World* 15:3 (Fall 1987): 16–19.

———, and Ana María Díaz-Stevens. "Religion and Faith Among Latinos." In *Handbook of Hispanic Cultures in the United States*, Felix Padilla, ed. Houston, TX: Arte Public Press (in English) and Madrid: ICI (in Spanish), (March 1993).

———. "Latino Identity and Catholicism." In *History of Hispanic Catholicism*, vol. 3. Jay Dolan, ed. Notre Dame: University of Notre Dame Press, in press.

Tomasi, Silvio. *Piety and Power: The Role of Italian Parishes in the New York Metropolitan Areas, 1880–1930*. New York: Center for Migration Studies, 1975.

Vallier, Ivan. *Catholicism, Social Control and Modernization in Latin America*. Englewood Cliffs, NJ: Prentice-Hall, 1970.

Vidal, Jaime. "Popular Religion Among the Hispanics in the General Area of the Archdiocese of Newark." In *Nueva Presencia*. Newark, NJ: Archdiocesan Office of Pastoral Planning, 1988, 235–348.

———. "Puerto Rican Catholicism." In *History of Hispanic Catholicism*, vol. 2, Jay Dolan, ed. Notre Dame: University of Notre Dame Press, in press.

17

Crack Kids: An Emerging Educational Dilemma

Patricia G. Tweeddale

Drug use is a problem in urban society and its schools. A new dimension of this problem is the use of illicit drugs by pregnant women and the resulting effects on their unborn infants. Crack/cocaine use, in particular, is approaching epidemic proportions, and its effects on infants in utero are creating a new population of schoolchildren exhibiting heretofore unseen problems. According to *U.S. News and World Report*,[1] this epidemic is the result of a shrewd and enormously successful marketing strategy by drug traffickers, with the result that crack, with subsequent addiction, has become easily accessible and initially affordable for the poor. The urban poor are the most severely affected, and a subgroup, women of reproductive age, is exposing a new generation to in-utero polydrug effects. While not limited to undereducated, poor, and minority individuals, the crack epidemic particularly affects these groups. Crack use and other problems associated with poverty—such as various types of chemical abuse, teen-age pregnancies, low birth-weight infants, single-parent families, and child neglect and abuse—all occur more frequently in particular groups of individuals and populations at inordinate risk, educationally, socially, and physically.[2] The accelerating incidence of these conditions raises serious questions about the ability of the public schools alone, as presently structured and financed, to deal successfully with this ever-increasing population of children. To educate and usher these afflicted children into the mainstream of American society will require alternative programs.[3]

The effects of cocaine on the developing fetus, although not completely understood, are toxic and result in long- and short-term consequences. Cocaine is a central nervous system (CNS) stimulant that blocks neuronal uptake of norepinephrine, resulting in increased heart rate and blood pressure. Due to its low molecular weight and high water and fat solubility, cocaine readily crosses the placenta. Numerous variables affect just how much of the drug reaches the developing fetus. According to Flandermeyer, "The extent of placental drug transfer depends in part upon the gestational age of the placenta; transfer is fastest during the first and third trimesters and slowest during the second."[4] Because of the relatively low pH of fetal blood (cocaine is a weak base) and the low fetal level of plasma esterases (blood enzymes) that metabolize the drug, cocaine may accumulate in the fetus. The literature reports numerous obstetrical effects of cocaine. Some of these include increases in the incidence of spontaneous abortion (*abruptio placentae*), prematurity, and intrauterine growth retardation (IUGR), all of which have been reported after exposure to cocaine during pregnancy.[5]

Further, not all of the effects of cocaine on the neonate are currently known.[6] Some, however, are found consistently and have been well documented throughout the medical literature. For example, neonates from one study of forty-six cocaine- and polydrug-using mothers had an increased rate of prematurity, intrauterine growth retardation, and smaller head circumference than did the drug-free comparison group. (It is important to realize that in the neonate, head circumference is synonymous with brain size.) That report further stated that "data confirm previous reports of increased placental hemorrhage, including *abruptio.*"[7] There are also numerous studies regarding the effect of cocaine on the fetal brain.[8] Chasnoff et al. found that cocaine exposure in only the first trimester, when women frequently are unaware of their pregnancy, "does put the newborn at-risk for neurobehavioral deficiencies compared with drug-free infants."[9] Chasnoff states that "cocaine's action in blocking norepinephrine and dopamine re-uptake in the developing fetus could interfere with neuronal development. And Grimm hypothesizes that such interference could leave the infant impaired in his/her ability to cope with common environmental demands at some point in later life."[10] Still other brain studies describe cerebrovascular accidents, subarachnoid hemorrhages, cerebral infarct, seizures, CT scan abnormalities, other radiographic abnormalities (i.e., in ultrasonography, magnetic resonance imaging), and an in-utero hemorrhagic intracranial lesion. One infant from a mother who snorted large quantities of cocaine just prior to delivery acquired a brain hemorrhage in the caudothalamic area (an area of the brain related to fine motor coordination). However, the implication of such a lesion, related to future neurobehavioral development, is uncertain.[11] Yet another study showed damage to the frontal lobes and basal ganglia, alterations that might not surface until after the first year of life, "when more complex visual-motor and social cognition tasks are required of the preschool and school-age child."[12] It is noted that this type of cerebral injury is uncommon in other than the drug-exposed population. Spires et al. state that "the implications of such [brain] lesions for future neurobehavioral development is unknown."[13] In yet another medical study there has been extensive follow-up of these pediatric casualties. In this research it was found that 75 percent of cocaine-afflicted infants had an I.Q. of less than 100 in the first year, with associated abornmal visual-motor coordination. Furthermore, the author states, certain "structural brain lesions are concentrated in areas that may not show impaired functions until school age."[14] Thus, the potential for long-term, as well as short-term, dysfunction in the development of these children is quite evident. Additionally, many handicaps will not become apparent until school age, and the extent of the developmental anomalies may take years to evaluate.

Small-for-gestational-age babies or small-for-date babies are perhaps the single most common problem among infants born to cocaine-using mothers. The small-for-date (SFD) infant is described as undersized in weight, length, and head (brain) circumference. The birth weight is generally regarded as being at least 30 percent under the expected normal weight, the equivalent of more than two standard deviations of mean weight for a given nursery. By four years of age the mean weight and height were between the tenth and twenty-fifth percentiles, with head circumference and bone age paralleling linear growth.[15] This study also investigated the neurological and intellectual sequelae for ninety-six small-for-date infants. Major neurological defects were uncommon. However, in 25 percent of the sample, there was minimal cerebral dysfunction characterized by hyperactivity, a short attention span, learning difficulties, poor fine motor co-ordination, and hyperreflexia. Electroencephalogram (EEG) abnormalities were noted in 59 percent of the boys and 69 percent of the girls. Speech defects appeared in 33 percent of males and 26 percent of females. The average I.Q. was 95 for boys and 101 for girls. Regarding school performance, 50 percent of males and 36 percent of females did poorly. One-third of the children with I.Q.s over 100 were failing consistently at school.[16] Harvey et al. also studied babies who were small for gestational age.[17] They divided the sample into two groups: (1) those who had slow head growth in utero starting before twenty-six weeks and continuing until near term and (2) those whose head growth slowed later in gestation. The former group had cognitive scores significantly lower than those of control children, while the latter group fell within the normal growth range. Those affected with earlier gestational slow head growth were evaluated at a mean age of 5.1 years and were found to have less ability to understand, carry out instructions, and copy and classify given shapes than normal children of the same age. A schoolteacher's assessment was that "they have particular problems with reading and writing, especially the boys, who were also thought to be clumsy."[18] Poor school performance, lower scores on intelligence tests, behavior problems, and other handicaps among the small-for-gestational-age babies are quite extensively referenced, particularly in the British literature.[19] With this in mind, the fact that a typical finding with crack-using mothers is that their babies are frequently small-for-gestational-age infants becomes rather ominous.

In the United States, Hill and Tennyson have carried out extensive studies on the effects of in-utero drug exposure, including alcohol, anticonvulsant drugs, neurostimulants (crack/cocaine), marijuana, tobacco (smoking or chewing), anticoagulants, antihypertensives, organic solvents, aminopterin, narcotics (heroin and methadone), and nonnarcotics (phenobarbital, diazepam, marijuana, phencylidine, and so on).[20] They state the following:

Infants having a birth weight of less than the base percentile are considered undernourished (small-for-gestational-age) and represent those infants at the highest risk for long-term neurological and mental morbidity. Recent evidence has shown that a child demonstrating any clinical degree of retarded intrauterine growth rate regardless of birth weight has a 42 percent chance of having some deficit in mental ability (i.e., mental retardation, attention deficit disorder, or specific learning disability). The need for special education in the intrauterine growth retardation (IUGR) infant was 27 percent compared to 0 percent in non-growth-retarded infants.

These authors summarize their lengthy studies as follows: "Neurobehavior can also be adversely affected by maternal drugs. Although symptoms may be limited to the first months of life there is some evidence that this abnormal behavior is a reflection of in-utero neurological insult which becomes evident later as poor organizational, perceptual, reading, and mathematical skills, or even mental retardation" (p. 136).

In summary, the medical literature classifies neonates who are born prenatally exposed to drugs as "fragile" infants with very low stimulus thresholds. They have physical abnormalities that cover a wide continuum from low birth weight and small head (brain) circumference, to eye anomalies such as strabismus (24 percent as contrasted with 2.8 percent to 5.3 percent of the normal population), to adverse effects reported on the neonatal auditory system (reflective of abnormalities in brainstem conduction time) and other malformations, including the genitourinary tract, respiratory tract (particularly an increased incidence of sudden infant death syndrome or SIDS), gastrointestinal and cardiovascular malformations, and brain lesions and infarction.[21] This continuum of congenital anomalies clearly shows the deleterious effects of crack/cocaine, alone and in combination with other illicit drugs, on the developing fetus.

While no single profile can describe every perinatally exposed-to-drugs (PED) child, the following can provide a generalized array of the most likely descriptors that consistently appear in some combination (two or more) in a PED infant.

Small head (brain) circumference (microcephaly)

Low birth weight

Decreased length

Small for gestational age (SGA)

Increased rate of distress at delivery

Low Apgar scores (<7 at one and five minutes)

Low scores on other neonatal assessment tests (Brazelton)

Fragile infants—easily overloaded by environmental stimuli

Tendency to shut out rather than interact with external stimuli

Irritability and tremulousness

Poor motor orientation and state regulation behaviors (orientation-interaction)

Abnormal reflexes

Imbalance in muscle tone usually displayed as hypertonicity

Abnormal startle response

Poor tolerance for oral feeding

Diarrhea

Increased rate of sudden infant death syndrome

Difficulty in ability to attend to and actively engage auditory and/or visual stimuli

Strabismus (24 percent occurrence in drug-exposed infants compared with 2.8–5.3 percent reported in the general population)

Genitourinary malformations (prune belly, hydroureter/hydronephrosis, hypospadius, bilateral inguinal hernias).

These neonates, born at risk due to in-utero drug exposure, then discharged to an environment that often places them at even greater risk throughout their childhood development, enter the school system with a plethora of special needs.

As part of the school system, perinatally exposed-to-drugs children are a special category of children who are not "just" at risk but are at risk in multiple ways. They often have mothers who are head of the family, whose earnings are below the poverty level, who are addicted to at least one chemical, and who may or may not be recovering. The child has already been exposed in utero to crack/cocaine and other drugs. This has likely left the child with one or more handicapping conditions, including, but not limited to, compromised cognitive abilities, emotional disorder, developmental delays of one or more kinds, and possibly some type of physical abnormality. This newest group of seriously at-risk students may or may not fit the categorization requirements necessary for placement in special education programs. They will, however, greatly expand the number of seriously at-risk students in the public school system. The schools then are potentially in a position whereby they can take an assertive role in bringing together a new and different approach to deal with the problem. Almost all communities offer a variety of services that are aimed at responding to the problems of their youth. However, these services are provided in such a fragmented way that benefits are minimized. Crack kids may have provided a "window of opportunity" for the school system by their increased numbers and the public's growing awareness of their problems. Nevertheless, their needs often go beyond anything that schools are capable of providing.

While many of the above conditions qualify a child for inclusion in programs that fall under the aegis of PL 94–142 or PL 99–457, there is not presently a clear profile that places the PED child in a separate and special category. Additionally, identification of the PED child not only is inadequate but under present conditions is likely to occur months or even years too late for the necessary early intervention. Thus, the child under these present circumstances will be even further behind, possibly hopelessly behind, before intervention and compensatory programs are provided.

There are three problems in identification that would be aided by more consistent public policy. The first concerns the lack of agreement about PED profiles and identification practices.[22] The second is the absence of a communitywide tracking process. The latter tracking could easily be addressed on a statewide, even national basis, by using a system similar in design to the one now employed for tracking the children of migrant workers. The third problem involves the development of assessment tools that measure both current conditions of the infant and the risk due to environmental factors. All of these problems are exacerbated by the narrowly defined criteria permitting developmental services to be offered. Older PED children may also be misdiagnosed due to a set of federal criteria in a single classification. These issues must be addressed by state and national policy if the PED problem is to be effectively contained and treated.

Additionally, intervention programs for the PED child will not be successful as single-agency programs, because these programs are often competitive and are, at best, multi-disciplinary/agency programs managed by an unspecified and probably self-selected agency bureaucracy and are supported with short-term and limited funding. Effective programs must be long-term funded, possibly by the federal government, and operated in a transagency fashion by a designated and well-trained transdisciplinary lead agency.

An excellent example of an urban school program crated specifically to address the crack kid problem was initiated by the Los Angeles (LA) Unified School District in 1987. This pilot program at the Salvin School was intended to serve a small, selected group of PED children and their families. It was the intention of the program to develop education strategies useful in any classroom to meet the needs of PED children. The program began with a single classroom and by 1991 expanded to four classrooms serving over forty children ages three to six years. The teachers at the school carefully include both student and the family as part of their "team." When possible they operate with other agencies, including university personnel. Using a multidisciplinary (MD) approach, the teacher takes the lead role and becomes the advocate for the child. The story of a student who had been in one foster home for a four-year period and was then placed by the social agency in another is somewhat typical. Following the second placement, the teacher noticed difficulty in school, worked with both the social worker and the original foster family, and got the child returned to the original family. The child's behavior soon improved.

Three major aspects of the school program include (1) the development of a structured, stimulus-reduced program, (2) the establishment of a nurturing/ritual routine, and (3) use of achievement gain as opposed to a deficit model for assessing the child. The establishment of strong attachment between the child and the teacher is a high priority, and to that end the child stays with the same teacher for a two-year period.

At the Salvin School, which houses this pilot program as well as many other special education programs for the LA district, I observed many incidences of behavior reinforcing the above description. The following are examples.

A "classroom" at the Salvin School consisted of a large classroom area, two smaller work areas, and what appeared to be an outdoor patio space adjacent to a larger playground area. The classroom space had six–eight learning centers. The two other work areas had tables and accoutrements for teacher-pupil inter-action. The patio area had four picnic tables and a sandbox. In effect, this pilot center classroom was not dissimilar to any classroom found in most urban, prekindergarten school systems.

During this period of observation, the classroom and learning centers each focused on multisensory opportunities to explore learning skills (listening, ma-nipulating, viewing, assembling, discovering, and so on). The individual centers were arranged comfortably to accommodate three students, and materials were in carefully delineated spaces. The materials were of the size and density that would be characteristic for any preschool kindergarten classroom, exhibiting those standards recommended by the Southern Association on Children Under Six.[23]

There was easy flow from one center to another with very natural directive openings (L-shaped, U-shaped) to each center. Seating in the classroom was at small stools and tables and was occasionally in small groups on the floor around the teacher. There were spaces for withdrawal or "time out," complete with cushions for winding down or even sleeping. There were no bells. The lighting was, for the most part, natural lighting. The location of the programs was in a part of a larger facility (school) but enjoyed its own sense of privacy. There was no evidence of special physical or environmental uniqueness to this program compared with other preschool programs.

One observed characteristic of the children was varying abilities to stay on task for a reasonable amount of time. Also, some of the children seemed spon-taneously to demand attention without regard to the task at hand. Most of the children seemed easily distracted. However, many professionals in early child-hood education would not view this as outside the parameters of average early childhood behavior patterns.

What was quite obvious, in terms of behaviors, was the interaction between teacher and/or aide and the individual student. For example, there were regular urging and solicitation of responses to assigned tasks, such as: "That's good," "That goes there," "Where will we put this?", "Turn it around," "Isn't that pretty?", "Good!", "Put the crayon in the cup." In a group activity led by the teacher, there were an extensive description of what was going to be done, explanation of what was being done, and signaling of the next activities, punc-tuated with individual invitation to focus by use of the specific given names of students. This included requests to perform specific active contributions to the activity and recognition for doing so. Emphasis was placed on the process of demonstrating appropriate responses, rather than rightness or wrongness of an answer. One could describe the teacher-student interaction as being almost ''programmed,'' even though the interaction was clearly spontaneous. There was constant and continual reinforcement by the teacher and the aide regarding what the student was doing, what the task goal was, what would happen upon completion, and how soon the task accomplishment would occur. There were specific activities that were prescribed in moving from one center-type activity to another, such as individual listening to favorite audiotapes, reclining and resting, and arts/crafts types of individual work. All of the children were engaged in a task, with a teacher or aide in close physical proximity providing constant calming encouragement (a low tone of voice and intermittent touch). The children were responsive to, and comfortable with, the teacher/aides and the learning environment.There was nothing obvious in their particular early childhood development that would be anticipated for at-risk children in general. The length of time necessary to achieve readiness for placement in the regular classroom is most likely the largest variable unique to this group.

The administrator of the building in which the program is housed indicated that the program did not present any particular demand on his time or any administrative challenges that were different from the routine ones associated with being the principal of a special education complex in the large urban school system of Los Angeles. He indicated that his background as a special education teacher and a regular education teacher, administrator of a regular school, and administrator of a special education center probably prepared him with the necessary equanimity to serve the Salvin School and its pilot project. He commented on the high quality of professional performance by the staff of the program and their ability to operate with minimal supervision from him. He further commented on the positive relationship and support of the assistant superintendent for the pilot program.

The Los Angeles Unified School District has experienced a significant reduction in budget allocations over the last four years. In the initial two years of the pilot program's existence, staff allocations were significantly above the standard early childhood special education averages. The program at the Salvin School went from four teachers, four aides, twenty hours of psychological services, and sixteen hours of social services, pediatric services, and nursing services to, in its third and fourth years, experiencing cutbacks in all areas, but particularly in nursing and psychological services.

In its fifth year, the program struggles with only two teachers, two aides, and minimal psychological and social service support. What impact this will have remains to be seen. It does point out the vulnerability of programs with high personnel costs due to the labor-intensive nature of the service during a budget crisis in a school district. What may be called to attention, as well, is the vulnerability of programs such as this when across-the-board cuts are used as an approach to budget resolution, as opposed to prioritized decisions.

What was very clear in discussions with the personnel from the Los Angeles district is the absence of inclusion of school personnel in the interagency approach to delivery of service. While there is within the district clear evidence of an interdisciplinary approach to delivery of service, the transdisciplinary agency model does not exist. This may in part be explained by the ongoing focus on infants and mothers that occurs primarily during the prenatal and postpartum periods, with the major concern being survival of the infant and rehabilitation of the mother.

One support response coming from the institutions of higher learning in California consisted primarily of support to the school system in terms of providing pediatric evaluation services to the children in the pilot program and social services in the form of personnel and space. Additionally, research services, both for longitudinal study of the pilot group and for ongoing current sociological and developmental research, were provided. This linkage between the University of California at Los Angeles and the Los Angeles Unified School District was a result of a personal friendship between a concerned pediatrician at the University Medical Center and the superintendent of the Los Angeles schools. Both individuals mutually recognized the impending challenges and agreed to set in motion a pilot venture.

THE TRANSDISCIPLINARY APPROACH

Of particular interest to schools in urban settings is the introduction of a different concept of early intervention delivery systems. First developed in 1976 by the United Cerebral Palsy National Collaborative Infant Project, Woodruff and McGonigel describe a transdisciplinary (TD) approach to early intervention that goes beyond inter- and multidisciplinary approaches.[24] In the TD approach, each disciplinary role incumbent learns about and is able, to some extent, to function and think within the disciplines of the other team members. The team consists of members from the appropriate disciplines and includes the child's family (primary caretaker unit). One agency and agency/discipline professional become the lead agency/professional providing and coordinating all services with the help and assistance of the TD team. Once operational, the TD approach conserves professional time and resources, as well as avoiding redundancy of services and duplication of time and effort of the client and primary caretaker. Some further discussion of the transdisciplinary/agency model is appropriate at this time (an excellent and detailed explanation of the transdisciplinary model is found in Woodruff and McGonigel.) Taking up the theme of the team approach and team building, Woodruff and McGonigel distinguish among multidisciplinary, interdisciplinary, and transdisciplinary agency.[25]

DISCIPLINES AND TEAM BUILDING

This discussion is based on Woodruff and Hanson.[26]

In order to accomplish the transdisciplinary agency approach, there are six "separate but related processes": role extension, role enrichment, role expansion, role exchange, role release, and role support.[27] At the role extension phase, team members (speech, occupation, physical therapists, nurses, teachers, parents, primary care providers, and social workers) engage in "self-directed" efforts to learn the roles of other team members. In role enrichment, team members learn about other disciplines and their contributions to the intervention program. Role expansion requires "pooling ideas and exchanging information."[28] Role exchange and role release are perhaps the most time-consuming and ego-difficult elements of the transagency team-building process. During role expansion team members learn and practice (under supervision) critical skills of other professional team members. This process is very time-consuming and requires great professional commitment to the transdisciplinary/agency process and the PED intervention goals and purposes. Finally, role support involves the continued support, interaction, and contribution of all team members in relation to the lead service provider, who cannot and should not assume the sole responsibility.

Historically, multidisciplinary and interdisciplinary approaches have failed to serve many clients successfully. This is often because several separate but needed agency/professionals require repetitive, redundant, and overlapping data from the client. Sometimes, separate agencies provide services in the same categories. Yet essential services may not be provided on the basis that another agency has or should have provided that service. Multiple agency service provision may result in outcomes of neglect or in redundancy of services. Multiple services that are fragmented and noncooperative produce a feeling of misuse, unimportance, and defeat. Such conditions leave the client or caregiving family feeling neglected and underserved.

Because of the present "cumbersome system," the transagency approach is a logical approach. Macro Systems comes close to this transagency concept in what they recommend as a cross-agency or multidisciplinary program.[29] They suggest that legal specification of the "lead agency" would prove beneficial to the service delivery process, the mother, the PED child, and the family/caregiver unit. Further, they suggest that every "drug-exposed child," once identified, should be eligible for the entire range of social-medical services: "multiple and interrelated problems facing the families of drug-exposed children necessitate . . . a wide range of interrelated or trans-agency services."[30] Halfon agrees, stating that programs must be interdisciplinary, bridging the multiple agencies involved.[31] Woodson is explicit, stating that federal government policy "should increase appropriations . . . in order to activate such services."[32] The implementation of a TD approach represents a radical restructuring of the delivery of services by all agencies, but particularly by the school system. The current movement towards site-based management of schools is an excellent opportunity to facilitate the change process. It is important that urban school administrators recognize and utilize this window of opportunity for enhancement of effectiveness.

In the midst of movement to implement reform in public education, while at the same time responding positively to calls for accountability by frustrated taxpayers and parents, public education is being besieged by the entry of increasingly large numbers of at-risk students, many of whom are at risk due to use of crack/cocaine by their birth mothers. Addressing the educational needs of these relatively newly identified children presents an expected and unanticipated challenge to an already overwhelmed public education system, particularly in urban settings. These children must be served and served well if the schools are to meet the demands of state accountability. Yet answers to the problems of service must be reached within parameters of limited, if any, increase in real dollar support for education. The labor-intensive requirement of providing appropriate learning opportunities for these children means they are expensive services. At the other end of the challenge is the recognition that this population, if unsatisfactorily served, presents relatively higher costs to the community and to society in the future. Answers are, as of yet, not forthcoming.

NOTES

1. The men who created crack, *U.S. News and World Report*, (19 August, 1991).

2. Insights (1990), Cultural misalignment and emerging paradigms, *Southwest Educational Development Laboratory* 24:3.

3. M. W. Kirst & M. McLaughlin (1989), Rethinking children's policy: Implications for educational administration, *Policy Bulletin*: 1–8.

4. A. A. Flandermeyer (1987), A comparison of the effects of heroin and cocaine abuse upon the neonate, *Neonatal Network*, 6(3):42–48.

5. I. J. Chasnoff, W. J. Burns, S. H. Schnoll, & K. A. Burns (1985), Cocaine use in pregnancy, *New England Journal of Medicine* 313(11):666–69. A. S. Oro & S. D. Dixon (1987), Perinatal cocaine and methamphetamine exposure: Maternal and neonatal correlates, *Journal of Pediatrics* 111(4):571–78.

6. I. J. Chasnoff (1989), Cocaine and pregnancy implications for the child (editorial), *Western Journal of Medicine* 150(4):456–58.

7. Oro & Dixon.

8. I. J. Chasnoff et al. (1986), Perinatal cerebral infarction and maternal cocaine use. *Journal of Pediatrics* 108(3):456–59; N. E. Chaney, J. Franke & W. B. Wadlington (1988), Cocaine convulsions in a breastfed baby, *Journal of Pediatrics* 112:134–345; M. C. Spires, E. F. Gordon, M. Chaudhuri, E. Maldonado & R. Chan (1989), Intracranial hemorrhage in a neonate following prenatal cocaine exposure, *Pediatric Neurology* 5(5):324–26; M. Rivkin & H. E. Gilmore (1989), Generalized seizures in an infant due to environmentally acquired cocaine, *Journal of Pediatrics* 84(6):1100–1102.

9. I. J. Chasnoff, et al. (1989), Cocaine: Temporal patterns of cocaine use in pregnancy, *Journal of the American Medical Association* 261(12):1741–44.

10. Ibid.; V. E. Grimm (1987), Effect of teratogenic exposure on the developing brain: Research strategies and possible mechanisms, *Developmental Pharmacological Therapy* 10:328–45.

11. Spires, Gordon, Chaudhuri, Maldonado, & Chan.

12. S. D. Dixon & R. Bejar (1989), Echoencephalographic findings in neonates as-

sociated with maternal cocaine and methamphetamine use: Incidence and clinical correlates, *Journal of Pediatrics* 115(5):770–78.

13. Spires, Gordon, Chaudhuri, Maldonado, & Chan.

14. S. D. Dixon (1989), Effects of transplacental exposure to cocaine and methamphetamine on the neonate, *Western Journal of Medicine* 150(4):436–42.

15. P. M. Fitzhardinge & E. M. Steven (1972), The small-for-date infant. II: Neurological and intellectual sequelae, *Pediatrics* 50(1):50–57.

16. P. M. Fitzhardinge & E. M. Steven (1972), The small-for-date infant. I: Later growth patterns, *Pediatrics* 49(5):671–81.

17. D. Harvey et al. (1982), Abilities of children who were small-for-gestational-age babies, *Pediatrics* 69(3):296–300.

18. C. E. Parkinson, S. Wallis, & D. Harvey (1981), School achievement and behavior of children who were small-for-dates at birth, *Development of the Medical Child Neurology* 23:41–50.

19. Harvey et al.

20. R. Hill & L. Tennyson (1986), Maternal drug therapy: Effect on fetal and neonatal growth and neurobehavior, *Neurotoxicology* 7(2):121–39.

21. I. Chasnoff (1988), Cocaine: Effects on pregnancy and the neonate, in I. Chasnoff (Ed.), *Drugs, Alcohol, Pregnancy and Parenting* (Boston: Kluwer), 97–113; M. G. Neerhof et al. (1989), Cocaine abuse during pregnancy: Peripartum prevalence and perinatal outcome, *American Journal of Obstetrics and Gynecology* 161(3):633–38; A. Hadeed & S. R. Siegel (1989), Maternal cocaine use during pregnancy: Effect on the newborn infant, *Pediatrics* 84(2):205–10; Chasnoff, et al. "Perinatal cerebral infarction and maternal cocaine use;" L. Shih, et al. (1988), Effects of maternal cocaine abuse on the neonatal auditory system, *International Journal of Pediatric Otorhinolaryngology* 15:245–51.

22. Macro Systems, Inc. (1991), *Programs Serving Drug-Exposed Children and Their Families*. Washington, DC: Department of Health and Human Services.

23. J. P. Bauch (Ed.) (1988), *Early Childhood Education in the Schools* (Washington, DC: National Education Association).

24. G. Woodruff & M. J. McGonigel (1988), Early intervention team approaches: The trans-disciplinary model, in J. Jordan et al. (Eds.), *Early Childhood Special Education: Birth to Three* (Reston, VA: Council for Exceptional Children), 163–81.

25. Ibid.

26. Ibid.

27. Ibid.

28. Ibid.

29. Macro Systems, Inc.

30. Ibid.

31. N. Halfon (1990), *Testimony Before the U.S. House Select Committee on Children, Youth and Families* (Washington, DC: U.S. Government Printing Office).

32. R. L. Woodson (1990, June 17), *Testimony Before the Senate Subcommittee on Children, Family, Drugs, and Alcohol* (Washington, DC), 21.

SELECTED BIBLIOGRAPHY

Bauch, J. P. (Ed.) (1988, September). *Early Childhood Education in the Schools*. Washington, DC: National Education Association.

Chaney, N. E., Franke, J., & Wadlington, W. B. (1988). Cocaine convulsions in a breastfed baby. *Journal of Pediatrics* 112:134–35.

Chasnoff, I. J. (1989). Cocaine: Temporal patterns of cocaine use in pregnancy. *Journal of the American Medical Association* 261(12).

Chasnoff, I. (1988). Cocaine: Effects on pregnancy and the neonate. In I. Chasnoff (Ed.), *Drugs, Alcohol, Pregnancy and Parenting*. Boston: Kluwer.

Chasnoff, I. J., (1986). Perinatal cerebral infarction and maternal cocaine use. *Journal of Pediatrics* 108(3).

Chasnoff, I. J., Burns, W. J., Schnoll, S. H., & Burns, K. A. (1985). Cocaine use in pregnancy. *New England Journal of Medicine* 313(11).

Dixon, S. D., & Bejar, R. (1989). Echoencephalographic findings in neonates associated with maternal cocaine and methamphetamine use: Incidence and clinical correlates. *Journal of Pediatrics* 115(5).

Dixon, S. D. (1989). Effects of transplacental exposure to cocaine and methamphetamine on the neonate. *Western Journal of Medicine* 150(4).

Fitzhardinge, P. M., & Steven, E. M. (1972). The small-for-date infant. II: Neurological and intellectual sequelae. *Pediatrics* 50(1).

Flandermeyer, A. A. (1987). A comparison of the effects of heroin and cocaine abuse upon the neonate. *Neonatal Network* 6(3).

Grimm. V. E. (1987). Effect of teratogenic exposure on the developing brain: Research strategies and possible mechanisms. *Developmental Pharmacological Therapy* 10.

Hadeed, A., & Siegel, S. R. (1989). Maternal cocaine use during pregnancy: Effect on the newborn infant. *Pediatrics* 84(2):205–10.

Halfon, N. (1990). *Testimony Before the U.S. House Select Committee on Children, Youth and Families*. Washington, DC: U.S. Government Printing Office.

Harvey, D. (1982). Abilities of children who were small-for-gestational-age babies. *Pediatrics* 69(3).

Hill, R., & Tennyson, L. (1986). Maternal drug therapy: Effect on fetal and neonatal growth and neurobehavior. *Neurotoxicology* 7(2).

Insights. (1990). Cultural misalignment and emerging paradigms. *Southwest Educational Development Laboratory* 24:4–6.

Kirst, M. W., & McLaughlin, M. (1989). Rethinking children's policy: Implications for educational administration, in *Policy Bulletin* (Bloomingdale, IN: Consortium on Educational Policy Studies).

Macro Systems, Inc. (1991). *Programs Serving Drug-Exposed Children and Their Families*. Washington, DC: Department of Health and Human Services.

The men who created crack. (1991, August 19). *U.S. News and World Report*, 44–53.

Neerhof, M. G., (1989). Cocaine abuse during pregnancy: Peripartum prevalence and perinatal outcome. *American Journal of Obstetrics and Gynecology* 161.

Oro, A. S. & Dixon, S. D. (1987). Perinatal cocaine and methamphetamine exposure: Maternal and neonatal correlates. *Journal of Pediatrics* 111(4).

Parkinson, C. E., Wallis, S., & Harvey, D. (1981). School achievement and behavior of children who were small-for-dates at birth. *Develop. Med. Child Neurology* 23.

Rivkin, M., & Gilmore, H. E. (1989). Generalized seizures in an infant due to environmentally acquired cocaine. *Journal of Pediatrics* 84(6).

Shih, L. (1988). Effects of maternal cocaine abuse on the neonatal auditory system. *International Journal of Pediatric Otorhinolaryngology* 15.

Spires, M. C., Gordon, E. F., Chaudhuri, M., Maldonado, E., & Chan, R. (1989). Intracranial hemorrhage in a neonate following prenatal cocaine exposure. *Pediatric Neurology* 5(5).

Woodruff, G., & McGonigel, M. J. (1988). Early intervention team approaches: The trans-disciplinary model. In J. Jordan, *Early Childhood Special Education: Birth to Three*. Reston, VA: Council for Exceptional Children.

Woodson, R. L. (1990, June 17). *Testimony Before the Senate Subcommittee on Children, Family, Drugs, and Alcohol*. Washington, DC: GPO.

VI

PEDAGOGICAL PROBLEMS

18

The Nature of Pedagogy

Stanley William Rothstein

To those who still have unrealistic attitudes toward the curriculum in public urban schools, the work of European theorists should be instructive. As urban children fail in math and science, as exceptional children find it harder and harder to participate in least restrictive environments, the urban schools seem to move further and further from their stated goals. This is not surprising, given the theorists' view that urban schools are characterized by inculcation and a need to reproduce the status quo in classrooms and society. The urban schools, in these studies, mindlessly pass on an arbitrary cultural design, and schoolteachers arbitrarily teach the speech and language of the well-to-do. Teachers assume, apparently, that they are merely passing on those elements of our language and culture that are of the highest order. They seem unaware of their role in passing on the culture of the dominant classes, without examining the power that lies behind it. Urban educational systems perform these economic and social functions without being aware of them: they are compelled by society to pass on the social relations that exist between people in urban schools and labor markets.

The question we need to answer here is a practical one that may be difficult to apprehend empirically: do pedagogical actions in urban schools lead to symbolic violence and control? The answer to this question must begin with an analysis of pedagogic action, the central relationship in the schooling experience. In such interaction children are regularly subjected to symbolic violence and control; in the act of instruction an arbitrary language and cultural habitus are dictated to students. Teachers and students learn to accept these value systems and symbols without question; they are exposed to them at birth and later in state institutions of learning.

The language and culture of children from the lower and working classes are most flagrantly excluded from this arbitrary language and cultural system. The power teachers exude is symbolic, in Pierre Bourdieu's sense, because it tends to mask the power of dominant groups that impose their meanings on education.

It is symbolic control in Basil Bernstein's sense, because it adds its own force to these insights and understandings, giving them a legitimacy that further masks the power relations existing in urban schools and the workplace.[1]

From the outset, then, the distinctive nature of pedagogic action needs to be defined. We know that the teacher's power to determine what will be studied in classrooms is impositional in nature, allowing for the inculcation of arbitrary cultural values. Some scholars have noted that the arbitrary language and culture of urban educational systems determine the kind of social and psychological experience teachers and students have in their classrooms.[2] This provides us with an insight into why some students succeed while others fail in their academic levels of achievement: such success or failure is associated with the different social and scholastic backgrounds of students. Both success and failure are affected by the distance between a student's home culture and language and the culture and language of the urban schools he or she attends.[3] This variance is the source of the inequalities in academic achievement of children from different social origins and sexes.

It may be argued, along with Bourdieu, that cultural and linguistic competencies, or capital, stratify social classes and knowledge in state urban schools, that the schooling of youth is closely related to the social, economic, and industrial structures in society. But that would seem only to prove a commonsense understanding of urban schooling's effects. That there is an organic need of social systems to reproduce themselves seems self-evident on the surface. Our workplaces and urban schools are more and more given over to an educational production of knowledge that seems most interested in maintaining and reproducing the linguistic and cultural basis of present-day social structures through familial and pedagogical indoctrination.

Again and again we discover the hidden nature of pedagogical action: it is the ultimate form of symbolic violence and control in mass society. Again and again our efforts at inculcation are centered on the pedagogical act in families and urban schools: the distance between these two habitus (scholarly mastery of scholarly language and the habitus inculcated by the family) is a primary predictor of student success in urban schools.[4] (*Habitus* is used here to refer to the product of the internalization of the principles of a cultural arbitrary that has no support in logic or rational thought.) We recognize, along with Bourdieu and Jacque C. Passeron, that urban schools demand a competency in an arbitrary cultural and linguistic habitus they themselves cannot provide for the masses of children from working- and lower-middle-class families. Such competencies and understandings can be provided only by a child's family and are achieved through a form of linguistic and cultural osmosis rather than in formal classroom lessons. The educational system, therefore, gives an unfair advantage to those who already possess a substantial advantage, by valuing highly the culture and language of elite classes and seeking to reproduce their beliefs, values, and relations in society and the workplace. Thus educational advantage confirms and legitimizes the positions of those who have inherited cultural and linguistic "capital" from parents, and the status quo becomes an overwhelming force in the schooling of urban youth.

What is the role of schoolteachers in these processes of symbolic violence and social control? Teachers transmit their versions of this arbitrary culture and language they have learned to imitate and admire, without thinking about what they are doing. Only occasionally do some see the effects their impositional behaviors are having on the self-systems of students.

In the normal scheme of things, this emphasis on the beliefs, values, and style of the elite forces people to value highly their experience and worldviews. Knowledge, both social and academic, gives some students an advantage over others, and the problems of social and economic inequality are passed on from one generation to the next. What are the consequences for minorities and women? Women are unequally selected, according to their social origin and sex.[5] Their test scores reflect more than just the consequences of previous training in families and classrooms, more than just their social origins or sex. They also represent the fact that students have or have not been eliminated, that they are or are not part of the army of drop-outs who are the shame of urban schooling in the advanced, industrial nations.

The irony of these findings is that the linguistic and cultural learnings in the family are capable of explaining, in a systematic way, the relations that come to exist between teachers and pupils in urban schools. If we can choose any one set of variables to explain the stratification realities of urban education, it is the student's acculturation and language proficiency and their effects upon the selection process.[6] The influence of language shows itself in the earliest years of family life and schooling when the use of linguistic capabilities are used to measure and assess students' competencies and worth. These never cease to be felt, identifying and segregating students in terms of race and socioeconomic class.

That there are other forms of communication in classroom life is not to be doubted. We know from numerous studies that pedagogic action of parents and teachers provides, along with richer and poorer vocabularies, a "complex set of categories, so that the capacity to decipher and manipulate complex structures, whether logical or aesthetic, depends partly on the complexity of the language and world views transmitted by the family."[7] But the cultural boundaries of an individual's life are set by the beliefs, values, and understandings of the world he or she learns in families. So we may postulate that educational failures and dropouts can be expected to increase as one moves toward students in socioeconomic classes most distant from the arbitrary language and cultural practices of the urban schools, that is, from the language of ideas and schooling. These ideas provide us with a sociocultural perspective for understanding an individual student's success or failure in urban schools. In urban schools, for example, success or failure could be measured as a relationship among a student's possession of cultural and linguistic capabilities, his or her father's occupation, and the family's level of academic achievement.

But an understanding of the disparity that exists between the achievement scores of men and women requires further analysis. We now have several studies in Europe and the United States attesting to a constant superiority of men over women. These outcomes have been traced to a systematic social conditioning wherein women are streamed into lower-status careers while men are encouraged to study medicine, science, and law. These studies indicate that women, principally through the processes of initial familial and educational streaming, are victimized by their social origin and sex: the educational establishments they attended predetermined their educational fate, much as the fate of minority children was determined by forced incarceration in urban ghetto schools. But these first socialization experiences are reinforced by subsequent learnings and career choices that assure them of less opportunity and success than their male counterparts.

Still, Bourdieu noted that those who survive the selection process in higher education was constantly changing according to new criteria governing elimination. This tended to weaken the relationship between social origin and linguistic competence. Nevertheless, the sons of senior executives were on the top of the university system, studying high-status disciplines. Social origin, with its initial socialization and learning patterns, could not be considered as a factor capable of explaining every attitude, opinion, and practice in an individual's life. The constraints of the selection system had to be understood by examining particular urban educational systems at different moments in their history and development.

It should be noted, too, that Bourdieu did describe an array of social characteristics and associations that defined the first experiences and conditions of children from different social classes. He did this in order to understand better the different probabilities that the various educational experiences would have for them and the significance for individuals in different social classes of finding themselves in situations of greater or lesser prestige and status. For children of manual workers, for sons of laborers, it was highly improbable that they would study Latin and Greek in urban schools; it was more probable that they would have to work, if they decided to stay in urban schools and pursue a career in higher education.

It may be argued from this that our urban educational systems are devoted to a pedagogy that affects the way children see themselves, their families, and their occupational possibilities. But that would lead us back to the idea that social classes in France, England, the United States, and elsewhere require a selection system that has its roots in familial and urban educational experiences of children. That there are stronger and weaker classes of people, affecting the ways each lives in the society, is seldom contested. Our urban educational systems are more and more exclusively involved in providing a pedagogy that is received as symbolic control or violence by students from lower-class families, and these pedagogical practices appear to mirror conditions in the world of work. This accounts for the huge failure rates urban schools report each year.

More and more, we are coming to understand how the process of social reproduction strengthens the existing culture and social relations of familial, social, and educational institutions. We assume that previously held ideas of class struggle and conflict have some basis in fact. Our urban schools resemble the factories and bureaucratic work environments, preparing youth for a working experience that emphasizes worker subordination.

Where do these ideas lead us? Where is urban schooling in the process of social reproduction that all social systems strive to accomplish? What is the relationship between urban education and the political, economic, and social structures of modern industrial society?

In every effort of the state to educate its young there is an effort to perpetuate the culture and arbitrary assumptions of influential groups and classes; as a function of inculcation, social communication, and legitimate social selection, relations between the classes are maintained in each generation. All efforts to school the urban young are a profoundly conservative endeavor, Emile Durkheim taught more than a century ago. But how can this justify current pedagogical practices in urban schools, where symbolic violence and control are accompanied by authoritarian organizational structures and where the adoption of the crudest forms of coercion and control persist even as we approach the twenty-first century? What have urban schoolteachers done when they provided a legitimation for the social inequality and transmissions of power and privilege from one generation to the next? How can pedagogical practice escape the debilitating effects of such antidemocratic institutions and practices?

PEDAGOGIC AUTHORITY AND WORK

The intolerable irony in our dissatisfaction with current pedagogical work in urban schools is that we have largely ignored the ways in which they have exerted symbolic violence and control in order to legitimate the social relations that exist in modern industrial society. If I were to choose one characteristic of urban education in Western society, it would be the concealment of the power relations that exist in urban schools and the larger social system. There are, of course, many ways to legitimate existing cultures. What is the nature of authority in a particular society? In whose interests does it perform its work? How are such authority and power legitimized in the eyes of citizens and workers? These issues have been studied by Max Weber and others and provide us with a deeper understanding of the social movement from feudalism to capitalism that has occurred over the past few centuries. They point to legitimate culture as a consensual one having its roots in traditional, charismatic, or legal-rational practices. In times of great ferment and change, charismatic leaders and authorities often come to the fore, receiving validation from the personality or message of leaders. Then an attempt is made by those who follow the charismatic leaders to sustain their teachings and organizations. This has been done by resorting to traditional forms of domination in the past, but in our own period, legal-rational authority, based on laws and the bureaucratic organization of Western society, has become ascendant.

We can suppose, then, that urban schooling's authority rests on legal-rational sanctions and the traditions that have grown up around it. These sensitize us to the symbolic violence and control of the schools' culture, assuring us that they reinforce the predominant assumptions and dispositions of society itself. In France, the right and power to administer symbolic violence and control through pedagogical action are given to state and private academic institutions: these can and do use their authority to inculcate the arbitrary culture they cherish.

Ultimately, urban schools have no other choice but to reproduce the principles of the arbitrary culture of the state and society. This is because the language and culture of schooling are imposed by groups and classes who are in control— groups considered important enough to have their values and social relations reproduced by the next generation of citizens. Their worthiness is enhanced, in modern society, because they have apparently delegated to a neutral agency (urban schools) the authority to perform this essential task of social reproduction. It is possible, then, to measure academic success in terms of whether schooling does or does not perform its primary function of inculcation, whether it does or does not reproduce the existing culture and social relations of production.[8]

That pedagogic work can be boring is obvious. If it does not last over many years, however, important sources of pedagogic power and control are lost. Educators and politicians are the ones who define when a youth has had enough schooling. They decide when he or she has had enough competence in the arbitrary curriculum and culture of the urban schools, when enough training has occurred so that an educated person exists. In addition, they use pedagogic discipline as a substitute for social control and physical constraint: they force children to sit and attend by bringing sanctions against those who fail to accept and internalize the culture and arbitrary pedagogical actions of teachers. Pedagogic work is a form of symbolic coercion and constraint, an action that forces students to sit in classrooms long after they have dropped out intellectually and emotionally. The longer the process of enforced schooling by educators, the easier it is to conceal the truth of the arbitrary language and culture that state urban schools impose on students. Every movement of the dominant educational and social forces in society is toward legitimacy, attempting to validate its own values, history, and language while excluding those of the immigrant and urban poor. Those from the poorer classes find themselves excluded from the benefits of schooling because they are subjected to a symbolic experience that questions their self-worth and competency.[9] Compulsory education forces the dominated classes to recognize and accept the schools' version of knowledge and know-how. Pedagogic work produces a primary culture and approved language that are characteristic of the group or class that controls the economic and social power of the nation. These groups or classes identify and transmit valid knowledge and behavior from one generation to the next. As in pedagogic action, the degree of effective pedagogic work is a function of the distance between the language and culture urban schools have inculcated into their students and the previous language and pedagogic actions of parents. The success of a student depends on his or her family and preschool years, even though urban schools perpetuate the ideology that all children start schooling on an equal footing. The acquisition of language, skills in solving everyday problems, kinship relationships, logical forms of thinking and worldly perspective are mastered during a youngster's formative years, when he or she learns the language, culture, and class position of his or her family. These beliefs, attitudes, values, self-concepts, and perspectives are symbolic in nature and tie one to a particular class in society, predisposing children unequally toward a symbolic mastery of the pedagogic action and work in classrooms.

URBAN EDUCATIONAL SYSTEMS

The question we need to answer today is an important one, though it cannot be answered by research alone: can an educational system survive without reproducing the social relations of educational and economic production? The central function of state schooling is inculcation; the central social function is reproducing the conditions of educational work in schools and in the workplace.[10] State-supported schools live by the largesse and direction they receive from the political sectors of the nation; they are duty-bound to validate the conditions and values of society and to segregate those who do not live up to their highest standards.

The function of reproduction excludes knowledge that would lead to dissatisfaction with the way things are in schools or the workplace: such understandings would make it more difficult to create and maintain the institutional conditions that allowed students to accept the economic and social system. Educational systems cannot be understood by researching the historical and social conditions of a particular educational system. Durkheim, who sought to understand the nature of urban educational systems by looking backward toward the early Christian habitus and Greco-Roman heritage, disagreed.[11] Looking at the organizational structures and practices schooling adopted as it tried to solve the problems of a particular period, he used history as a study of an evolving life form. More recently, other social and educational theorists have come to believe that only by examining such structures more intensely could they come to see and understand the social forces that gave rise to different historical situations and educational processes. Only then could one examine educational structures and their relationship to ongoing forces in other sectors of society.

Progress made by an educational system—such as paying teachers, organizing and training them systematically, the standardization of educational organization over a wide area, examinations, civil service status, and so on—was all part of the bureaucratic establishment and institutionalization of pedagogic work. Durkheim identified the medieval university as the first educational system in Europe because it had within its structure evaluation methods that validated the results of inculcation (the diploma). This evaluation component was Durkheim's primary consideration because it united the pedagogic action of inculcation and forced it into a more homogeneous, standardized pattern. Max Weber might have added that such urban educational systems were also characterized by a cadre of specialized personnel whose training, recruitment, and careers were controlled by the institution and who found, in the educational system, a way of maintaining their claim to a monopoly of legitimate inculcation of the arbitrary habitus or culture of the urban school and society.

Since urban educational systems cannot perform their essential function of inculcation unless they produce and reproduce the structural and relational conditions for their own pedagogical work, a habitus as homogeneous and durable as possible in as many students and teachers as possible is necessary. Its external functions of cultural and social reproduction force it to produce a habitus as close as possible to the cultural arbitrary that it was funded and mandated to produce.

The need to assure homogeneous and orthodox school work forces the educational system to move toward standardized training for both teachers and their students. Standardized curriculum, pedagogical methods, and tests are used to measure students against one another. The tools of teaching that the educational system uses are not only aids in the performance of pedagogic action but also ways of limiting the goals, perspectives, and content of classroom work. Textbooks, syllabi, manuals—all have the effect of unifying what is taught in different classrooms by different teachers. The need to codify and systematize the pedagogic communication and urban school culture is conditioned by the demands for homogeneity and orthodoxy in increasingly strained, mass societies. All learning in urban educational systems is done within the framework of an essentially apprenticeship system in which the student is socialized out of his or her ignorant condition over a period of many years. This binds the graduates, teachers, and students to the educational system and to the economic and social system.

The institutionalization of pedagogic action is characterized by an obsessive concern for self-reproduction. There is an inadequacy of research training and inquiry methods up and down the grade system. There is a programming of the norms of research and the objects of inquiry so that the interests of the status quo are served. Urban educational systems are relatively autonomous institutions monopolizing the legitimate use of symbolic violence and serving groups or classes whose cultural arbitrary they reproduce.

NOTES

1. Pierre Bourdieu and Jacque C. Passeron (1977), *Reproduction in Education, Society and Culture* (Los Angeles: Sage Publishers), 54–67.

2. Ibid., 4–7.

3. Pierre Bourdieu (1979), *The Inheritors: French Students and Their Relation to Culture* (Chicago: University of Chicago Press), 3–12.

4. Bourdieu and Passeron, 31–35.

5. Bourdieu, 1–28.

6. Bourdieu and Passeron, 73.

7. Ibid., 73–74.

8. Ibid., 35–37.

9. Stanley W. Rothstein (1987), "The Ethics of Coercion," *Urban Education* 22 (1):53–72.

10. Bourdieu and Passeron, 54–67.

11. Emile Durkheim (1956), *Education and Sociology* (New York: Free Press).

19

Mathematics, Science, and Urban Education

David Eli Drew

When compared with the education received by students in a variety of countries throughout the world, American science education can best be described as mediocre.[1] Furthermore, the very groups that are overrepresented in our cities—the poor, the disadvantaged, and people of color—are severely underrepresented in classrooms where mathematics and science are taught. Science education not only is vital for an increasingly technological society but also has become a vehicle through which the inequalities of our society are perpetuated and exacerbated.

Fortunately, research in a range of disciplines has suggested solutions for these problems. The disciplines include educational research (e.g., studies about cooperative learning), cognitive psychology (e.g., studies about the impact of self-esteem and self-efficiency), sociology (e.g., the links between reference group interactions and achievement), and the history of science (e.g., some of history's most powerful insights have come from ''unlikely'' people).

The single most important change that is required involves a national consciousness-raising. Teachers, parents, and the students themselves must recognize that virtually every child has the capacity to master mathematics and science and should be taught these subjects. This is true for females as well as for males, for poverty-stricken students as well as those from more affluent backgrounds, and for persons of every ethnicity. Beyond consciousness-raising, the research results provide guidance as to how the reform of science education can proceed most effectively.

THE URBAN CONTEXT: POVERTY'S PERNICIOUS EFFECTS

Several years ago I spent a day in the classroom of a gifted junior high school teacher, the late Charlie Koepke, in Ontario, California. His principal described to me both the enthusiasm and excitement Charlie's students felt about science and how this experience stood in stark contrast to their lives outside school. Their homes and neighborhoods were filled with violence or the fear of violence. For many of those students school had become a safe haven.

You cannot discuss urban education in America without discussing poverty. I will not repeat here the alarming statistics about the levels of poverty in America's cities, since they are presented elsewhere in this volume. But I will note that many separate stress factors afflicting a child growing up in poverty have a cumulative effect. These include not only fearing violence in the neighborhood or the family but also finding no adult at home after school. Poor people are more likely to be sick, in part because of poor nutrition, and less likely to afford good health care. (Perhaps the single most effective public policy initiative to improve math and science education would be a massive escalation of programs providing prenatal nutrition to poor women.) Drug and alcohol abuse are much more frequent. The list goes on.

It costs more to live in a poor neighborhood than it does to live in an affluent neighborhood. In a classic article called "Keeping the Poor Poor," Paul Jacobs detailed the irony of the extra costs associated with being poor.[2] Housing is more expensive, on a per-square-foot basis. Since banks have retreated from the most poverty-stricken ghettos, the simple act of cashing a check becomes an expensive exchange. While there are loan sharks who will advance money at unbelievable rates and who demand to be paid back on time, the usual middle-class avenues for obtaining credit are not open to the poor. Not only do they pay higher rates when they do qualify for loans, but their property is seized more quickly if they are late with payments. Like the banks, the major supermarket chains have abandoned the inner city, so residents frequently shop at convenience stores and small mom-and-pop markets where food products and other essentials cost much more.

Consider, further, that many urban students, particularly in a city like mine, Los Angeles, have migrated to the United States with their families under very difficult circumstances. A Los Angeles elementary school teacher, John Lantos, recently observed that in his classroom: "I will watch Sharona, from Tehran, who was shot at by soldiers as she escaped with her family over the Makran Mountains into Pakistan. I will watch Mayra, who endured the sullen stares of border guards and three days of hunger and thirst as she and her mother rode rickety buses up the twisted spine of Central America. I will watch Vinod, who wrote that what he missed most about his native India was his baby cow, born the day he left." Lantos marvels that these students, faced with so many challenges, persevere and try to learn. "I will miss my young heroes and heroines, because that is what they are. In a country crazed with violence, in a country whose elected leaders have all but abandoned them, these children have risen above their circumstances and performed heroically. They have noble qualities, all of them. Their accomplishments made me feel exalted."[3]

Table 19.1
Achievement Scores by Nation for 13-Year-Olds (Average Percent Correct)

Country	Science	Mathematics
Korea	78	73
Taiwan	76	73
Switzerland (15 Cantons)	74	71
Hungary	73	68
Soviet Union (Russian speaking schools in 14 Republics)	71	70
Slovenia	70	57
Emilia-Romagna, Italy	70	64
Israel (Hebrew-speaking schools)	70	63
Canada	69	62
France	69	64
Scotland	68	61
Spain (Spanish speaking schools except in Cataluna)	68	55
United States	67	55
Ireland	63	61
Jordan	57	40

Source: Archie E. Lapointe, Nancy A. Mead, and Janice M. Askew, *Learning Mathematics* (U.S. Department of Education and the National Science Foundation, 1992). Archie E. Lapointe, Nancy A. Mead, and Janice M. Askew, *Learning Science* (U.S. Department of Education and the National Science Foundation, 1992).

THE INTERNATIONAL CONTEXT: HOW DOES THE UNITED STATES STACK UP?

In the past twenty-five years there have been a number of comparative international studies of educational achievement. Typically about twenty countries have been involved, and the sample of students has been in the hundreds of thousands. Typically, the students have been tested in elementary school (at about the age of ten, in high school (at about the age of fourteen), and in the last year of secondary school (at about the age of eighteen). The dismal performance of American students had been widely reported in the U.S. press, particularly the finding in most evaluations that U.S. high school seniors rank at or near the bottom of the pack. For example, Table 19.1 presents data from the most recent international assessment on the mathematics and science achievement scores of American students relative to those from seventeen other countries.

In my judgment, American mathematics and science achievement is bad (and must be improved), but not as bad as this table would lead you to think. Certainly, these most recent results are consistent with findings from the other international assessments conducted in recent decades. But two methodological considerations must shape our interpretation of these data. First, the samples across countries are not comparable because different proportions of the school-age population attend school in different countries.

Those countries that weed out weaker students prior to secondary school have an advantage in international comparisons with countries that attempt to make science available to the entire adolescent population. Second, while the researchers attempt to minimize or eliminate test item bias, the item selected for the test may more closely correspond to the curriculum in some countries than in others.

Writing about an earlier international study, John Eichinger noted that different countries have different science curriculum structures, which make comparisons less meaningful. For example, American high school students study a different subject each year while European students learn a little about each subject each year. Eichinger observed, "Since the test questions were based on a combination of stated or approximated national curricula, students from countries such as the U.S., which have no official or unofficial national curricular standards, may be at a disadvantage."[4]

Eichinger concludes his review: "As a science teacher, I must ask myself the following question after reading the IEA study: Can a single 24 to 30 item test possibly be an accurate index to the curriculum in my classroom, in all other American science classrooms, and in the science classrooms of 16 other countries? The degree of disagreement in my answer should be proportional to the degree of skepticism that I exercise as I interpret IEA's results."[5]

In these evaluation studies, U.S. students typically perform in the middle of the pack when they're in elementary school but fall to the bottom of the pack by the senior year of high school. This could mean either that the performance of U.S. students deteriorates or that the elementary school performance is a more accurate measure, because the percentages of the school-age population in school are comparable at that time. I believe the latter interpretation is correct, particularly because in some of the studies the performance of high school seniors in the top 1 percent or top 5 percent of each country was compared, and American students then performed at, or just below, the middle.

In summary, the evidence appears to indicate that when the proportion of the school-age population still attending school is controlled, U.S. students perform at, or just below, the middle rank. Furthermore, while it's hard to estimate accurately the impact of test item bias (and the data available about this vary from study to study), it's possible that this factor might increase the true U.S. ranking somewhat.

However, the net result of these statistical adjustments is to upgrade the relative performance of U.S. students from "disastrous" to "mediocre."

Furthermore, in the analyses to estimate the effects of differing national school attendance rates, an interesting fact emerges. While the United States has a very high percentage of eighteen-year-olds in school relative to other countries, the percentage of those in U.S. schools who study mathematics and science is very low! The statistics on the relative percentage of American students who study advanced mathematics, for example, calculus, are even more disturbing.

One of my former doctoral students, Dr. Margarita Calderon, now is a faculty member at the University of Texas at El Paso. For a number of years she directed the remedial center there. Students who are having trouble in a variety of subjects, including mathematics, come to the center for tutoring. The center hires under-graduates and graduate students as tutors. In reviewing the hiring decisions made by the center over a number of years. Dr. Calderon observed that they rarely hired Americans to tutor in math. Rather, they tended to hire tutors who were from three countries: Malaysia, India, and Mexico. Most of the Mexican students at the University of Texas, El Paso, come from Juarez. Juarez and El Paso are twin border towns, and Juarez is about a mile from El Paso across the Rio Grande River. While it's possible that those Mexican tutors are from the more affluent sector of Juarez, it appears that a young person who goes through the Juarez school system emerges with a much better knowledge of mathematics than the same young person would if he or she attended school a mile away in the United States! In fact, some of the teachers from Juarez have been providing guidance to the American teachers about mathematics instruction.

STUDENT INTEREST IN SCIENCE

The number of students who find science interesting seems to shrink as they progress through the school system. R. F. Yager and J. E. Penick presented data to illustrate this point and concluded: "The more years our students enroll in science courses, the less they like it. Obviously, if one of our goals is for students to enjoy science and feel successful at it, we should quit teaching science in third grade. Or perhaps we should try teaching it differently."[6]

Carl Sagan recently commented: "Every now and then, I'm lucky enough to teach a class in kindergarten or the first grade. Many of these children are curious, intellectually vigorous, ask provocative and insightful questions, and exhibit great enthusiasm for science."[7] But when he visits a high school class, the students are much less interested. Somewhere between kindergarten and high school they have lost their enthusiasm. Some research suggests that the danger area may be junior high school.

F. James Rutherford was the director of a project that prepared a report for the American Association for the Advancement of Science about the teaching of science and math in the United States. He comments, "You have to know something is wrong when teaching something as exciting as science can result in most of us disliking it."[8]

THE UNDERREPRESENTATION OF WOMEN AND PEOPLE OF COLOR

At every link in the science education pipeline, from grade school to grad school, women and people of color are underrepresented. Furthermore, their percentages decline even further as students progress through the pipeline. That is, women and people of color are even more underrepresented in graduate school

Table 19.2
U.S. Citizen Ph.D.'s in Natural Science and Engineering

		White		Asian		Hispanic	
Year	Total	Men	Women	Men	Women	Men	Women
1985	8161	5797	1587	224	80	83	34
1986	8090	5675	1654	240	83	96	41
1987	8216	5652	1709	279	83	109	43
1988	8685	5960	1862	290	72	141	46
1989	8811	5824	2060	324	93	127	48
1990	9249	6205	2134	310	86	143	67
1991	9281	6150	2110	353	128	152	61

		Black		Am. Indian	
Year	Total	Men	Women	Men	Women
1985	8161	69	29	13	9
1986	8090	53	33	20	11
1987	8216	60	33	23	7
1988	8685	63	33	21	6
1989	8811	72	38	25	9
1990	9249	68	35	15	2
1991	9281	87	46	25	9

Source: "Scientific Minority and Woman Power," *Science* 256 (June 1992): 1765.
Note: Totals include minority groups not listed.

and subsequent professional life than they were in elementary and secondary school. Table 19.2 presents some data to illustrate this.

An analysis by the American Mathematical Society and the Mathematical Association of America reported that only 363 out of 804 mathematics doctorates awarded in 1987–1988 (45 percent) were awarded to Americans. (Ten years earlier 634 math doctorates had been awarded to Americans.) Of the 363, only four were African-Americans!

In a thorough and definitive article about "Women in Science and Engineering," physicist and historian Stephen G. Brush asks: "What is preventing more women from going into science and engineering? There is no simple answer to this question. In the past two decades overt discrimination may have become covert, but it is still effective. And some new factors have emerged to reinforce the old obstacles."[9]

Among the obstacles Brush cites are the negative popular culture stereotype of the scientist as a nerd, textbook portrayals of scientists and engineers that disproportionately discuss and picture males, wide-ranging publicity about the so-called mental inferiority of females, inadequate precollege preparation, biases in the Scholastic Aptitude Test, cutbacks in financial aid, inappropriate teaching methods, sexist attitudes of professors and students, and the tradition of combative interactions among scientists.

Jadwiga S. Sebrechts began an article in the *Journal of NIH Research* with a question:

What do the inventors of the following have in common?

- The cotton gin
- The microelectrode
- Nerve growth factor
- Nuclear fission
- COBOL computer language
- Apgar score
- Smallpox inoculation
- Tetracycline

A clue: It's the same thing that is common to the scientists who identified and catalogued more than 300,000 stars, who co-founded the Marine Biological Laboratory at Woods Hole, Mass., who founded ecology, who made the calculations necessary to split the atom, and who invented the branch of mathematics known today as functional analysis.[10]

The answer, of course, is that all these scientists were women.

Bernadine Healy, director of the National Institute of Health, has said, "The astonishing thing is that young women pursue careers in science at all!" Healy sees one exception to the discouraging, subtle, and not so subtle biases against women in American schools and colleges: "All women's colleges lose fewer of their science majors to other fields. Based on my own personal experience, I believe that women's colleges can engender an environment and a mind-set in which there are no barriers based on gender, an environment that encourages women to pursue 'nontraditional' fields—like science and medicine."[11]

THE IMPORTANCE OF SCIENCE EDUCATION

These statistics are particularly disturbing because science education is of vital importance in the preparation of scientists and engineers, the training of skilled workers, and the development of science literacy.

There is considerable debate currently about whether the United States faces a shortage of qualified scientists and engineers. Two propositions are indisputable: the pipeline of future scientists begins with elementary and secondary education, and we need a more diverse population of scientists and engineers. Presently the population of scientists and engineers is almost exclusively white and male. But work in the history of science and the sociology of science suggests that a more diverse technological work force may lead to more creative discoveries, perhaps the introduction of new paradigms. People from different cultural backgrounds and women bring new frames of reference to the analysis of scientific problems.

Studies repeatedly report that American business and industry find lacking the technical skills of workers who have graduated from our school systems. In fact, one national commission found that many employers deliberately have "dumbed down" the technical requirements for skilled workers so as not to demand more in jobs than can be achieved.

The Industrial Revolution of the nineteenth century transformed a rural Ameican economy dominated by farming into one dependent on heavy manufacturing. The automobile became the cornerstone and symbol of this economy, following the development of the assembly line by Henry Ford. The number of people whose jobs centered about the automobile—manufacturing the parts, putting the vehicle together, selling it, repairing it, reselling it, financing it—was staggering.

In the second half of the twentieth century, American society is again undergoing a radical change, this time because of an information revolution. Like the farmer, the blue-collar worker is now receding both as a symbol and as a reality. The smokestack industries are now being replaced by service-oriented, information-processing businesses. These changes have created massive educational needs for both workers and executives.

While in college, I worked in a machine shop next to an old, skilled European craftsman who ridiculed those of us who operated automatic lathes. If that proud craftsman is alive today, he must be shaking his head in wonder at the precision of industrial products effortlessly turned out by the current computer-based machinery. (Insiders call this CAD/CAM—computer-aided design/computer-aided machining.)

Blue-collar workers who find themselves unemployed when manufacturing industries are replaced by information-processing firms or when an auto plant is moved from, say, southern California to South Korea have been labeled "displaced workers." A vivid example of the threats to skilled workers by automation is provided by the newspaper business. Setting type had been a challenging craft, difficult to master. Now it's all done easily with computers.

In this new economy, business and industry transcend national boundaries. Robert Reich comments:

The software engineer from Belmont, Mass., working on a contract for Siemens, which is financed out of Tokyo, the routine coding of which will be done in Bulgaria, the hardware for which will be assembled in Mexico, is a true citizen of the global economy. Her stake in the future productivity of the kid who lives 10 miles away in Chelsea, Mass., is quite low. It is now possible for this symbolic analyst to experience a rising real income even though the rest of the people of the nation experience falling real incomes. We are no longer in the same economic boat, so to speak.[12]

Reich adds, "The competitiveness of Americans in this global market is coming to depend, not on the fortunes of any American corporation or on American industry, but on the functions that Americans perform—the value they add—within the global economy."[13]

Reich argues that the work demanded by information-based society will require what he calls "symbolic analysts," people skilled in pattern recognition and other symbol manipulation work. He suggests that many American children—he estimates 15 to 20 percent—are being well educated for symbolic analytic work, despite the ills that have befallen the American educational system. He argues that, in contrast, "Japan's greatest educational success has been to assure that even its slowest learners achieve a relatively high level of proficiency."[14]

Anthony Patrick Carnevale, Leila J. Gainer, and Ann S. Meltzer, authors of a 1991 book, *Workplace Basics: The Essential Skills Employers Want*, note:

There is no question that employers today are focusing more and more on an employee's ability to compute at increasing levels of sophistication. The reason for this is simple— technology requires it. Moreover, the introduction of sophisticated management and quality control approaches such as statistical process control (SPC) demand higher math- ematical skills. Ironically, as occupational skill-level requirements climb, higher edu- cational dropout rates and worsening worker deficiencies in computational skills are appearing.... Employers already are complaining of their workers' computational skill deficiencies, particularly those evidenced by miscalculations of decimals and fractions, resulting in expensive production errors.[15]

Carnevale et al. comment further on the research about the economic impli- cations of deficiencies in mathematical skills manifested by American workers: "Similarly, in 1988 Motorola conducted a study that showed that a Japanese student can be moved into the workplace at an employer cost of $0.47, while an American student's transition costs the employer $226. This is primarily due, says Motorola, to the emphasis on statistics and applied diagnostics in Japanese schools."[16]

Beyond what students need to become scientists, engineers, or skilled workers in the new globalized economy, they need an excellent education so that they can become scientifically literate. They will be called upon to make all kinds of choices about their personal lives that require familiarity with scientific concepts and the ability to make decisions, for example, whether to have a mastectomy or a lumpectomy if breast cancer is detected, whether it's financially wise to get a service contract with their new VCR, whether they should listen to the advice given by astrologers, and so forth.

In China, the constitution of the People's Republic specifically discusses sci- ence education policies. In the United States, 21 percent of the adult population believes that the sun revolves around the earth.

MATHEMATICS IS THE FILTER

Consider the following widely held beliefs about mathematics: "Americans are better at math than people from other countries, except Asians"; "Now that we have calculators and computers nobody (except scientists) needs to learn mathematics"; "Most women can't do math."

In fact, each of the above statements is false, but each is a myth that has become firmly embedded in American culture. In a ranking of things that most Americans hate, fear, and detest, mathematics rates right up there with Saddam Hussein, taxes, and politicians.

Mathematician John Allen Paulos has argued that Americans suffer from what he calls "innumeracy," the inability to deal with numbers and mathematics, a deficiency he describes as parallel to illiteracy. He observes; "In fact, unlike other failings which are hidden, mathematical illiteracy is often flaunted: 'I can't even balance my checkbook,' 'I'm a people person, not a numbers person' or 'I always hated math.' Part of the reason for this perverse pride in mathematical ignorance is that its consequences are not usually as obvious as are those of other weakness."[17]

Research is revealing that mastery of mathematics may be the single factor most related to an individual's success in college and beyond. Furthermore, virtually everyone can learn advanced mathematical concepts, even those who start late. The negative attitudes about math achievement are based on incorrect assumptions about who can learn this subject.

I believe that avoidance of math is the hidden factor that explains a surprising percentage of the career decisions made by young people. There are people who want to be doctors and dentists but choose other careers so that they won't have to take math in college. An academic counselor at a large technical university who works with community college transfers reports that she repeatedly is told, "I'd like to major in _____, but I can't do math so I'm going to become a teacher instead." Think of the introduction that future teacher's students will have to the joys of arithmetic and mathematics.

A recent College Board study about success in the SATs and college concluded that the key factor was mathematics.[18] In fact, Donald Stewart, the president of the College Board, said, "Math is the gatekeeper for success in college."

THE "STRANGE" CONCEPT OF APTITUDE

Several years ago I was talking with a colleague who is a math professor in China. He made a very telling point. He noted that virtually everybody in China learns advanced mathematics while only a few do so in the United States. He said that in China it's assumed that everyone can master calculus and is expected to do it. In America, he said, you have this "strange concept of aptitude."

We approach teaching differently depending on whether we assume that (1) virtually everyone can master our material, and the challenge is to present it in a manner that allows people to do so or that (2) this material is tough, and only a few of the best and brightest will be able to learn it. Most math teachers embrace the second philosophy. Put another way, the question is whether mathematics is a scarce resource to be doled out only to the most able or whether it's an abundantly available resource that can be used to empower most people in our society.

Aptitude and intelligence tests are most useful in situations where access to resources, for example, admission to college, must be limited to only a few, and a legitimate basis for identifying those people is needed. (Of course, the test should be free of gender, ethnic, and economic biases.) But these tests are not needed in situations where the resources are not scarce. Furthermore, the widespread use of such tests can be extremely destructive if they send the incorrect message to those who are not selected that they are incapable of learning the material. When this happens, a device that was created to allocate scarce resources has become the instrument that destroys the self-image and aspirations of many students.

ACHIEVEMENT, SELF-CONCEPT, AND ASPIRATIONS

Contributing to the problem are the attitudes and expectations held by some teachers about the capabilities of girls and people of color. I teach about multivariate statistical analysis in our Ph.D. program at the Claremont Graduate School. I have encountered many students, especially women and students of color, who feared math and were sure they could not do it. (As you may know, most graduate students dread statistics and put if off as long as possible.) Virtually all of these students then discover they are capable of understanding and conducting sophisticated statistical analyses like hierarchical multiple regression. In conversation, I often find that their negative self-image goes back to an elementary school teacher with a sexist or racist attitude, a person who thought that "girls can't do math" and managed to traumatize a student who now must be convinced about her real ability. Sheila Tobias has studied "math anxiety" and has shown how and why this affliction is particularly prevalent among women.[19]

Many people have become aware of the extraordinary accomplishments of Jaime Escalante. This mathematics teacher at Garfield High School in East Los Angeles successfully prepared many Latino and other students from poor families to take the Educational Testing Service Advanced Placement test in calculus. The movie *Stand and Deliver* told this story well. But the most important message from this experience is not that Jaime Escalante is an extraordinary and successful teacher, although this certainly is true. The message is that high school students whom most educators might have considered incapable of mastering calculus did master it when they were taught by such a creative instructor.

It's disturbing that many teachers erroneously believe that certain kinds of students can't do math. This becomes tragic when the students themselves incorporate those devastating myths into their self-concept and then lower their aspirations, thereby shortchanging what they can do with their lives.

Without question, the best information available about college students comes from the Cooperative Institutional Research Program (CIRP) conducted by UCLA's Higher Education Research Institute. Substantial data about more than 7 million college freshmen have been collected during the past twenty-five years. This includes information about freshman major and career aspirations. When plotted over a twenty-five-year period, the percentage of freshmen choosing mathematics dropped precipitously. Mathematics is not attracting students. In part, this is because many math professors have the attitude, "We'll see who's tough enough to survive and flunk the rest out."

In recent analyses I conducted with the CIRP data I examined mathematical self-concepts, specifically the percentage of students who rated their own mathematical ability as being in the top 10 percent of college students. The results are both fascinating and disturbing. Among Anglos, 24 percent of the men thought they were in the top 10 percent while 10 percent of the females placed themselves there. Among African-Americans, 14 percent of men and 8 percent of women thought they were in the top 10 percent; among Chicanos, the figures were 28 percent of men and 8 percent of women. Finally, among Asians, 40 percent of the men and 24 percent of the women thought they were in the top 10 percent of college students on mathematical ability.

In a further analysis I examined only those students who actually were in the top 10 percent of this sample in mathematical ability, as measured by their score on the SAT quantitative test. The cutoff for this sample was a score of 670, which actually is higher than the threshold that marked the top 10 percent of those who took the test during that year (high school seniors in 1984), which was 580. Thus, this is a conservative definition, and these students actually may have been in the top 5 percent. Furthermore, they would have received a report from the Educational Testing Service indicating their score and their percentile. Despite this, only 49 percent of the women freshmen who were in the top 10 percent believed they belonged there. Furthermore, four years later about half of those 49 percent no longer considered themselves to be in the top 10 percent in math ability. Only 23 percent of the women who actually were in the top 10 percent believed that they were in the top 10 percent in both their freshman and senior years!

SOLUTIONS

During the past decade there have been many task force reports and studies detailing what is wrong with American education. The first and most widely quoted was *A Nation at Risk*. There also have been a number of curriculum and educational reform initiatives launched. Few reform movements aimed at the schools are likely to have a massive impact because of the fundamentally de-centralized nature of American schooling. Key policy decisions are made in thousands of separate school districts by thousands of school boards. However, several efforts in science education are worth noting.

A new science literacy program has been developed by faculty members at thirty-six liberal arts colleges using a $20 million grant from the Albert P. Sloan Foundation.[20] The instructors use dramatic examples from real life to illustrate scientific principles. For example, Wellesley College physicist Theodore Ducas rode an elevator up and down forty floors of a Boston skyscraper while standing on a scale and videotaping the scale. He then showed his class how these data could be used to identify the position and acceleration of the elevator at any given time.

Project 2061 (named for the year that Halley's comet next returns to Earth) is a massive, long-term effort sponsored by the American Association for the Advancement of Science.[21] The project has been organized in three stages: defining curriculum goals, developing sample curricula, and implementing curriculum change in schools throughout the country. Stage I has been completed and yielded a volume specifying goals and objectives, *Science for All Americans*. Luther Williams, head of Education and Human Resources at the National Science Foundation, said about this volume, "For the first time we have a total representation of what should constitute science education."[22] Presently curriculum development is being carried out at six sites: Pennsylvania, Wisconsin, Georgia, Texas, and California (two sites).

Another project is sponsored by the National Science Teachers Association and titled Scope, Sequence, and Coordination (SSC). While this project is also large, it is being implemented more rapidly. Curriculum reform already is under way in three sites—California, Iowa, and Texas. The SSC's guiding principles are that (1) information is learned in thematic blocks and (2) students learn concrete ideas before moving to abstractions. For example, students conduct density experiments, simultaneously learning some physics, chemistry, and biology, as opposed to separate courses in physics, chemistry, and biology. One criticism of this approach is that most teachers are specialists in one discipline and may be surprisingly weak in the other disciplines.

Iowa program director Robert Yager comments: "Traditionally kids were told, 'Learn this and you'll find it useful.' But it wasn't useful. Now we turn that around." Yager has also commented on how the courses can stimulate student interest. For example, one course focused on the ozone threats. "To their teacher's amazement, the students were soon clamoring for information: 'What's an atom? What's a molecule? What does pH mean?' The class became the community ozone experts."[23]

These two efforts and a parallel effort in math education, spearheaded by the National Council of Teachers of Mathematics, share certain themes: less memorization, greater emphasis on hands-on activities, a greater focus on students' questions and the ideas they bring, linking science to society's problems, and emphasizing the scientific process and how problems are solved.[24]

The Education and Human Resources Directorate (EHR) of the National Science Foundation (NSF) is engaged in a massive funding effort aimed at dramatically increasing the participation of underrepresented students in the science and engineering pipeline. According to Dr. Joseph Danek, the person with responsibility for managing this array of programs: "These funds should not be considered add-ons. These activities are central to what the educational system in this country is all about."[25]

The spectrum of programs includes several targeting precollege education and several for colleges and universities. In the former category are Comprehensive Regional Centers (where universities take the lead), Partnerships for Student Achievement (where school districts take the lead and in-class activities are emphasized), and summer camp programs. In the latter category are the Research Career for Minority Scholars program (which focuses on awards at the departmental level) and a much larger program, the Alliance for Minority Participation program (AMP). In the AMP program statewide efforts link universities and colleges, and curriculum change is a key feature. Each state receives $1 million a year from the National Science Foundation, which is matched by $1 to 2 million from other sources each year. The funding for each state lasts five years. There presently are eleven implemented AMP programs. NSF's national objective is to increase the number of underrepresented minorities getting bachelor's degrees from 13,000 to 50,000 by the year 2000.

As important as these efforts are, three changes are fundamental to the improvement of science education in the cities:

- We now know that students learn best when working in cooperative study groups with their peers.

- We need to attract the most-qualified young people into teaching science and mathematics and to reward them appropriately.

- We must recognize that virtually all students, regardless of ethnicity or gender, can master mathematics and science. We should expect and require them to do so.

COOPERATIVE STUDY GROUPS

The most exciting research about how people learn math was carried out by a graduate student at Berkeley. Uri Treisman, while a teaching assistant in calculus courses, observed that the African-American students performed very poorly while the Chinese students excelled.[26] He did not accept the conventional wisdom that the low achievement rates of the African-American students were due to such factors as their parents' poverty or the poor schools they attended as young children. He thought maybe it had to do with how they studied, what they studied, and with whom. So Treisman spent eighteen months observing both the Chinese and African-American students. He found the Chinese spent longer hours studying than other students and that they frequently studied together in groups, for example, working out extra homework problems as a group. Treisman then developed an experimental workshop in which he replicated these interaction and study patterns with the African-American students. The results were astounding. These African-American students went on to excel in calculus.

Treisman found that when you look at students who entered college with given SAT performance level, his workshop students consistently outperformed both Anglos and Asians. A central component of the workshop approach was to stretch the students to excel by giving them extra, advanced problems. While these African-American students had been experiencing difficulties and failure in the preworkshop era, they were high school valedictorians who resented and rejected an approach based on remediation. In short, one key to Treisman's success was his focus on self-concept. The students were treated like the winners they could be, not like helpless losers.

Wait a minute, a critic might say. Those African-American students already were good enough to be admitted by Berkeley. Would these methods work in other colleges and universities, and would they work with students of other ethnic backgrounds? My colleague Martin Bonsangue and I received a grant from the National Science Foundation to explore these questions. Dr. Bonsangue gathered data about a workshop program based on the Treisman model that has been implemented at Cal-Poly Pomona.[27] In fact, this institution has the oldest and best-established workshop program in the country. The results show precisely the kind of dramatic improvement from the Cal-Poly workshops that Treisman found at Berkeley. More specifically, the calculus achievement of Latino workshop students improved dramatically. Furthermore, Bonsangue was able to measure longitudinal effects beyond simply assessing performance in the calculus course itself. Once again, he found dramatic positive effects associated with workshop participation. For example, participants were significantly less likely to drop out of advanced calculus courses and science, mathematics, and engineering majors.

TEACHING AND THE CURRICULUM

Good teaching involves knowing what methods are effective. However, despite considerable evidence about the value of laboratory and field experience, a recent national study by the Educational Testing Service found:

- Only 35 percent of the seventh graders and 53 percent of the eleventh graders reported working with other students on science experiments at least on a weekly basis.
- Over half of the third graders and more than 80 percent of the seventh and eighth graders reported never going on field trips with their science class.
- Sixty percent of the seventh graders and 41 percent of the eleventh graders said they never had to write up the results of science experiments.[28]

Obviously, curriculum is very important in science education, and we go to great lengths to teach people how to be good teachers. But we must think carefully about how we can draw better young people into careers as science teachers.

Given that part of the problem may be the kinds of science and math teachers students encounter in their elementary and secondary education—and that part of the solution may be better teacher recruitment and training—other data from the CIRP might be of some interest. These data suggest that most undergraduates planning teaching careers these days are education majors. But the data indicate that this was not true twenty years ago. In other words, fifteen or twenty years ago a high school student was much more likely to be taught by a young teacher who had been a math and physics major in college. Today the same student might well have a teacher who has had more course work in education than in math and physics.

There clearly has been a decline in the quality of science and math teachers as a side effect of the women's movement. Increased career opportunities for women during the past two decades have meant that intelligent young women, happily, no longer are constrained to careers in teaching, nursing, and one or two other fields. The result is that the educational system has lost the "hidden subsidy" that resulted from the fact that so many bright young women who once chose teaching now feel free to choose other careers.

Several years ago I was asked to testify before a subcommittee of the U.S. House of Representatives about mathematics and science education. A number of other science policy experts presented as well. However, the most vivid and memorable testimony was a presentation given by Kent Kavanaugh, a teacher from a suburb of Kansas City. Mr. Kavanaugh had received a highly coveted teaching award from the president of the United States in the Rose Garden of the White House. He stated:

The month before I left for Washington, D.C., to receive the Presidential Award, I averaged 40 hours a week at my job—not my teaching job, my second job as an analytical chemist for the Mobay Corporation of Kansas City. I must work at two or more jobs to make ends meet and to try to pay for college tuition for my son who graduates this spring. Because of this, I often come to school physically and mentally worn out. I am not the exception, I am the rule.[29]

The most effective teaching does not take place when a mechanical model is employed. Learning involves active engagement by the learner. He or she must incorporate the new material, and this means linking the new material to the existing body of knowledge, based both on experience and prior learning, that the student brings to the classroom. This makes it all the more important that teachers at both the precollege and college level find ways to connect to the frame of reference in the student's mind. In my experience, the method that seems most promising is the frequent use of metaphors or stories.

The instructor must learn about the student's frame of reference to improve the quality and effectiveness of teaching. The benefits of doing this are reciprocal. Scientific research, theorizing, and model building are enriched and may be transformed if we learn more about precisely these same cultural perspectives that previously underrepresented groups bring to the table.

CHANGING EXPECTATIONS

The research by Treisman and Bonsangue and the work at Harvard by Richard Light have revealed pretty clearly what works in college instruction.[30] There is evidence that these findings also apply at the precollege level. Robert Reich has observed that, in America's best classrooms:

Instead of individual achievement and competition, the focus is on group learning. Students learn to articulate, clarify, and then restate for one another how they identify and find answers. They learn how to seek and accept criticism from peers, solicit help, and give credit to others. They also learn to negotiate—to explain their own needs, to discern what others need and view things from others' perspectives, and to discover mutually beneficial resolutions. This is an ideal preparation for lifetimes of symbolic-analytic teamwork.[31]

Students learn more effectively when they engage in a dialogue with other students (and with their instructors). They also learn more when they are expected to excel, not approached as being in need of remediation. Almost thirty years ago, the Coleman Report findings foreshadowed these results.[32] At the time, the work of James S. Coleman and his associates was the largest social science study ever conducted. Self-esteem and self-efficacy are central to educational achievement and the development of meaningful educational and career aspirations. In math and science and, for that matter, in every educational enterprise, we should use a talent development model rather than a model of exclusion. Furthermore, these workshop group studies are reminding us that learning is a social and psychological process, not a mechanical process.

Equity 2000, an intervention project of the College Board, is attempting to increase the percentage of minority students who go to college. The project, which will impact over 200,000 students, brings together local educators and national experts. Since prior research has shown the links between mathematics attainment and college attendance, the focus is mathematics instruction and encouraging more young people to take more math. An important component of this intervention effort is educating instructors about the capacities of young people from minority backgrounds to master math. In that regard, results from the first year of the project are instructive. According to the College Board, the percentage of students that the teacher believed were capable of passing algebra or geometry increased dramatically, tripling in the case of geometry. In the pilot city of Forth Worth, Texas, the number of students who took algebra increased 36 percent during a one-year period.

A fascinating study by Professor Robert Rosenthal of Harvard University suggested that the expectations teachers have about a student's potential exert a strong impact on his or her learning.[33] In his prior research Rosenthal had discovered how researchers, for example, experimental psychologists studying white rats in mazes, unconsciously biased seemingly scientific observations in support of hypotheses they expected. If researchers could unknowingly bend objective phenomena to match their expectations, couldn't the same be true of teachers?

Rosenthal and his colleagues next selected some elementary school students totally at random. The researchers then informed the teachers that these students had tremendous intellectual potential of a kind that had not been revealed on standard intelligence tests. Once the teachers held these expectations about these otherwise typical children, the students' grades improved dramatically. It turned out that the teachers were spending more time with them and were predisposed in subconscious ways to perceive the students as doing well. Furthermore, student performance responded to this extra treatment.

This study by Rosenthal has been the subject of some methodological controversy. But the idea is intriguing and powerful and has spawned many other studies. Perhaps many children fail in school because their teachers expect them to fail.

The world of art provides a good metaphor about discovering the potential that lies within each student. Here is a description from a book about Eskimo Aivilik art: "The carver . . . rarely sets out, at least consciously, to carve, say, a seal, but picks up the ivory, examines it to find its hidden form and, if that's not immediately apparent, carves aimlessly until he sees it, humming and chanting as he works. Then he brings it out: seal, hidden, emerges. It was always there: he didn't create it; he releases it; he helped it step forth."[34]

Peter Drucker has observed: "What one human being does, other human beings can do, too. It's a law of human affairs that today's record becomes tomorrow's commonplace. . . . My 18-year-old grandson, who was a high school miler, ran the mile in 3.57—and he was not even considered very good. I was better. I just didn't run as fast because nobody else had run as fast. That's normal for human beings. Raise the standards, and everyone runs faster."[35]

NOTES

Preparation of this chapter was supported, in part, by a grant from the Kluge Foundation.

1. To avoid repetition of the cumbersome phrase "mathematics and science education," I use the term "science education" throughout this chapter.

2. Paul Jacobs, Keeping the Poor Poor, in *Crisis in American Institutions*, 6th ed., Jerome H. Skolnick and Elliott Currie, eds. (Boston: Little, Brown, 1985), 113–23.

3. John Lantos, Farewell to a Classroom of Young Heroes, *Los Angeles Times*, June 1991.

4. John Eichinger, Science Education in the United States: Are Things as Bad as the Recent IEA Report Suggests? *School Science and Mathematics* 90, no. 1 (January 1990): 37.

5. Ibid., 38.

6. R. E. Yager and J. E. Penick, Perceptions of Four Age Groups Towards Science Classes, Teachers, and the Value of Science, *Science Education* 70 (1986): 355–63.

7. Carl Sagan, Why We Need to Understand Science, *Parade Magazine*, 10 September 1989, 10.

8. R. Connel, Report Seeks Changes in Teaching of Science and Math, *Los Angeles Times*, February, 1989, 26.

9. Stephen G. Brush, Women in Science and Engineering, *American Scientist* 79 (September–October 1991): 404.

10. Jadwiga S. Sebrechts, The Cultivation of Scientists at Women's Colleges, *Journal of NIH Research* 4, no. 6 (June 1992): 22.

11. Bernadine Healy, Women in Science: From Panes to Ceiling, *Science* 255 (1992): 1333.

12. Robert Reich, Harnessing Human Capital, *U.S. News & World Report*, 22 April 1991.

13. Robert Reich, *The Work of Nations: Preparing Ourselves for the 21st Century* (New York: Knopf, 1991), 172.

14. Ibid., 228.

15. Anthony Patrick Carnevale, Leila J. Gainer, and Ann S. Meltzer, *Workplace Basics: The Essential Skills Employers Want* (San Francisco: Jossey-Bass, 1990), 23.

16. Ibid., 23.

17. John Allen Paulos, *Innumeracy: Mathematical Illiteracy and Its Consequences* (New York: Hill and Wang, 1988).

18. American Association for the Advancement of Science, *Science for All Americans: A Project 2061 Report on Literacy Goals in Science, Mathematics and Technology* (Washington, DC: Author, 1989).

19. Sheila Tobias, *Overcoming Math Anxiety* (New York: Norton, 1978).

20. R. Pool, Who Will Do Science in the 1990s?, *Science* 248 (April 1990): 433–35.

21. American Association for the Advancement of Science, *Science for All Americans*.

22. E. Culotta, Can Science Education Be Saved?, *Science* 250 (December 1990): 1327–30.

23. E. Marshall, The Reform Agenda: Emerging Consensus, *Science* 250 (December 1990): 1329.

24. Ibid., 1327.

25. Ibid.

26. Philip Uri Treisman, *A Study of the Mathematics Performance of Black Students at the University of California, Berkeley*, 1985, Ph.D. diss.

27. Martin V. Bonsangue and David E. Drew, *Long-Term Effectiveness of the Calculus Workshop Model* (Washington, DC: National Science Foundation, 1992).

28. John A. Dossey, *The Mathematics Report Card: Are We Measuring Up?* (Princeton, NJ: Educational Testing Service, 1988).

29. American Association for the Advancement of Science, *Science for All Americans*.

30. R. J. Light, *The Harvard Assessment Seminars* (Cambridge, MA: Harvard University Graduate School of Education and Kennedy School of Government, 1992).

31. Robert Reich, *The Work of Nations: Preparing Ourselves for the 21st Century* (New York: Knopf, 1991), 233.

32. James S. Coleman et al., *Equality of Educational Opportunity* (Washington, DC: U.S. Government Printing Office, 1966).

33. Robert Rosenthal, *Pygmalion in the Classroom* (New York: Holt, Rinehart and Winston, 1968).

34. Edmund Carpenter, Federick Varley, and Robert Flaherty, *Eskimo* (Toronto: University of Toronto Press, 1959), cited in Roach Van Allen, Let Students Have Their Say, *The 49th Yearbook of the Claremont Reading Conference* (Claremont, CA: Claremont Graduate School, 1985).

35. Peter Drucker, Performance, Accountability, and Results, in *Educating for Results* (Baltimore, MD: National School Boards Association, 1992).

20

Education, Society, and the School Dropout

Charles Milligan

Why students leave school before graduation has vexed teachers, administrators, parents, and students since the notion of education for all became an actuality in the late 1950s. The reality that most students graduate from school has left educators even more preoccupied with the question of why some students do not stay in school.

In the past, as educators attempted to understand the magnitude of the dropout problem, theoretical models began to appear. One of the consequences was the classification of students using one or more factors. Such risk factors supposedly disclose to educators which adolescents are more likely to leave school prematurely. Although they were designed to identify and predict the student who is likely to drop out, no typical profile of a dropout exists. Two students with the same personal characteristics and family backgrounds may both be classified as being at risk of dropping out, yet one will graduate and one will not. Being at risk would refer to the portion of the school population that consistently shows a lack of the necessary intellectual, emotional, and/or social skills to take full advantage of the educational opportunities available to them. Often these students become disenchanted, ultimately openly or passively reject school, and thereby drop out.

School systems and communities continue to point their fingers accusingly at one another, trying to assign blame for the escalating number of school dropouts.[1] No one seems to agree on just which adolescents are dropping out of school or how many of them there are. Two reasons why children are dropping from school come to mind: the students lack ambition, and too many parents today find it necessary to work longer hours, thus increasing the time children are left unsupervised by either parent. While these excuses are commonly heard around school campuses across America, they have very little empirical support.

As an advanced civilization, Americans have always wanted to believe that every individual is able to accomplish any goal. Because of the key role of education in determining position and condition in adult life, a fundamental concern of educational policy since 1965 has been to see that educational opportunity is available to all Americans.[2] On the surface, the solution to poverty seems to ride squarely on the shoulders of education. Perceiving education as the ultimate answer, Peter F. Drucker reports:

Today we cannot get enough educated people. We realize that our economic progress, our defense strength and our political position in the world depend more and more on constantly increasing the supply of higher educated people both in quality and in quantity. In the past the question has always been: How many educated people can a society afford? Today the question is: How many people who are not highly educated can a society afford?[3]

It is the purpose of this chapter to challenge the accuracy of the above statement by looking at (1) the dropout through history, (2) society's interaction with the dropout, and (3) the poverty that is presumed to be the result of a lack of education. Typically this is done through the eyes of researchers who have little connection to the real problems faced by many of the students who leave school. In this regard, it is intention of this researcher to review the endless cycle of the failure to achieve a secondary education and poverty, not from the viewpoint of a researcher, but through the eyes of a dropout.[4]

Society, poverty, and education are three portions of our civilization that cannot be separated. They are hopelessly bound together, all independent, yet dependent on one another. With all the complexities presented by each separate issue, policymakers have used shot-in-the-dark tactics that have, to this date, failed to eliminate the drop-out problem or explain why there is a problem. An analysis of the statistical data on dropouts reveals two separate issues: (1) many of our children are not completing high school, and (2) a disproportion of those not completing school are from the minority population. It is believed that these separate issues have hindered America's educational system in responding to the problem of dropouts. Since 1965 American policymakers have treated the problem of dropouts as if it were in a vacuum.

Viewing our educational system as a sociological institution offers a means to explain the multifaceted dilemma of school dropouts. Dropping from school is not the problem; it is merely a symptom of a much larger problem: inequity in our social system. Students today leave school for far different reasons than they did fifty years ago. Examining the social institution of education provides a starting point to understand better the drop-out dilemma.

EDUCATION AS A SOCIAL INSTITUTION

Thomas Jefferson, while serving as minister to France in 1786, wrote to his friend George Wythe that he was elated that the Virginia legislature had finally agreed to enact the statute for religious freedom that he had proposed seven years earlier. He was distressed, however, that the most important bill before the state legislature had not passed. This bill called for "the diffusion of knowledge among the people." Jefferson beseeched his friend to "preach, my dear Sir, a crusade against ignorance; establish and improve the law for educating the common people. Let our countrymen know that the people alone can protect us against these evils, and that the tax which will be paid for this purpose is not more than the thousandth part of what will be paid to kings, priests and nobles who will rise up among us if we leave the people in ignorance."[5] Jefferson encouraged education, seeing it as a way for the "preservation of freedom, and happiness" and a release from "ignorance, superstition, poverty and oppression of the body and mind in every form."

Education in modern times became the way for society to prepare the common man better for the task of survival. The educational system technically offers perfect equality of opportunity. In theory, success in school depends exclusively on intelligence, effort, and merit unconnected to social background. Yet, through a fusion of economic and cultural forces, the class system is able to convert this paltry egalitarian institution into an instrument of class privilege.

The benefits of a high school education were offered to all except those few who were thought to be too handicapped or unable to cope with the demanding curriculum. This curriculum was one of the primary means by which children were separated and stratified. The curriculum is comprised of (or dictated by the reigning political leaders to comprise) subjects, skills, values, and behaviors that were sanctioned and preferred by society. It provided a convenient way for educators to select out "substandard" students, while socializing them to play out their social and occupational roles in a corporate society.

This type of selecting out had a profound effect on minority students, as well as any student from a family of low social economic status. By standardized tests, grade point averages, and teachers' opinions, these students have been routinely encouraged (and in some instances required) to take less challenging courses. While educators use the term *tracking*, *sorting* would seem more appropriate. Sorting out the segments of the population that will forever remain a floor mat for a class society becomes the result of this process.

This sorting process is inherent in American public education; it occurs through both formal, institutionalized practices and informal, less obvious methods. Most school systems include special tracking for the "gifted" or highly motivated students, where such students are separated and placed in different schools or classrooms. The informal and, in my belief, more damaging sorting of students occurs within classrooms and administrators' offices when teachers and administrators make decisions and judgments that affect the students' educational futures. Although these decisions may seem relatively insignificant, the cumulative effect can have a lasting impact. For some students this can be devastating, shaping their lives forever.

There exists no better view than that of Emile Durkheim to explain the idea of education as a social process. According to Durkheim, "Education is the influence exercised by the adult generation on those not yet ready for social life. Its object is to arouse and to develop in the child a certain number of physical, intellectual, and moral states which are demanded of him by both the political society as a whole and the special milieu for which he is specifically destined."[6] If this impact is perceived as negative, the influence used by adults becomes an instrument of destruction, not socialization.

Throughout Durkheim's lectures and writings, one idea occurs repeatedly—education exists as a social process. From the outset, Durkheim makes the assumption that man is motivated and dominated by his natural egoism. This seems to stem from Thomas Hobbes's definition of man, which states he has unlimited desires and consequently requires discipline. Man, Durkheim says, "destroys himself less frequently when he has things to concern him other than himself."[7] The more society keeps people engaged, the less destructive they will be. Discipline, then, becomes a strong theme for Durkheim. The first and foremost mission of the education system becomes to accustom individuals to submitting to discipline. The system could then be valued by whether or not the masses followed the rules set down by those (in the Weberian sense) who are in authority.

As industrialization improved the status of those in the middle class, individuals could no longer differentiate the limits between the possible and the impossible, the just and the unjust, and the legitimate and illegitimate hopes of those that were immoderate. Becoming aware of their own unlimited desires, individuals assumed that other individuals had the same desires, seeing them only as means of achieving their own ends. Durkheim believed that this discrepancy between the desires of the individual and the ability to achieve them was the major cause of alienation from society.

Durkheim viewed the person as only an imprint of an impersonal conscience and granted only secondary significance to the individual. The education system, therefore, exists only as a means to make an individual more "human" through interaction with others. Society implants in each individual, through this interaction, an aspect of itself so that, in effect, it creates him or her. The success of this interaction can be measured to the extent that an individual defines himself or herself in terms of the society.

In Durkheim's opinion, each individual becomes convoluted into the whole (society) through an integration process called education. "Society is the highest end; and in order that it be stable, individuals must be content in their special milieux. The state, therefore, must remind teachers constantly of the ideas and sentiments that must be impressed upon the child to adjust him to the milieu in which he must live."[8]

Durkheim's paradigm of education is rather simple: our system exists to indoctrinate the next generation with the thoughts of the previous generation. At first appearance this could be easily accomplished, but when you match teachers (previously socialized individuals) with children (who have ideas of their own or who have been socialized differently), a severe conflict arises.

Durkheim professed that there was a breakdown in the controls and social solidarity that accompanied the industrial age. If there was a breakdown in controls, where and when did it occur? In retrospect, it does not appear that what Durkheim saw was a breakdown. What he saw was more like the growing pains of industrialization and the newfound desires that were just being cultivated. Karl Marx might have said that the anomic reaction was caused by a change in technology and ownership. There does, however, appear to have been a breakdown, but it occurred much later.

The loss of social control appears to be traceable to a single event that occurred 22 June 1944: the signing of the Servicemen's Readjustment Act of 1944, commonly called the GI Bill. This event, more than any other, did more to break down the class structure than did the Bread and Peace Marches in 1917 Russia.

After World War II, a college education was seen as a ticket to a good job or entry into one of the professions (lawyers, doctors, and so on). The question of access to higher education became a major issue to the public. It was no secret that admission to a college or a university was not based solely on ability. Although more children were in school than ever before, it was nonetheless true that some never had a chance to go to college because the elementary and secondary schools they attended were too inadequate to provide decent preparation. The GI Bill changed much of that. The concepts of the GI Bill were not born from a well-meaning government trying to assist the returning veteran. Rather, it was the product of a secret commission, formed by President Franklin Roosevelt, to establish a strategy for dealing with the massive numbers of war-hardened veterans meandering around the country looking for work.[9] Believing that the veterans would not be willing to go from the fighting lines to the soup lines, many Americans feared that an armed revolution would be in the making, if this issue was not confronted.

If someone had correctly estimated the number of veterans who would use their benefits, I am sure another remedy would have been sought. Before the war, enrollment in higher educational institutions stood at 1,364,815.[10] By the fall of 1947 that number had grown to 2,338,226. Ten years later, when the last veteran had drawn his check, 2,232,000 men and women had attended college under the GI Bill.[11]

During this period many of the elites in this country cried out against wholesale education. Harvard's president at the time, James B. Conant, worried that the GI Bill would cause a lowering of academic standards; he preferred to see a bill that financed the education of "a carefully selected number of returned veterans." No matter what the criticism, one thing was certain: for three years (1946–1948) almost half of this country's college graduates were recipients of the GI Bill. Many elitists in America became apprehensive that even our economy could not absorb the increasing number of college graduates.

Using Durkheim's logic, we can see that these college graduates acquired new desires, far outreaching the old ones. But it is my belief that the prior socialization had worked sufficiently enough, for the most part, to keep them in their place.

Their children, however, are a different story. We know them as the "baby boomers."

Coming from a more educated set of parents, these children became disconnected with Durkheim's vision of school as a place to become disciplined. The baby boomers received mixed messages between school and home. This hybrid of the indoctrination scheme replaced the more docile and obedient youth with a more rebellious, undisciplined one. These youths became the new dropouts. They no longer left school to work the farms or support the family; they were leaving school for much different reasons.

CAUSES?

Viewing education as a social process, the dropout takes on a different social role. This new role shows that the reasons have changed for the dropout over the years. While a slow increase in high school graduates occurred from 1900 (11 percent) to 1940 (25 percent), it was not until 1950 that 50 percent of the students enrolled in high school actually graduated.[12] The combination of Sputnik, McCarthyism, and ambitious commercial publishers seemed to bring the problem of school dropouts into national focus. Inspired by fears for national defense, the federal and private foundations poured funds into many education reform projects.

The mood during the 1960s was confidence and optimism. America's elementary and secondary schools were adjusting to the new demands of the post-Sputnik era. For the first time, the problem of educational change was jointly attacked by federal agencies, university scholars, big-city school districts, and almost everyone else in the field.

As graduation from high school became the norm,[13] the national drop-out rate of 25 percent became a crucial issue for educators. Solving this problem became an educational priority during the early 1960s. With the passage of the Economic Opportunity Act of 1964, high school completion was stressed as a requisite for all citizens.

When the decade of the 1960s opened, the problems of the schools seemed solvable; by the late 1960s, the waning of national self-esteem was evident in the schools. Where once there had been a clear sense of purpose about educational goals, now there was uncertainty. During this time, many federally funded studies attempted to determine the actual number of dropouts. The primary focus of these studies was on who dropped out, rather than how to prevent students from dropping out.

As researchers began the task of performing an actual head count, dropouts began disappearing from the demonstrations and the "Woodstocks." The society of the 1960s had found a place for these dropouts: Vietnam. While World War II saw an average soldier twenty-five years of age, Vietnam's soldier was nineteen.

The year 1970 found a nation attempting to heal itself from the devastation of ten years at war. Again the dropout was not missed. As the military stopped drafting, recruitment hit an all-time low. The dropout was lured into the service with promises of job security and technical training.

As our society survived the 1970s and began 1980, a new twine of socialization encircled the dropouts: economic competitiveness. In addition, President Ronald Reagan slammed shut the military door on dropouts, no longer allowing them to be recruited into the service. With a rising trade deficit, educators offered a grim forecast: the reservoir of academically cultivated workers would shrivel, while jobs necessitating intellectual proficiency would increase. This growing gap has raised the eyebrows of the powerful and elite of this country, and the drop-out issue vaulted to the forefront of American politics. Even President George Bush wants to be heralded as the "Education President." At the nation's Governors Conference, all fifty governors signed a commitment that by the year 2000, 90 percent of our youths would graduate from high school.[14] There were many recommendations on how to accomplish that goal, all of which came with very expensive price tags!

For the majority of adolescents who drop from school, the great American dream is a collage of unfulfilled expectations. Well-paying jobs, for those who fail to graduate, have dwindled or ceased to exist entirely. Blue-collar occupations, those most closely associated with dropouts, have fallen from 67 percent (1970) to 44 percent.[15] As the national employment picture moves to a service-oriented economy, more sophisticated skills are needed in our increasingly technological society.

Sixteen thousand school districts across the United States compile statistics each year on the growing number of dropouts. However, it appears that no two school districts count dropouts the same way. Most administrators claim that they merely follow state and local guidelines to calculate the annual number of dropouts. Mostly, their statistics are inaccurate, and in fact the method used to calculate the rate changes from year to year. Some school districts do not even count them.[16]

In several school districts across America, the dropouts are calculated by subtracting the number who graduate from the total enrollment three to four years earlier. Such "completion rates" are hardly an adequate substitute for drop-out rates. They do not take into account students who move to other districts or leave school temporarily.

Realizing that this statistical nightmare had reached its peak, Congress charged the National Center for Educational Statistics (NCES) to develop a precise statistical description of the dropout in the United States. Although the year-to-year system will not be in place until the fall of 1992, the NCES issued the second "regular" report to the president and Congress on dropouts and retention rates.[17] In the 1988–1989 school year, the most recent reliable figures available, 682,000 American children dropped out of school.[18] Based on a 180-day school year, that's about 3,789 students a day![19]

The figures presented by the NCES are, in my opinion, very conservative.

Many researchers feel that a significant number of students never get counted. A study performed in Chicago found that 5.5 percent of the district's eighth grade students never started high school. Because they were not the legal age to leave school (sixteen), they became officially "lost" in the bureaucracy.[20] Using the data provided by the school district, researchers tracked approximately 29,600 students who completed the eighth grade in the spring of 1987. It revealed that 1,600 or 5.5 percent never entered the ninth grade.

I believe that, on some level, one must assume that the data presented by the government are very conservative. Some estimates of the drop-out rate are as high as 27 percent.[21] One new dimension to consider when discussing dropouts is the completion rate. Completion rate is the actual percentage of students who complete the high school curriculum. This excludes general equivalency diplomas (GEDs) and alternative methods of obtaining a high school diploma. This figure stands at 64 percent. That means that a full 36 percent of our children fail to graduate through the normally established system.

Although the statistical picture is important, it is equally important to draw conclusions and propose possible solutions to this problem. In my opinion, the NCES numbers can be used to establish a valid, though conservative, picture of who drops from school. Then and only then can meaningful programs be established to address adequately this national dilemma. Before the establishment of any worthwhile program, there needs to be some type of agreement on precisely who is dropping out of school.

Many of the conclusions drawn about dropouts have been based purely on untruths and myths. William James once observed that the chief use of statistics is to refute the figures of other statisticians. It is not the intention of this author to refute any research, but rather to focus the light on the seemingly unnoticed, substantial group of adolescents leaving school.

WHY THE MAJORITY LEAVE SCHOOL

When asked why they dropped from school, dropouts are far from silent. The following are some of their documented reasons for leaving school:

• I left because of overall boredom. I wanted to get on with life.
• The teachers and counselors told me I was stupid.
• Not enough individual help.
• I needed more challenging classes.
• I didn't like school. I hated it there. It felt like a dummy zoo.

While some may judge these responses as being sour grapes, the fact that 46 percent return within four years to complete high school should get our attention. Not surprisingly, students who were polled five years after they had dropped out cited 43 percent of the time, that the teacher was the reason they had dropped out.[22] Most students view their teachers as being unhappy with their jobs, disgruntled, bored, and boring.[23] Poor teachers erode students' confidence and their fragile sense of acceptance from their peers. Students go to great lengths to avoid teachers they feel put them in uncomfortable or humiliating situations. In a study at California State University, students' self-esteem was significantly lower after exposure to teachers over a school year.[24]

In a pilot study recently conducted on fifth, sixth, seventh, eighth, and ninth graders, only 25 percent reported that they wanted to be smarter. Fifty-one percent reported that school caused the most stress for them. When asked whom they would tell if they planned to run away from home, 70 percent said a friend, 6 percent said a counselor, 24 percent said no one. No one would tell a teacher.[25] Throughout the 100 or so periodicals, books, and articles reviewed, there was not one mention of the fact that students do not seem to like teachers. It is my belief that students in the middle and upper grades who drop out of school simply do not like teachers.

Most students "at risk" of dropping out, based on their background, prior experience, and behavior, do not drop out. Drawing a sketch of the dropout we find that he or she

1. is white,

2. is from an English-speaking home,

3. had both parents living together,

4. had never repeated a grade, and

5. received Cs or better as grades.

WHY THE MINORITIES LEAVE SCHOOL

The characteristics of the typical dropout do not always reflect the population with the highest rate. Drop-out rates are higher for blacks and Hispanics than for whites and Asians. When comparing or interpreting minority drop-out rates, special consideration must be given.

First, although blacks drop out at higher rates than whites, the difference has narrowed considerably in the last twenty years. Since 1968, the difference in drop-out rates for blacks and whites has shrunk from thirteen percentage points to two percentage points.[26] Still, black students continue to drop out at higher rates than do whites; however, when parent education and other background factors are the same, black students drop from school at roughly the same rate as white students.

Second, the drop-out rate for Hispanics remained unacceptably high during the same fifteen-year period. The problem may have something to do with the fact that 36 percent of all Hispanics in the United States are immigrants, and half of those immigrants arrived in the last ten years. Using Census Bureau data, Ben Wattenberg found that American-born Hispanics, on the other hand, are twice as likely to hold white-collar jobs.[27] Further studies may indicate that, at least for the Hispanic population, there may be a solution to their drop-out problem. As the population of first-generation Hispanics born in America increases, so may their graduation rate.

Blacks and other minorities have certainly had the time to assimilate into our society. Whey have their rates remained so high? The answer is a complex issue that rests at the feet of our society. Until the need for civil rights legislation disappears from humanity, I fear that the minorities may never recover. Today's society responds to minorities with indifference, and because our educational system is a social process, it too fails to meet the needs of the diverse population that it professes to serve.

RESTRUCTURING OF SCHOOLS FOR DROP-OUT PREVENTION

Our society is undergoing a social revolution as profound as its technological one. This transformation, as far-reaching as any in history, is as fundamental as the emergence of democracy, the growth of public education, or the rise of capitalism. This phenomenon is the way people interact with one another for mutual benefit. How does this affect the student who drops out? Given the choice of leaving or staying in school, it is the belief of this author that at least 50 percent or more leave school because they simply cannot get along with those given the responsibility to teach them.

These adolescents are not dropouts, they are "pushouts," pushed from school by an unresponsive system that cannot or will not change.

Schools function much like the nineteenth-century factories they were originally designed to resemble.[28] Batches of boys and girls still move like cattle from room to room where each teacher dumps a little more on each student. Most sociologists agree that the average adolescent today deals with many more adult decisions than ever before.

Our grading system and curriculum function much the same way as they did at the turn of the century. Although psychologists and educators repeatedly point out the problems and misinterpretations that commonly stem from the traditional report cards, no alternative method of evaluating student's work has gained wide acceptance. Additionally, there is no research evidence to support grades as a measure of achievement.[29]

Even the way we administer discipline is outdated. Recent studies indicate that up to the ages of ten or twelve, children develop higher self-esteem in learning environments where the discipline is firm and demanding.[30] These same children, however, suffered deleterious effects upon their self-esteem when the discipline remained the same during their teen years.

The emphasis upon completion in our education system is also said to take its toll on our children.[31] The competition in many academic arenas is as deadly as it was for the Roman gladiators. Many a parent has handed back a proud son or daughter a B report, only to say, "Well, just keep trying; I'm sure you will get that A if you try hard." That may have been the child's maximum effort.

Children learn they are but one of many and that their individual concerns will not be addressed in school.[32] The education system incorporates the value systems of military and penal institutions and of psychiatric hospitals into the daily life of a student.

As we recognize that education is a social process, any criterion for educational criticism and construction implies a particular social idea. That idea is expressed as a society by making provision for participation by all its members on equal terms and securing flexible readjustment of its institutions through interaction of the different forms. One such form is an education system that gives individuals a personal interest in social relationships and controls and the habits of mind that secure social changes without introducing disorder.[33]

Referring to disequilibrium or imbalance, Jean Piaget noted that when a person encounters difficulty in assimilating an object or event, due to inadequate cognitive structures, a conflict or interdisturbance occurs, accompanied by an uneasy feeling.[34] This author does not believe that it is necessary for disequilibrium to accompany every new learning situation. We have long accepted that biological growth is nonlinear. If it is accepted that intellectual growth is nonlinear, why is our education system set up in such a linear fashion, thereby aiding disequilibrium?

If the learning situation allowed for the development of a cognitive structure prior to inundating the learner with new material to assimilate, accommodation could occur without disequilibrium. This theory, I believe, graphically depicts the reason that the typical adolescent leaves school.

The perfect learning situation may well have been articulated by John Dewey almost seventy-five years ago. Dewey knew that the direction of education should agree with the natural impulses of the young. For this to occur, a school education should be valued to the extent by which it creates a desire for continual growth. Essential to that growth are five major objectives for educators to strive for: (1) that the pupil have a genuine situation of experience, a continuous activity in which he or she is interested for its own sake; (2) that a genuine problem develop within this situation as a stimulus to thought: (3) that the student possess the information and make the observation needed to deal with it; (4) that a suggested solution occur that the student shall be responsible for developing in an orderly fashion; (5) that the opportunity and occasion be given to test the idea by application, making its meaning clear, so that the student discover for himself or herself its validity.

The solution for our minority students is more complex than that for other pushouts. The inability to adapt to our culturally biased educational system has left many of our minorities not only uneducated but bitter. Special training for teachers to deal with this cultural diversity is a must. With the increasing minority population, steps are already being taken to confront this problem. Special certificated programs and required course work in student diversity are in place. But is it too little, too late?

The economic model that Drucker presented has never materialized. At the time Drucker made his analysis, it seemed reasonable to assume there would always be a place for someone who was highly educated. Today, however, the supply of educated people far outnumbers the jobs available in our society. Schools are not necessarily the best place for learning. Many countries have developed a system of apprenticeships to serve better the needs of their students.[35] At sixteen, these students work at some trade for two to three days a week and spend the remaining time in a traditional academic classroom. Businesses across America are calling for a similar system. The development of such a system would benefit many of the pushouts before they became a statistic, both majority and minority students.

THE ENDLESS CYCLE OF POVERTY

The American system has been driven by profit to build steel skyscrapers for stock brokerage firms while the cities decay, to spend billions of dollars while children go hungry. Capitalism has always been a failure for the lower class. The problem now is that it no longer is functioning for the dropouts. A recent analysis of the 1990 census shows that the poverty rate for families that are headed by young parents who have dropped out of school has increased from 39 percent to 64 percent and their median income in constant dollars has plummeted by 46 percent.[36]

In our distressed times, many are looking to the educational system for a better way of life. A fundamental proviso of the American social pledge has always been that education is the means by which an adept and motivated citizen can expect to advance his or her position and condition in life. Through the education process, an attainment of knowledge occurs theoretically, leading down the path to security and success. Those not reaping the benefits were (and are) considered lethargic and inept, doomed to live in poverty.

When the American system can no longer offer its young a secure future, it will indeed be in trouble. The threat of unemployment has always been perched on the doorstep of the poor; it now lurks outside the white-collar workers' and professionals' homes. When this happened only to the poor, it was functional; there were always the jails. What this may mean for the new generation is that a college education may not be a guarantee against unemployment. When this unemployment and poverty begin to engulf the middle class, anarchy could begin.

If we look at the shift in wealth and employment, it is not difficult to believe that the distribution of wealth is controlled, that educational opportunities are manipulated, and that employment chances are conveniently arranged in order to eliminate many of the citizenry. With this understanding, the pivotal question becomes, Will the middle class continue to enjoy the trickle-down effect of the elite? As our society moves into the twenty-first century, it had better move slowly. World markets may not like subsidizing the standard of living in America.

Education has not met the needs of many Americans. Unless more is done, the current move toward restructuring schools will do little more than spend millions of tax dollars. The Committee on Economic Development declares that "most school reform is piecemeal and conflicting."[37] The report goes on to cite academic failure as the result of societal problems such as "poverty, family instability, substance abuse and racial discrimination."

Americans experience a quality of life shared by few other cultures. We live in a democratic society where we are taught that our ultimate proclamation of citizenship is going to a voting booth every four years to choose between two white, well-off, Anglo-Saxon males who have inoffensive personalities and orthodox opinions. This voting ritual surrenders our strengths, demeans our abilities, and eradicates the very persona of self. However, from time to time, Americans rebuff that idea and rebel.

These rebellions, so far, have been contained. The American order is the most ingenious system of controls in world history. With a country so rich in natural resources, talent, and labor power, the system can afford to distribute just enough wealth to just enough people to limit discontent by the minority. It is a country so authoritative, so immense, so agreeable to so many of its citizens that it can provide freedom of dissent to the few who are not satisfied.

This control in American society is dispersed through a complex array of societal labyrinths. The voting system, work situation, family, church, school, and the mass media are all pieces of a vast puzzle held together by the glue of patriotism. This strategy of control mollifies opposition with reforms, isolating people from one another.

One percent of the nation owns a third of the wealth.[38] The rest of the wealth is distributed in such a way as to turn those in the 99 percent against one another: small property owners against the poor, black against white, native-born against the new immigrant, educated and skilled against the illiterate and unskilled. These assortments of would-be patriots have felt indignant about, and committed carnage against, one another with such savagery as to obscure their common predicament as sharers of the leftovers in a very opulent country.

Against the reality of that desperate, bitter battle for the resources made scarce by those in power, many have been left behind. The poverty-stricken citizen's predicament in America has not been the lack of a will to fight; rather, through the socialization process, this group of Americans has been led to believe that there is no reason for them to fight.

CONCLUSIONS

This chapter began by looking at education as a social process through the eyes of Durkheim. He revealed that the government, which is the institution that represents all classes and interests of society and represents society as an organized whole, has gradually become the conscience of education, using it as the instrument by which society attains its goals. Ideals change with time, and social institutions alter to conform to them. Therefore, education should be an ever-varying process to prepare the individual to adjust to an ever-changing environment.

These sociological misfits called dropouts have not bought into the system's socialization process. Though each has defected for different reasons, the end results are the same. When a society wishes to know if its education process is successful, it cannot be measured in CAP scores, SAT scores, or Graduate Record Examination (GRE) scores. It can be measured by the extent that it prepares its citizens for the task of survival in its society. If we wish to measure our success, a mere head count of the dropouts in America shows the painful reality of a failing system. To address effectively this social phenomenon of dropouts, social scientists need to form more than just one model of the dropout. Then and only then will our society move toward a solution to the problem of dropouts.

NOTES

1. G. Mortenson (1990), *High school graduation and college participation of young adults by family income background*, Ames, IA: American College Testing Program.

2. L. E. Gladieux and T. R. Wolanin (1976), *Congress and the colleges, the national politics of higher education*, Lexington, MA: Lexington.

3. Peter F. Drucker (1979), The new majority, *Society*, 2, no. 16, 290.

4. In March 1969, this author dropped from school and joined the Marine Corps. While this is not an autobiography, it is a sample of the feelings and emotions not often depicted in quantitative research.

5. G. Lee (1961), *Crusade against ignorance: Thomas Jefferson on education*, New York: Teachers College Press, 99–100.

6. Emile Durkheim (1956), *Education and sociology*, Glencoe, IL: Free Press, 71.

7. Emile Durkheim (1951), *Suicide: A study in sociology*, New York: Free Press, 68.

8. Durkehim, *Education and sociology*, 71.

9. Kevin Olsen (1974), *The G.I. Bill, the veterans, and the colleges*, Lexington: University Press of Kentucky.

10. Washington Government Printing Press (1968), *Digest of educational statistics*, 68.

11. Olsen, 43.

12. D. Schreiber, B. A. Kaplan, and R. Strom (1965), *Dropout studies: Design and conduct*, Washington, DC: National Association of the United States.

13. H. Allen and L. Quay (1982), *Truants and dropouts: Encyclopedia of educational research*. New York: Macmillan.

14. R. Walker (1990), *Governors set to adopt national educational goals*. Educational Week, 16 February.

15. U.S. Department of Labor (1990), *Employment and Earnings*, Washington, DC: Government Printing Office.

16. An example of this is my own experience. I quit high school in the winter of 1968. During this research my curiosity became acute as to how Clarksville High School

in Clarksville, Tennessee, counted dropouts. I was informed by the County Board of Education that as of February 1990 they did not count kids who left school.

17. National Center for Education Statistics (1990), *Dropout rates in the United States: 1989*, Washington, DC: Government Printing Office, NCES 89–609.

18. U.S. Department of Education (1990), *Digest of education statistics 1990*, Washington, DC: Government Printing Office, NCES 91–660.

19. This number is the total number of Americans eighteen years or younger who do not have a high school diploma or equivalent and are currently not enrolled in any school.

20. E. Flax (1989), Dropout data emphasize problems in the middle years, Education Week, 3, 21 April.

21. Massachusetts Advocacy Center (1988), *Before it's too late*, Boston: MIT Press, Center for Early Adolescence. July.

22. A. Hahn (1987), Reaching out to America's dropouts: What to do? *Phi Delta Kappan*, 4, December, 256–63.

23. L. Olsen and M. Moore (1982), *Voices from the classroom: Students and teachers speak out on the quality of teaching in our school*, Oakland, CA: Citizens Policy Center.

24. C. Milligan (1989), *The effects of teacher self-esteem on school dropouts*, master's thesis, California State University Fullerton.

25. This was a study performed by this author. The reason for the study was to provide experience at collecting data. This is unpublished and merely for experience. The results to the questions were, however, interesting enough to mention.

26. U.S. Department of Commerce (1989), *School enrollments—social and economic characteristics of students: October various years*, Washington, DC: Bureau of Census.

27. B. Wattenberg (1989), American hispanics, *U.S. News and World Report*, 10 September, 14.

28. S. Rothstein (1987), Schooling in mass society, *Urban Education* 22, no. 3, 277.

29. L. Kutner (1989), Why report cards may be highly overrated, *Orange County Register*, June, J7.

30. J. Buri, P. Louisele, T. Misukanis, and R. Mueller (1988), Effects of authoritarianism and authoritativeness on self-esteem, *Personality and Social Psychology Bulletin*, 14, no. 2, 271–82.

31. J. Nichols (1989), Competition said to diminish academic achievement, *Education Week* 16, 25.

32. S. Rothstein (1984), *The power to punish*, Lanham, MD: University Press of America.

33. J. Dewey (1916), *Democracy and education*, New York: Macmillan.

34. H. Ginsberg and S. Opper (1988), *Piaget's theory of intellectual development*, Englewood Cliffs, NJ: Prentice-Hall, 208–56.

35. S. Hamilton (1990), Calling for an American system of apprenticeship, *Education Week* 42, 422.

36. S. Erving (1991), *Vanishing dreams: The plight of America's young families*, Washington, DC: Children's Defense Fund.

37. Committee on Economic Development (1990), *The unfinished agenda: A new vision for child development and education*, Washington, DC: Bureau of Census.

38. G. W. Domhoff (1983), *Who rules America now?* New York: Simon and Schuster, 42.

VII

WHAT CAN BE DONE?

21

What Needs to Be Done?

Stanley William Rothstein

Equal educational opportunity is one of the most fashionable slogans of our time and one that is most misunderstood. At first glance, nothing appears more popular than these appeals for greater equity in the schooling of the working and immigrant families of the United States. Dare anyone raise a voice against these democratic values? Yet the schools continue to select children into tracks that lead to universities or the lower levels of work in our society. "Something is wrong," say those who have studied these things. "Our children should be doing better." This is because these people fail to look behind the clever slogans to the realities of school life in a competitive, industrial ethos. Evidently those who call for equalization of opportunity are unaware of the history and primary tasks of educational systems.

In fact, it is no secret that there have been, and continue to be, two separate educational systems in the United States. The fight to eliminate racial and socioeconomic segregation flares up, now and then, then dies down as people get used to things being "the way they have always been." What the latest calls for affirmative action and equity in schooling are up against is the unequal and competitive value system that is embedded in modern capitalist society.

Educational systems must change from agents of the state into genuine centers of individual renewal. But this idea runs counter to the goals of the state and the history of urban schooling as it has developed in the last 300 years. The possibility of reforming urban schools and creating oases for children has been a fantasy from the start. It has fallen victim to the realities of uncertain labor markets and the need for new workers as old ones wear out. The very idea of equal opportunity for all students was declared to be unsound by no less an educational authority than Woodrow Wilson. As president of Princeton in the early years of this century, he wrote that America needed to educate only a tiny fraction of its population. The rest were to be trained to do the work their betters demanded of them. The theory of leveling the class differences among Americans was rejected on the grounds that children had to be prepared for realistic roles in the bursting, class-bound industrial society.

Thus, the demand for equity was pushed aside, and the children of the urban and immigrant poor were trained in the essentials of good citizenship and work habits. As this form of education has persisted for more than 100 years, it is not surprising that the children and grandchildren of those who were schooled in the past are dissatisfied with present-day practices. The content and pedagogical work of the 1800s are alive and well in America's schools, stuffing children full of facts that will be obsolete long before they graduate from high school.

If these comments are on the mark, urban educational systems have entered a critical stage in their growth and development. Educators have attempted to justify their efforts even as citizens on the right and left have condemned their work in urban and suburban schools. Some educators have begun not to look to the state but to act in the best interests of their students. The democratic instincts of some of these educators have permitted them to empower students and teachers to try out new ways of teaching and learning, with varying consequences. Some have developed new ways of working with "at-risk" children, seeking to understand why children drop out of school. Others have found ways of using the expertise of universities to reach out to the teachers and children in inner-city situations. Indeed, if making the schools more human and more humane is an important area of school reform, then new forms of pedagogy need to be practiced. If teachers are to become more effective in their work with children, then more sophisticated programs of education will have to be devised for them. Why should we continue to train teachers who are ignorant about the nature of family relationships? Why should we ignore what we know of human personality when such knowledge could help us to structure more effective schools? Why shouldn't we confront the realities of schooling's links to the state and labor market? Why shouldn't we admit that teaching to prepare for tests has deadened classroom experiences and turned off successive generations of children to academic learning and pursuits?

Those who want to change things in our urban schools will have to open their eyes to the problems that face us and the economic system we seek to serve. If we opt to teach children, we have to be prepared for those who will say that such ideas are positively dangerous for schools and society.

Nevertheless, within the framework of these oppressive conditions, many educators and teachers are groping for new ways of serving their students. In this last section we review the work they have done in dealing with the chronic and continuing problems of crime, violence, gangs, and drug abuse in urban schools and neighborhoods. Then we look at the nagging and persistent problem of literacy and reading comprehension among the urban and immigrant boys and girls in inner-city schools. Both chapters deal with what educators have done to ameliorate these social problems and what still needs to be done. Then professors at California State University, Fullerton, describe outreach programs they have developed to involve minorities in their educational experiences. Finally, we examine the principalship as it is and the changes that may be necessary if it is to survive into the twenty-first century.

22

Crime, Violence, Gangs, and Drug Abuse: What Urban Schools Can Do About Them

William L. Callison and Nancy Richards-Colocino

This chapter is intended to offer a clear statement of the problems schools face in helping students at risk of substance abuse from dropping out or joining gangs and to identify solutions that have worked to ameliorate these problems in other schools.

The following highlights of research in a Los Angeles area district indicate the tragic proportions of the drug abuse problem:

- By age eleven, 11.7 percent of students report being intoxicated at least once.
- By age sixteen, 52 percent report being intoxicated at least once.
- By age eight, 40 percent of the students report experimenting with drugs.
- Of eleventh graders 7.4 percent report daily use of marijuana, and 39.3 percent report engaging in the extremely dangerous practice of using two or more drugs at the same time during the last six months.[1]

Results of a review of records and needs assessment surveys completed by staff and parents showed that over 37 percent of K–12 students showed problems with chronic school failure, discipline, and attendance, were children of alcoholics, and/or were educationally disadvantaged. Also, over 60 percent of the students had no skills to cope with peer pressure for substance abuse.

Immigrant parents do not understand the criminal justice and/or the educational system. When confronted with the legal system, parents lack trust and understanding of how the system works. They often come from a country where law enforcement and government institutions are corrupt. They need education about the legal system, juvenile justice system, law enforcement, and the expectations of American institutions in general. In a telephone survey conducted by the district of Santa Ana, California, 97 percent of parents support curriculum instructing students on the dangers of drugs and alcohol, 50 percent of parents were unaware of counseling programs, 61 percent were unaware of gang prevention programs, 45 percent were unaware of parenting classes, 40 percent were unaware of the drug education program, 80 percent were unaware of the drop-out prevention program, 72 percent were not involved in community groups, and 54 percent were aware of district committees, but only 2 percent participated. Ninety-two percent of the parents surveyed approved of district programs. This gives evidence that parents need assistance in getting more involved in their children's education, but frequently because of cultural and linguistic differences, they do not know how.

As a result of this needs assessment, Hispanic School District is implementing a highly successful curriculum-based, K–12 Substance Abuse Prevention Program funded from the district's general fund and from the Drug-Free Schools and Communities Program. While this program has been successful in reducing substance abuse—especially at the school level—needs assessment and research indicate there is a significant need for prevention programs focusing on high-risk youth, parent education, and a community-based campaign.

Several factors are increasing national concern about dropout, substance abuse, gangs, and violence in urban schools, including effects of the increasing world-wide economic competition and a decrease in jobs available to nongraduates in the business world.

The 1990 census indicates 34.8 percent of all students between fifteen and seventeen have dropped out or been placed in classes at least one year below their age group.[2] This is an increase from a comparable figure of 29.1 percent in 1980. Some 32 percent of white students fell into this category while for blacks the percentage was 48 percent and for Latinos, 48.6 percent.

A bipartisan commission of prominent American businessmen, educators, and labor leaders said recently that "the United States productivity crisis can be solved only by radically restructuring both the country's educational system and its basic manufacturing philosophy along the lines of industrialized nations of Western Europe and Asia.[3] Presidential candidate Ross Perot expressed similar views.[4]

The commission, headed by former U.S. labor secretaries William E. Brock III and F. Ray Marshall, said the United States must quickly invest tens of billions of dollars in public schools and on-the-job training to emulate its overseas competitors, whose workers are far better educated and handle a broader range of responsibilities, resulting in more productive companies and higher-quality goods and services. Brock and his colleagues conducted interviews with 2,000 peoples in 450 businesses in the United States, Europe, and Asia to gather their data. Brock said, "By silently accepting America's descent into a low-skill, low wage economy, we are on the brink of sentencing our children and ourselves to a lower standard of living."[5]

Kevin Phillips indicates that, in terms of changes in average family income, only families in the ninth and tenth deciles showed improvement from 1977 to 1988. All other families showed declines, with those at the bottom, in the first decile, showing the greatest decline, 14.8 percent.[6] At the very top, on the other hand, the top 1 percent showed at 49.8 percent improvement! To say it another way, the United States has now passed France with the dubious distinction of the greatest gap of any industrial nation between the top 20 percent and the bottom 20 percent in family income. More to the point, in 1988 45.3 percent of New York City residents over the age of sixteen could not even be counted as labor force participants because of poverty, lack of skills, drug use, apathy, or other problems. They did not even reach the bottom 20 percent because they had no income. What can we do to help these young people at the lowest level of our society?

The commission's recommendations for education called for a national program that would require all students to obtain certificates of academic achievement at age sixteen, a system of apprenticelike certification for older students who do not go on to a four-year college, and a requirement that businesses spend an amount equal to 1 percent of their payroll on worker training. The best companies in the world "reduce bureaucracy by giving autonomy to 'front line' workers." Team production is a key element in increased productivity.

The implication for those of us in education is a need to accelerate our present movement toward competency assessment with instruction focused on weak areas that research has shown to be critical. For example, the commission suggests that the United States establish a system to allow an orderly school-to-work transition for non–college-bound students, which would be implemented through a national system of industry-based standards professionally to certify young men and women.

On 25 September 1990, new vocational education amendments were passed by the U.S. House of Representatives, titled the Carl D. Perkins Vocational and Applied Technology Education Amendments of 1990. There are four major changes: (1) a shift away from traditional job skills toward learning academic and other kinds of thinking skills and for linking thought with action; (2) increasing focus of resources on districts with the greatest need for reform and improvement; (3) districts rather than states to be largely responsible for designing their programs; and (4) a distinction made for the first time between secondary and post-secondary funding levels, which will allow funds to be targeted at either level.[7]

The biggest change is one of mission—from de-emphasizing preparation for full-time jobs to technical preparation for two-year post-secondary technical education. This change reflects what is happening in the job market. Most vocational students do not now get full-time jobs upon graduation from high school; only 30 percent did in 1988.[8] They go on to two-year technical education to prepare for the more complex jobs in an increasingly high-tech society. For the secondary schools the theme should be an emphasis on "learning to learn," accompanied by problem-solving skills that can apply in many work situations.

Dropout and substance abuse together are the key factors preventing students at risk from completing high school. There are many other situations that place students at risk, of course, such as pregnancy, child abuse, and suicide. Many urban districts are now working to integrate their established efforts for dealing with students likely to drop out with the "new" efforts in substance abuse prevention. As the research cited later in this chapter indicates, two-thirds of the abusers drop out, so there is good reason to integrate these activities. It is important that the individuals responsible for substance abuse and drop-out prevention both report to the same senior administrator in order to assure sound coordination of the two efforts. There is a considerable overlap in the behaviors of the dropout and the abuser, such as poor attendance, low grades, and poor self-image, and consequently both types of students will be placed in interventions that address these problems in a well-run system.

Once drop-out–prone students are identified, four types of programs can serve them. We will describe them and then provide a summary of strategies to use in substance abuse prevention. Many districts like to place their initial thrust at the middle school level because (1) the problem behaviors are quite visible at this age, unlike the elementary level, and (2) substantial success can be achieved in these grades, whereas there is less payoff in later years.

DROPOUTS

We frequently see articles indicating that urban schools often have drop-out rates of 50 percent or more. Communities placing pressure on school districts to deal with the rising number of dropouts raises the issue of how they are counted. An article by Floyd Morgan Hammack in the *Teachers College Record* from Columbia University describes in detail differing methods school districts use to compute their drop-out rate.[9] Many districts do not find it advantageous to list a high drop-out rate when they can compute a lower one using these and other techniques. They are often funded on the basis of the number of students attending school at present. If another funding method—for example, one that emphasized student proficiency in basic skills—was utilized, the reporting behaviors would change. A survey of over 600 employers taken in 1983 indicated that 82 percent of all jobs screened out candidates with no high school diploma.[10] Given the costs to business of teaching employees basic skills cited above, we can predict that the percentage of dropouts screened out will increase in the years ahead. This factor is exacerbated by the increasingly technical demands placed on employees by complex technologies that business must use to compete effectively with advanced industrial nations. The problem is serious, even monumental, when one considers the complexity of attempting to improve schools where 50 percent or more of the students are dropping out. Jonathan Peterson, writing in the *Los Angeles Times*, suggests another dimension of our problem. Not only do we need relevant training for students based on today's needs, but these needs are changing rapidly. "Every year, one out of eight jobs in the United States is newly created, and one out of nine is eliminated, as employers respond to the shifts in technology, consumer demand and competitive realities."[11] Not only do we have to keep updating our vocational opportunities for students, but we need to emphasize technology. Peterson, in the same article, quotes another researcher, William Johnston, of the Hudson Institute, as follows: "The haves and have nots in the year 2000 are going to be defined by their skills. . . . It's going to be the technologically able versus the technologically unable."[12] These skills are needed just to survive. To do well, people will need to "be able to manage people, adapt to technological change, think analytically and communicate effectively." The use of technology in periods of conflict, such as the war with Iraq, underlines the need for students to acquire these survival skills.

SUBSTANCE ABUSE

Students report pressure from peers to use drugs and alcohol in elementary school as early as fourth grade. These young people are at risk not only because of pressure from peers but because substance abuse has been shown by research to be a symptom of socioeconomic deprivation, parental abuse or neglect, inadequate health care, and cultural alienation.[13] It is important for educators to understand that our best hope for success with young people with a tendency toward substance abuse is to intervene early. This requires us to identify potential abusers through indicators such as disruptive behaviors, defiance of rules, hyperactivity, nervousness, talk about drugs, avoidance of contact with others, depression, and irritability. Characteristics such as frequent drunkenness; friends who use alcohol, marijuana, and other drugs; drug sale offenses; pickups by police; and sales of drugs have been used by some districts to identify abusers.

THREE COMMON MISTAKES IN DEALING WITH AT-RISK STUDENTS

Many urban school districts attempt to deal with low-achieving students through flawed strategies that include (1) retention in grade, (2) tracking, and (3) assignment to special education classes. Recent research indicates that retention does not show consistent learning benefits when the records of retained students are compared with those of age-mates who are not held back.[14] Not only does retention not do what we hoped, but it actually contributes to dropout, according to G. Natriello's research.[15]

The research of J. Goodlad and others indicates that tracking may, over time, actually increase the gap between top and bottom students rather than decrease it.[16] This appears to result primarily from teacher expectations being reduced when they teach the lower tracks. Since successful change tends to be incremental, J. McPartland and Robert E. Slavin suggest five steps to use in reducing tracking:

1. Postpone between-class homogeneous grouping until as late in the grade span as possible; rather, utilize within-class groups for math or reading.

2. Limit tracking in the later grades to those basic academic subjects where differences in students' prior preparation will hurt whole-class instruction.

3. Improve placement criteria and add resources where tracking is used.

4. Try new incentives that may encourage students to take challenging courses rather than stay on a lower track, such as pass-fail grading.

5. Retain separate classes for gifted, limited-English, and special education students at each grade level, even as you reduce tracking.[17]

The primary mistake in special education placement is to designate low-achieving students as learning disabled (LD) merely because of low achievement when there are no other LD characteristics. Whether this is done through poor placement procedures or to attract greater instructional resources, it is poor policy. Typically the result creates a funding limitation, which in turn precludes students who really do need special education from obtaining it.

In our view, secondary schools and their students are seriously threatened by the increase of substance abuse and dropout. Perhaps new assumptions and important changes are in order.

NEED FOR NEW ASSUMPTIONS

First, we must move away from the notion that reducing the percentage of dropouts is "the schools' problem." In our national survey of state departments of education to identify promising drop-out prevention and recovery programs, we found that of the initial twelve high school programs put into our database, eleven had work experience components. The single exception had a component that offered students assistance in locating appropriate employment at the end of the program. We need to collaborate with business and industry.

Second, programs that require cooperation from business and community agencies, such as those to reduce substance abuse and dropout, need to be planned jointly with them from day one. The senior author, as one of the creators of the successful dropout recovery program Upward Bound, knows from long experience that linking to agencies in the community can work only when there is true collaboration in the project design.

Third, we wait in vain for funding from the federal government to provide the primary resources to attack these problems. There will never be a return to massive federal intervention funding such as we had in the 1960s. The senior author, as former coordinator of the National Dropout Prevention Network, is familiar with strategies that the various states are using or planning to use to address this issue. Every state we know about is using a plan that relies on schools to find the needed resources at the local level to supplement state and federal funding.

Fourth, G. Wehlage and R. Rutter suggest that programs should be inventive and engage discouraged students, perhaps through approaches that include more than narrow vocational skills. Programs should emphasize personal and social development and be relatively small (25–100 students, 2–6 teachers).[18] This would apply to substance-abusing students as well.

Fifth, no matter what type of program we develop for preventing dropouts and substance abuse, we should identify students as early as possible. The model we use for dropout prediction was developed by Jack P. Sappington, one of our colleagues.[19] One can predict potential dropout at the fourth, sixth, and ninth grades with an accuracy rate of 79 percent or better. Student characteristics used are all available in the student's cumulative file. They include absences, grades, reading scores, mobility, citizenship, juvenile delinquency, special education history, physical disability, and grade retention.

TYPES OF DROPOUT PROGRAMS

Dropout programs that are receiving the most attention involve students in a variety of settings for education and work experience. There are four types identified by David Stern:

1. Regular academic curriculum leading to local diploma. An example of this is the Warren County High School program in Glasgow, Kentucky. Students meet with tutors during the latter part of class periods when they are experiencing problems and are given special counseling and help with their academic assignments.
2. Remedial academic curriculum leading to diploma equivalent. California now has a dozen school districts using the computer-based instruction program NOVANET to offer basic and other high school skills to students who have returned to learning centers after dropping out. They achieve the GED (General Educational Development) diploma through this approach.
3. Specialized vocational curriculum leading to job placement. Connecticut, through its Vocational-Technical School System, provides Bilingual Vocational Training Programs, which offer job-entry and trade-related skills taught bilingually; job-specific language using English as a second language approach; preventive counseling and life-coping skills; case management of trainees' problems such as child care and transportation; and job development and placement.
4. Regular academic curriculum combined with a vocational education. The Boston Compact consists of an agreement between employers and the school system to place students in jobs if the school system meets its quotas in terms of school attendance and reduction of drop-out rates. Students who have satisfactory school attendance can qualify for summer jobs and, in some cases, move into apprentice programs upon graduation from high school.[20]

TYPES OF SUBSTANCE ABUSE PREVENTION PROGRAMS

Substance abuse prevention programs that demonstrate the most effectiveness use comprehensive strategies to reduce risk factors and collaborate with resources outside the school setting.[21] Program components should always be linked to the risk factors as described by the publication by the California Department of Education's *Not Schools Alone* publication.[22]

Program Components	**Risk Factors**
1. *Planning process.* Involve school, family, peer, and community representatives to plan and monitor a comprehensive program.	All risk factors
2. *School policy.* Ensure clear and appropriate policies for prevention, intervention, and disciplinary action.	All risk factors, especially: • Early antisocial behavior • Easy availability of gateway and other drugs • School discipline regarding drug use • School transitions • Poor school climate
3. *In-service training of staff.* Provide general awareness training for staff and community and intensive training for core staff who will implement the plan.	All risk factors, especially: • Early antisocial behavior • Lack of student involvement • Poor school climate • Little commitment to school • Academic failure • School transitions
4. *K–12 curriculum on drug abuse.* Select and implement a curriculum for alcohol and other drug prevention that includes life skills, a no-use message, and the stages of drug use, appropriate to children's cognitive and social development levels and the culture and values of the community.	All risk factors, especially: • Academic failure • Early antisocial behavior • Lack of opportunities for students' involvement • Greater influence by, and reliance on, peers than parents • Little commitment to school • Early first use
5. *Parental involvement and education.* Provide workshops for parents on prevention, child development, risk factors, and intervention.	• Low expectations of children's success • Lack of bonding or closeness to parents • Use of tobacco, alcohol, or other drugs by parents or parents' positive attitudes toward their use. • Lack of clear expectation for children's behavior.

6. *Programs for early intervention and student assistance.*

Establish school-based student assistance programs for students with problems associated with substance abuse or needing support from peers.

7. *Intervention and community involvement.*

Identify community resources, establish working relationships and an intervention plan that provides a full range of services to drug-using youth and their families, including reentry to school following treatment.

8. *Peer group programs.*

Establish peer group programs at all grade levels, including instruction in refusal skills, support groups, student leadership, peer tutoring, peer assistance, cross-age teaching, dramatic presentation. Select responsible positive adults as advisors.

9. *Positive alternatives for student activities, recreation, and social development.*

Provide opportunities for leadership and activities to promote positive alternatives for students, such as school and community drug-free events and job and volunteer service opportunities.

• Academic failure

• Easy availability of drugs

• Antisocial behavior

• Use of tobacco, alcohol, and other drugs by parents and parents' positive attitudes toward their use

• Association with peers who use drugs or sanction their use

• No relationship with caring adults beyond the family

• Lack of employment opportunities

• Lack of involvement and leadership in school

• Abundance of liquor outlets

• Easy availability of drugs

• Little commitment to school

• Lack of involvement and leadership opportunities

• Greater influence by, and reliance on, peers than parents

• Early first use

• Association with peers who use drugs or sanction their use

• Use of gateway or other drugs by parents and parents' positive attitudes toward their use

• Lack of involvement, employment, and leadership opportunities

• Alienation and rebelliousness

• Association with peers who use drugs or sanction their use

• Greater influence by, and reliance on, peers than parents

GANG AND VIOLENCE PREVENTION STRATEGIES

Strategies shown to prevent the problem of youth gangs were addressed at a recent state conference on gangs as reported by Western Center for Drug-Free Schools and Communities.[23] Effective strategies include:

1. Overcome community denial that gangs exist.
2. Develop a network of community resources to address different aspects of the gang problem in a comprehensive manner.
3. Adopt effective, school-based strategies, including:
   a. Establish clear expectations about acceptable behavior
   b. Maintain visible staff on campus to create a sense of safety
   c. Involve parents

We need not only to focus on drop-out prediction, substance abuse, and gang prevention much earlier in the student's school career but to look as well at the type and amount of contact students have with their teachers. In many urban school districts even our elementary and middle/junior high schools have become large and impersonal. This is especially true for students who don't do well in the typical school environment. The following set of recommendations are aimed at middle school students at risk, but they certainly would benefit all students at risk.

Middle School Task Force Recommendations for Students at Risk

1. Local school boards should mandate at least one extended time block daily in two or more of the core curriculum subjects during the middle grades to ensure that:
   a. Every middle grade student is known personally and well by one or more teachers.
   b. Individual monitoring of student progress takes place systematically so that teachers and counselors can quickly identify learning difficulties and take corrective measures.
   c. Cooperative learning strategies are implemented as a means of building strong positive peer group relationships and reinforcing essential educational values and goals.
2. Superintendents should give leadership in helping principals devise means for reducing the pressure of large, complex schools, which leaves many students with a sense of anonymity and isolation. Particular attention should be given to organizational and scheduling concepts that are student-centered and maximize opportunities for strong personal bonds among smaller numbers of students and teachers throughout the full span of the middle grade years.
3. Local school boards should authorize and fund peer, cross-age, and/or adult tutorial and mentor programs in the middle grades as a proven response to the needs of many at-risk students.
4. The state department of education and local district curriculum departments should assist teachers in devising instructional strategies that allow students with basic skills deficiencies to engage in learning experiences that develop higher-order thinking skills; these strategies should correspond with core curriculum goals and should enable students to learn in regular classrooms; and learning experiences should be consistent with the maturity and interest levels of young adolescents.

5. Principals should give leadership in creating cultural support systems for students—particularly those with limited-English proficiency—whose self-identity is threatened through the loss and implicit devaluing of their native language; teachers and counselors should understand the psychological trauma involved in the transition from one language to another and the bearing that this phenomenon has on the negative attitudes and values of some categories of at-risk students.

6. Teachers, counselors, and principals should continuously model behavior that affirms their commitment to the basic mission of those who work in the middle grades; to enjoy young adolescents and to create conditions for academic success and educational commitment for every student.[24]

OBJECTIVES SHOULD BE BASED ON RESEARCH

Research indicates that 30 percent of all children experience school adjustment difficulties, stress, and behavior problems that are predictors of future maladjustment and drug use.[25] Therefore, prevention and early intervention projects that utilize research-based intervention strategies addressing specific risk factors show greater effectiveness.

Association with Drug-Using and Gang-Affiliated Peers

Association with drug-using and/or gang-affiliated peers has been one of the strongest predictors of adolescent drug use and gang involvement. This may be viewed as a peer-supported phenomenon reflecting the importance of peers during adolescence.[26] Therefore, the positive utilization of peer groups for assistance or for positive alternative activities can be highly effective in promoting a drug-free, healthy life-style. In addition, the use of support groups led by trained professionals from school or community can be an effective strategy to promote insight and support of change in an adolescent's behavior and attitudes.

Family Role and Socialization Deficits

The family role in preventing drug use and gang affiliation among adolescent youth has been well documented. The importance of family socialization includes the adult as a role model for the youth of the family. H. B. Kandel, S. S. Martin, and C. Robbins[27] found that three factors help predict youth initiation into drugs: parent drug use, parent attitudes about drugs, and parent and child interactions. Parental "use" seems to act as an impetus to experimentation, according to most findings.[28] Parent support of gang life-styles and sibling membership in gangs are the most potent reasons for gang affiliation. Parents are quietly molding their child's behavior; therefore, prevention projects need to provide positive modeling through training parents or by using substitute models, such as mentors.

Lack of School Interest and Achievement

Poor school performance, though not always leading to drug use, is a common antecedent to drug initiation.[29] L. N. Robins noted that drug users are noticeably "underachievers."[30] Academic failure in late elementary grades exacerbates the effects of early antisocial behavior. D. J. Hawkins, D. M. Lishner, and R. F. Catalano[31] found that such factors as how much students like school, time spent on homework, and perception of the relevance of course work are also related to levels of drug use,[32] confirming a negative relationship between commitment to education and drug use, at least for adolescents in junior or senior high. To intervene, a district can use core and support staff at the school sites to screen and assist students who seem to be academically weak or failing.

USE OF THE RISK FACTOR MODEL

William Callison's recent project with twelve school districts confirms the validity of a risk approach, which combines risk factors for dropout and risk factors for substance abuse together for analysis and intervention.[33] It is based on the work of Hawkins at the University of Washington.[34] The California State Department of Education strongly urges that districts use his model in the development of prevention projects.

This model is derived from research on heart disease, in which risk factors are characteristics in an individual or in his or her environment that increase the likelihood of developing heart disease. If risk factors for drug abuse, such as antisocial behavior, association with drug-using peers, family management practices, and academic failure, can be assessed along with resiliency or protective factors, such as involvement in church activities and strong attachment to parents and school, appropriate programmatic interventions can follow. Protective factors are important even if they represent only the opposite end of the risk factor continuum, because protective factors buffer the effects of risk indicators. A list of these important risk and protective factors follows:

Risk Factors

1. Laws and norms favorable toward behavior

2. Availability of drugs and alcohol

3. Extreme economic deprivation

4. Neighborhood disorganization

5. Physiological factors

6. Early and persistent problem behaviors (i.e., aggression, conduct, hyperactivity)

7. Family history of alcoholism and parental drug use

8. Poor and inconsistent family management practices

9. Family conflict
10. Low bonding to family
11. Academic failure
12. Low degree of commitment to school
13. Peer rejection in elementary grades
14. Association with drug-using peers
15. Alienation and rebelliousness
16. Attitudes favorable to drugs
17. Early onset of drug use

Protective Factors

1. Strong attachment to parents
2. Commitment to schooling
3. Regular involvement in church activities
4. Belief in the generalized expectations, norms, and values of society
5. Low affiliation, autonomy, exhibition, impulsivity, and play
6. High achievement, cognitive structure, and harm avoidance

ADAPTATION OF RISK FACTOR MODEL BY A SCHOOL DISTRICT

The Hawkins risk factor model has been adapted by the Irvine Unified School District in Irvine, California, in a project called Strategies for Resiliency. Irvine is a rapidly growing city of over 100,000 with a strong commitment to prevent or ameliorate many of the big-city problems associated with growth. A summary of the middle school project is described.

Summary of Project

Purpose: to demonstrate the effectiveness of comprehensive holistic prevention and early intervention strategies to reduce risk for alcohol and other drug use and increase resiliency in high-risk middle school youth.

Goals: (1) to decrease the incidence and prevalence of drug and alcohol use among high-risk youth, (2) to reduce risk factors for using alcohol and other drugs as they impact on individual high-risk youth and on the environments in which high-risk youth and their families function, (3) to increase resiliency and protective factors within high-risk youth and within their families and communities in order to reduce the likelihood that youths will use alcohol and other drugs.

Activities: (1) to develop a systematic, multidimensional identification of at-risk students, (2) to provide effective prevention and early intervention programs for middle school students, (3) to collaborate with the community to provide outreach services to families of high-risk students, (4) to provide training and educational resources for school staff, (5) to develop, evaluate, and disseminate effective strategies.

Evaluation: (1) assessment of student attitude and risk behaviors, including alcohol and other drug use, antisocial behaviors, personality factors, self-esteem, and resilient attitudes or behaviors as measured by parent, teacher, and student self-reports, the Risk Assessment Survey, the Family Apgar Scale, the Rosenberg Self-Esteem Scale, and various locally developed instruments; (2) assessment of basic skills improvement as measured by academic GPA and CTBS test scores; and (3) attendance as measured by district records. Process evaluation measures include the effectiveness of trainings, manuals, and curriculum in meeting project implementation goals.

Intervention Approach

The intervention objectives of the project are to decrease antisocial, aggressive behavior and develop prosocial behaviors; to decrease the tendency to associate with drug-using peers due to passive behavior and lack of alternative activities; to improve parental drug-free information, attitudes, and skills related to family management, value systems, modeling, and communication of no-use message; to increase student achievement and interest in school activities; to improve health and health attitudes; to increase awareness of personality needs and develop healthy alternatives and resources for high-risk students who may be sensation-seekers, be cognitively impulsive, isolated, and highly tolerant of deviance, and/ or have low self-esteem.

A dual-level intervention system will provide prevention to all middle school youth and identification of at-risk and high-risk students, facilitating their referral to school-based early intervention and community-based treatment programs.

The first level of intervention is the district's alcohol and drug abuse prevention program, provided to all middle school students through health class, teacher advisement, homeroom, elective classes, assemblies, small group counseling, and positive peer-led activities (such as the Conflict Resolution Program and Youth to Youth Conferences).

The second level of intervention will provide identification and early intervention for students at risk for developing drug abuse problems, by evaluating the students' risk levels and providing interventions to increase resiliency and prosocial development. Risk and resiliency levels will be evaluated along the continuum of risk, thereby permitting a nonlabeling, proactive intervention program.

Defining Risk in Students

Research has found that there are many paths to drug abuse;[35] therefore, interventions must also address these specific areas. A student's risk factors may be related to problems with school, family, peers, or personality and may be a combination of these areas. Students must also be identified by the degree of risk, as strategies that work with at-risk students may not work with high-risk students. A definition of these groups as used in the project follows.

At-risk students have a limited number of risk factors. They may be students with low self-esteem; passive or aggressive students who are experiencing peer pressure problems; children who lack realistic information on destructive aspects of drugs; children experiencing failure in school or with behavioral or antisocial problems. They may be children of substance abusers and genetically at risk, representing the 25 percent of children affected by alcohol risk characteristics.

High-risk youth experience multiple risk factors. These students have multiple problems with attendance, discipline, family, self-esteem, or academics and/or are observed, reported, and/or self-reported to have alcohol and other drug use problems at school or in the community. These students' school problems may be academic, behavioral, social, or personal. Family problems may be due to living in dysfunctional or abusive family environments, such as homes where alcohol and/or drug abuse occurs or has occurred. Other indications of high risk are: child of a substance abuser; victim of physical, sexual, or psychological abuse; dropping out of school; becoming pregnant; being economically disadvantaged; committing a violent or delinquent act; experiencing mental health problems; attempting suicide; experiencing long-term physical pain due to injury; or experiencing chronic failure in school.

Evaluation Results

The Strategies for Resiliency project has shown promising reduction in risk factors as it enters its third year of evaluation. The project is based on research by N. Richards-Colocino[36] that used the Hawkins risk factor model to develop a risk factor survey that successfully discriminated between alcohol and other drug users and nonusers in the student population. Using a discriminate function analysis design, a total of 81.6 percent of students were correctly classified as users or nonusers on this self-report survey. The classifications also correlated well with student record data containing risk factor information.

Current evaluation of the Strategies for Resiliency project indicate that this comprehensive intervention system decreases risk factors in students and decreases the use of alcohol among the targeted middle school students.

COMPUTER-ASSISTED RISK IDENTIFICATION AND INTERVENTION

As risk factor assessment is used with greater numbers of students to drive prevention and intervention activities, the efficient management of the process becomes an issue. One solution to scoring, analyzing, prioritizing, and grouping students is to automate the process through the use of Scantron forms and computerized decision models called expert system software.

For example, the Irvine school district and others in southern California are identifying students at risk and placing them into appropriate interventions using expert system software called Comprehensive Risk Assessment.[37] It is available for both Macintosh- and IBM-compatible computers. An expert system is a kind of artificial intelligence program that mimics human logic within a specific area of expertise, in this case, the characteristics of at-risk students. The approach uses Scantron forms where students self-report the needed data, which are then put through the scanner, thus eliminating the time-consuming process of gathering data from each student's cumulative folder. The data are then automatically entered into the software, thus saving the time needed for data entry in our earlier system. The expert system further makes possible another big time-saver, automatic scheduling of identified students into appropriate interventions. These recent developments save large amounts of time and expense, dramatically reducing the time required for a student study team or the equivalent to complete student placements.

Application of Elliott's Gang Reduction Model

Gang participation develops when young people come from a home with poor socialization patterns, weak linkage to positive students and school staff, and strong ties to delinquent youth. The most common path leading to gang participation is the situation where the youth comes from a home background with weak socialization to his or her community's values, has not developed bonds to positive students or teachers at school, but has developed linkage to delinquent youth in the community.[38] Researchers describe this as a path where there is joint occurrence of weak conventional controls and, at the same time, reinforcement for delinquent activity.

These situational characteristics also lead to drug use. Consequently, many strategies for reduction of substance abuse are appropriate for reduction of gang involvement for particular students.

One key to antigang efforts is statewide legislation. For example, in 1982 California passed the Victim's Bill of Rights, which is Article I, Section 28(a) (c) of the California Constitution. It states, among other rights for law-abiding citizens, that "all students and staff of public primary, elementary, junior high and senior high schools have the inalienable right to attend campuses which are safe, secure and peaceful." The importance of this legislation will be immediately apparent to well-trained school administrators. It provides a defensible legal basis for protecting their students against foreseeable criminal activity, like that carried out by gangs. Gangs are by definition groups that are involved in criminal activities.

Operation Safe Schools: An Innovative Gang Reduction Model

The Orange County (California) Department of Education, with the assistance of the California Office of Criminal Justice Planning, created Operation Safe

Schools (OSS) in 1987. Its purpose is to offer participating school districts an "early intervention, prevention education program tailored to assist school districts in maintaining safe, secure and peaceful school environments."[39]

Some of its objectives include creation of a curriculum that teaches students their responsibilities in maintaining school safety, since many gang members do not consider the consequences of their illegal activities on their families, neighborhood, or school unless they have been pointed out to them. OSS provides intervention at school sites, such as dealing with anger, and utilizes positive role models. Student leaders are trained as peer assistants, since the term *peer counselor* offends many trained counselors, and in-service training is offered to school staff to help them work with gang members.

OSS also provides parenting classes and teaches students how to network to protect themselves. Most critically it provides specific model rules and regulations to use in analyzing school policies regarding student attire, disruptive behavior, drug involvement, and appropriate disciplinary procedures. It is important that students not be typed as "gang members" since young people who are seeking to protect themselves by appearing to wear colors may not, in fact, be gang members. The gang label may prevent a student from building a constructive life in future years. The identification some experts use to locate students who may be gang members includes police data, such as first arrest, number of arrests in a lifetime, number of arrests in the past year, and use of colors if a knowledgeable staff member is involved.

Other OSS activities include linking to community-based organizations that work with schools to encourage after-school events as well as creating cooperative relationships with police and other law enforcement agencies to increase prevention activities that address the relationship between antisocial group membership and drug abuse. The development of school-business partnerships to create positive alternatives for students is helpful, as is the creation of an advisory board with members from schools, law enforcement, community, church, and private agencies.

There are seven steps in the implementation of the OSS model on a school campus. These include:

1. The selected school's principal chooses school staff to participate in a results-oriented advisory group.
2. OSS professional staff work with the advisory group to develop a comprehensive plan of action, which is then submitted to the site principal.
3. The principal/district staff modify and approve the plan prior to implementation.
4. OSS staff provide in-service training for selected personnel at the school site.
5. Implementation of the plan proceeds.
6. The advisory group evaluates the plan's results and submits recommendations for improvement to the principal/district staff.
7. The principal/district staff review the recommendations and approve follow-up.

Evaluation of the effort can be measured, with expectation for improvement in the following:

Improved attendance

Improved grades and test scores

Increased attendance in higher education institutions

Decreased discipline problems

Decreased violence and vandalism

Decreased drug and alcohol abuse

Reduced negative peer pressure reported

Improved student self-image

Enhanced decision-making skills observed

Program objectives achieved

The Los Angeles Unified School District Model for Alcohol and Drug Prevention

The Los Angeles district and several other urban school district prevention programs were summarized by the Western Regional Center of Drug-Free Schools and Communities.[40] The uniqueness of the Los Angeles Model is reflected in its development within the district's health education program. Students in grades seven and ten take a required health course that includes information about substance abuse. In the early grades, the program concentrates on drug safety and social skills behavior relative to gateway drugs. Current funding for drug prevention has assisted the district in making prevention efforts more widespread and greater in scope, including early intervention, support groups, and parent involvement.

Collaboration with Others

Parent support groups operate at some schools, and parent education is conducted through the Impact and Drug Alcohol Resistance Education (DARE) programs. Students participate in peer programs and take an active role in program development. For example, students developed a series of antidrug media spots through the Tobacco Utilization Prevention Education project.

In addition to students and parents, different agencies in the community are involved with the district's prevention program. The Los Angeles County Drug and Alcohol Program Office includes partnership with over eighty agencies, including ones that target minority groups in alcohol and other drug use prevention. Among other things, these agencies help lead support groups on campus. There is also collaboration with the American Heart and Lung Association in tobacco prevention programs.

The Drug Alcohol Resistance Education program, which was developed in conjunction with the Los Angeles School District and the Los Angeles Police Department, has been in the district since 1983. DARE is a part of a comprehensive K–12 health education curriculum where every grade level is involved in the district's school-based prevention program. The prevention program involves a social skills approach and includes law enforcement (DARE and SANE), teacher-led prevention, parent education, Drug Alcohol Tobacco Education coordinators at the elementary, middle, and high school sites, and 2nd STEP, Discover Skills, and TUPE programs. The district's early intervention program includes impact at the junior and senior high schools and on-site counseling by social workers at the elementary schools.

In an urban district, high-risk youth are a special focus. There is also a focus on drugs and gangs to deal with violence and high-risk behavior in students. Identification of high-risk youth is targeted at the elementary level, with a special focus on particular grades and student populations.

Dr. Matthew Rich, the coordinator for the Los Angeles program, cites several elements that make the program unique, including the emphasis on comprehensive health education using a social skills approach, targeting elementary grades, an effective delivery system, being school-based with teacher buy-in, and police department involvement.

Evaluation of the program supports is success, as seen in decreased arrests, a lower drop-out rate, and less reported drug use as indicated by surveys used throughout the state.

Duarte Community Prevention Model

One of the most successful drop-out and substance abuse prevention models in California is operating in the Duarte Unified School District, Duarte, California. Duarte schools are virtually a microcosm of the schools in Los Angeles County, a multiethnic population that is predominantly Latino. The district has been recognized by the California State Department of Education for its exemplary drop-out prevention efforts.

Project Aims. The aims of the District At-Risk Management Project, funded by the U.S. Department of Education, are to develop a computer management system that will (1) identify potential substance abusers and potential dropouts and (2) use an expert system, Comprehensive Risk Assessment[41] to connect identified students at risk with appropriate interventions to reduce student risk levels.

Accomplishments. This project developed an at-risk management system to complement the identification of students at risk that was in place. It added early intervention of school staff to assist youth who may become substance abusers and/or dropouts. The Duarte Primary Prevention and Early Intervention for High Risk Youth Program is an innovative design that has established effective drug and alcohol abuse prevention and successful interventions. This at-risk management system has made a significant impact on reducing student drug use by creating a computerized delivery system for drug abuse prevention and intervention that utilizes the latest research to predict potential abusers and dropouts. It utilizes a computerized identification system that, in turn, automatically links students with great need to effective interventions.

Project activities were developed during the past eight years and from a review of the current literature on high-risk and substance-abusing students. Components respond to the research findings, particularly the research on high-risk factors for adolescents.

Description of the Delivery System. The Duarte Primary Prevention and Early Intervention for High Risk Youth Program offers a comprehensive, holistic approach for preventing alcohol and other drug use by elementary school students and is being evaluated over a period of two years. The project addresses the needs of the student, the family, the school, and the community, in a comprehensive approach to prevention, through the following:

Student

1. Identification of behavioral and academic deficits and provision for peer tutoring, support group, and social skills and health curriculum.

2. An increase in social skills, peer-resistant strategies, decision-making skills, and self-esteem.

3. An increase of bonding to home and school, with positive role models (star performers and lecturers).

4. An increase in academic performance and confidence in interacting with peers at school and home.

5. A decrease in antisocial behaviors.

School

1. Teachers, counselors, and administrators are gaining prevention knowledge, skills, and curriculum.

2. Staff are being more sensitive to students' problems.

3. New dimensions of health are allowing more challenging physical fitness programs for risk-taking youth and provide extracurricular activities (hikes, trips).

4. School is providing a comprehensive program to address cognitive, social, health, and personality concerns, as well as providing curriculum and materials.

5. Programs are addressing family needs for parenting skills and drug prevention education.

6. Schools are providing paraprofessional prevention specialists who interact with high-risk students, parents, and community.

Community

1. Prevention Committee with membership from schools, parents, police, health agencies meets monthly to reinforce an antidrug-use message for students.
2. The spirit of unity and responsibility is being strengthened and expanded by this concerted effort to prevent youth from experimenting with substances.
3. Businesses are cooperating in offering responsible advertising that discourages drug use among youth.

Family

1. The need for better family management techniques and parenting skills is being met through active parenting classes.
2. Parents are gaining knowledge about drug use and ways to cope with children who have problems or are using.
3. Parents who need resources will gain help and support.

A coordinated intervention system that identifies high-risk juveniles or students with chronic drug abuse problems and facilitates their referral to an established intervention system or drug abuse treatment program has been developed.

A high-risk student or one with a chronic drug abuse problem is defined as a student having problems with attendance, discipline, family, self-esteem, or academics and with observed, reported, and/or self-reported substance abuse problems at school or in the community.

A data-gathering system involving students, parents, school personnel, and community resources to identify students who need help has been developed, including:

1. A database of all students in the district identifying the lower quadrant based on academics, low test scores, and students exhibiting at-risk behaviors.
2. A referral form for teachers who have identified a problem with a student and a procedure for handling referrals and tracking disposition of each referral.
3. An information system to let referring teachers know the disposition of the referral.
4. A plan for sharing information with parents of students.

Interventions Available for Linkage with Students Identified. The types of intervention services offered through the Duarte Primary Prevention and Early Intervention for High Risk Youth Program include:

1. Individual and group counseling with prevention specialists directed toward improved social skills, increased interest in, and information about, drug-free activities and group support of nonuse, and when indicated, referral to community counseling services.

2. Family intervention, counseling, and referral, including active parenting classes.

3. Presentations on special topics of student concern and drug abuse, utilizing comprehensive health curriculum materials and visiting experts.

4. Development of school-sponsored activities for high-risk students, such as adventure courses, field trips, and after-school programs.

5. Referral to, and support for, use of available community resources.

A follow-up procedure tracking participants as they progress through middle and high school, providing important research information about the support needed for continued nonuse of drugs and alcohol, has been initiated.

The objectives of the DUSD (Duarte Unified School District) project are:

• To decrease antisocial, aggressive behavior and develop prosocial behaviors.

• To decrease the tendency to associate with drug-using peers due to passive behavior and lack of alternative activities.

• To improve parental drug-free information, attitudes, and skills related to family management, value systems, modeling, and communication of no-use message.

• To increase student achievement and interest in school activities.

• To improve health and health attitudes.

• To increase awareness of personality needs and develop healthy alternatives and resources for high-risk students who may be sensation-seekers, cognitively impulsive, isolated, highly tolerant of deviance, and/or have low self-esteem.

• To improve attitudes, skills, and use of resources to achieve individual goals.

This project is now beginning its second year in the district's five elementary schools. It will be expanded to include the junior and senior high school students.

SUMMARY

Many of the programs and research presented have implications for urban school districts that want effective programming to prevent and intervene with troubled adolescents. Because at-risk adolescents have a tendency to engage in a variety of dysfunctional behaviors, it is clear that good intervention programs serve students with more than one type of problem. For example, gang prevention programs should include a strong drug education component based on what we know about drug use by gang members.

One effective way to address the various problem behaviors is to identify and seek to decrease risk factors while increasing protective factors where possible. This means that effective programs must be comprehensive, using specific strategies that decrease risk in the particular individuals being served. Identification of risk is a very important factor prior to initiating a prevention or intervention program for an adolescent. However, the identification must not result in labeling that serves only to identify the problem rather than change it. In fact, if a prevention or intervention program can identify risk factors and intervene with sound strategies without damaging labels, it is almost assured of success.

NOTES

1. Based on a confidential report made available to the primary author.

2. Staff Report, *School Enrollment-Social and Economic Characteristics of Students* (Washington, DC: U.S. Census Bureau, 1992).

3. Bob Baker, *Los Angeles Times*, 19 June 1990.

4. *Los Angeles Times*, 5 June 1992.

5. Brock, William E. and F. Ray Marshall, US Government Printing Office, 1989.

6. Phillips, Kevin, *The Politics of Rich and Poor*, New York, NY, Random House, 1990.

7. John G. Wirt, "A New Federal Law on Vocational Education: Will Reform Follow?", *Phi Kappan* 43 (February 1991): 465–469.

8. Kenneth Gray, "Vocational Education in High School: A Modern Phoenix?", *Phi Delta Kappan* 23 (February 1991): 48–56.

9. Floyd Morgan Hammack, "Large School Systems' Dropout Reports: An Analysis of Definitions, Procedures, and Findings," *Teachers College Record* 3 (Spring 1986): 12–14.

10. A. Malizio and D. Whitney, "Educational Credential in Employment: A Nationwide Survey," paper presented at Lifelong Learning Conference, College Park, MD, 1984.

11. Jonathan Peterson, "Service Jobs Dominate the Economy," *Los Angeles Times*, 24 September 1987.

12. Ibid.

13. Eric N. Goplerud, *Breaking New Ground for Youth at Risk: Program Summaries* (Washington, DC: U.S. Government Printing Office, 1990).

14. L. Shepard and M. Smith, *Flunking Grades: Research and Policies on Retention* (London: Falmer Press, 1989).

15. G. Natriello, A. M. Pallas, E. L. McDill, J. M. McPartland, and D. Royster, *An Examination of the Assumptions and Evidence for Alternative Dropout Prevention Programs in High School* (Baltimore, MD: 1988). Center for Social Organization of Schools, Johns Hopkins University.

16. J. Goodlad, *A Place Called School* (New York: McGraw-Hill, 1983).

17. J. McPartland and Robert E. Slavin, *Policy Perspectives: Increasing Achievement of At-Risk Students at Each Grade Level* (Washington, DC: U.S. Government Printing Office, 1990).

18. G. Wehlage and R. Rutter, *Evaluation of a Model Program for At-Risk Students*. National Center on Effective Secondary Schools, University of Wisconsin, Madison, WI, 1986.

19. Jack P. Sappington, *The Predictive Strength of Nine School-Related Indicators for Distinguishing Potential Dropouts*. Ph.D. diss., United States International University, San Diego, CA, 1979.

20. David Stern, "Dropout Prevention and Recovery in California," paper written for the California State Department of Education, Sacramento, CA, 1986.

21. D. J. Hawkins, D. M. Lishner, and R. F. Catalano, "Childhood Predictors of

Adolescent Substance Abuse,'' *Etiology of Drug Abuse: Implications for Prevention* (Washington, DC: U.S. Department of Health and Human Services, 1985); Bonnie Benard, Anthony Fafoglia, and Jan Perone, "Knowing What to Do—and Not to Do—Reinvogorates Drug Education," Association for Supervision and Curriculum Development Curriculum Update, February 1987.

22. California Department of Education, *Not Schools Alone* (Sacramento, CA: Office of Healthy Kids, Healthy California, 1991).

23. Western Regional Center Drug-Free Schools and Communities, *Substance Abuse Among Juvenile Delinquents and Gang Members* (Portland, OR, Prevention Research Update, Northwest Regional Educational Laboratory, 1990).

24. Report of the Superintendent's Middle Grade Task Force, *Caught in the Middle, Educational Reform for Young Adolescents in California Public Schools* (Sacramento, CA: California State Department of Education, 1987).

25. E. L. Cowen, M. Zax, L. D. Izzo, and M. A. Trost, "Prevention of Emotional Disorders in the School Setting," *Journal of Consulting Psychology* 30 (1966): 381–87.

26. D. J. Hawkins, D. M. Lishner, and R. F. Catalano, "Childhood Predictors of Adolescent Substance Abuse," *Etiology of Drug Abuse: Implications for Prevention* (Washington, DC: U.S. Department of Health and Human Services, 1985).

27. H. B. Kandel, S. S. Martin, and C. Robbins. "Applications of a General Theory of Deviant Behavior: Self-Degradation and Adolescent Drug Use," *Journal of Health and Social Behavior* 23, no. 4 (1982): 274–94.

28. J. V. Rachal, L. L. Guess, R. L. Hubbard, S. A. Maisto, E. R. Cavanaugh, R. Waddell, and C. H. Benrud, *Adolescent Drinking Behavior*, vol. 1, Sample Studies, Research Triangle Institute, Research Triangle Park, 1980, 1982.

29. R. J. Jessor and S. L. Jessor, *Problem Behavior and Psychological Development: A Longitudinal Study of Youth* (New York: Academic Press, 1977); Kandel, Martin, and Robbins.

30. L. N. Robins, "The Natural History of Drug Use," *Evaluation of Treatment of Drug Abusers, ACTA Psychiat. Scand.* 62 (1980): 284.

31. Hawkins, Lishner, and Catalano.

32. Alfred S. Friedman, "Does Drug and Alcohol Use Lead to Failure to Graduate from High School?", *Journal of Drug Education* 15, no. 4 (1985): 27–42.

33. William Callison, David Crabtree, Pamela Ehlers, Antoinette Evans, Nancy Richards, Gene Sakanari, and Deborah Youngblood, "Identifying Characteristics of Students at Risk of Substance Abuse," presentation of master's thesis and doctoral research to the Partnership Academy Committee Substance Abuse Project members, Orange Unified School District, 24 April 1990.

34. Hawkins, Lishner, and Catalano.

35. E. R. Oetting, and F. Beauvais, "Common Elements in Youth Drug Abuse: Peer Clusters and Other Psychosocial Factors," *Journal of Drug Issues* 22, no. 2 (1987): 133–51.

36. N. Richards-Colocino, *School-Based Assessment of Students at Risk for Drug Abuse*, Ph.D. diss., United States International University, San Diego, CA, 1991.

37. Comprehensive Risk Assessment, software produced by Students-at-Risk, Inc., 1260 Brangwyn Way, Laguna Beach, CA 92651.

38. D. S. Elliott, Donald Huizinga and S. Menard, *Multiple Problem Youth: Delinquency, Substance Abuse and Mental Health Problems* (New York: Springer-Verlag, 1989).

39. Orange County Department of Education, *Operation Safe Schools* (Costa Mesa, CA, D.C. Department of Education 1992).

40. Western Regional Center of Drug-Free Schools and Communities, *Urban Profiles in Prevention*. Portland, OR: Northwest Regional Educational Laboratory, September 1991.

41. Comprehensive Risk Assessment.

23

Reading in the Urban Environment

Norma Inabinette

By 2000, we've got to, first, ensure that every child starts school ready to learn; second, raise the high school graduate rate to 90 percent; the third, ensure that each American student leaving the 4th, 8th, and 12th grades can demonstrate competence in the core subjects; fourth, make our students first in the world in math and science achievements; fifth, ensure that every American adult is literate and has the skills necessary to compete in a global economy and exercise the rights and responsibilities of citizenship; and sixth, liberate every American school from drugs and violence so that schools encourage learning.[1]

Reading is a critical skill necessary not only for success in school but for survival in the world. Reading ability in the twenty-first century will not only determine the quality of life, as it has in the past but will influence the very existence of it. As we move into the communication age, one's ability to process information in written form will determine how well one can carry out the normal daily activities that thus far have not demanded high literacy skills. It is now believed that by the year 2000, the average American must have reading skills at the fourteenth grade level to be a fully functioning citizen.[2]

While the demands for increased reading ability grow steadily, too many of our school-age children are handicapped because they lack the basic skill of reading.[3] This lack of ability to process print is seen most dramatically in the urban school setting, where both the quality of the schools and life in general make learning a challenge. In order to understand the impact a lack of reading skills can have, it is important to understand what reading is and what factors support or hinder growth in reading.

READING: A DEFINITION

Reading is the process of constructing meaning from print. This process is complicated and complex, requiring the smooth coordination of several interrelated sources of information. Most importantly, the author's meaning can be understood and assimilated only if it matches the language and experience of the reader. When the reader is able to match his or her background and knowledge with those of the printed work, meaning construction begins.

Reading Is a Language Process

The process of reading begins when children first encounter oral language. As they are exposed to vocabulary and contextual language, they begin to assimilate that language for their own use. Language is an active process of involvement that is learned in the natural settings of the home and the neighborhood, with children hearing both vocabulary and sentence structure as they occur with daily use. By the time children enter formal education, they should have a strong conceptual vocabulary (words whose meaning is clearly understood) and an understanding of the syntax (word order and use in sentences) and semantics (subtle shades of word meaning), as well as the purpose and influence, of language. This oral language knowledge is then transferred to the printed page as the learner gains knowledge of the printed symbols that represent oral speech and a basic understanding that print is a representation of oral language. It is extremely important that children be immersed in language at an early age so that the conventions of language are learned well.[4]

Reading Is a Constructive Process

The reader must bring to the reading act knowledge about the subject matter that acts as prerequisite information to the text reading in order to construct meaning from the words found there. No text can supply all of the information on a topic that is needed. Authors assume that the reader has some basic information (background knowledge) that will fill the gaps that the author does not cover in the text. Good readers use their inferencing skills to supply the unstated information. Since all readers do not share the same experiential or knowledge base, interpretation of a piece of print will vary from reader to reader depending on the extent of prior knowledge and familiarity. Readers who bring a great deal of information to the text will take away more than readers whose background knowledge limits their understanding of the text content.

Reading Is a Fluent Process

To be a fluent reader, word identification and word analysis skills must be automatic. The reader must have mastered enough of the mechanics of reading to make word recognition and attack rapid, automated processes so that reading energy is not spent in the basic decoding skills of reading but rather in the comprehension of reading.

To become fluent readers, children begin by learning the fundamental skills of word identification. Through repeated practice and reading of materials that contain the basic vocabulary of our language, they learn to use phonic skills (sound/symbol relationships that allow for very basic word attack) and structural analysis skills (word part skills that allow for use of root words, affixes, and familiar word parts for more rapid word identification) to analyze words that are not instantly recognized as sight words. Words that the reader sees often will become sight vocabulary requiring no analysis at all because the reader has stored them as whole images and can recall them as such. These basic skills are then combined with the ability to use context (the sense of the sentence) and configuration (the general shape and form of the word) to determine rapidly what a word is when it is encountered in print. Once these mechanical skills are mastered, reading of words (or phrases) becomes so automatic that the reader does it both rapidly and without conscious effort. Fluency of language is essential if the words read are closely to resemble oral language. If fluency is achieved, the reader has a good chance of making sense of the printed material because the language flows just as it does orally.

Reading Is a Strategic Process

Readers need to monitor their speed and intensity of reading with the purpose they have established for reading. Content texts (social studies, science, and so on) that contain a great deal of compressed information and unfamiliar vocabulary need to be read more slowly than narrative stories read for pleasure or material scanned to provide specific information. Strategic readers know when they are not understanding the text and employ ''fix-it'' strategies to back up and reread or consult other knowledge sources for background knowledge.[5] Skilled readers set purposes for themselves based on the extent of their knowledge and/or familiarity with the text material and their basic learning needs. Reading to study may require more time and a slower rate than reading to learn material, so that purpose and, therefore, pace will vary.

Reading Is a Motivated Process

Motivation is the key to learning and the essential ingredient in reading success. Reading must be a pleasurable and fulfilling process, or understanding will not take place. To be motivated, the reader must have command of the skills of reading, interest in the content of the material read, and teachers who are willing to instill excitement about reading. While children enter the educational system anxious and eager to learn to read, they often lose their enthusiasm when exposed to materials that are too difficult or instructional situations that do not prepare them for learning. Motivation and enthusiasm for reading must be supported at all levels of learning and must involve not only the reader but the home and school as well.

Reading Is a Lifelong Process

Reading is not a skill completed in the first three grades, where traditionally efforts have been spent on teaching the mechanics of processing print. Reading is a continuous process that barely begins with the conclusion of the formal education of children. As children move through the educational system, the needs for more sophisticated reading, combined with the continuous maturity of their intellectual abilities, alter the reading purposes. Practice throughout life makes readers more adept at using information, analyzing related information, and building mental schemas (bundles of associations in the mind)[6] that make the reading process more effective. Continuous practice is needed for reading skills to be maintained and honed so that learning through the use of reading skills can be maximized. Our schools must face the challenge of preparing students to learn to read at every step of the educational process. As purposes for reading and unfamiliarity with material change, reading instruction must be continued to help readers become independent, fluent processors of text.[7]

BASIC NEEDS FOR READING

Reading is a cultural phenomenon that begins early and continues throughout life.[8] Because of this, basic needs exist that influence the quality of reading mastery that will occur. Too often with urban populations, the basic needs are not met to the extent needed to produce strong, efficient readers. A surprising number of children enter school already at risk for failure because of their underpreparedness for the educational process. Children of the inner city are likely to be at-risk learners, given the paucity of their environments, compared with their counterparts in nonurban settings. Poverty, with all of its implications, is a common feature in the inner city. Children born into impoverished homes grow up in danger of compromised development due to low birth weight, malnutrition, recurrent and untreated health problems, physical or psychological stress, and learning environments that do not provide stimulation and language development for learning.[9] Since literacy requires that children have basic, fundamental needs met before learning develops, urban children are likely to be doomed to failure within a literate-based society.

Emerging Literacy

Reading begins with the development of emerging literacy. The home becomes the child's first teacher.[10] Parents and their interaction with their children become the single most influential ingredient in school success and the foundation for emerging literacy.[11] In the home children receive language models that enable them to learn the structure and influence of language that will later be translated into facility with print.

Experiences with hearing oral language and subsequently with language in print establish the foundation for later learning. Preparation for reading requires an environment in which children experience sound language models in order to develop concepts and facility with language. Through verbal interaction with family and neighbors, children learn the use of language as well as its structure. Through language they gain experiences about the world. Literacy is developed as the family reads to children, talks to them, explains concepts to them, and shares the love of reading and respect for books. Too often in inner-city environments, parents are unprepared for the task of developing literate children due both to parental lack of facility with language and to the social/economical demands that control their lives. Inner-city environments often prohibit caregivers from providing for their children the experiences that are required to build the basic knowledge necessary to match "book learning" with children's conceptual frameworks. Children who experience life only with the inner city lack the facility and flexibility to develop concepts outside the boundaries of their limited environment.

Basic Needs

Children who are to become good readers require that their basic needs for food, shelter, health, and safety be provided. Children who come to school hungry, frightened for their physical safety, or insecure because of the effects of dysfunctional families or neighborhoods are unable to concentrate on the act of reading. Not only do children face the daily tasks of learning underprepared in terms of language and concepts, but they share their concentration with thoughts of hunger, fatigue, anxiety, and insecurity. It is difficult for children to face the reading book with undisturbed energy when they are concerned about a family member arrested during the night, a drive-by shooting, a high-starch breakfast, and the lack of sleep they had with four other persons in the bed. Reading requires that children devote their total energies to the act of reading, or reading development suffers.[12]

Background Experiences

Students need background experiences for learning to read. As prepared learners we are able to read about places, people, and things that we have not experienced personally. While many of the reader's experiences involve vicarious interaction with text, there must be a strong relationship between the new and unfamiliar and what is already known. It is critical that readers have at least some exposure to the concepts included in the printed matter, or they are not able to glean appropriate information from the text. Children of the inner cities most often come to school lacking the hands-on experiences that make it possible for them to relate to the vicarious experiences encountered in books. When children are restricted to their neighborhood block or even their apartments because of the dangerous conditions of their environments or live in family structures that lack the economic facility to provide them with out-of-neighborhood experiences, they have little opportunity to sample people, places, and events they might be exposed to in books. If one examines the kinds of books used with children, including the new thrust toward the use of children's literature, one can see the unreality of these materials compared with their experiental background. Although many children in the general population may not have experienced a farm as such, visits to zoos, neighborhood pets, and stories read to them prepare them to transfer learned concepts to new areas of learning. However, if the reader's background does not include zoo trips, pets, or even stories about animals, it is difficult to relate to the smell, feel, and sound of a farm, much less the function and purpose of one. The experiences that most youngsters take for granted (going to the market, attending a movie, driving to the country, and so on) may be as foreign to inner-city children as a trip to Mars.

Appropriate Curriculum

Students need appropriate curriculum for reading development. While good readers wish to explore new and interesting printed materials, they most often choose those materials that at least in part match their own experience so that understanding and application of information come easily. Children in the urban area too often are asked to read materials that have no bearing on their lives and have no relationship to reality as they see it. While young children may be eager to read about new places, people, and things, older students are less inclined to be enthralled with topics that are far removed from their world. Reading materials need to match the interests and needs of the reader. This is not to imply that the curriculum needs to be restricted to the structure of their environment, but certainly it needs to reflect their interests, experiences, and goals. Effort can then be made to provide new experiences and goals so that the curriculum can be expanded as students grow and mature. Curricula must provide for these children both materials that are relevant and immediately applicable to their lives and a sound foundation of justification for learning those that do not. While it may be noble for children to learn about the attributes and contributions of ancient Greek civilization, the nobility of Greek culture loses its impact when the inner-city child is caught up in the immediate basic needs of survival.

Motivation

Children need to be motivated to read. Too often in the inner-city environment, reading does not hold priority in the home and therefore eventually loses its place as a priority in school.[13] Children of the inner city need teachers and materials that will relate to their lives and motivate them to tackle the job of deciphering and understanding print. More than any other group, urban children need to become part of the "literacy club" that will encourage them to use print to enrich their lives.[14] They need to be inspired to use printed materials to gain information, satisfy their daily needs, answer their questions, and provide for them pleasure and satisfaction. Inner-city children need to want to read, need to see reading as an essential ingredient to the quality of their lives, and need to feel the joy and satisfaction reading can provide them. They need to be convinced that reading and learning are the keys to open the doors that lead them out of the poverty and negativism that hold them prisoners in the inner city.

WHAT CAN BE DONE

Reading growth and development are influenced by a myriad of factors. Many of the difficulties in learning to read in the inner-city environment are often beyond the scope and control of the school. The educational system cannot control the home or neighborhood factors that impinge on learning, although attempts have been made to ease the impact of them. Harold Hodgkinson describes our educational system, especially that which services the inner-city populations, as a house with a leaky roof.[15] Repairing the damage to the carpets and walls (the quality of education the school supplies) will be futile if the leak (societal failings, poverty, fear, and so on) is not repaired. Society and economic poverty have inflicted on our inner-city children tremendous deficits in their preparation. With the rise in the number of homeless, drug-exposed, neglected and abused, and dysfunctional families and catastrophic illness and other societal ills, the inner-city child is in danger of being doomed, more than ever, to a life of restricted opportunities and illiteracy.[16] For too many children the family is not the protector, advocate, and moral anchor, and the neighborhoods are places of menace rather than support.[17] It will take the concerted efforts of government, business, and medical and social service facilities, as well as the schools, to overcome the dramatic negative impact of the inner city. While the school plays a significant, though often small, part in the total makeup of the child, the schools can take steps to provide the best possible learning environment for children.

Early Preparation

Early preparation is essential. Because children in the inner city come to school unprepared for the act of reading, readiness for reading must begin very early—long before the traditional public education sequence normally begins. These early intervention programs are essential if we are to prevent the problems that later develop as underprepared children move through the traditional educational system. It has become obvious in recent years that the seeds for school failure and high school dropouts are sown very early and are measurable as early as third grade.[18] Emerging literacy programs can provide inner-city children with a foundation, language, and experience base that will give them additional tools for learning when they begin the formal process so that failure becomes not the norm but the exception. Although the importance of early intervention has long been acclaimed, it has recently been publicly voiced in the *America 2000* plan for education, whose first goal is that "all children in America will start school ready to learn."[19] While Head Start programs were once evident in communities, their numbers have dwindled. The need for such programs now seems more critical. If youngsters are to enter school equipped with the language and experiences for learning that are necessary for success, then facilities for providing such language and experiences must be put in place. Children must be read to, talked to, listened to, conversed with. They must experience the everyday occurrences that are reflected in our reading material and taken for granted by most of the middle-class population. They must be shown how to cut, paste, use crayons, answer questions, shop in a store, cross a street, brush their teeth, and the countless number of things children do that prepare them for learning. Preschool programs must provide not only learning experiences but security and routine for stability, health in the form of vaccinations, nutrition and exercise, and love and respect that build in children a sense of self-worth. Without preschool preparation, our inner-city children will struggle continuously to compete in a system for which they have antiquated tools. It is essential that the public realize that monies and effort spent on remediation pay off less well than prevention programs that allow children to begin school with a chance of success.[20]

Parent Involvement

Parent involvement in the learning-to-read process is critical. Because parents function as children's first and perhaps most influential teacher, it is essential that parents be both prepared for helping their children and motivated to do so. Children spend only 9 percent of their childhood in school, with 91 percent spent in the home/neighborhood setting. Parents cannot be excluded from the learning process, or the school system's efforts are overwhelmingly diluted. Parents create the attitude about reading and school, set the example by reading to their children, using appropriate language structures and vocabulary, referencing books when discussing topics, asking and answering questions, listening, describing, relating the unfamiliar to ideas already understood. To leave parents out of the educational process is like leaving the flour out of the cake. However, with parents who may themselves not be ready for learning, the task of being their children's home "teacher" becomes formidable. Programs must be designed that will make parents part of the school curriculum planning and instructional strategies, motivate them to be involved, and provide them with the knowledge they need to take on the home instructional/preparation tasks with success and confidence. Instruction, support, materials, techniques, and encouragement must be a part of the creation of home environments that foster learning.

The Best Teachers

Inner-city children need the very best of teachers. Often inner-city schools are staffed with teachers who see their responsibility as warden rather than teacher. They assume the role of disciplinarian, modifier of behavior, controller of disruption as opposed to provider of information and inspiration for better futures. Qualified and talented teachers can be recruited to the inner city if they are prepared for the culture shock they will encounter and have a burning desire to change the lives of children whose potential is often buried under layers of poverty, fear, and anger. Universities and school districts must work together to provide programs for potential inner-city teachers that will equip them with an understanding of the behaviors exhibited by inner-city youngsters, hands-on experience with already well-qualified, exceptional master teachers, and the best possible teaching skills. Teachers entering the doors of inner-city schools must be informed, competent, motivated professionals whose interest is in working with the needs of that group of learners.[21]

High Expectations

Expectations for learning must be high. Curricula in many of our nation's schools have been "dumbed down" to accommodate children whose ability to learn and whose language are perceived not to match those of the general population. They are often considered to have inferior skills, and the lowering of standards for acceptable learning has occurred. In fact, for too many of our schools "our current ceiling for students is really much closer to where the floor should be."[22] Some educators are proposing that the failure of the nation's schools is housed not in restricted budgets or poor materials and instructional programs but in the lowered expectations teachers have for students.[23] In particular, inner-city faculties have created school curricula that have been watered down to the point where even the slowest of learners is not satisfied. Inner-city schools seldom fully challenge the potential of the youngsters enrolled there. Time and energy are spent on behavioral control rather than on the advantages of graduating inner-city youngsters with skills that will allow them to enter the mainstream of American economic competition. Inner-city youngsters are often presented with outdated materials, with methods that do not provide the readiness for reading necessary to understand the texts, and with limited application of new skills learned. They are often involved with reading programs that emphasize word attack skills rather than comprehension and critical thinking[24] and are given few independent skills in order to make them self-reliant utilizers of language. Inner-city school staff must create visions of human potential for these children so that common goals and instructional directions are shared by all faculty, parents, and students alike. It is critical that these children be provided with the best possible reading proficiency skills and the highest of expectations so that the immeasurable potential of these children can be unleashed.

Functional Curriculum

Curriculum must be functional and related to needs. While the country discusses the attributes of cultural literacy,[25] it has become apparent that inner-city children need to be prepared for life after school by being exposed to a functional curriculum that prepares them for economic and social success. With the competition for jobs in this country and an unemployment rate in the double digits, it becomes apparent that public schools must prepare students for the realities of work. Seventy-five percent of all those listed on the unemployment rolls lack reading and writing skills that would make them employable in anything but labor-intensive positions.[26] It has been recorded that unemployment leads to increased mortality rates, higher suicide rates, and higher rates of admission to mental hospitals.[27] Recognition of the needs for a fundamental curriculum has been noted in state curriculum proposals that include functional reading skills and work experience as part of the high school curriculum.[28] Curricula that do not prepare the inner-city child with skills for both literacy and job success have failed gravely in accomplishing their mission.

Communication Skills

Communication skills must be developed. In an age where one's ability to communicate through oral and printed language is critical, the basic school program must emphasize this need. It is especially critical with a group of students who have not had the language advantages of most middle-class youngsters. To accommodate this need, the schools must institute a strong integrated language arts program.[29] Traditionally we have taught reading, writing, speaking, listening, and spelling as separate subjects. The result has been a fragmentation of the curriculum and a disjointed use of language skills among children. An integrated language arts program would provide inner-city children with an opportunity to be producers and consumers of language in sensible, meaningful ways. They would develop their skills by reading, writing, speaking, and listening about the same topics. As they read, they would converse with each other, write responses, listen to their peers. The learning day would be built around the interaction and mutual support of those language skills they need to develop to compete with language-rich students. The development of language skills should not concentrate only on basic mechanical reading and writing skills. While basic word attack, grammar, sentence structure skills, and so on are essential, too often the instruction of inner-city children stops there. These students require much practice in utilizing basic skills, but they deserve instruction beyond the basics. They have the need and the right to be instructed in critical thinking and the metacognitive processes (self-regulation and self-awareness) of learning in order to do more than gain surface comprehension of materials. All communication skills must be fully developed to allow them to compete in a world where communication skills will determine success or failure.

Print-Rich Environment

A print-rich environment is necessary. Paucity of printed material not only characterizes the homes of many inner-city youngsters but also describes their schools. Children deprived of books, magazines, junk mail, catalogs, and so on grow up with the concept that reading is neither critical nor very useful to their existence. Without available materials, family and neighborhood members do not model the importance of literacy, and its value is lost early in the developmental years. Since most of these children will not have families with the means to supply them with a plethora of printed material, such environments must be provided. Public libraries, preschool bookshelves, free reading books for families, and story reading sessions at neighborhood locations all need to be abundant and convenient for the inner-city child and family.

Decrease in the drop-out rate is essential. In recent years, drop-out rates have steadily climbed until inner-city areas have as many as 28 percent of their students leaving school before graduation.[30] Although the factors contributing to the drop-out rates are many, failing grades, inability to read, low test scores, inability to identify with school, and the resultant low self-esteem are among the most serious considerations.[31] To overcome the effects at the end of the educational continuum, we need to identify students early in the system and provide for them the remedial (or prevention) help, summer reading programs, special classes, supervised homework labs, and encouragement needed to meet their needs. Business and industry must unite with educational facilities to provide resources and personnel to support at-risk youngsters. Children allowed to fail within the system and then prematurely leave that system are doomed to a life of poverty and hardship. Dropouts find themselves out of the mainstream of economic and social flow. It should be the primary goal of inner-city schools to retain students until they have the skills necessary for being productive, contributing citizens. Without this goal, we will continue to allow our students to step out of the academic life that could mean escape from the inner city and an end to the vicious cycle of economic and cultural poverty that has been perpetuated.

CONCLUSION

In the past, urban populations have, for the most part, received less than the best possible education. Now it becomes apparent that if we are ever to raise the standards and hopes of urban children, we must arm them with reading and language arts skills that will allow them to be active participants in the world. We can no longer afford, either financially or emotionally, to feed them. We must teach them to fish so they can feed themselves. Education, adequate reading skills in particular, is the key to creating for them opportunities to move away from the cycle of poverty and depression that mark the lives of too many children. Without the help of education, these children will continue destructive behavior as adults, thus producing generation after generation of the corrosive effects of long-term poverty.[32] Urban children deserve the right to read, to process printed information that will allow them to become competent, contributing citizens. If we refuse to heed the call, the riots of 1967 and 1992 will continue to remind us of how we have failed our children.

NOTES

1. *America 2000: An Education Strategy* (Washington, DC: U.S. Department of Education) 1991, p. 3.

2. Jeanne Chall, *Stages of Reading Development* (New York: McGraw-Hill) 1983.

3. Steve Cahn, "Restoring the House of Intellect," *American Educator*, 5: 12–13, Fall 1981, pp. 37–38.

4. Y. Goodman and M. Haussler, "Literacy Environment in the Home and Community," *Roles in Literacy Learning: A New Perspective* (Newark, DE: International Reading Association) 1986, pp. 26–32.

5. T. Jacobowitz, "AIM: A Metacognitive Strategy for Constructing the Main Idea of Text," *Journal of Reading*, 36, 1990, pp. 620–24.

6. S. Darling, "Family Literacy Education Replacing the Cycle of Failure with the Legacy of Success," *Kenan Trust Family Literacy Project* (Louisville, KY: Kenan Trust) 1988.

7. Jeanne Chall, *Stages of Reading Development* (New York, NY: Harper and Row) 1984.

8. Richard Anderson, Elfrieda Hiebert, Judity Scott, and Ina Wilkinson, *Becoming a Nation of Readers: A Report of the Commission on Reading* (Washington, DC: National Academy of Education) 1985.

9. Committee on Economic Development, *Children in Need: Investment Strategies for the Educationally Disadvantaged* (Washington, DC: Council on Economic Development) 1987.

10. Dolores Durkin, *Children Who Read Early* (New York: Columbia University Teacher College Press) 1966.

11. *What Works: Research About Teaching and Learning* (Washington, DC: U.S. Department of Education) 1987.

12. Albert Harris and Edward Sipay, *How to Increase Reading Ability* (New York: Longman) 1990.

13. E. Gray, "Identification and Intervention Strategies for Preschool, Kindergarten, First and Second Grade Children at Risk for Reading Difficulties," *Review Literature*, 70, pp. 66–84.

14. Frank Smith, *Insult to Intelligence* (Portsmouth, NH: Heinemann) 1986, pp. 37–39.

15. Harold Hodgkinson, "Reform Versus Reality," *Phi Delta Kappan*, 32, September 1991, pp. 9–16.

16. Committee on Economic Development.

17. *America 2000.*

18. Commission for Students at Risk of School Failure, *Young Children Living in Risky Circumstances: Addressing the Needs of At Risk Students During the Early Learning Year*, 1990.

19. *America 2000*, p. 10.

20. Select Committee on Children, Youth and Families, *Children and Families in Poverty: The Struggle to Survive* (Washington, DC: U.S. Government Printing Office) 1988.

21. A. T. Henderson, "Parents Are a School's Best Friend," *Phi Delta Kappan*, 70, 1988, pp. 148–53.

22. Jane Stallings and Linda Quinn, "Learning How to Teach in the Inner City," *Educational Leadership*, 49, November 1991, pp. 25–27.

23. Asa Hilliard, "Do We Have the Will to Educate All Children?", *Educational Leadership*, 49, September 1991, pp. 31–36.

24. Daniel Singal, "The Other Crisis in Our Schools," *Atlantic*, November 1991, pp. 14–24.

25. *What Works*.

26. E. D. Hirsch, *Cultural Literacy: What Every American Needs to Know* (Boston: Houghton Mifflin) 1987.

27. Raymond Nickerson, *Adult Literacy and Technology* (Champaign, IL: Center for the Study of Reading) 1985.

28. W. Rumberger Russell, "High School Dropouts: A Review of Issues and Evidence," *Review of Educational Research*, 57, 1987, p. 113.

29. California High School Task Force, *Second to None* (Sacramento: California Department of Education) 1992.

30. Kenneth Goodman, "Whole Language Research: Foundations and Development," *What Research Has to Say About Reading Instruction* (Newark, DE: International Reading Association) 1992, pp. 46–49.

31. National Center for Educational Statistics, *Digest of Education Statistics* (Washington, DC: U.S. Department of Education) 1990, Table 393.

32. N. L. Gage, "Dealing with the Dropout Problem," *Phi Delta Kappan*, 72, December 1990, pp. 280–85.

BIBLIOGRAPHY

Applebee, Arthur, Judity Langer, and Ina Mullis. *Who Reads Best?* (Princeton, NJ: Educational Testing Service, 1988).

Brophy, Jere. "Successful Reading Strategies for the Inner-City Child." In Ryan and Cooper Kaleidoscope, *Readings in Education* (Princeton, NJ: Houghton Mifflin, 1988), pp. 296–302.

Brunner, J. "The Role of Dialogue in Language Acquisition." In Jarvella Sinclair and Henry LeVelt (eds.), *The Child's Conception of Language* (Berlin: Springer-Verlag, 1978), pp. 241–56.

Carta, J. J. "Education for Young Children in Inner-City Classrooms." *American Behavioral Scientists*, 34, 1990, pp. 440–53.

Cuban, Larry. "The At-Risk Label and the Problem of Urban School Reform." *Phi Delta Kappan*, June 1989, pp. 780–801.

Eitzen, D. Stanley. "Problem Students: The Sociocultural Roots." *Phi Delta Kappan*, April 1992, pp. 584–90.

Grant, Carl. "Urban Teachers: Their New Colleagues and Curriculum." *Phi Delta Kappan*, June 1989, pp. 764–70.

Hodgkinson, Harold. *All One System: Demographics of Education from Kindergarten Through Graduate School*. (Washington, DC: Institute for Educational Leadership, 1985).

House Select Committee on Children, Youth, and Families. *Current Conditions and Recent Trends* (Washington, DC: U.S. Government Printing Office, 1989).

An Imperiled Generation: Saving Urban Schools (Princeton, NJ: Carnegie Foundation for the Advancement of Teaching, 1988).

Kirsch, Irwin, and Ann Jungeblut. *Literacy: Profiles of America's Young Adults* (Princeton, NJ: National Assessment of Educational Progress, 1989).

Leinhardt, Gaea. "What Research on Learning Tells Us About Teaching." *Educational Leadership*, 49:7, April 1992.

Monahan, Joy, and Bess Hinson. *New Directions in Reading Instruction* (Newark, DE: International Reading Association, 1988).

Roscow, La Vergne. "How Schools Perpetuate Illiteracy." *Educational Leadership*, 49, September 1991, pp. 41–44.

Samuels, S. Jay, and Alan Farstrup. *What Research Has to Say About Reading Instruction* (Newark, DE: International Reading Association, 1992).

Schorr, Lisbeth. *Within Our Reach: Breaking the Cycle of Disadvantage* (New York: Doubleday, 1988).

U.S. Department of Education. *Schools That Work: Educating Disadvantaged Children* (Washington, DC: U.S. Government Printing Office, 1978).

Walberg, Herbert, Michael Bakalis, Joseph Best, and Steven Baer. "Restructuring the Nation's Worst Schools." *Phi Delta Kappan*, 16, June 1989, pp. 802–5.

24

Involving Minorities in Urban Education

Paul W. Kane and Helen Parcell Taylor

THE BACKGROUND

Underrepresentation of minority individuals in the teaching profession has been identified as a major problem in teacher education in the United States today (Kennedy, 1991). While the percentage of minority students in the nation's public schools is on the rise, the percentage of minority teachers is decreasing. In fact, it is expected to drop to less than 5 percent by the year 2000 (Weiss, 1986). It is predicted that if current demographic trends continue, this teaching force of 5 percent nonwhite teachers will be teaching a national population of students who are one-third nonwhite (Hawley, 1989).

This disparity between the number of minority teachers and minority students already exists in California. During the 1988–1989 school year, the number of minority students in the state's public schools surpassed 50 percent (Kennedy, 1991). The trend is even more noticeable in the public school districts in the immediate vicinity of California State University, Fullerton (CSUF). During October 1991, three public school districts within the university's service area were surveyed. Information was gathered regarding the minority status of the teachers currently employed in these districts and the makeup of the student population. Of the nearly 2,500 teachers working within these three school districts, only 14 percent were minorities. The minority pupil population in two of the districts surveyed exceeded 50 percent while minority students made up 93 percent of the student population in the third district. This particular district projected a need to hire 1,740 new minority teachers within the next decade. Compounding the potential problems presented by such a concentrated minority population was the finding that over 62 percent of the students were of limited English proficiency. At the same time, within the entire state of California, only 8,000 teachers hold bilingual credentials or certificates, far short of the 20,000 needed in the state to meet the educational needs of the student population.

Another researcher has made similar predictions. She too has noted that as the number of minority students continues to grow throughout the nation, the number of minority teachers is decreasing. She predicts that by the year 2020, 39 percent of the school-age population nationwide will be minority and that the percentage of minority teachers during that same time span will drop from 12 percent to 7 percent of the total (Irvine, 1989).

Yet the current enrollments of both African-American and Hispanic under-graduates in institutions of higher education indicate that the above trends will not be easily altered if teacher training institutions continue with business as usual. With African-American college enrollment decreasing 8 percent and His-panic enrollment dropping 10 percent during the years 1976–1985, some steps must be taken to attract minority students not only into universities but also into teacher education programs (Yopp, Yopp, and Taylor, 1991).

Recent literature dealing with teacher preparation has emphasized collaborative and partnership models of training between universities and public school districts (Goodlad, 1990). In such programs, university faculty test whether their theories hold up against the realities of teaching; public school teachers learn new teaching techniques; and student teachers train in schools that are really models of good teaching. The close working relationships that exist in such collaborative models between faculties in the public schools and the university help to assure that teacher training becomes a partnership among peers, each contributing in unique ways to improve the training of the novice teacher. The Holmes Group, a consortium of nearly 100 American research institutions, holds that the bond between the university and public school will ensure that "teachers, adminis-trators, teacher educators, and administrative educators should work together to make fine schools for children that will also be realistic, challenging, and sup-portive settings for the field studies of prospective teachers and for the rising professionalism of practicing teachers" (Holmes, 1990).

What follows is a description of a series of collaborative efforts between a large, public university, California State University, and the major urban school district within the university's service area. The steps taken by California State University, Fullerton, and the Santa Ana Unified School District (SAUSD) to bring about this educational partnership illustrate how each segment can con-tribute its strengths and thus assist the other as each pursues its educational objectives in joint collaboration.

THE LEARNING CENTER

The Department of Secondary Education at CSUF has developed over the last twenty years a program that is heavily field-based and operated in conjunction with neighboring public school districts. The secondary education faculty believe that the best method of delivering teacher education is through a collaborative partnership with school districts, such as that recommended by the Holmes Group and John Goodlad (Holmes Group, 1990; Goodlad, 1990). In order to achieve these ends, the program uses a "Learning Center" concept. Districts selected to participate in the credential preparation program are designated as Learning Centers.

The Learning Center is supported by a faculty team from the Secondary Education Cooperative Teacher Education Program (SEC TEP), made up of the Learning Center resident instructor (district staff member), university field coordinator (preservice course work professor), methods professors (art, business education, english and foreign languages, social science, mathematics, music, physical education, and science), and university supervisors. Methods courses and university supervision are delivered by the various university departments. The team is under the direction of a coordinator of secondary education. Each team is responsible for covering all areas of instruction and supervision that are normal parts of the credential experiences for teacher candidates. The resident instructor, who is a district staff member, represents the Learning Center district in the program, acts as liaison person between the district and the university, assists in student placement in the district, and plans and participates in on-site seminars for students. The university field coordinator, a full-time faculty member from the Department of Secondary Education, is assigned to the Learning Center for one-half to three-fourths of the faculty's teaching load.

Through joint planning between the university faculty member and the resident instructor, students are assigned to appropriate master teachers and school sites and provided with an extensive review of the operations of the district. District teachers also act as members of the screening committees of the university that review credential candidate qualifications and deny or grant admittance to the credential program. The district also provides the necessary space to instruct and train the potential teachers. Most importantly, the district provides specialists from among its personnel to instruct on specific topics. For example, the person involved in gang control presents a workshop on the subject. Other specialists cover such topics as classroom management, various learning/teaching styles, legal issues, and motivational techniques. The joint planning and presentations by university and district personnel ensure that the objectives of the credential program are timely, current, applicable, and of special interest to the teacher candidates in this preparatory stage of their careers.

Thus local districts have a long and successful history of close collaboration with the university in the training of teachers. This fact has allowed each segment to be responsive to the needs of the other and has increased the flexibility of each unit to modify its programs when necessary. Support from top administrators, dean, and superintendent ensures that needed resources are available for program continuance and improvement. Finally, the nearly twenty years of this cooperative venture in teacher preparation have increased the level of communication between the members of each segment so that lengthy preliminaries, which are often needed when new ideas or ventures are to be considered, are not necessary because of the high level of trust and partnership that already exists between the university faculty and district personnel. This trust and communication allow each unit to respond very quickly to emerging events important to each.

CHANGING DEMOGRAPHICS

Orange County, California, where CSUF is located, is undergoing a rapid change in student demographics similar to what is occurring in many areas of the United States. At present, nearly 50 percent of the county's public school students are minorities. Yet 91 percent of the county's teachers are of European-American background. We are witnessing an important turnabout whereby the minority is, in fact, the majority in many areas. The implications of this change for public education and the preparation of the teaching force carry significant ramifications for the entire educational establishment (Pinar, 1989). Recognition of the changes is only a first step in bringing about the necessary alterations that can allow students to receive the best education that is possible.

The SAUSD is the most urban district within the county. With an enrollment over 47,000, it is the eighth largest district in the state. The district is composed of twenty-seven elementary schools (grades K–five), seven intermediate schools (grades six–eight), four high schools (grades nine–twelve), one independent study campus, and one continuation high school. The present student population makeup is as follows: 7 percent white, 85 percent Hispanic, 7 percent Asian, and 2 percent African-American. Among these students, 62 percent are of limited English proficiency. Santa Ana, as well as almost every other school district, is faced with a major problem—where can teachers with similar characteristics to the student population be found? For example, less than 9 percent of the current students in the CSUF credential program are minorities.

RECRUITING MINORITY TEACHERS

A critical problem facing schools of education across the nation is how to increase the pool of minority applicants for admission to teacher education programs. Continuation of current trends will only exacerbate the problem by increasing the number of nonminority credential candidates while the number of minority public school students skyrockets.

The close collaboration developed over nearly two decades between CSUF and SAUSD allowed each agency to define the problem quickly, develop plans to meet the challenge, and engage the resources of both agencies to implement new programs. This close collaboration between university and large urban school district provides a model for university-district partnership that can be replicated elsewhere. Examples that follow illustrate the advantages that are possible from such close cooperation.

Of the approximately 500 credential candidates that CSUF trains each year, only 9 percent are minorities. At the same time, neighboring school districts are expanding their minority student population at a very rapid rate. How could the pool of potential minority teacher candidates be increased? Joint discussions between CSUF and SAUSD centered on several possibilities.

As is the case in many school districts throughout the United States, great numbers of English-speaking teachers rely mainly on bilingual teaching aides to assist in their heavily minority classrooms. These aides often have extensive classroom experience, want to work with students, and have language skills needed by English-limited students. Yet most of these aides are not college graduates and thus not eligible for teaching credentials. Given this scenario, CSUF initiated a program to assist those aides interested in becoming credentialed teachers. Efforts were made actively to recruit bilingual aides into the credential programs. The university provided individual counseling to meet the unique needs of each aide. Some were directed to the community colleges to begin their academic training. Those eligible were encouraged to apply to CSUF. Intensive academic counseling, as well as financial aid counseling, was provided. Stipends were made available to assist with tuition and book costs. Currently sixty-six instructional aides are involved with the project. The group is 79 percent Hispanic, 13 percent white, 3 percent African-American, 3 percent Asian, and 1 percent Hawaiian. Eighty-five percent of the aides are bilingual. Since this program is only in its second year, no aides have reached the credential stage of the program. However, 7 percent of the aides are currently enrolled in a university, while 93 percent are attending community colleges. It is anticipated that students will begin to enter the teacher credential program within two years.

A parallel effort to attract minority students into the secondary credential program is also being conducted by CSUF in the SAUSD. This effort, called the Teacher Track program, targets minority high school juniors and seniors who are CSU-eligible for recruitment efforts.

The Teacher Track program is coordinated by the university secondary teacher track coordinator, who is a member of the secondary education faculty and is responsible for the day-to-day management and delivery of the program to the district; maintaining program communications between the district and the university; developing and supplying materials for academic preparation and career and academic advising to high school project advisers and students; delivering in-service training to high school project advisers; securing and scheduling monthly teacher education speakers/activities for the district; appointing high school project advisors to lecturer status and enrolling students in the university for college credit; arranging a field trip to campus each semester; and coordinating the evaluation of the program's activities and accomplishments.

The district and the university cooperatively select a project adviser for each high school. The project adviser at each high school is trained and coordinated by the secondary education coordinator of the Teacher Track. The project adviser is the site coordinator for the Teacher Track at each individual high school. The adviser has the major responsibility for recruiting students interested in teaching and supervising all Teacher Track activities that take place at the school or that involve Teacher Track students from that particular school. Advisers are the principal support and resource for Teacher Track students. The advisers provide the channel through which the Teacher Track can deliver services to participants. The Teacher Track advisers are teachers, counselors, and/or administrators within the SAUSD. They are responsible for identifying and enrolling students who participate in the Teacher Track; delivering academic preparation to enrolled students at the local high school; assisting students with career and academic advising for entrance into the teaching profession, scheduling and coordinating the field component of the program; and coordinating monthly district presentations delivered by the university. The Department of Secondary Education appoints project advisers at the rank of lecturer and pays them for their teaching and advising.

Each student attends a weekly class taught by the project adviser. In these classes, students learn about educational pedagogy and learning concepts. Once each month the class is taught by a university education professor. Class activities include maintaining a journal, viewing videotapes of model instruction, readings, and discussions. Students are also provided with help with their own study skills. In addition, each student enrolls in a college-level class—The Teaching Experience: Exploration. Tuition fees for the university class have been waived by the CSUF president. Finally, the students are required to tutor elementary, junior high, and senior high students for a total of forty hours during the semester. A highlight of the program is a field trip to CSUF, where students attend workshops, visit university classes, and have the opportunity to speak one-on-one with students currently enrolled in the secondary credential program. To date, more than 250 students have participated in the Teacher Track program. In addition, the advisers coordinate and supervise all Teacher Track activities at the school site. Again, since this program is only in its second year, no students have reached the CSUF teacher training program at this time. Yet, follow-up studies indicate that 100 percent of the students who have completed the program are interested in teaching as a career, and nearly 50 percent of them credit participation in the Teacher Track program as being the key reason why teaching is now their career objective.

Each of these joint university-public school efforts is designed to increase the number of minority teachers and to provide credentialed teachers in numbers that more closely reflect the demographic profile of the public school districts that surround CSUF. This need for more minority teachers in the public schools is great both locally and nationally. All students need contact with minority teachers to help prepare them to live and work in an increasingly multicultural, multiethnic society. Minority teachers can serve as role models of successful, contributing members of society for minority students and reflect the growing diversity among professionals and authority figures throughout society (Alston 1988). Children's attitudes toward school, their academic accomplishments, and their views of their own and other's worth are influenced by their contact with teachers who represent power and authority in America (Task Force on Teaching as A Profession, 1986). Integrated teaching staffs also give all students the opportunity to witness cooperative interaction between nonwhite and white teachers of equal status.[13] At least one researcher points out that the increasing alienation and school failure of minorities are related to the decline in the number of public school minority teachers who "bring to the classroom unique, culturally-based pedagogical approaches that are often compatible with the learning needs of their minority students" (Irvine 1989). A quality education requires that all students be exposed to the variety of cultural perspectives present in the nation at large. Such exposure can be accomplished by a multiethnic teaching force in which racial and ethnic groups are included at a level of parity with their numbers in the population. In our pluralistic society, it is beneficial for both minority and majority children to have contact with minority teachers.

FINANCIAL SUPPORT OF STUDENTS

Close collaboration between university and public school district permits other exciting and mutually rewarding activities to occur. Preliminary surveys of potential minority teacher education candidates mentioned financial concerns as the most serious roadblock to pursuing a teaching credential. Recognition of this need brought about joint planning between the university and the neighboring school districts to apply for, and receive, a state-approved internship credential program. This program allows teacher candidates to be hired by districts as interns and be paid while they complete the state requirements for the credential. Through this joint program the school districts will be able to hire candidates with qualifications that fit the district's needs, and the university will be able to attract students (most often minorities) into its credential programs.

A CSUF/Santa Ana Internship Advisory Board was organized, made up of CSUF staff, district personnel, principals, teachers, and bargaining agents. The advisory board participated actively in the design and development of the internship program's philosophical orientation, educational goals, and content emphases. Since the implementation of the internship program, the board has met faithfully each semester to review the program and its graduates and make suggestions for improvements.

Application for financial support through state, federal, and private grants has also been stimulated through the collaborative efforts of the school districts and the university. Each segment is able to use the expertise of the other when applications are made. More importantly, the past history of close cooperation permits the rapid response to possible funding ideas and the quick writing of the grant proposals themselves. The Teacher Track program is such an example. Funds were obtained that benefited the district and the university. This program has been so successful that the Department of Secondary Education will continue the program even when funding ends.

JOINT GRANT APPLICATION

Another example of cooperation is the grant proposal CIMATE (Ciencia, Maematica, Tecologia), designed to increase the number of underrepresented ethnic minority students entering secondary teaching in the fields of science, mathematics, and technology. At present, less than 1 percent of the minority candidates recommended for secondary credentials by CSUF are in these subject areas. Yet these are precisely the academic areas where districts have the greatest need. The intent of the grant, therefore, is to identify high school students currently in the SAUSD who have aptitude in these subject areas and to provide them with experiences similar to those presently available in the Teacher Track. Special emphasis will be on tutoring these students in areas needed and mentoring them with science and mathematics faculty from the university. The goal of the program is to attract and eventually train eighty high school minority students per year from the SAUSD for possible employment as credentialed teachers in science, mathematics, and technology within the district. Again, the needs of the SAUSD and the university stimulated each to search for ways to solve and finance their educational needs. Similar relationships also have begun to emerge in other districts as the level of cooperation spreads. Currently another local school district has approached the Department of Secondary Education to apply jointly for federal dollars to meet the needs of the growing number of minority students in that district. Joint university and district planning, writing of the grant, and, if funded, implementation illustrate again the advantages of close association between the two educational segments.

PUBLIC SCHOOL TEACHERS AS UNIVERSITY INSTRUCTORS

Another benefit of close collaboration has emerged and has been especially helpful to the academic departments of the university. From time to time there is a need to hire part-time instructors to meet student demands for additional classes or to complete the teaching loads of faculty on leave. Since the department already hires local district personnel as resident instructors in its credential program, the precedent for employing teachers from cooperating districts has a long history. Close working relationships, as earlier described, ensure that university administrators know the skills of participating teachers while at the same time these teachers are familiar with the instructional needs of the university. Thus district personnel are hired as resident instructors and Teacher Track advisers. In addition, an English-as-Second-Language specialist from the SAUSD is a lecturer in the department teaching the multicultural class that is a requirement for all secondary credential candidates. Also two other public school faculty teach our mandated introductory course on explorations of teaching as a career. The close working relationships between the university and the districts allow these opportunities to exist for qualified public school personnel. Everyone comes out a winner. University students study with practitioners who are very familiar with our program and who are able to combine pedagogical theory with everyday classroom practice. Also the university has instructors who can bring immediacy to the curriculum. The teachers benefit because of the study and research needed to prepare for teaching the class. The interaction is two-way. The public school classrooms become on-site laboratories where university professors can hone their instructional skills while teaching in the district's classrooms.

PROFESSIONAL DEVELOPMENT SCHOOLS

The level of collaboration between CSUF and SAUSD has led to the formation of a professional development school, as suggested in the Holmes report. This group concluded in its very influential report that collaboration between public schools and institutions of higher learning is a must if teacher education programs are to improve, become more rigorous, and be connected "to liberal arts education, to research on learning and teaching, and to wise practice in the schools" (Holmes, 1990). The Holmes group envisioned professional development schools as centers of inquiry on topics related to the problems of teaching. This sentiment is also strongly supported by statements made by the Association of Teacher Education in its report *Distinguished Company*. This report called for shared leadership, shared reflection, and shared planning between universities and the public school systems. (Association of Teacher Educators, 1991).

Regardless of the many benefits, this increased level of collaboration does not come easily. S. Chira has pointed out that potential problems present in the collaborative process must be anticipated, planned for, and overcome if the procedure is to succeed. The bureaucracies at all levels must approve the changes. Principals and teachers at the local school sites must be committed. Universities must support the faculty, who spend more time in the public schools during the retention-tenure process, which usually rewards publications but not active involvement in the public schools. Finally, funding to support the changes must be provided (Chira, 1990). Anticipating the possible obstacles that may need to be overcome focuses the attention of the participants on the means to advance their cause while at the same time minimizing difficulties.

From this expanded base, the Professional Development School (PDS) was established in Santa Ana. A survey of needs, close and constant discussion, and intensive planning have begun to bring about results. One junior high school has been targeted to receive increased in-service training for its teachers. University faculty are conducting seminars on the junior high campus. Precredential candidates are being assigned to the school. Mentor teachers are acting as master teachers to the credential candidates. Grant proposals are being developed jointly by all the participants in the PDS.

It is anticipated that this is only the beginning of the possibilities that may emerge from collaboration. Health needs of students and parents may be targeted by the Department of Nursing at CSUF. Other CSUF academic units may wish to focus on other special needs within the SAUSD. For example, the requirements of special students might be addressed by the Department of Special Education, while the Department of Health Education, Physical Education and Recreation might investigate ways that students might be helped by their departments' areas of academic specialties. The possibilities continue to become apparent. Counseling needs of the district population might concern the faculties in the Departments of Counseling and Human Services. Once thought is given to the linkages between a public school district and a local university, the possibilities are endless. Moreover, the increased participation in the local communities seems to generate an increased interest and excitement among the personnel involved in carrying out the various components of the concept.

The impetus for the establishment of the PDS came from the superintendent of the SAUSD and the dean of the school responsible for the credentialing of teacher candidates. Each person built upon the already close working relationship that existed between the two segments and agreed the PDS would be used to meet the needs of each unit. Stress was placed on a collaboration that would use the experts of the district and the postsecondary institution to develop teachers who are prepared to teach in districts such as the SAUSD and to offer continuing in-service training to currently employed credentialed teachers. With these goals, the PDS is currently developing projects designed to aid in the learning of public school students, student teachers, and school and university faculty.

It soon became apparent to those involved in planning that other members of the educational community must be included to enhance the goals of the various components of the educational community. Since many of the public school students attended the local community college, Rancho Santiago, prior to enrolling in four-year institutions, Rancho Santiago must be involved. Also the nearby campus of the University of California, Irvine, not only sent student teachers to the SAUSD but also was very active in grants and in-service training with the district. Thus it became apparent that close collaboration soon leads to increased partnerships once the pattern of cooperation is explored, accepted, and implemented.

PROJECT STEP

STEP is a broad-based academic collaboration joining the Santa Ana public school district with three local colleges and universities (Rancho Santiago College, California State University, Fullerton, and University of California, Irvine) for the improvement of the academic preparation of minority youth for success in higher education.

The major goals and activities of Project STEP are to address the needs of all students for literacy and critical thought in the areas of mathematics, science, and language arts through enrichment of the district curriculum and staff development programs; to foster greater student commitment to preparation for college admissions with the assistance of a comprehensive guidance curriculum and academic support programs; and to disseminate the lessons learned from the partnership model. The infrastructure created by the STEP Administrative Council commits the top leadership of each educational segment to work together to address common concerns shared by the educational community and brings educational reform directly into the classroom. School/college faculty teams work together to strengthen the curriculum, counselors teach lessons in the classroom from the guidance curriculum developed by an intersegmental task force, and parents are involved with school and university faculty in an elementary school evening workshop called Family Math. What has become increasingly clear is the appropriateness of the role of postsecondary institutions in providing a variety of resources and joining with the K–twelve sector to alleviate the serious segmental isolation that exists regarding common academic preparation concerns.

Project STEP represents a significant effort to reconstruct the relationships among the various units of education to promote improved academic preparation for all students and provide the nation with a working collaborative model. The project was first launched with the SAUSD in 1983, when it was estimated that only 10 percent of the district seniors were pursuing postsecondary education. In response to annual surveys since 1987, 65 percent of the seniors now report that they are attending college. Data from the registrars of the STEP postsecondary partner institutions indicate that over 40 percent of the SAUSD seniors enroll at one of these three campuses.

What really makes Project STEP unique is the level of interinstitutional cooperation among the school district, community college, and universities involved and the universal commitment to action by the project leaders. They work together to promote academic excellence and equity through joint activities in curriculum enhancement, professional development, and student academic support and guidance. Each partner institution takes leadership responsibility for one or more of the STEP task forces, which are programs designed to form an integrated matrix of support for students, faculty, parents, counselors, and administrators. The secondary education field coordinator of the Santa Ana Learning Center heads the STEP Task Force on Professional Development Center/ Schools, and the secondary education mathematics methods professor/university supervisor heads the Task Force on Mathematics.

Project STEP currently receives external funding support from the Carnegie Corporation of New York and the Fund for the Improvement of Postsecondary Education (FIPSE) and significant support from all of the participating institutions.

PROJECT SAFEMAP

SAFEMAP (the Santa Ana Unified School District and California State University, Fullerton), headed by the CSUF secondary education methods professor/ university supervisor of mathematics student teachers, is a three-year project focusing on the mathematics instruction received by students in grades K–five.

This project places special emphasis on minority students, specifically Latino students, in the SAUSD. The project is funded by the National Science Foundation ($408,500) with California State University, Fullerton, as the contractual institution (Pagni, 1989).

One of the goals of SAFEMAP is to train a cadre of teachers to become leaders in mathematics education in the district. The four components of the SAFEMAP experience for teachers are mathematics content; mathematics methodology, such as problem solving and some learning styles such as cooperative group learning; family math; and the use of technology such as computers and calculators. To date 220 teachers have participated in the SAFEMAP project. Teachers have met on weekends once a month for two years. SAFEMAP instructors are provided with a substitute one day each month to plan the upcoming session. Each participant is given a copy of the text and receives a stipend of $2,000 ($500 per semester) and twelve units of university credit at reduced cost, which can be used to renew their credentials or for district salary credit (no cost) to move up on the salary scale (Andrini & Pagni, 1992).

SAFEMAP won the California State School Board's Gold Bell Award for a district wide program. It has evolved into a successful model to be disseminated to other districts, counties, and states.

MATHEMATICS DIAGNOSTIC TESTING PROJECT

The Mathematics Diagnostic Testing Project (MDTP) was formed as a joint project of the California State University and the University of California in 1977. Its mission included the determination of mathematics competency areas necessary for success in calculus, the development of diagnostic tests for those competency areas, and the establishment of a communication network with California high schools to provide information to them about their students' mathematical preparedness for college mathematics and science courses. Accomplishments have included development, implementation, and scoring of diagnostic testing determining calculus, precalculus, intermediate algebra, and elementary algebra readiness. The California State University, Fullerton, mathematics department, headed by professors who teach the secondary education mathematics methods courses and supervise the secondary mathematics student teachers, provide MDTP services to the Santa Ana Unified School District. In addition to providing tests and scoring services to Santa Ana schools, they provided some consulting services to teachers and offered a means of communicating curricular and pedagogical ideas. All of these activities facilitate interaction between secondary and postsecondary mathematics instructors.

DWIGHT D. EISENHOWER MATHEMATICS GRANT

The Dwight D. Eisenhower Mathematics Grant, headed by two SEC TEP mathematics methods professors/university supervisors, seeks to eliminate tracking and to increase the number of high school students successfully completing a college preparatory mathematics program through a system change in grades four–twelve in the content covered, in the delivery of that content, and in the assessment methods. The target groups are all teachers of grades four–twelve in the Santa Ana Unified School District and all students in the Santa Ana Unified School District. It attempts to eliminate certain mathematics courses that have traditionally been a "dead-end" track and to increase the number of high school students successfully completing a college preparatory mathematics program.

Participating teachers take four university mathematics courses, which are taught in a way that models the 1991 California Mathematics Framework and the National Council of Teachers of Mathematics Curriculum and Evaluation Standards and designed to meet the needs of teachers that teach large numbers of culturally diverse students. District administrators complete a full-semester course that covers a sample of the content and methodology taught to the participants over a two-year period of the project. Each course is taught by a team of instructors composed of one university mathematician and two kindergarten–twelve instructors.

At the end of the project, a large number of teachers will have participated in this extensive program of professional development, which will enable them to provide leadership in producing a systemic change in the content covered, in the delivery of that content, and in assessment methods in mathematics. Also an example for the reorganization, delivery, and assessment of the mathematics content taught at the university level will have been established (Pagni, Shultz, & Golan, 1992).

CENTER FOR THE COLLABORATION FOR CHILDREN

The spirit of cooperation and joint activity between multiple agencies suggests ever new areas that may be considered and new relationships that can be fostered. Other local districts have seen the PDS in operation and now wish to establish a similar operation in their districts. At present, two neighboring districts have begun preliminary discussions with the intention of eventually setting up a PDS in their service areas. Furthermore, the relationship with school districts and the university is now expanding beyond the school district boundaries. Segments of local communities are being brought together to address common concerns and ways that the university-community partnership can address these needs. One such unit has been developed, has received outside funding, and is currently engaged in activities that at present seem without limit. The Center for the Collaboration for Children (CCC) has been established at CSUF. The center's goals are to use the disciplines of the university to help children and families in a collaborative way that will bring the resources of the university and the multitude of social agencies to bear on the problems facing children in our society. Workshops have been held for social service and health care agencies. Other institutions of higher education have agreed to participate in the center. The goal of an interdisciplinary and interagency approach to all things related to children and families is nearing fruition.

STAFF DEVELOPMENT

A professor of multicultural education at CSUF is involved in yet another example of collaboration. She is currently doing staff development work with faculty clusters of secondary, junior high school, and elementary teachers in the SAUSD. Information has been presented on "Developing Academic English Across the Curriculum" and "Meeting the Needs of a Changing Student Population." The issues of culture and of language proficiency have particular implications for teaching a diverse student population, particularly groups of Asian and Hispanic students. Following the sessions, teachers meet in small groups to discuss how the strategies presented can be implemented in their classes. The district selects the discussion leaders for these groups.

In addition, teachers from another large Los Angeles basin high school, who have already been trained by the multicultural professor, have presented sample lessons in their subject areas to the SAUSD teachers. To date, between 600 and 700 faculty members have been trained.

CONCLUSION

School, community, and university collaboration does work. It requires time, effort, funds, and commitment from all participants. Communication must be open, frank, and honest at all times. The needs of each segment must be stated early, and common objectives must be agreed upon. Resources must be forthcoming to meet the common commitments. But the results of such collaboration can be greatly rewarding. Each group brings its expertise to the meeting table. The discussion of ideas enlarges the perspective of all participants and creates an energy that encourages new and unique approaches to problems that emerge. Such collaboration can often be slow, sometimes frustrating, but the end result can lead to a revitalized group of participants eager to get on with the tasks at hand.

BIBLIOGRAPHY

Alston, D. (1988). *Recent Minority Classroom Teachers: A National Challenge*. Washington, DC: National Governor's Association.
Andrini, Beth, and Pagni, David. (1992). *SAFEMAP Brings Confidence, Joy, and Understanding to Elementary Mathematics Teachers*. Unpublished manuscript.
Association of Teacher Educators. (1991). *Distinguished Company*. Reston, VA: NAASP.
Chira, S. (1990). "Teacher Education: Realities of Present and Dreams of Future," the *New York Times*, August 29.
Goodlad, J. (1990). "Better Teachers for Our Nation's Schools." *Phi Delta Kappan*, 72, pp. 32–36.

Hawley, W. (1989). "The Importance of Minority Teachers to the Racial and Ethnic Integration of American Society." *Equity and Choice*, 5, 76–81.

Holmes Group. (1990). *Tomorrow's Schools: Principles for the Design of Professional Development Schools*. East Lansing, MI: Holmes Group.

Irvine, J. (1989). "Beyond Role Models: An Examination of Cultural Influences on the Pedagogical Perspectives of Black Teachers." *Peabody Journal of Education*, 4 Summer, pp. 243–275.

Kennedy, M. (1991). "Policy Issues in Teacher Education," *Phi Delta Kappan*, 72, pp. 43–50.

1988–89 Annual MDTP Report. A joint project of the California State University and the University of California and a project of the California Academic Partnership Program, pp. 1–12.

Pagni, David L. (1989). "Project SAFEMAP: An Innovative Approach to Assist Minorities in Mathematics." *Journal of Educational Issues of Language Minority Students*, 4 Spring, pp. 85–89.

Pagni, David, Shultz, Harris, and Golan, Ana. (1992). *California State University, Fullerton and Santa Ana Unified School District Mathematics Proposal*. Fullerton, CA.

Pinar, W. (1989). "A Reconceptualization of Teacher Education." *Journal of Teacher Education*, 72 January/February, pp. 86–94.

The Student Teacher Educational Partnership Project (STEP). (1990). *To Advance Learning: A Handbook on Developing K–12/Postsecondary Partnerships*. Irvine: University of California.

Task Force on Teaching as a Profession. (1986). *A Nation Prepared: Teachers for the 21st Century*. Washington, DC: Carnegie Forum on Education and the Economy.

Weiss, S. (1986). "Where Have All Our Minority Teachers Gone?" *NEA Today*, 5, pp. 1–5.

Yopp, H., Yopp, R., and Taylor, H. (1991). "The Teacher Track Project: Increasing Teacher Diversity." *Action in Teacher Education*, 2, pp. 32–39.

25

The Principal in Urban Schools

Walter F. Beckman

Principals are key factors in successful urban schools, and the degree to which they meet the current and future challenges determines the degree to which these schools can be effective. There are no simple solutions to complex school problems and the countless demands on the urban principal. In fact, the problems and the demands facing the school may be so staggering that the principal's need for imagination, innovation, and initiative may be more than at any other time in the recent past. Mandates for improved school quality and broader services are forcing the need for a new principalship.

Certainly no single chapter can contain all the necessary answers for the instant success of urban principals. This chapter is intended to take a rapid look at what the principal faces within the urban school, what his or her role is, the necessary tools of the position, a quick look at administrator preparation, and what needs to be done to achieve success.

URBAN SCHOOLS

What can we say about urban schools today? Where are they in their development, and where are they going? It is difficult to answer these kinds of questions. It is easier to say where they are not and where they do not seem to be going. They do not appear to be teaching the immigrant and urban poor children of America what they need to know to escape their poverty, and they do not seem to be institutions of equity and social justice. Urban schools have a record of failure that stretches back more than 100 years. They have never provided their students with the personalized education they so desperately needed. They have never used multicultural or multilinguistic approaches with much success.

Most people agree that urban schools are too big and too impersonal. Their curriculum is riddled with linguistic and cultural biases; their teaching methods are archaic by any standards. The funding base of urban schools is woefully inadequate when compared with that of middle- and upper-middle-class suburban schools. Classrooms are usually characterized by the continuously talking teacher and silent, uninvolved children. The idea of stuffing children full of facts persists, even though the research indicates that such "facts" are obsolete before students can get through the system. (Rothstein)

Many teachers are increasingly demoralized and frustrated. In many cases they are ill equipped to work with divergent groups and ever-changing demographics. Concerns for safety and other dimensions of the changing urban environment affect schools as well. New methodologies and technologies appear relentlessly, but these usually lack implementation because of scarcity of human and material resources.

In spite of what might be conservatively called the crisis in urban education, there are enlightened teachers and discerning schools that make a difference. It is readily apparent that where there are quality schools, the distinction is likely to be in the leadership qualities of principals who understand our rapidly changing society.

We should remember that the one and only purpose of the school is education—education used in its broadest meaning of the growth and development of children and service to society through the community, state, and the nation. The school should be one of the greatest social institutions ever conceived by humankind, and its continued existence can be justified only by its service to the broader society. Everything done by the school through its administrators, teachers, facilities, and curriculum should be looked upon as service to its children and its community.

The role of the principal is far greater than the administration of the routine tasks of the school. Far more important is the role of leading the school toward the attainment of the goals for which it exists. Thus, every phase of the program and activities of the school should be motivated by, and coordinated through, the educational leadership of the principal working in cooperation with the school staff and the community.

The program of the urban school has increasingly expanded and become increasingly difficult. To dispense factual knowledge and to develop elementary skills are not enough. The adjustment of students to the stresses and strains of modern life has become a pressing need that is no longer met easily by the home, church, community, or any of the informal means of generations past. While the school is usually reluctant to assume increased responsibilities, it has been unable to avoid at least part of the task of helping to guide the growth and development of the individuals whom it serves. Though subject matter and skills are no less important than in the past, they are of little use to a frustrated, emotionally upset individual whose attitudes, understandings, and appreciation are confused. Thus the more humane curriculum and the additional objectives of "attitudes," "language control," "understandings," and "values" have placed a tremendous challenge before the modern urban school. As always, teaching, if it is to be effective, must be both a science and an art.

The increased knowledge of the learning process, sociological concepts, nutrition, and psychological concepts has discredited many of the old concepts of teaching and has opened many new possibilities for a better and more effective educational program. The principal must help the urban teacher to establish a new vision of teaching. Teachers, of course, must know the subjects they teach and how the child grows and develops, but they must also know urban children— how they adjust to the culture, what their interests are, and how to develop their potentialities. Teachers must see education as a process by which the students can, in spite of a suspect environment, be led and motivated to the goals set for themselves in terms of their individual needs. Teachers must see the curriculum as a means that includes subject matter, meaningful experiences, and varied methods by which pupils gain needed knowledge, skills, understanding, attitudes, appreciation, and interests that help them live a happy and productive life. In addition, the program of the school must be functional in terms of the needs of the urban community and its people.

This may seem too ambitious, but unless the urban schools accept the challenge of the times and make sincere efforts to improve their programs to attain such goals, our profession will have failed and our society will continue to languish. One of the greatest tasks of the urban school is to develop and maintain a dynamic program that meets the individual and social needs of the community. This statement has been said over and over again, but too little has been done to translate the ideal into practice. The task is not an easy one, and any great degree of success can come only through the coordinated efforts of all the stakeholders— parents, community leaders, business leaders, politicians, and educators. The operational word is *coordinated*, and this indicates a major responsibility of the principal. The urban school program must become the means whereby the entire school is stimulated to be constantly sensitive to changing needs, and it must demonstrate courage and initiative in developing better ways to meet the needs. The principal is the leader and the coordinator who sees to it that all aspects of the school and all individuals work together toward the major educational goals.

One of the great needs today is for a more functional program of education throughout the urban schools. Yet the question remains as to how this can be achieved. While no one answer can be given, nor can any infallible formula be offered, there are certain fundamental principles that should offer some guidelines.

The major instrument of learning in the program of any school is the teacher. No matter how elevated the ideals of the principal, no matter what the needs of the community, no matter how fine a curriculum framework or course of study may be developed, the implementation of all these must be through the teachers. The best teaching requires an interested, enthusiastic, and understanding teacher. It should be obvious that these characteristics cannot be obtained through coercion or by executive order. The urban principal must help teachers find interest, attain broad understandings, achieve confidence in a sometimes hostile environment, and find the satisfactions inherent in effective teaching. Only through self-activity does a teacher become a good teacher. No principal can make a person be an effective teacher. A principal can only help through motivation and stimulation, cooperation on teaching problems, and opportunities for understanding.

The success or failure of the urban school depends largely on the leadership of the school principal. The importance of the principalship has often been underestimated by educators and by the greater society. Instead of being regarded as a key position of leadership in the functioning of the educational program, it has sometimes been looked upon as an educational technician position or as a reward for long service as a teacher. However, research clearly indicates that the principal significantly makes a difference in the degree of quality of a school.

THE ROLE OF THE URBAN PRINCIPAL

A great deal of friction and conflict in urban schools may arise if the principal does not possess a broad, well-conceived philosophy of education that features the needs of schools in current and future environments. This lack may result in instability of the organization, inconsistency in policies and practices for the urban setting, misunderstandings between faculty and students, and lack of parent and community support. Not only does it produce turmoil throughout the organization, but it results in too many examples of inequity or "savage inequalities" mentioned by the author Kozol. (Kozol) It is difficult for teachers to do their best work unless they feel certain that their efforts are congruent with an underlying philosophy that pervades the school and not just empty expressions that are used on special occasions. First and foremost it is the principal's role to activate an operational school philosophy and create a school climate and a vision that will lead to urban schools' equaling the best of education anywhere.

The good principal is the most potent force in building the quality school. The urban community, the professional leaders, and the front-line teachers exhibit a strong tendency to judge the school by its principal. Unquestionably, the principal's leadership, achieved cooperatively with the faculty and the urban community, determines the standards and establishes the tone and eventual quality of the school. School stakeholders hold the principal largely responsible for the quality of the school. Thus, he or she receives credit or blame for the results of the school. The principal's philosophy, insights, interests, and actions may modify, create growth, and promote change, or they may delay, inhibit, and confine the school's mission. Currently, urban schools are endeavoring to adapt their programs to meet seemingly overwhelming problems. The principal is in a particularly strategic role to lead in these efforts to improve urban schools.

The school's goals and objectives give direction and purpose to all of the stakeholders who are associated with the school, and they help to identify the numerous activities that need to be accomplished by a successful school. Therefore, the principal must become involved with the various goals and objectives that have been developed for the school. These should evolve as a basic part of the principal's vision for the direction of the urban school.

Education, as well as most facets of society, has been quick to state what the aims of education should be, along with quick-fix school improvement. The literature is replete with new ways of reaffirming old goals. Nevertheless, certain school goals seem to emerge, hold constant in some cases, and reemerge in others. A current representative sampling of such goals includes development of knowledge, development of basic skills, problem solving, learning how to learn, personality development, values, citizenship, multicultural and ethnic diversity, and world understanding.

As the principal and other school colleagues consider the question of what the goals of the school should be, they should also be aware of the expectations of the urban stakeholders. These expectations should be clearly received, studied, and evaluated. The stakeholders need to recognize that students will more than likely face quite different problems in the future from those of today's adults. This uncertain future needs to be addressed today in an educationally sound manner that will help students confront a world of change.

The urban principal must be cognizant of the basic elements of the administrative process and have a thorough understanding of appropriate application of those elements. Richard A. Gorton lists thirteen administrative processes: problem identification, diagnosis, setting objectives, decision making, planning, implementing, coordinating, initiating, delegating, communicating, working with groups, evaluating, and problem solving. (Gorton) To some degree these and other processes need to be met head on by the principal.

There are many opinions as to the role of the urban principal, but a number of roles emerge very frequently in the literature. One role is organizational leader; some classify this as the role of a manager. The organizational leader initiates, coordinates, and implements activities, procedures, and policies of the school. Much of this is accomplished by helping the other stakeholders to complete their tasks and reach their goals in an effective and efficient manner.

A second role is "authority figure." The principal is the backer of discipline rules of the school, albeit at times through teachers, vice principals, or other staff members. From the principal, teachers and staff members expect actions that support the school's rules, their decisions, and the interests of society. In the broadest context the principal assumes the role of the ultimate protector of the school, no matter what degree of participation and collaboration the other stakeholders have.

Third, the role of instructional leader goes with the principalship, even though it may in practice be more myth than reality. The expectation by most theorists, educators, parents, and governance leaders is that the principal is or should be the instructional leader. The biggest disagreements with this role are when and how to be the instructional leader.

The role of assessor or evaluator of the many facets of the school falls to the principal. In this role the principal evaluates people, situations, progress, programs, and ideas. Understanding of evaluation and evaluation models is critical to the success of the principal and the school.

A commonly accepted fifth role of the principal is facilitator. The principal facilitates situations where the satisfaction and climate of the organization are positive. This manifests itself in high satisfaction and good climate as perceived by students, teachers, parents, community, and educational leaders. It is currently accepted that the concepts of satisfaction and climate are distinctly separate and that both are of critical value. James Keefe's work with the National Association of Secondary School Principals on Comprehensive Assessment of School Environments-Information Management System (CASE-IMS) clearly indicates the importance of these two concepts. (Keefe)

Last, the role of mediator has evolved as one of the major functions of the principal. The principal assumes this role in many different forms, such as ombudsman, dissuader, conflict mediator, and persuader. Complex values, different cultures, group demands, and rapidly changing demographics create an environment that demands great principal expertise in this role.

SKILLS, FUNCTIONS, PROFICIENCIES

Specific roles and tasks of the principalship have been gradually superseded by lists of skills, functions, and proficiencies. Many times these rubrics are more descriptive of the qualities that the principal needs to function best in his or her position. The real world of the urban principal is often quite different from the environment described in the literature. To think that we can effectively develop the perfect model for all is naive. However, there are a number of credible studies on the effectiveness of school principals. We need to look at a few of the more successful studies.

The National Association of Secondary School Principals (NASSP), through its development of an assessment center project, identified twelve generic skill areas that can be assessed and that have been found to be necessary to be a successful principal. This comprehensive process assesses the generic skills through intensive activities that typically face a principal. Among the many benefits of the process is the assignment of operational definitions to the generic skills. These skills and their definitions are:

1. Problem Analysis: ability to seek out relevant data and analyze complex information to determine the important elements of a problem situation; searching for information with a purpose.

2. Judgment: ability to reach logical conclusions and make high-quality decisions based on available information; skill in identifying educational needs and setting priorities; ability critically to evaluate written communications.

3. Organizational Ability: ability to plan, schedule, and control the work of others; skill in using resources in an optimal fashion; ability to deal with a volume of paperwork and heavy demands on one's time.

4. Decisiveness: ability to recognize when a decision is required (disregarding the quality of the decision) and to act quickly.

5. Leadership: ability to get others involved in solving problems; ability to recognize when a group requires direction, to interact with a group effectively and to guide it to the accomplishment of a task.

6. Sensitivity: ability to perceive the needs, concerns, and personal problems of others; skill in resolving conflicts; tact in dealing with persons from different backgrounds; ability to deal effectively with people concerning emotional issues; knowing what information to communicate and to whom.

7. Stress Tolerance: ability to perform under pressure and during opposition; ability to think on one's feet.

8. Oral Communication: ability to make a clear oral presentation of facts or ideas.

9. Written Communication: ability to express ideas clearly in writing; to write appropriately for different audiences—students, teachers, parents, and others.

10. Range of Interests: competence to discuss a variety of subjects—educational, political, current events, economics, and so on; desire to participate actively in events.

11. Personal Motivation: need to achieve in all activities attempted; evidence that work is important to personal satisfaction; ability to be self-policing.

12. Educational Values: possession of a well-reasoned educational philosophy; receptiveness to new ideas and change. (Hersey)

Edgar Kelley, speaking of the implications for universities of the NASSP assessment process, stated: "Given society's demands for improved practices in education, coupled with research findings that have shown the performance of the principal to be critical for effective schools, and with career demographic data which support forecasts of a need to train and select new principals for America's schools, the principals who are trained during the period between 1985 and 1995 are likely to be the single most important determinant of the quality of American education during the early part of the twenty-first century." (Kelley) This statement rings true for the principals of urban schools.

The National Commission for the Principalship identified twenty-one domains, which they grouped into four areas. The functional domains address the organizational processes and techniques by which the mission of the school is achieved. They are (1) leadership, (2) information collection, (3) problem analysis, (4) judgment, (5) organizational oversight, (6) implementation, and (7) delegation. The programmatic domains, which focus on the scope and framework of the educational program and reflect the core technology of schools, instruction, and the related supporting services, are (8) instructional program, (9) curriculum design, (10) student guidance and development, (11) staff development, (12) measurement and evaluation, and (13) resource allocation. The interpersonal domains acknowledge the critical value of human relationships to the satisfaction of personal and professional goals and to the achievement of organizational purpose. They are motivating others by (14) sensitivity, (15) oral expression, and (16) written expression. The fourth domain is the contextual domains that reflect the world of ideas and forces within which the school operates and explores the (17) intellectual, (18) ethical, (19) cultural, (20) economic, and (21) political and governmental influences upon schools, including traditional and emerging perspectives. They are the philosophical and cultural values, legal and regulatory applications, policy and political influences, and public and media relationships. (Thomson) These domains suggest a knowledge base for principals that recognizes the centrality of instruction and the requirements of decentralized structures for informed functional and interpersonal leadership.

Karolyn J. Snyder and Robert H. Anderson found themes from research studies and placed them in ten models for school planning, development, and evaluation. These themes provide task and process directions for school development activities. In all cases the principal is in the locus of control. Important themes for the urban principal have been abstracted from their work.

Organizational planning includes the following:

1. School Planning. In effective schools, teachers and principals translate collective concerns into specific, achievement-oriented school improvement goals. Improvements are planned by the entire staff in response to needs and changes in the school environment. Collaborative decision making creates a healthy school climate, which tends to foster a sense of community. Responsibility for total program success is shared by the entire staff.

2. Team Planning. In effective organizations individuals work in the context of both permanent and temporary work groups. Effective schools develop creative approaches for grouping teachers into working teams. Team success seems to hinge on the leader's ability to maximize member assets.

3. Individual Performance Planning. In successful organizations a high-level goal orientation exists for individual performance that is linked to the organization's goals. In successful schools, both school and teacher goals tend to guide teacher performance. Role expectations are clear, and teachers are held accountable for student performance in effective schools. A goal structure for performance discharges responsibility for contributions to organizational success and provides a framework for work activity, skill development, supervisory feedback, and performance evaluation.

Staff development includes the following:

4. Staff Development. Staff development programs that are school-based and linked to improvement goals are the most effective. In successful schools, staff development is viewed as an essential to improvement efforts and is planned by teachers and principals together to address skills that are transferable to the classroom.

5. Clinical Supervision. In effective schools principals conduct frequent formal and informal observations to coach teachers in their development of instructional skills. Effective teaching behaviors guide supervision practices as principals and teachers seek to improve teaching and, subsequently, raise the levels of student achievement.

6. Group Development. Principals initiate and sustain group participation. In effective schools the staff is cohesive, has purpose, and collectively seeks program improvement. Cooperation and satisfaction are important to all of the participants.

7. Quality Control. In successful schools, principals control a complex web of staff

interactions. The staff is held accountable for results, individually and collectively, in a supportive atmosphere.

Program development includes the following:

8. Instructional Management. In effective schools, principals communicate a system of instructional standards to teachers, coordinating schoolwide curriculum and instruction. Teachers plan and carry out programs together, providing a climate of high-achievement expectations for all students. In successful schools teachers are able to alter outdated methods of instruction or to adopt new practices when the expectation of such change exists and where teachers frequently exchange ideas and support each other in the instructional improvement process.

9. Resource Development. Making productive use of resources is central to effective organizational productivity. Principals of successful schools plan for, organize, and distribute resources to their staffs. Effective principals are able to secure adequate material and human resources in spite of seeming constraints. High levels of parent and community involvement tend to facilitate student achievement. Involved schools have a greater awareness of community issues. Involvement results in increased satisfaction between parents and the school.

School evaluation includes the following:

10. Assessing Achievement. Principals of successful schools develop schoolwide assessment models that include student evaluation, program evaluation, team evaluation, and personnel evaluation. The assessment model allows all participants the opportunity of individual and collective involvement in the process. (Snyder and Anderson)

In a pragmatic sense, one must look at certain basic properties of the work of the principal. A systematic understanding of the nature of principals' tasks may be necessary to understand the roles, focus, and operations of that position. In a simple but extremely important analysis, Kent Peterson looked at three central features of the work of principals as they went about their daily work. Brevity of tasks characterized the work of principals. Most activities were short and quick, with activities ranging in the hundreds during a given day. Brevity of the activities of the job says a lot about selection, training, and organizing of the principal. A second property of the work of principals was variety. The variety ran from evaluating teachers to supervising custodians, to say nothing of working with parents and children. Not only was there a great variety of tasks, but many of them used a wide variety of technologies, for example, budgeting and public relations. He found that principals need a wide repertoire of cognitive skills to handle the vast array of tasks. Third, the work of principals was very fragmented. It is not unusual for one activity to interrupt another. In fact, it was rare to have one activity completed without interruption. A competent principal must be able to cope with task fragmentation. (K. Peterson)

The urban principal not only must be able to cope with brevity, variety, and fragmentation but also must be able to organize the school so that longer-range tasks of planning, implementation, and assessment of goals can be accomplished. This is not easy to do, but knowing the nature of the job helps in training, development, and restructuring of the principalship.

PREPARATION PROGRAMS

The principalship is in need of radical changes, emphasizing behaviors that influence instructional practice, new curriculum, and school development. Unfortunately, practices within school districts and university training programs still largely reflect an outdated orientation. If urban school principals are going to be successful, we need to address how we select, prepare, and retrain principals. Obviously, we need to find educators who can develop the knowledge, skills, and proficiencies to fit the previously stated roles. We then need to ensure preparation and development programs that accomplish this mission. Let us take a brief look at what is working.

The most sophisticated and promising selection process is the National Association of Secondary School Principals' assessment center project. (Hersey) This procedure has been validated and used widely in recent years. The process's flexibility can easily focus on the unique needs of urban principals. This widely use technique can be the linchpin for successful selection and promotion models.

A very encouraging development program for principals is the California School Leadership Academy. This statewide training plan focuses on many of the skills, competencies, and processes outlined earlier in this chapter. The implementation of this development design proves that massive retraining designs can be accomplished.

An exciting plan for the preparation of principals is the model recommended by the NASSP Consortium for Performance-Based Preparation of Principals. Their recommendations are not only timely but designed to stimulate greater involvement of professors, practitioners, and other educational stakeholders in the improvement of programs for the preparation of principals. The following list is taken from the consortium's recommendations. (Keefe)

1. Each university that prepares principals should offer a comprehensive and systematic program.

   - Identify program goals and objectives based on entry-level expectations for principals in the geographic area served by the program.

   - Determine goals and objectives reflecting admission requirements and the instructional content of the preparation program.

2. Principal preparation programs should include a strong performance-based component.

3. University departments should make use of the NASSP consortium rating exercise for regular program evaluation.

4. University professors should embrace the "opportunity for renewal" implicit in the instructional analysis of the consortium rating exercise and the skill development of Assessment Center technology. The process should be viewed as staff development as well as program evaluation.

5. At both the admission and instructional stages, the reasons for employing various practices and procedures should be carefully examined, that is, tradition, market analysis, department or professor preferences, and so on. Outmoded or unjustifiable practices should be modified as appropriate.

6. Personalized, performance-based programs should be planned for students from the diagnostic analysis of generic and task-specific skill needs.

   • Academic content should flow from the diagnosed needs of all students.

   • Various types of simulation and clinical activities should be used to meet the specialized needs of individual students.

7. Field experiences should be structured to develop or enhance the generic and task-specific skills of individuals.

   • No activity is field-based unless the primary instructional emphasis lies at the application level of experience.

   • Practitioners should be carefully screened before being authorized to work with candidates in field settings. The university might confer clinical appointments on field supervisors/mentors.

   • Both the quality and the variety of field experiences are important. Adequate resources must be budgeted to support quality field/clinical training.

8. New materials for performance-based instruction (simulations, case studies, and so on) must become an institutional and national priority. Materials should be validated in terms of the NASSP Assessment Center dimensions or the task behaviors common to all principal preparation programs.

9. Instruments and procedures for diagnostic assessment of generic skills and for monitoring field-based performance should be given greater attention in preparation programs. Both formative and summative assessment is needed to measure student skill levels—during the program, at the time of completion, and at entry-level placement in administrative positions.

The design, delivery, and dynamics of the preparation program are essential to forming a basic foundation for urban principals. Urban school leaders need to start with the best background that the profession can give them.

ACHIEVING SUCCESS

There are promising techniques, procedures, and practices for urban principals seeking to achieve success. Work with total quality management, the linking of alternative assessment, and techniques of effective schools are, to name a few, worthwhile approaches for urban schools. Much needs to be said for a clarion call for an adequate financial structure for education. This is particularly true of urban schooling. Because of space limitation a look at some of the features and ideas of the supportive environment concept follows.

This approach deals with the psychological climate of the learning situation and urban schools and suggests the following question: What do principals need to know as they go about their business?

Since they must deal with people all the time, it seems reasonable to say they need some knowledge of human beings and how they react to working in medium- or large-sized organizations.

Supervisors must also deal with groups of people, so they should know something about how groups influence their members, how they form informal structures that work for or against the formal structures of the urban school organization.

They must deal with staff members who are working with others in complex organizational settings, so they should know about organizational theory and leadership and the ways in which individuals respond to the constraints of such organizations.

They must help staff members to identify and solve their personal and job-related problems, so they should have a knowledge of the helping process and how to work best with multicultural students and teachers as individuals. Principals must also provide instructional support and management for staff members, so they should know something about how this can be done most effectively.

School leadership is a way of learning about and using information so that supervisors and staff members can become more aware and effective in their work and more secure in their psychological well-being. This way of looking at the leadership process must emphasize communication skills.

The way a principal faces a staff member or parent can be done in a skillful or unskillful way. Here are some superficial skills that supervisors should know about.

First, skilled supervisors always try to face the client or staff member directly, (Ridley and Asbury, 1988), showing the other person that they are completely involved with them and their problem. In our culture this says to the other person: I am listening to you; I am available now. Turning one's body sideways lessens one's degree of contact and involvement with the other person. Turning one's eyes sideways seems to tell the other that you are not really interested in what she or he is saying! So microskills can be very important.

A second skill follows: always adopt an open position or posture when you talk to the client or staff member. Crossing one's legs or arms can be seen by others as defensive postures. They tell the other that we are less involved with them and what they are saying. An open position or posture can say to the other that you are not upset by what she is saying and that you want to hear more. Of course, you could be very involved with the person who is talking and still cross your arms and legs. But the important question is this: Am I conveying to this other person how involved I really am? Or am I making it possible for this person to misunderstand my attitude because of the way I sit?

In our society, leaning forward toward the other person shows interest and concern for what is being said. When both the supervisor and the staff member are leaning toward one another, they show their mutual involvement in what is being said. Leaning too far toward the other can backfire, however. You may violate the personal space of others and cause them to draw back and become defensive or frightened. It can be seen as trying to become too intimate too soon.

Eye contact is a must in American society, and steady eye contact can be a good thing. This is another way of telling clients or staff members that you are with them, that you are sharing their interests and concerns. Conversely, looking away to the side can be seen as a lack of interest and involvement and should be avoided.

Finally, the supervisor should come to the meeting in as relaxed a frame of mind as possible. Being at ease tells the other that you are not nervous or preoccupied. If you move about in your seat or seem distracted facially, the staff member will wonder what's making you so uncomfortable. Using your body effectively is a first step in being a skilled supervisor. But, of course, that is only the beginning. All these skills will not work if they are used without thinking about the relationship that the skilled supervisor must develop with staff members or clients. The most skilled approaches will be seen as manipulation or worse.

So supervisors will have to do more than mechanically position themselves when they speak to others. Communication with their staff members ultimately depends on nonverbal communications and their ability to attend to those with whom they work. They can ask themselves certain questions as they meet with clients and staff members.

- Do I like the person I am talking to? If I do, how well am I listening to what he or she is saying?
- What am I saying on a nonverbal level, and how is this person responding? Is he or she taking a defensive position or showing, by body language and presence, liking and trust for me, too?
- Are we acting as though we are not paying complete attention to one another? Is either one of us distracted by other concerns? If there are distractions, what am I doing to deal with these problems?

FEELING EXPRESSION SKILLS

Most people, as children, are taught to repress many of their feelings and early attitudes. Many come to terms with these forgotten and frozen attitudes when they reach adulthood, putting them in some perspective. Others, however, do not. The supervisor's purpose is to help staff and others to understand these feelings and attitudes to they can function more effectively in their work. This helps staff to become more aware of their own reasons for doing things and helps them to think more about the children they serve. This is one way that a supervisor can help staff to respond to one another and to the children in a meaningful way, one way they can grapple with their mutual problems and unresolved feelings emanating from past conflicts.

Few programs in educational administration deal with these deeper, psychological problems. Their approaches are not rooted in recent research or knowledge about the human ego. They do not encourage supervisors and staff members to reflect upon their behavior and emotions; they do not provide approaches that allow staff to help children develop inner controls over their feelings and behaviors.

If being an urban school supervisor means anything today, it means changing the old-fashioned communication systems in schools and replacing them with new ways of listening and learning. Since few supervisors ever develop knowledge and skills in this area, it is easy to see why most leadership experiences in schools are so unpleasant and unrewarding.

So it is important to discuss what school supervisors must know if they are to establish more supportive environments for their staff and students. Just learning these insights, understandings, and skills will help urban supervisors work with their staff more effectively, but it will not create good learning environments. That requires still more knowledge, insights, empathy, and understanding.

Consider the idea of group membership, which is crucial to an understanding of urban schools. Researchers have separated educational leaders into formal and informal types, both operating in the same organization. The school supervisor has been designated by the state and is the legal-rational authority in the school building. But leadership is sometimes assigned to those who can best serve the needs of people at particular times and places. In the classroom or staff's lounge, many of the staff who are followers in faculty meetings become informal leaders who create positive or negative feelings in other staff members. This ability of individuals to shift from the role of follower to that of leader is often observed in schools and corporate structures. Because of this, theory and research into small group life have come to see the leadership role as a shared function, rather than a quality assigned to a particular individual. Nobody can be the ''cool and competent'' person all the time, yet this is often the front that supervisors are asked to present in their everyday dealings with people. Some situations demand personal knowledge about students; others require highly developed skills and insights from staff or counselors. Theoretically, the supervisors should be those who can do things best for a group or school. But in many schools today, the authorities are always assigned to leadership roles even when there are others who have greater skills and insights about certain difficulties or problems. How can supervisors be trained to understand group structures and the changing roles of leadership? What must they do in order to work with informal groups effectively? The questions do not lend themselves to easy answers or short cuts. Yet ways of identifying positive and negative groups and leaders to exist; methods of expressing and neutralizing conscious and subconscious emotions also exist and are important in helping supervisors improve their communication and relations with others. A sound communication system provides the supervisor with reliable information about what is really happening inside the building. It allows her or him to make decisions based on a deeper understanding of the staff's personal goals and aspirations. (Rothstein, 1993).

The wellspring and power of organizational energies are released when people are encouraged to identify and resolve problems that come up in their work. New ways of doing things are accepted more easily when they are the result of participation and consensus. While many preach participative management, few provide strategies and structures that take into account the demands of the organization or the expectations of staff members and children. The process of establishing greater trust and participation is rooted in democratic values and ideals. How to hear others clearly, how to encourage them to talk freely about themselves and their problems—these are other important concerns for urban principals.

How to use questioning and group meetings to increase staff involvement and responsibility; how to help staff and students identify and resolve mutual problems in the classroom; how to deal with poor solutions and ineffective staff; how to help faculty set goals and standards for their work performances; how to use mutual and ongoing evaluations to gather information needed for informed, intelligent decisions—these are other areas that must be considered by the practicing school administrator. Some of these ideas come from the writer's years as a teacher and supervisor. Some are the common legacy of research that has accumulated over the past few decades or so. Yet these skills, insights, and understandings are worthless, as many learned leaders have surely learned to their sorrow, unless they are used in the right context by school supervisors who are willing to spend more of their energies on developing better personal relationships with the people around them.

CONCLUSION

New approaches to the urban schools can provide conceptual frameworks for developing new models. While working collaboratively, urban principals need to ensure that educational practices become increasingly integrated as they focus on specific goals. The principal and the many stakeholders can develop a capacity for continuous self-renewal and for satisfying, productive educational outcomes. Thus, urban schools can become rebuilt into vigorous social agencies for society as their workers develop the ability to collaborate and to define regularly the needed tasks in their educational mission. Collaborating around goals, refining conditions, and adapting to changing environmental expectations become the work ethic in a productive school.

Peter Drucker has stated that knowledge is the true capital of a modern society. (Drucker) If this is true, our society cannot afford to squander the vast potential of the urban schools. This is but one of many reasons for developing the best leadership for these schools. Vito Perrone has said, "Teaching, after all, is about knowing children well." The principalship is about knowing all people well.

BIBLIOGRAPHY

Bacharach, Samuel B. 1990. *Education Reform*. Boston: Allyn and Bacon.
Blumberg, Arthur. 1989. *School Administration as Craft*. Boston: Allyn and Bacon.
Drucker, Peter. 1989. *The New Realities*. New York: Harper and Row.
Gorton, Richard A. 1983. *School Administration and Supervision*. Dubuque, IA: William C. Brown.
Hersey, Paul W. 1986. *NASSP's Assessment Center: Selecting and Developing School Leaders*. Reston, VA: National Association of Secondary School Principals.
Keefe, James W. 1985. *Performance-Based Preparation of Principals*. Reston, VA: National Association of Secondary School Principals.
Kelley, Edgar A. 1986. "Implications for Universities." In *NASSP's Assessment Center: Selecting and Developing School Leaders*, (47–50), ed. Paul W. Hersey. Reston, VA: National Association of Secondary School Principals.
Kozol, Jonathan. 1991. *Savage Inequalities*. New York: Crown.
McCleary, Lloyd E., and Scott D. Thomson. 1979. *The Senior High School Principalship, vol. 3: The Summary Report*. Reston, VA: National Association of Secondary School Principals.
Perrone, Vito. 1991. *A Letter to Teachers*. San Francisco: Jossey-Bass.
Peterson, Kent. 1981. "Making Sense of Principals' Work." Paper presented to the annual meeting of the American Education Research Association, Los Angeles.
Ridley, Norman L., and Frank R. Asbury. 1988. "Does Counselor Body Position Make a Difference?" *School Counselor* 23, 253–58.
Rothstein, Stanley W. 1991. "Supportive Supervision: Leadership for the Twenty-First Century." In *The Principal as Chief Executive Officer*, ed. Andrew E. Dubin. London: Falmer Press.
Rothstein, Stanley W. 1993. *The Voice of the Other: Language as Illusion in the Formation of the Self*. New York: Praeger.
Schon, Donald A. 1987. *Educating the Reflective Practitioner*. San Francisco: Jossey-Bass.
Sergiovanni, Thomas J. 1991. *The Principalship: A Reflective Practice Perspective*. Boston: Allyn and Bacon.
Snyder, Karolyn J., and Robert H. Anderson. 1986. *Managing Productive Schools Toward an Ecology*. Orlando, FL: Academic Press.
Thomson, Scott D. 1990. *Principals for our Changing Schools*. Fairfax, VA: National Commission for the Principalship.
Ubben, Gerald C., and Larry W. Hughes. 1992. *The Principal*. Boston: Allyn and Bacon.

Selected Bibliography

Altenbaugh, Richard J. "Our Children Are Being Trained Like Dogs and Ponies: Schooling, Social Control, and the Working Class." *History of Education Quarterly* 21 (Summer 1981): 644–679.

Bernstein, Basil. *Pedagogic Discourse, Vol. 4 Class, Codes and Control*. London: Routledge, 1991.

Bourdieu, Pierre. *The Inheritors: French Students and Their Relation to Culture*. Chicago: University of Chicago Press, 1979.

Bowles, Samuel, and Gintis, Herbert. *Schooling in Capitalist America: Educational Reform and the Contradictions of Economic Life*. New York: Basic Books, 1976.

Braverman, Harry. *Labor and Monopoly Capital: The Degradation of Work in the Twentieth Century*. New York: Monthly Review Press, 1974.

Chasnoff, Isidore J., Burns, William J., Schnoll, Samuel H., and Burns, Kenneth A. "Cocaine Use in Pregnancy." *New England Journal of Medicine*, 313(11) (1985).

Cremin, Lawrence. *Transformation of the School*. New York: Knopf, 1961.

Cubberley, Elwood P. *The History of Education*. Cambridge, MA: Houghton-Mifflin, 1920.

Cubberley, Elwood P. *Public Education in the United States*. Cambridge, MA: Houghton-Mifflin, 1934.

Darder, Antonia. *Culture and Power in the Classroom: A Critical Foundation for Bicultural Education*. Westport, CT: Bergin and Garvey, 1991.

Drotar, Dennis, Crawford, Peggy, and Bush, Marcy. "The Family Context of Childhood Chronic Illness: Implications for Psychosocial Intervention." In Myron G. Eisenberg, LaFaye C. Sutkin, and Mary A. Jansen, eds., *Chronic Illness and Disability Through the Life Span: Effects on Self and Family*. New York: Springer, 1984.

Dubin, Andrew E., ed. *The Principal as Chief Executive Officer*. London: Falmer Press, 1991.

Edwards, Nathan, and Richey, H. G. *The School in the American Social Order*. Boston: Houghton-Mifflin, 1963.

Erickson, Erik H. *Identity and Crisis*. New York: Norton, 1968.

412

Selected Bibliography

Foucault, Michel. *Discipline and Punishment: The Birth of the Prison*, trans. Alan Sheridan. New York: Pantheon Books, Doubleday, 1961.

Freire, Paolo. *Pedagogy of the Oppressed*. New York: Seabury Press, 1970.

Goodlad, John. *A Place Called School*. New York: McGraw-Hill, 1983.

Goodlad, John. "Better Teachers for Our Nation's Schools." *Phi Delta Kappan* 72 (1990).

Greer, Colin. *The Great School Legend*. New York: Basic Books, 1972.

Hawley, William. "The Importance of Minority Teachers to the Racial and Ethnic Integration of American Society." *Equity and Choice* 5 (1989).

Hodgkinson, Harold. *All One System: Demographics of Education from Kindergarten Through Graduate School*. Washington, DC: Institute for Educational Leadership, 1985.

Holmes, Irvine J. "Beyond Role Models: An Examination of Cultural Influences on the Pedagogical Perspectives of Black Teachers." *Peabody Journal of Education* 53 (1989): 33–75.

Hummel, Robert C., and Nagle, John N. *Urban Education in America*. New York: Oxford University Press, 1973.

Jacobs, Paul. "Keeping the Poor Poor." In Jerome H. Skolnick and Elliott Currie, eds., *Crisis in American Institutions*, 6th ed. Boston: Little, Brown, 1985.

Karabel, John and Halsey, Arthur H. (eds.) *Power and Ideology in Education*. New York: Oxford University Press, 1977.

Katz, Michael S. *The Irony of School Reform*. Cambridge, MA: MIT Press, 1964.

Katz, Michael S. "The New Departure in Quincy, 1873–1881." In Michael B. Katz, ed., *Education in American History*. New York: Praeger, 1973.

Lewis, W. David. *From Newgate to Dannemora: The Rise of the Penitentiary in New York 1796–1848*. Ithaca, NY: Cornell University Press, 1965.

Nasaw, David. *Schooled to Order*. New York: Oxford University Press, 1979.

Nasaw, David. *Children of the City: At Work and at Play*. New York: Oxford University Press, 1985.

Rothstein, Stanley W. *Identity and Ideology: Sociocultural Theories of Schooling*. Westport, CT: Greenwood Publishing Group, 1991.

Rothstein, Stanley W. *The Voice of the Other: Language as Illusion in the Formation of the Self*. Westport, CT: Praeger Publishers, 1993.

Sagan, Carl. "Why We Need to Understand Science." *Parade Magazine*, 10 September 1989.

Sage, Daniel D., and Burrello, Leonard C. *Policy and Management in Special Education*. Englewood, NJ: Prentice-Hall, 1986.

Schultz, Stanley K. *The Culture Factory*. New York: Oxford University Press, 1973.

Treadway, Peter G. *Beyond Statistics: Doing Something About Dropping Out of School*. Stanford, CA: Stanford University Press, 1985.

Turnbull, Ann P., and Schutz, Jane B. *Mainstreaming Handicapped Students: A Guide for the Classroom Teacher*. Boston: Allyn and Bacon, 1979.

Tyack, David. *Turning Points in American Educational History*. Waltham, MA: Blaisdell, 1967.

Tyack, David. "Bureaucracy and the Common School: The Example of Portland Oregon 1851–1913." In Michael Katz, ed., *Education in American History*. New York: Praeger, 1973.

Waller, Willard. *The Sociology of Teaching*. New York: Russell and Russell, 1961.

Index

About the Contributors

LOUISE ADLER is a professor of educational administration at California State University, Fullerton, who has specialized in studies of minority group responses to public school curricula.

ANTHONY M. STEVENS-ARROYO is a social scientist specializing in liberation theology and its effects on Latinos living in urban centers. He is a professor at the Graduate School and University Center of the City University of New York and director of PARAL: Program for the Analysis of Religion Among Latinos at the Bildner Center for Western Hemisphere Studies.

RICHARD J. ALTENBAUGH is a noted educational historian who has written widely on the teaching profession and its evolution from the preindustrial period to the present. He is a faculty member at Slippery Rock University.

WALTER F. BECKMAN is a professor and chairperson of the Department of Educational Administration at California State University, Fullerton. His writings have focused on assessment processes in selecting and training school administrators in urban centers.

H. WARREN BUTTON is a distinguished historian and former editor of the refereed journal *Urban Education*. He is a professor at the University of Buffalo, State University of New York.

WILLIAM L. CALLISON is a social scientist and author of many books on the uses of technology in modern educational practice. He is a professor in the graduate Department of Educational Administration at California State University, Fullerton, and is currently studying the drop-out problem in urban schools.

NANCY RICHARDS-COLOCINO is Director of Guidance Resources, Irvine Unified School District, Irvine, California. She has designed and implemented federal- and state-funded substance abuse grants and research projects and has been a social worker and school psychologist. She has a private practice as a marriage and family therapist.

ANTONIA DARDER is an important social theorist specializing in the culture of the teacher and its effects on the educational experiences of minority children in urban schools. She is a professor at Claremont Graduate School.

DAVID ELI DREW is a professor of sociology and quantitative studies at Claremont Graduate School. He is a noted researcher and theorist who has written widely on the problems of science education in the United States.

ANDREW E. DUBIN is a professor of educational administration at San Francisco State University and a social scientist studying the experiences of special needs children in urban settings and schools.

JANE WHEELER-DUBIN is a marriage and family counselor in San Francisco. She teaches courses on the special needs child at San Francisco State University.

LAURENCE IANNACCONE is a noted political scientist who has written widely on urban school boards and their politics. He is a professor at the University of California at Santa Barbara.

NORMA INABINETTE is a professor in the graduate Department of Reading at California State University, Fullerton. She is a specialist in ameliorating the problems of reading retardation in urban schools.

JACQUELINE JORDAN IRVINE is a writer and researcher who has specialized in the relationships between teacher perceptions and the enormous failure rates of minority children in public schools. She is a professor in the Division of Education at Emory University.

PAUL W. KANE is chair of the Department of Secondary Education at California State University, Fullerton. He has been dean of the School of Human Development and Community Services and specializes in the sociology of education and the adolescent experience in urban schools.

FRANK W. LUTZ is a distinguished political scientist and theorist who has written several books on the governance and politics of urban school boards. He is director of the Center for Policy Studies and Research in Elementary and Secondary Education at East Texas State University.

CHARLES MILLIGAN is a school administrator in the Tustin Unified School District in Southern California and a recent recipient of the Ph.D. from Claremont Graduate School. His research interests are in school dropouts and the relations between schooling and society.

ANTONIO NADAL is deputy chairperson of the Department of Puerto Rican Studies at Brooklyn College. He teaches in the Bilingual Teacher Education sequence at the college and has been a consultant and evaluator of bilingual programs for many years.

MILGA MORALES-NADAL is the director of the Bilingual Personnel Training Program at Brooklyn College. She has taught and counseled for many years in New York City schools and written several papers on bilingual education. She was formally a reporter for the U.S. edition of *Claridad*, a newspaper published in Puerto Rico.

LAURENCE J. NEWMAN has been a teacher and administrator in the New York City school system. He is a doctoral student and adjunct professor at Hofstra University in the Department of Administration and Policy Studies.

STANLEY WILLIAM ROTHSTEIN is a social critic and theorist who has used multidisciplinary approaches to the nature of schooling in mass society and the role of language in the development of identity and social relations in urban schools. He is a professor in the graduate Department of Educational Administration, California State University, Fullerton.

CHAROL SHAKESHAFT is a noted researcher and theorist specializing in the role of women in educational governance. She has written and lectured widely about these issues and gained national attention with her book *Women in School Administration*. She is a professor in the Department of Administration and Policy Studies at Hofstra University.

ANA MARÍA DIAZ-STEVENS, studying liberation theology in urban centers and its effects on Latino children, is a professor in Puerto Rican Studies at Rutgers University.

HELEN PARCELL TAYLOR is coordinator of secondary education at California State University, Fullerton, and an associate professor. She has had extensive experience in recruiting minority high school students in math, science, engineering, and education.

KIP TELLEZ is a faculty member in the Department of Curriculum and Instruction at the University of Houston. His expertise is in curriculum politics in urban schooling.

PATRICIA G. TWEEDDALE is a doctoral student at the Center for Policy Studies and Research in elementary and secondary education at East Texas State University.

JOSEPH G. WEERES is chairperson of the Graduate Department of Educational Administration at Claremont Graduate School.

DARLENE ELEANOR YORK is a doctoral student at Emory University, working on teacher perceptions of minority children.